JAPANESE NEW RELIGIONS
In Global Perspective

CURZON STUDIES IN NEW RELIGIOUS MOVEMENTS

Editor: Judith Coney

This Series is interested particularly in any innovative religious group that has established itself in the last fifty years. We welcome high-quality, original research contributions from across the globe, based on sensitive, in-depth research methods. Preference is given to the publication of material on religious groups which have not so far been documented. All the books in the Series address the theme of religion and society. The Series is mainly comprised of monographs exploring and extending existing theories about religion and society. It also includes edited collections designed to focus, in particular, on cross-cultural themes and draw together research findings from across the world.

Proposals or scripts for the Series will be welcomed by the Series Editor or by the Chief Editor, Curzon Press.

JAPANESE NEW RELIGIONS
In Global Perspective

Edited by
Peter B. Clarke

CURZON

First Published in 2000
by Curzon Press
Richmond, Surrey

Editorial matter © 2000 Peter B. Clarke

Typeset in Sabon by LaserScript Ltd, Mitcham
Printed and bound in Great Britain by
TJ International, Padstow, Cornwall

British Library Cataloguing in Publication Data
A catalogue record of this book is available from the British Library

ISBN 0–7007–1185–6

CONTENTS

NOTES ON CONTRIBUTORS

Alfred Bloom is Professor Emeritus at the University of Hawaii and Institute of Buddhist Studies, Berkeley. He has taught World Religions and Buddhism at the Universities of Oregon and Hawaii. He was the Dean of the Institute of Buddhist Studies, and received ordination, at Nishi Honganji in 1990. His publications include *Shinran's Gospel of Pure Grace*, 1965; *Shoshinge: The Heart of Shin Buddhism*, 1986; *Strategies of Modern Living: A Commentary with Text of Shinran Shonin: The Journey to Self-Acceptance*, 1994.

Gary Bouma is Professor of Sociology at Monash University, Melbourne.

Peter B. Clarke is Professor of History and Sociology of Religion and Director of the Centre of New Religions at King's College, University of London. His publications include *Japanese New Religions in the West* ed. P. Clarke and J. Somers, 1994 and *New Religious Movements in Western Europe – An Annotated Bibliography* ed. E. Arweck and P. Clarke, 1997.

Catherine Cornille is Professor of Comparative Religion at the Catholic University of Louvain. Her publications include *The Phoenix Files West: The Dynamics of Inculturation of Mahikari in Europe* in Japanese Journal of Religious Studies 18, 2–3, 1991; *Different Forms of Spirit Meditation in Mahikari and Shinnyoen: Shamanism East and West*, in Syzygy, Vol. 1 No. 4, 1992 and *Jesus in Japan: Christian Syncretism in Mahikari*, in *Japanese New Religions in the West*, ed. P. Clarke and J. Somers, 1994.

Tina Hamrin is Research Fellow at the Scandanavian Research Institute at Stockholm University. She has published *The Dancing Religion in a Japanese-Hawaiian Immigrant Environment via Healers and Shin Buddhist Clergy to Nationalistic Millenarianism*, 1996.

Sanda Ionescu is Research Scholar on Japanese New Religions in the West at the Centre of New Religions, King's College, University of London.

Louella Matsunaga is Lecturer in the Anthropology of Japan at the University of Oxford.

Ari Pedro Oro is Professor of Anthropology at the Federal University of Rio Grande, Porto Alegre, Brazil.

Wendy Smith is Senior lecturer in Japanese Studies at Monash University, Melbourne.

Shiva Vasi is a Doctoral Student in Anthropology at Monash University, Melbourne.

Acknowledgements of Other Contributors

The editor is very grateful to all the various movements and their members who helped to provide information for use in this volume. Thanks also go to Sonia Crivello for her assistance with copyediting and with compiling the index, and to Keishin Inaba for his help with editing and correcting the Japanese.

Peter B. Clarke

Japanese New Religions Abroad

A Case of 'Reverse' Globalization

Peter B. Clarke

This volume contains new research on a wide range of aspects of Japanese new religions abroad, particularly in Australia, Europe, and the Americas, since the 1960s, and hopefully will contribute to our understanding of the globalization process as a cultural phenomenon, and particularly to what might be termed the reverse influences in that process.

A multifaceted process, globalization has long been widely seen as unidirectional. As an economic idea it is described as a gradually expanding capitalist system that originated in Europe in the sixteenth century and began to spread out from there to other parts of the world in a necessary search for bigger markets and on the back of the technologies it developed and the political aspirations it espoused to drive it forward. A second dimension to globalization is also directly relevant to the issues raised in this volume, that is globalization in the sense of the spread of modern means of communication which facilitate the rapid exchange of ideas and information to every part of the world, including the Web and the satellite-based land mobile services which enable communication even in the absence of land based cellular services. With this alternative route for terrestrial calls fully operational nowhere will remain isolated from personal contact through geography, lack of land based technological infrastructure, or natural structures.

The third dimension to globalization, the cultural dimension, is the most relevant of the three to this research. From this perspective globalization is popularly seen as a process whereby one cultural form expands relentlessly and destroys, as it does so, the essence of every other culture that it encounters. The resurgence of Islam in Iran in the 1970s and 1980s has been interpreted as a response to such a process. Such an understanding of cultural globalization greatly oversimplifies the process.

If global culture is defined as the outcome of the interaction between regional cultures, some of which have acted as catalysts where the pace,

1

form and content of modernization are concerned, this would appear to be heuristically more valuable than unidirectional perspectives which interpret it as the impact of the creative and dynamic, emerging from one single source, on the traditional and static.

The dynamic interaction of cultures, which is a central element of globalization, leaves nothing the same and often leads to a deepening in understanding and appreciation of the particular or to its idealization, or to a belief in its uniqueness and universal significance. In the interface between the particular and the global both are in a state of flux and both act as agencies of change. The making of Japanese Buddhism (Anesaki, 1930), of Japanese Christianity (Mullins, 1999), of Indonesian and Moroccan Islam (Geertz, 1968), and of Christianity in South Africa (Sundkler, 1961) illustrates this point. Japanese Buddhism is not reducible to beliefs and practices that are exclusively Japanese; it transcends them and yet is distinctive and different largely on account of the way it has been shaped and moulded by the Japanese cultural, intellectual and social context. As Gombrich (1994: 22) observes in his account of his impressions of Japanese Buddhism:

> What concerns me is something more startling for a Buddhologist: that for each sect (in Japan) the content of its own text or texts is virtually co-terminous with the range of Buddhist ideas. In all Buddhist traditions particular monks and their pupils have specialized in sets of texts; in the days before writing when large bodies of material had to be preserved orally, this was a practical necessity. However, in those far-off days no Buddhist would have been unaware that the different bodies of text were complimentary, and in particular that the *vinaya* and the *sutras*, dealing with conduct and doctrine respectively, were both equally essential for all members of the Sangha. Not so, however, in Japan. There the *vinaya* is the exclusive cultural property of one tiny sect the (Ritsu): they learn that text alone and no other sect learns the *vinaya* at all'.

In his study of Japanese Christianity Mullins (1999) explains the process whereby the veneration of the ancestors, which had no place in Christian missionary theology and ritual, was made a central feature of worship by local Christian churches, much as it was in the Ethiopian and Zionists Churches of South Africa (Sundkler, 1948). Mullins (1999: 109) notes that in sharp contrast to Protestant missionary policy, many indigenous movements allow their members to retain the traditional Buddhist altar in their home and encourage members to pray in front of this altar with non-Christian family members. Speaking of how Moroccan Islam acquired its distinguishing features, that is its 'moral severity', 'magical power,' 'aggressive piety' and enthusiasm for saints, Geertz (1968: 9) writes:

'It is out of the tribes that the forming influences on Islam in Morocco came, and the stamp of their mentality remained on it, whatever Arabo-Spanish sophistications urban religious scholars, *locking themselves away from the local current* (my italics) were able, in a few selected corners, and for a few chromatic moments, to introduce'.

And in his discussion of the impact of Islam on Indonesian culture Geertz (1968: 11) concludes that it 'did not construct a civilization, it appropriated one'.

All religions with universal goals are constantly subject to domestication, producing continuously new variations of the universal in the particular and the converse also holds, as is illustrated in the case of Islam's development in contemporary western Europe (Clarke, 1998). Where they appear to have radically changed the cosmology and belief system of a society they have in fact acted more as catalysts than as suppliers of original ideas, as Horton's (1971) analysis of the emergence into prominence of the notion of the Supreme Being in African thought convincingly argues. Particular and ethnic religions which are carried to diverse and different cultural locations by migration, or by trade and commerce, or by soldiers serving abroad as in the case of the Greco-Roman religions, or by wandering priests and ulema, tend, for their part, to assume a more pan ethnic character.

The dynamic nature of this interactive process notwithstanding, whatever aspect of globalization is considered – the economic, technological or cultural – there is a tendency to use the term as a synonym for westernization and to see it as originating in the West and moving out from there in other directions. Such a perspective neglects the contribution to the creation of modern, global society made by non-western societies, and hence the use here of the term 'reverse influences' to describe the focus and scope of this volume.

To adopt such a perspective is not to imply that the Japanese experience of modernization was, as some contend, unique and uninfluenced by the western process, but to counteract the misleading notion that the West performed the roles of dynamo and exemplary centre of this process which has been subsequently imitated globally. This is not to agree with the view often expressed that Japan modernised without westernizing, which is clearly an oversimplification. Over time Japan did produce an atypical version of modernization. As Eisenstadt (1995: 159) comments, it became a society 'that was highly controlled yet non-totalitarian, indeed formally and to some extent actually a democratic society'. The distinctive and unusual character of the Japanese modernization process is not easily explained. To quote Eisenstadt once more (1995: 159):

How can we then explain these characteristics of modern and contemporary Japanese society – the modes of regulation of behaviour, of structuration of the major arenas of social life, of the overall cultural programme of modernity that has developed in Japan? How can we explain this rather unusual combination of features specific to the institutions of modern and contemporary Japanese society?

Searching for an explanation Eisenstadt focuses on the particular historical and cultural features of Japan and its highly developed adoptive-adaptive mechanism for managing outside influences which enable it to remain distinctive and apart from the wider world. He believes that the influences of Confucianism and Buddhism from China, though paramount in shaping the cultural development of Japan, never succeeded in making her part of their world, but were transformed in radically different ways to ensure that they made a fit with the Japanese ethos. More recently Gray (1998: 170 ff) has stressed the uniqueness of the Japanese modernization process, maintaining that it was rooted in the cultural, ethical and social history of Japan and grounded in a trust, as opposed to a contract, culture, and in a full employment culture, as opposed to one that used unemployment as an economic regulator.

Both scholars appear to have overemphasised the degree of uniqueness and to have neglected the diversity of opinion and response to modernization and westernization in Japan, which, where its ethos, self image and identity are concerned, is too often portrayed as static, impermeable and impenetrable, as an unassailable fortress. Culture cannot be hermetically sealed off from other areas of life. Japanese modernization involved developments in education, the military, banking, commercial law, and in several other spheres, all of which were modelled on western systems, and if the cultural traditions and social structure of Japan did not radically change accordingly to produce convergence with the West in these areas, they were considerably modified by such innovations, as the heated controversy in Japan surrounding the extent and desirability, or otherwise, of westernization shows.

Many in Japan not only believed that the country in being modernized was also being thoroughly westernized and that this was both inevitable and desirable, and quoted Spencer's Principles of Sociology to support their position (Waswo, 1996: 94). Influential writers were wildly enthusiastic about this kind of development. The controversial, avant-garde, and, some would say, prophetic writer, Tanizaki Jun'ichiro (1886–1965), who later in life was to move back to more traditional tastes, was a great enthusiast of westernization in the 1920s. He was also imbued with the spirit of positivism, and even saw a silver lining for progress in the devastating Great Kanto earthquake of 1923 which measured 7.9 on the Richter scale and in which over 100,000 people in the Tokyo area – the epicentre was 50 miles from Tokyo city – tragically lost their life.

Deeply concerned at first at the destruction and loss of life caused by the quake, Tanizaki later began to look upon it as an opportunity to rebuild Tokyo on western lines and make of it 'a decent place' with:

'Orderly thoroughfares, shiny, newly paved streets, a flood of cars, blocks of flats rising from floor to floor, level on level of geometric beauty, and threading through the city elevated lines, subways, streetcars. And the excitement at night of a great city, a city with the amusements of Paris or New York, a city where life never ends. Then, and then indeed, the citizens of Tokyo will come to adopt a purely European-American style of life, and the young people, men and women, will all wear Western clothes. *This is the inevitable trend of the times*, (my italics) and whether one likes it or not this is what will happen' (Citation from: Keene, 1984: 750).

Others, by contrast, opposed the inroads being made into Japan by foreign ways and did much to invent or reinvent what they believed were unique forms of Japanese cultural identity to counter them. These inventions and reinventions were underpinned by a philosophy which propounded the opposite thesis to that which maintained that everything sophisticated, advanced and modern inevitably flowed from West to East. It was asserted that Japan represented more fully the universalizing values claimed by the 'other', the West. From this it followed logically that Japan had the capacity to produce an original and authentic form of modernization that would be in keeping with its own essential values and that Japanese culture would, therefore, gain nothing by succumbing to the universalizing pretentions of Western culture.

Though highly contentious, this notion of Japan as the original and unique source and agency of its own industrialization and modernization undoubtedly performed a useful function in lending moral support to the development of an indigenous strategy to control the force and scope of westernization, which some individuals, associations, and political and religious movements, including Omotokyo and many of the Japanese New Religions established between c1890–1945, found intolerable, and detrimental to the Japanese spirit and way of life. As Bellah (1968) points out, westernization remained a problem for right wing and left wing elements alike in Japan, both of which strove in their different ways to rid the country of the 'bad taste of the modern', particularly in the form of the modern spirit, which, they felt, was embedded in Anglo-American culture.

Japan found westernization more difficult to integrate and domesticate than previous waves of cultural penetration in the past such as Buddhism. And the domestication of outside influences has become progressively more difficult, particularly during the last quarter of a century. With Japan's new constitutional arrangements modelled on those of the United States which came into effect in 1946 and its arrival at the centre of world economic affairs since the 1960s, unprecedented levels of pressure have been placed on its ability to adapt, shape and mould incoming attitudes, comportment and orientations toward the world and bring them into line with its own view of how life should be lived. When insular and distant from the centre, Japan had more time to deliberate and make choices about how it should respond to other cultural influences, whereas now, being more directly involved in every aspect of global life, its capacity to apply its integrative principles to such influences has been considerably diminished. The process of the domestication of the 'other' has, however, remained an issue, as the *nihonjinron* debate about Japaneseness in the 1970s and 1980s made obvious, even if it was more of a thought experiment than a concrete strategy that effectively led to any slowing down of the process. Perhaps only economic recession can effect this.

These caveats notwithstanding, Japan has produced its own distinctive form of industrialization and modernization and has considerably domesticated the ever increasing tide of western cultural influences during the past 150 years. In this respect it illustrates the main effect of the process of economic and cultural interaction which is the globalizing of the particular and the particularizing of the global to produce something new. Seen from the perspective of religion it is clear that cultural globalization does not result in extreme relativism nor does it undermine the possibility of constructing genuinely universal religious teachings and objectives, that is teachings and objectives with implications agreed upon, shared and implemented by religions everywhere and designed for everyone. As Roberts (1995) suggests, doctrinally distinctive religions will increasingly seek to forge between themselves a global ethical system, a proposal discussed by the Parliament of World Religions that assembled in Chicago in 1993, and a shared theological critique of late modern Capitalism in the absence of a viable alternative. Such developments will inevitably impact on theological discourse. Indeed they already have, and can be seen in the different opinion of and attitude taken by Christianity since the 1960s to Islamic revelation, compared with the beginning of the 20th century.

However, the most obvious direct effect of globalization on religion to date is to be seen in the greater diversity and specialization to which it has greatly contributed. Previously, religions that were either theologically or ethnically indisposed, or unable, for political and other reasons, to expand outside their home base now have the opportunity to do so and to succeed in a new environment. For much of their history abroad Japanese new religions have been essentially ethnic religions, while in more recent times the opportunity to compete and offer yet another specialized version of spirituality has been greatly improved. In the case of Japanese new religions, as in the case of so many other religions, including the spread of Islam to Europe and North America (Clarke, 1998), both immigration and economic and legal factors have been behind their expansion abroad.

At first the Japanese new religions abroad showed little missionary intent. This is not usual where immigrants are the main carriers of a religion. Generally religions composed of immigrants pass through several stages beginning with a period of quarantine during which they act as the social cement of the newly established community. It is through the church or mosque, or synagogue, or temple, that the new comers network and provide each other with mutual support. Ideally, the period of quarantine is followed by a gradual process of assimilation dictated by the needs of the second generation. This process needs to be controlled, otherwise it will quickly lead to a reaction in the form of a radical reform movement. Also to shed too much cultural baggage too quickly can be counter-productive, for a movement that seeks to recruit outsiders a degree of specialization, strictness and exclusivity, can be important to its success in a global market.

As Japanese new religions go North and South and West in ever greater numbers they focus attention on the production, complex character and dynamics of global culture, and on the need to view this process from different angles rather than from a single vantage point in order to understand its contents, form and its effects which, below the surface, are bewilderingly diverse, making general explanations of the rise and decline, success and failure of religion in the modern world highly tentative at best.

Contributions

Catherine Cornille's contribution (pp. 10–34) is concerned with the universalistic and particularistic and/or nationalistic pretentions of Japanese new religions and with how these affect their organizational and administrative arrangements and their capacity to adapt to non Japanese cultures. In Cornille's opinion genuine universalism is rarely found in the case of the Japanese new religions in Europe, nationalism and ethnocentrism being pronounced features of the orientation and world view of most of these movements.

In the first (pp. 35–73) of her two contributions to this volume Louella Matsunaga examines whether the parallel expansion of Japanese companies and Japanese new religions (she focuses most of attention on the links between the Japanese company Yaohan and the Japanese company Seicho no Ie or House of Growth) can be interpreted as a modern form of cultural imperialism similar to the European Christian missionary expansion to Africa and elsewhere that accompanied trade in the eighteenth and nineteenth centuries. Another accompanying theme in this contribution is the process whereby, as they expand overseas, certain Japanese companies which in Japan resemble closely in ritual, organization and ethos new religions, become 'secularised' as they travel abroad and establish themselves in Europe and elsewhere. Of course, this is not always so as the case of Yaohan shows.

In their study of Mahikari and Zen in Australia (pp. 74–112) Bouma, Smith and Finlay note the difference between the way Japanese religious movements arrived there and Hinduism and Islam, which came as the religions of migrants. The carriers of Japanese movements were largely westerners. They further note that the rewards offered by the Japanese religions contrast with those offered by other religions: the former emphasise the tangible benefits to be enjoyed in the here and now – this is one of their most attractive and appealing aspects- while the latter stress that the real pay-off comes in another life.

Clarke addresses the theme of Japanese millenarianism in the first of his two main contributions (pp. 129–181). This is a unifying idea in almost every Japanese new religion and extensively developed in Omotokyo and Sekai Kyusei Kyo (Church of World Messianity). Clarke's main focus here is on the strategy devised by Messianity to turn Brazil into what he describes as a catalytic converter that will save the world from self-destructing by inspiring sound and sustainable ecological and environmental policies, which will in turn lead to the elimination of disease, poverty and crime. Ari Pedro Oro (pp. 113–128) also examines the activities of Messianity in Brazil providing a detailed case study of its appeal in the city of Porto Alegre, situated in the south of the country.

Other case studies include Sanda Ionescu's account (pp. 182–197) of Soka Gakkai (Value Creation Society) in Germany in which she discusses that rather rare achievement so far: the successful adaptation of a Japanese religion to a European context, in this case Germany, over the past thirty years. The paradox is that this most rigid, uncompromising and inflexible of Japanese new religions is the most successful at adapting to European conditions and at recruiting new members of European origin.

Louella Matsunaga's second detailed and lengthy contribution (pp. 198–239), based on extensive fieldwork, examines notions of health, illness and disease in Mahikari in Britain, and the interest in and appeal of these ideas and techniques. This complements several other contributions and in particular that of Tina Hamrin (pp. 240–256) who from intensive fieldwork in Hawaii on Tensho Kotai Jingu Kyo, popularly known as the Dancing Religion, reached the conclusion that this was essentially a healing religion. The questions of health and sickness also receive attention in Ari Pedro Oro's previously mentioned contribution on the Church of World Messianity which practices the healing technique of *johrei*, and in the Bouma, Smith, Finlay contribution on Mahikari in Australia. All these contexts point to a strong interest on the part of many in alternative ideas on the causes of sickness, in spiritual healing techniques, and in religion generally as a source of well-being.

Bloom (pp. 257–271) viewing it as a new religion in the American context, offers a perspective on why an old Japanese tradition, the Shin Buddhist tradition founded by Shinran (1173–1263), noted for its Calvinist like emphasis on faith alone, remains after over 100 years presence in the United States, 'a relatively unknown and misunderstood Buddhist tradition' (pp. 269).

The theme of the success and failure of Japanese new religions abroad is taken up and developed, as was previously mentioned, by Clarke in the second of his two main contributions which concludes the volume. This discussion is carried on against the background of Stark's general theory of the success and failure of religion (1996) is devoted largely to the development of Soka Gakkai, Tenrikyo, Messianity, Perfect Liberty, Seicho no Ie and Mahikari in the United States, Brazil and Europe.

References

Anesaki, M. (1930), History of Japanese Religion, London: Kegan Paul, Trench, Trubner and Co.

Bellah, R. (1968), 'Meaning and Modernization', in *Religious Studies*, Vol. 4 No. 1, pp. 37–47.

Clarke, P.B. 'Islam in Western Europe: Present State and Future Trends' in New Trends and Developments in the World of Islam, (ed) Peter B. Clarke, London: Luzac Oriental, pp. 3–41.

Eisenstadt, S.N. (1995), Japanese Civilization. A Comparative View, Chicago: Chicago University Press.

Geertz, C. (1968), Islam Observed, Chicago: Chicago University Press.

Gombrich, R. (1994), 'A Buddhologist's Impressions of Japanese Buddhism' in Japanese New Religions in the West, (eds) Peter Clarke and Jeffrey Somers, Eastbourne, Kent: Japan Library/Curzon Press, pp. 15–24.

Horton R. (1971), 'African Conversion' in *Africa* XLI (2), April, pp. 85–108.

Keene, D. (1984), Dawn to the West, New York: Holt, Rhinehart and Winston.

Mullins, M.R. (1999), Christianity Made in Japan. A Study of Indigenous Movements, Honolulu: University of Hawaii Press.

Roberts, R.H. (1995), 'Globalized Religion?': The Parliament of the World's Religions (Chicago, 1993), in Theoretical Perspective' in Journal of Contemporary Religion, Vol. 10. No. 2, pp. 121–139.

Sundkler, B.G.M. (1961), Bantu Prophets in South Africa, Oxford: Oxford University Press.

Waswo, A. (1996), Modern Japanese Society, 1868–1964, Oxford: Oxford University Press.

CHAPTER ONE

New Japanese Religions in the West

Between Nationalism and Universalism

Catherine Cornille

One of the characteristics which appears to distinguish the new Japanese religions from the traditional religions of Japan is their universalistic orientation and international missionary zeal. Shintoism, the native religion of Japan, focuses uniquely on the creation and the salvation of Japan and the Japanese,[1] and has been often used for nationalistic and ethnocentric purposes.[2] And Buddhism, which is essentially a universalistic religion, developed distinctly nationalistic traits when moving into Japan, propagating itself as the 'protector of the nation' and performing rituals in service of the rulers and for the prosperity of the people. Within the syncretism which came about between Buddhism and Shintoism in Japan, Buddhist divinities came to be regarded as manifestations of Shinto deities and thus came to be identified with the creation of Japan and with Japanese sacred places. While in China Zen Buddhism remained aloof of any association with kings or princes, in Japan it was embraced by the ruling warrior classes whose spirituality and ethos it shaped, and by whom it was in turn itself influenced. This exchange gave rise to some of the highest expressions of what is now considered as typically Japanese culture such as the tea-ceremony, different forms of martial arts and swordmanship, flower-arrangement, the nō-theater etc. Japan also gave rise to a truly indiginous school of Buddhism called Nichiren Buddhism, whose founder Nichiren (1222–1282) viewed Japan as the center of the world, or as the world itself. In his commentary on the verse of the *Lotus Sutra*: 'the Buddha appeared in the world', Nichiren stated: 'by "world" Japan is meant...', thereby also referring to his own role in the history of salvation. It may thus safely be said that 'Nichiren was a patriot, considering himself as the pillar, the eyes and the great vessel of Japan' (Kitagawa 1966:121). One of the most distinctive characteristics of what has come to be called 'Japanese Buddhism' is thus its nationalism.

While prior to its arrival in Japan, Buddhism had travelled a long way from India through China and Korea, Japanese Buddhism itself has, up till

10

the twentieth century, manifested little or no missionary zeal. The emergence of Japanese shrines and temples outside of Japan in the past hundred years have been mostly the effect of economic circumstances, first of deprivation and later abundance, leading to the emigration of Japanese workers and business-people to the West, where they continued to practice their faith. Trained priests were sent and temples were built mainly to cater to the needs of expatriate Japanese.[3] Thus, for example, Jodo Shinshu temples were built in Hawaii, the United States, Latin America and eventually also in Europe. While the Hongwanji Headquarters were ambivalent about sending missionaries to the United States, the two first Japanese Buddhist missionaries were dispatched in 1899, in response to an explicit plea from the Young Men's Buddhist Association of America:

> For those of us living in the United States there is no possibility of basking in the Compassionate Life of the Buddha. Not only are we unable to hear about the Bodhidharma in general, we are cut off from enlightenment through the teaching of Jodo Shinshu. Thus we are unable to understand and appreciate the heart and mind of Shinran Shonin. How we lament at such a state of affairs. Who would not lament? In the eight directions are non-Buddhist forces surrounding the Japanese Buddhists, and we cannot be at ease. It is as if we are sitting on the point of a pin; no matter how we move, we will be pricked. Our burning desire to hear the Teachings is about to explode from every pore in our body... (Quoted in Fields 1992:144).

The first Japanese Buddhist missionaries were thus sent not to convert Westerners to Buddhism, but to attend to the needs of their own followers abroad. The ceremonies were conducted mostly in Japanese, and until a few decades ago there was little or no effort to attract Westerners and to adapt to the Western context. As Shintoku Peel, a European Shin-Buddhist priest states: 'Whenever some Caucasian people became by chance interested in Jodo-Shinshu, they remained outside the Japanese collectivity. Theirs was an individual choice and standpoint and generally they were not too warmly welcomed in the Buddhist temples, which functioned not so much as places of religion, but more often as guardians of the Japanese cultural identity' (1985:99). Most of the early immigrants moreover strongly believed in the myth of the eventual return to Japan and saw no reason for any form of inculturation or adaptation of the faith to the new context. However, with the entry of second and third generation Japanese who often barely knew the Japanese language, and the occasional conversion of Americans and Europeans, the need was gradually felt to adapt the tradition more to its Western context. In the past few decades, Westerners, both male and female, have been ordained monks, nuns, and priests in the various schools of Japanese Buddhism, and gradually more interest has developed in the spreading of Japanese Buddhism in the West.[4]

While this broadening of horizon is a rather late development in Japanese Buddhism, and while the Shinto tradition remains essentially Japanese, the new religions of Japan have manifested from the outset a universalistic orientation. These religions emerged in largely three waves, the oldest dating from the middle to the end of the nineteenth century, the second flourishing after the Second World War, and the third, the 'new new religions' emerging in the past two decades.[5] The universalistic attitude of these religions is manifested in their teachings, practices and aesthetic expressions. The revelations or realizations of the founders of these religions are directed not only to the people of Japan, but to the whole world, and their practices are characterized by a universal accessibility of the means of salvation. On the aesthetic level, the international dimension is reflected in a mixture of Japanese and Western architecture and decor. Many of the new religions have also established international headquarters and more or less conscious missionary strategies.

On the other hand, many of the new religions have also retained explicitly nationalistic and ethnocentric tendencies, claiming Japan to be the origin of creation and the cradle of salvation and the Japanese to be the chosen people. They call for a return to traditional Japanese values such as submissiveness, obedience and sincerity and reinstate traditional practices such as the worshipping of ancestors and purification rituals. In this paper I shall look at how these seemingly contradictory tendencies toward universalism and nationalism coexist in those new religions which have developed missionary activities in Europe, and how this contradiction is resolved, if indeed it is.

Tenrikyo

'To every corner of the earth I will go to save'

The very oldest of the new Japanese religions is Tenrikyo, founded in 1838 by a peasant woman, Miki Nakayama. In the process of summoning the help of various shamanistic healers to cure her son's disease, she found herself possessed by the god *Tsukihi* or *Tenri-O-no-Mikoto* who requested that she become his living shrine. Her mission came to be understood as that of 'sweeping the dust of human hearts' (*Ofudesaki* XVII:11)[6] and bringing about a life of joy. Whereas the focus of Japanese religions at that time did not extend beyond the islands of Japan, Miki Nakayama was from the outset called to accomplish her mission 'throughout the world' (*Ofudesaki* XVII:11). This is reflected in the fifth stanza of the *Mikagura-uta*, the main hymn of Tenrikyo and part of its canonical literature, which states: 'Not only in Yamato, but to every corner of the earth I will go to save'. This universalism may be understood in relation to monotheistic beliefs which gradually developed in Tenrikyo. God came to be regarded as the creator and parent of all human beings: 'Being the creator of the world, all human beings are my children' (*Ofudesaki* IV:62) and 'All human beings are indeed brothers and sisters and there exists none who is an utter stranger' (*Ofudesaki* XIV:53). From this it followed that the salvation of the whole world became the expression of the love of God: 'When all human beings have accomplished the purification of their minds and come to live a life full of joy, I Tsukihi, too, will become cheered up. When I become cheered up, so will all human beings' (*Ofudesaki* VII:109–110).

The universalistic understanding of salvation in Tenrikyo is also related to its belief in the uniqueness of the foundress. While other religious traditions are not explicitly rejected, various statements in the texts of Tenrikyo imply that they have not captured the whole truth. In the very first verse of the *Ofudesaki*, God the Parent says, 'Looking all over the world and through the ages, I find no one who has understood my heart.' And the second verse of the prologue to the *Mikagura-uta* reads: 'It is natural indeed that man is ignorant of the truth, for I have not expounded it to him.' While it is thus suggested that God has not revealed himself fully in other religions, Miki Nakayama is presented in the very first revelation as the full manifestation of God: 'I am the Creator, the true and real God. I have the preordination for this Residence. At this time I have appeared in this world in person to save all mankind. I ask you to have Miki as My living Shrine' (Tenrikyo 1966:7).

These universalistic beliefs were put into practice in Tenrikyo through missionary activities, not only in Japan, but also abroad. According to the movement, the greatest service to the people (*hinokishin*) consists in 'conveying God's mind to other people.' And 'those who have devoted themselves to *hinokishin* in the above sense, finding in it the value of living, are called *yōboku* and are the ideal human image in Tenrikyo' (Tenrikyo 1981:190–191). Tenrikyo originally focused its foreign mission on Asia, sending missionaries at the end of the nineteenth century to Taiwan, Korea, Manchuria, Mongolia, Siberia, and China. This mission could be seen, at least initially, as the result of social and political circumstances, rather than as a conscious and calculated missionary policy. The first Tenrikyo missionaries to China and Taiwan followed the Japanese troops in the 1894 Sino-Japanese war. Others left Japan as a result of the Meiji persecutions of Tenrikyo and started to proselytize in other countries of Asia. Soon, however, international mission became a more conscious strategy: missionaries were sent to various continents and their hardships became part of the heroic lore of the tradition.[7] The first mission station in the West was established in London in 1908, and missionaries were also sent to North America and to Brazil prior to the second world war. In 1918, the Young Men's Asociation was founded which set itself as goal to form *arakitoryo*, or pioneer missionaries who bring the teachings of Tenrikyo where they have yet to be conveyed. In 1927, an Overseas Mission Department and a Foreign Language School were established in the

Tenrikyo headquarters. It was, however, only after World War II that the overseas mission became a policy for the whole movement. The Tenrikyo Missionaries Association was established which currently counts about eight hundred thousand members and whose mission is 'to experience the joy of single-hearted salvation, awakening to their duty as the instruments of Oyasama; to help one another in perfect union; and to engage actively in propagation work in order to realize a joyous life according to the will of God the Parent' (Tenrikyo 1986:155). Its activities include 1) constant use of the Scriptures, 2) spreading of the teaching and salvation, 3) transmission of faith, 4) *hinokishin*, 5) get-together of yoboku, 6) general meeting, 7) seminars and lectures, and others. The Tenrikyo Overseas Mission Department consists of nine subdepartments for the different areas of the world, and one translation department. In Europe, mission stations and overseas offices were established in Germany (Munich), Italy (Milan and Rome), England (London), the Netherlands (Haarlem), and France (Paris, Bordeau, Perpignan). The total number of members in Europe does not exceed one thousand, and half of these live in France, where the only Tenrikyo church is located. Most of the members of Tenrikyo in Europe are Japanese.

The Jiba as the centre of the world

While the term 'nationalism' in the strong sense may not be applicable to Tenrikyo, some of the teachings of the foundress have nationalistic undertones and have come to be used for nationalistic purposes in the history of Tenrikyo. These teachings relate mainly to the creation myth, which is at the heart of Tenrikyo doctrine and practice. According to this myth, the creation of the world took place at the Jiba, a place designated by the foundress and currently located in the city of Tenri, close to Nara. This is also emphasized in the *Ofudesaki* which states: 'There at the Jiba did I begin to create all the human beings of the world. The Jiba is the native place of all people. This shall be our eternal home' (XVII:7–8). The myth further specifies that 'Human beings were conceived at the Jiba of Origin 900,099,999 years before October 26, 1838 [date of the beginning of Tenrikyo]. After conceiving them in three days and three nights, Izanami-no-Mikoto stayed there for three years and three months, and gave birth in seventy-five days to those children in the following order: first in an area of seven *ri* square between what later became Nara and Hase; second in the rest of what later became Yamato Province; and third in what later became provinces of Yamashiro, Iga, Kawachi; and then in the rest of what later became Japan' (Tadasama 1983:95). Marking the exact place of the origin of creation is a pillar called the *kanrodai*, the axis mundi which forms the central point of worship within the movement. Every month, the story of creation is reinacted during the *Kagura-service* which is only performed around the Kanrodai, and only by a select group of 10 eminent members.

14

During this service, the ritual dancers wear animal masks and re-enact the creation story. The teaching and practice of the creation story are regarded as the very essence of Tenrikyo, as reflected in the following words from the *Ofudesaki*: 'If only I can teach the origin of human beings throughout the world, then I will work whatever kind of salvation. Indeed, with a single word I will save you from and and every matter' (XII:129–130). Members are encouraged to attend the Kagura service at the kanrodai as often as possible and are greeted with the words '*okaeri nasai,*' 'welcome home' or 'welcome back' upon arriving in the city of Tenri. The return to the Jiba and the participation in the Kagura Service is said to be 'the extension of God's work of creation' and 'the way to universal and perfect salvation in every respect' (Tenrikyo 1986:51). The ultimate goal of Tenrikyo is that of 'all people returning to Jiba, worshipping again around the Kanrodai' (Tadasama 1983:95).

While Miki Nakayama's emphasis on the Jiba as the place of creation and the origin of salvation may be regarded as no more than a classical example of the notion of the 'axis mundi' which may be found in most religious traditions, it may also breed nationalistic ideas and feelings. Even in the *Ofudesaki* itself, there are verses with more explicitly nationalistic connotations, such as the following:

> Until now, those of *Kara* have done as they pleased with *Nihon*. What can be done about the regret of God? Hereafter, *Nihon* will do as it pleases with those of *Kara*. Be aware of it, all of you. Root and branches of the same tree: branches will break, yet the root will prosper. Until now, those of *Kara* were said to be great, but from now on they will only be broken. Look at *Nihon*! It is thought to be tiny, but when the root appears, you will be overwhelmed with amazement. (III:86–90)

These verses were made much of in the 1930s and 1940s, when members of Tenrikyo were also swept up in the nationalistic ideology of the times. The terms *Kara* versus *Nihon* may refer to other nations versus Japan. In the various wars which Japan has fought since the Meiji era, members of Tenrikyo have mostly supported the imperial cause with fundraising and prayers (Ellwood 1982:52–60). The dancers of the Kagura-service use a fan imprinted with the Japanese flag.

However, the relationship between Tenrikyo and the state has often been tense, since its own creation story in many respects contradicts the official Shinto creation myth which forms the basis of the authority and the legitimacy of the Japanese emperor. Tenrikyo underwent official government persecution for many years, with passages from its sacred texts censured and the performance of certain parts of the rituals banned. It was not until after the Second World War that its sacred scriptures were published in their original form and that the whole Kagura ritual could be performed. Since the War, most potentially nationalistic terms and symbols have come to be interpreted in a more spiritualistic sense. Thus, in the official English translation of the *Ofudesaki*, the term *Nihon* is explained as 'deriving from a word that indicates the region around the Jiba, refers to the place settled by those whose use of mind and way of living are near the intention of God the Parent, who is one in truth with the Jiba' while the term *Kara* is said to mean 'the places inhabited by those whose use of mind and way of living are still distant from God's intention' (*Ofudesaki* 1993:267). And the read circle on the white surface, represented on the fan used in the Kagura dance is said to represent the sun, rather than the Japanese flag.

The Omoto New Religions

The Purification of the World

Sekai Kyusei Kyo and Mahikari are both off-shoots from one of the older new religions, Omotokyo. Within Omoto, strong universalistic tendencies were already manifested in its belief that 'all religions come from the same source,' a belief which it, in turn, inhereted from a Chinese sectarian religion called Do-in (Young 1988:263). This led to the foundation in 1925, by the co-founder of the movement, Onisaburo Deguchi, of *Jinrui Aizenkai*, also called 'Universal Love and Brotherhood Association' (ULBA). This organization was established in order to 'establish enduring peace by removing the barriers of race and religion, enhancing the true worth of all men, and promoting cultural advancement' (article III of its constitution). Deguchi viewed Omoto as 'the international religion' which would unite all other religions, and reinforced this idea by introducing the study of esperanto within the movement. While the use of esperanto is a distinctive feature of Omoto, the idea that all religions are unified in the one universal religion has been taken over by all religions decending from Omoto including Sekai Kyusei Kyo and Mahikari.

Both Sekai Kyusei Kyo and Mahikari are new Japanese religions with strong universalistic pretentions. After the Second World War, Okada Mokichi, founder of Sekai Kyusei Kyo changed the name of his movement from the 'Greater Japan Society of Kannon' (founded in 1934) to *Sekai Meshiakyo*, 'the Church of World Messianity' and finally to *Sekai Kyusei Kyo*, 'World Salvation Teachings'.[8] *Sukyo* Mahikari calls itself a 'supra-religious organization' and has developed an elaborate doctrine to demonstrate its own role as the fulfilment of all other religions. According to this doctrine, other Gods and religions belong to the era of water, while at this time the era of the fire-God has dawned. While both Sekai Kyusei Kyo and Mahikari believe in various lower gods and spirits, the emphasis is ultimately on one God who is the source of creation and salvation, and whom members address in their prayers. The founder of each of these religions is regarded by their followers as the messiah, or as the messenger of God. It is this belief in one God and in the founder as the unique channel of God's will which theoretically supports the idea of a universal mission.

Omoto, Sekai Kyusei Kyo and Mahikari all understand their univeral mission in ecological and aesthetic terms as the purification of the world or 'the Restoration of Man and the Environment' (theme of the ULBA conference, held in Feb. 1981 in Kyoto) and the establishment of paradise on earth. Both Sekai Kyusei Kyo and Mahikari are strongly opposed to the use of any fertilizers in farming and have invested much effort and many resources in research and information on natural farming and in the actual creation of natural farms throughout the world. The conception of purity operative in Sekai Kyusei Kyo and Mahikari also extends to the spiritual world where it is believed that the spiritual body of a person can be polluted by possessing spirits which are the cause of all kinds of diseases and misfortunes. Both religions thus practice a purification ritual called *johrei* in Sekai Kyusei Kyo and *okiyome* in Mahikari which consist of the chanelling of the Divine Light through the palm of the hand, and which is believed to have the power to avert evil and to cure diseases.[9] While the performance of this purification ritual is only one element in Sekai Kyusei Kyo, Mahikari has made it the heart of its teaching and practice, and has come to be known mainly as a healing religion. Any member who has been initiated is allowed and encouraged to apply *okiyome* to whoever is willing to receive it, regardless of age, sex, race, nationality or religion. Sekai Kyusei Kyo, on the other hand, puts more emphasis on an aesthetic understanding of salvation in terms of the creation of 'earthly paradises' and the stimulation of artistic creation.[10]

The universalistic teachings of Sekai Kyusei Kyo and Mahikari are given additional impetus through their millenaristic teachings, also inherited from Omotokyo. Okada Mokichi, the founder of Sekai Kyusei Kyo, believed that a new world or paradise had already been established in the spiritual world and was gradually breaking through on earth by means of the purifying power of *johrei. Johrei* is considered in this movement as the symbol of God's love and mercy in the period of transition, and as a way to avoid disasters before the establishment of the Kingdom. In Mahikari, this millenaristic belief acquired more apocalyptic overtones. Here too, a new 'sunshine civilization' is about to break through. However, prior to the dawning of this civilization, the world will be purified through what is called a 'baptism by fire,' understood as a series of various cataclysms. Only those who have joined Mahikari, and have thus already been purified, will be saved. The date for the coming of the new civilization is the end of the second millenium, and members are urged to exert themselves to save as many people as possible before this time. This is expressed in several of the

17

prayers of Mahikari such as the *Butsumetsu no yo* (the time of the end of the world):

> The time of the money-making and sight-seeing business is over. Now is the time for the land of the Origin of Sun (Hinomoto) to prosper with the work of God's Light. The time to protect the religious denominations and sects and tradition is over. Now is the Divine Era to participate in the Divine Plan and accomplish its goal. Obsolete is the world in which the protection of traditions and religious denominations is considered as the primary purpose. Now is the Divine Era of Sukyo in which the primary mission is the salvation of the people of the world.
>
> (Yokoshi Prayer Book 1986:198)

These millenaristic expectations and universalistic self-perception have brought about strong missonary activities in both Sekai Kyusei Kyo and Mahikari. The former established its first mission center outside of Japan in Hawaii in 1953. Since then it has continued its mission in North- and South-America, Canada, China, Taiwan, Korea, Thailand, France, Belgium, Portugal, etc. Mahikari established its first 'training-center' or *dōjō* in the West in Paris in the early seventies and has spread from there to Switzerland, Italy, Belgium, Germany, England, the Netherlands, Spain, and also to North and South America and to Africa. This called for the establishment of an international office in Japan, and a more systematic effort at translating the texts and prayers of the movement. While Sekai Kyusei Kyo has remained relatively small in Europe (a few hundred members), Mahikari has become one of the most successful new Japanese religions in Europe, counting about ten to fifteen thousand members of mostly European and African origins. This different success-rate is partly related to different approaches toward the transmission of Light and to different missionary policies. Both movements encourage their members to proselytize, making it a condition for one's own spiritual development and the upward mobility within the movement. But while Sekai Kyusei Kyo has profiled itself predominantly as a cultural organization (MOA) in the West and is somewhat reserved about the practice of *johrei*, Mahikari encourages its members to practice *okiyome* whenever and wherever possible. Members are thus more intensely engaged in the propagation of the teachings. Both religions attract not only Japanese and European members, but are also popular among Africans living in Europe.

Japan as the Cradle of Salvation

While Sekai Kyusei Kyo and Mahikari regard themselves – in line with Omotokyo – as international religions with branches throughout the world and members from many different nationalities, their teachings and

18

practices still manifest traces of implicit, and sometimes explicit national-ism. Onisaburo Deguchi, co-founder of Omotokyo, already advanced the idea (in the *Reigen Monogatari*) that there existed a 'deep connection' between Japan and the rest of the world. This meant that the islands of Japan are in fact a model for the rest of the world: Honshu representing Europe and Russia, Shikoku Australia, Hokkaido North-America, Kyushu standing for Africa, and Taiwan (at that time occupied by Japan) for South-America. Japan is thus given the special mission to transform itself and to save the rest of the world. This idea of the unique role of Japan in the plan of salvation of the world was taken over and elaborated by Mahikari. Okada Yoshikazu, founder of Mahikari, used myths and beliefs about the sunken continent Lemuria or Mu, which circulated among Rosicrucians and Theosophists[11] to argue that Japan was once the center of this original civilization and that the Japanese were the first of God's creatures.[12] From Japan, 16 princes were sent all over the world to form the 'five colored races'.[13] Thus, all languages, cultures, religions and civilizations originate in Japan. The idea that Japan is the center of creation is also elaborated in the book *Mahikari, Thank God for the Answers at Last* by A.K. Tebecis which is widely read among non-Japanese members of Mahikari:

> According to the revelations he (Okada) received from Almighty God the land that is now called Japan is the cradle of *all* major religions. The Taka Amahara ('high plain of Heaven') referred to in Shintoism is the country today called Japan, and is where Gods descended on earth and manifested in physical form. In other words, world history began in Japan. The first humans on earth were created in Japan, in Hidama (now called Hida) in the area of the city Takayama. Japan was the 'garden of Eden in the east' that is mentioned in the Bible (Genesis 2:8). The spiritual name of Japan is *Hi no Motosu Kuni* which means 'Country of the Origin of the Spirit'. Aeons of time later after civilizations had spread throughout the world, the continent in the Pacific Ocean (of which Japan was a part) became known as the Mu continent (1982:389–390).

According to Mahikari, it is thus the area of Hida which is the place of the origin of creation. The city of Takayama and the whole area of Hida have become important places of pilgrimage for the members of Mahikari. It is in Takayama that the 'Main World Shrine' or the *Suza* was built and the mausoleum for the founder was erected on a hillside in the Hida area. The headquarters of Mahikari are located near the Suza, and it is here that members attend the advanced course of Mahikari. The Suza itself is regarded as God's dwelling-place on earth and the source of salvation, understood as the return of the five colored races to the place of creation. While Mahikari has spread throughout the world and has attracted a considerable amount of non-Japanese members (about 150,000 of a total of

800,000 members according to 1996 statistics of the movement), still almost all prayers are recited in Japanese, and all rituals are performed in their original Japanese form. Ritual objects such as scrolls, statues and altars for the ancestors are exported from Japan to the various Mahikari centers abroad. Thus, the Mahikari training centers or *dōjō's* in the West have become exact replicas of their Japanese originals. Even though the prayer books provide vernacular translations, all members are required to recite prayers in the Japanese language. This is, according to Mahikari, because the language used in the prayers is not actual Japanese, but *kotodama*, 'the language of the Gods.'[14] Although attempts have been made to appoint local national leaders, the general regional leaders or *shidōbuchō* are all Japanese. This is because Mahikari is regarded as a theocracy, rather than as a democracy, and because Japanese leaders seem to be more submissive and reliable.

The belief in Japan as the origin of creation is related in Mahikari cosmology and soteriology to its role as the cradle of salvation. Biblical passages referring to the Light and to the idea that the 'Light must come from the East' (Gen. 3:24, Job 38:24, Isaiah 41:2, etc.) and to the Paraclete or the Spirit of Truth (John 16:7–8, 12–14) are said to refer to the founder of Mahikari and presented as evidence of the special role of Japan in the economy of salvation. To further accentuate the role of Japan, the story of the life of Jesus is retold and adapted to Mahikari purposes. According to the Mahikari version of the life of Jesus, he did not live and die in Judea, but travelled all over the world, and received the teachings which he later proclaimed in Judea from Shinto priests. He did not die on the cross, but he retuned to Japan where he married a Japanese woman and died at the age of 118.[15] Not only Jesus, but also the Buddha, Lao-tzu, Confucius, and Mohammed are said to have visited Japan, and to have gained their insights from Shinto sages.

The nationalism of Mahikari also manifests itself in its attitude toward the Japanese emperor. While the emperor himself denounced his divine status at the end of the Second World War, Mahikari continues to regard him as a direct descendent of Su-god, and a mediator between God and the world. Traces of Japanese imperialism may be detected in the belief that the role of the emperor applies not only to Japan, but to the whole world.[16] The divine mission of the emperor as mediator between God and the world is however shared in Mahikari with the founder who is seen as God's saviour. Salvation is thus conceived of as the unification of the five colored races under the emperor of Japan and the teachings of Okada Yoshikazu, referred to in the movement as Sukuinushisama or 'Lord Saviour'.[17]

In Sekai Kyusei Kyo, the importance of Japan in the plan of salvation is expressed predominantly in terms of its cultural and artistic superiority. Salvation is understood as the creation of paradise or of a world of truth, virtue and beauty, in which the latter plays an important role because it can be expressed by form. The creation of beauty is thus a work of salvation to which, according to the founder, the Japanese have been particularly called: 'Every race in the world has its own thought and culture. The national characteristic of the Japanese people is to give expression through the medium of beauty and thus to contribute to the development of culture. From this the future course of Japan is self-evident. I believe that eternal peace and prosperity will be brought about if we adhere to the above ideal.'[18] In order to live up to this ideal, so-called 'earthly paradises' have been created by the movement in Atami and Hakone. These art museums and Japanese gardens are regarded as sacred grounds, as places of pilgrimage, and as models for the rest of the world. This is reflected in the following words of the founder: 'If a pattern is worked out somewhere in the world, it will in time be imitated on a world-wide scale.'[19] The activities of Sekai Kyusei Kyo in the West have mainly focused on the export of Japanese culture through the organization of Japanese language courses, courses in *ikebana* or flower arrangement, Japanese theatre and of exhibitions of Japanese art. This has been done under the auspices of MOA, or Mokichi Okada Association.

The Nichiren New Religions

World Peace

While Soka Gakkai, Reiyukai, Rissho Kosei Kai and Nihonzan Myohoji are all new religions derived from the nationalist school of Nichiren Buddhism, their focus is not only on the salvation of Japan but of the whole world. Each of these religions has thus developed a universalistic reading of the Lotus Sutra, and has become particularly involved in the propagation of World Peace. Nichidatsu Fujii (1885–1985), founder of Nihonzan Myohoji, a smaller new religion, saw his mission in terms of bringing Buddhism back to India and spreading it throughout the world: 'Though some may regard them as obsolete teachings, the Buddhist doctrines against killing and violence will save today's world. We must go all over the world to preach these teachings with courage and confidence. Buddhism must find its way to Europe, too' (Nichidatsu 1974:134). This is expressed through the building of peace pagodas (*saiten-kaikyo*) throughout the world and through the practice of *gyakku-shodai*, beating the drum and chanting the *daimoku* ('praise to the Lotus Sutra) for peace. Members of the movement have been active in the defence of minority rights (such as those of the American Indians) and in protest marches against nuclear arms (such as the 1982 walk across the United States) and against war. Reiyukai and Rissho Kosei Kai have also been active in the attempts to abolish the production and testing of nuclear weapons. Rissho Kosei Kai played a major role in the sponsoring and the organization of the first World Conference for Religion and Peace in Kyoto in 1970, and the founder of the movement, Nikkyo Niwano, was the first president of the Asian Conference for Religion and Peace and is honorary president of the World Conference for Religion and Peace. The 'Niwano Peace Foundation' was established in 1978 'to contribute to the realization of world peace and the enhancement of culture'. Every year, the Niwano Peace Prize is awarded to a religious person or organization which has contributed significantly toward the establishment of world peace. For Rissho Kosei Kai, world peace and inter-religious dialogue are inseparable. Unlike some of the other new religions of Japan, it does not regard world peace as its own prerogative, or acceptance of the movement and its ideology as a condition for world peace. Soka Gakkai, the largest of the new religions in the Nichiren line, believes that world peace can be accomplished through the chanting of the *daimoku* in front of the *gohonzon* (sacred scroll with the names of various Buddhas and Bodhisattvas from the Lotus Sutra.) While all these new religions advocate world peace, there is little or no concrete analysis of the political, economical and social causes which inhibit its actual realization.

The international orientation of Soka Gakkai has come with the ascent to power of D. Ikeda in 1960. It is he who created Soka Gakkai International (SGI) and who has stimulated the propagation of the teachings of the movement outside of Japan. The first Soka Gakkai missionary was sent in 1960 to the United States, where the movement has become very popular, attracting to date (1996) a membership of about 300,000. The movement started in Europe in the early sixties, and has a membership of about 30,000, spread predominantly over England, France and Italy. Under the leadership of the second president, Toda Josei, Soka Gakkai developed an aggressive and notorious practice of proselytization called *shakubuku*, meaning 'to break and subdue'. This was done through argumentation, promises and threats and through the rejection and denigration of all other religions, especially Christianity. Every new member joining the movement had to promise to bring in three new members. In coming to the West, Soka Gakkai has somewhat modified and tempered this aggressive form of proselytization, and has come to understand *shakubuku* more in terms of sharing or testifying to the positive changes which membership may bring about. However, the exclusivistic attitude which characterized the teaching of Nichiren himself, and the practice of Soka Gakkai in Japan has continued within its international mission. While Rissho Kosei Kai has made the dialogue with other religions the heart of its mission in Europe, Soka Gakkai has involved itself very little with inter-religious dialogue.[20]

In Japan, proselytization or *michibiki* forms an integral part of the practice of members of both Reiyukai and Rissho Kosei Kai. To become a leader, a member must bring three or more new members into the movement, and a strong sense of respect and responsibility characterizes the relationship between the convert *michibiki no ko* (child) and the one who brought the person into the movement and who is called *michibiki no oya* (parent). In the West, a distinction is made within Rissho Kosei Kai between *michibiki*, which is understood in a broader sense as bringing people to 'religion' as the basis of world peace, and *taiken seppō-kai*, which consists of explicit proselytization with the purpose of converting people to the movement (Nehring 1992:248–255). This broader understanding of proselytization is related to its concern with inter-religious dialogue. In 1967, Rissho Kosei Kai started the 'Faith to All Men Movement' with the purpose of bringing people to their own faith. This is based on the belief that the Buddha Shakyamuni reveals himself in all religions. Hence, the mission of Rissho Kosei Kai in the West has mainly taken the form of dialogue centers, which in Europe are located in Germany (Frankfurt) and in Belgium (Moorslede). On the other hand, the teaching of Rissho Kosei Kai is also regarded as the universal truth which must be brought to every corner of the world. The goal of the movement is ultimately to spread the '*Sangha*', a notion which may be understood in the broad sense as referring to all those who do the will of the Buddha and live in harmony, or in the more narrow sense to the members of Rissho Kosei Kai (Niwano 1968:191). Reiyukai has developed more traditional missionary activities in the West and has between five hundred and one thousand members in Europe, spread over Italy, Spain, England and France. Besides building peace pagodas and beating the drum while chanting the daimoku, members of Nihinzan Myohoji are encouraged to practice *keta*, which consists of guiding others on the path while practicing oneself. The emphasis here is however on one's own practice and on the creation of world peace, which may account for the relatively small number of members in the movement (1500). The first peace pagoda of Nipponzan Myohoji in the West was inaugurated in Milton Keynes, England, in 1980. The movement also has a few members living in Paris.

The religious practice in all four of the new Japanese religious within the Nichiren tradition is focussed on the recitation of the *daimoku*, or the mantra '*nammyohorengekyo*' or 'praise to the Lotus Sutra' in Japanese. While all these religions strongly believe in the power of the mantra, they differ to a certain extent in their understanding of its functioning. In Soka Gakkai, it must be recited in front of the *gohonzon*, the sacred scroll on which verses of praise to the Lotus Sutra have been inscribed by the priests of the Nichiren Shoshu sect of Buddhism. Since its excommunication by Nichiren Shoshu, Soka Gakkai has acquired its own original *gohonzon*, painted by the famous sixteenth century priest, Nikkan Shonin. A more universalistic understanding of the *gohonzon* as the reflection of an internal reality, rather than as a magical object is also being developed. In Rissho Kosei Kai, the sacred object or the *gohonzon* is the statue of the Buddha in the *daisedō* or the Great Buddha Hall in Tokyo. For Nihonzan Myohoji, it is the mantra itself which holds the power. While the recitation of the mantra is the same in Japan and in the West, there is also a certain attempt to adapt to the local cultures. Thus, when Soka Gakkai started its mission in the United States, the first missionary, Masayasu Sadanaga, changed his name to George Williams. Soka Gakkai has also appointed local national leaders outside of Japan and has integrated the celebration of local festivals.

Japan as the model of peace

Even though the new Nichiren religions have broadened their missionary horizons beyond Japan, they have not completely rid themselves from all traces of nationalism. While they all propagate world peace, it is also believed that this peace can only be established by their own movement, and that it can only proceed from Japan. Nichidatsu Fujii, e.g., believes that Japan is called to establish world peace because, according to him, 'it is by nature a peaceful nation which has almost never engaged in any aggression toward other countries' (Fujii 1980:51). Japan establised a constitution renouncing war and arms after the Second World War because, Fujii argues, 'we aspired to become an example of a society and nation that lives an elevated life overriding the actual conflicts of interest for the sake of peace and well-being of humanity' (Fujii 1982:62). He interprets the current superiority of Japan within the context of the sequence of dominant civilizations mentioned in the Lotus Sutra: There is *sayuu-toomotsu* when the West is elevated and the East sunk down. This has been the situation for the past hundred years. The West has brought materialism and unabraidled economic expansion to the East, which cannot but lead to human extermination. For humanity to survive, the opposite movement must be brought about or *tooyuu-saimotsu*, in which the East must become dominant. The spiritual civilization of the East deals with the question of the mind and the heart and focuses on non-violence. And this spiritual civilization of peace must emerge from Japan because 'except in Japan, there is no longer a religion that ascribes to the belief of eliminating Western civilization and leading humanity in the reverse direction' (Fujii 1980:25–28). This religion is for Nichidatsu Fujii Buddhism, and more particularly his own version of Nichiren Buddhism. According to him, peace was thus to emanate from Japan through the building of peace pagodas or stupas all over the world.

While the importance of Japan in the process of the salvation of the world is less systematically elaborated in the other Nichiren new religions, there is still some soteriological importance attached to the country of Japan and to its culture. The fact that the mantra 'nammyohorengekyo' cannot be translated into other languages points to certain magical connotations attached to the language. Each of the new Nichiren religions has, or had a particular place of pilgrimage in Japan where the original mandala was

believed to be situated. This was for Soka Gakkai the *kaidan*, located in
Taiseki-ji. Since the separation with Nichiren Shoshu, however, the main
mandala has been moved to the headquarters in Tokyo. For Rissho Kosei
Kai, the main mandala is the statue of the Buddha, situated also in Tokyo.

Soka Gakkai has become prominent in Japanese politics through its
political party called Komeito, now Shinshinto. While the program of the
party cannot be said to be overtly nationalistic, Anson Shupe points out
that they argued 'that their grounding in the nationalist zeal of Nichiren
would restore Japanese pride and return the nation to its preeminent place
in the community of nations' (Shupe 1993:234). Soka Gakkai has also
adopted a highly militaristic organizational structure dividing the movement into some version of household (*setai*), squad (*kumi*), company (*han*),
district (*chiku*), region (*shibu*), general region (*shoshibu*), and headquarter
(*hombu*). This structure is also found in other new religions such as
Mahikari, and reflects a typically Japanese love of order and hierarchy.

Buddhist New Religions

Spirit Messages and Universal Mission

Shinnyo-en and Kofuku-no-Kagaku are two new Japanese religions which
have little in common besides the fact that they both claim to belong to the
Buddhist, but not to the Nichiren Buddhist, tradition. Shinnyo-en was
founded in 1936 (but officially recognized in 1953) by a Buddhist layman,
Shinjo Ito and his wife Tomoji Ito. Their religion can be regarded as a
popularized form of esoteric Buddhism in which the life history of the
founder and his family play an important soteriological role.[21] Kofuku-no-
Kagaku may be ranked among the new new religions as it was founded only
in 1986 by a business man, Ryuho Okawa (born in 1956), who from 1981
on had been receiving spirit messages and who came to believe in himself as
a (higher) reincarnation of the Buddha, and as the manifestation of the
highest Spirit, called 'El Cantare.' Both Shinnyo-en and Kofuku-no-Kagaku
attach great importance to the spirit world and view their universal mission
as a response to developments within this world. The main practice of
Shinnyo-en is called 'sesshin training' and consists of the interaction with
the spirit world through trained mediums called *reinōsha*. It was believed
that with the death of the wife of the founder in 1967, the power of
salvation, called *bakku-daiju*, through interaction with the spirit world was
made available to the whole world.[22] According to the teaching 'she
departed for the spiritual world to extend the salvation transcending all the
differences in languages, religions and nationalities.'[23] Kofuku-no-Kagaku
developed within ten years from a small study group to a religion with
universalistic pretentions through a development in the self-understanding
of Okawa from a medium for messages from a variety of spirits to the

incarnation of the highest spirit 'El Cantare'. The latter development took place in 1991, when he declared to his followers: 'It is El Cantare who stands before you and preaches the eternal Truth. I am the one who is given the highest authority on this earth' (Okawa 1995a:78). In 1994, Ryuho Okawa launched the 'big bang' campaign of world-wide mission with the following speech: 'The world is one. Human beings are one. The truth of the Buddha is the teaching to save the entire human race on earth. We will not rest until it reaches every corner of the world, deserts of Africa, Latin America, the lands of atheism, everywhere' (Okawa 1995b:29–30). This universality is regarded by Okawa as a necessary and important characteristic of any contemporary religion: 'Any religion that is now necessary or that will emerge or spread ought to contain universality . . . it should be a religion that could be readily accepted all over the world. . . . In the present age, however, the world is about to become one, and we should think that God's will might be that a religion that could unify the world is desirable' (Okawa 1993:161–163).

The international mission of Shinnyo-en has developed mainly through members who moved outside of Japan and continued their missionary activities abroad. While Shinnyo-en states that the fundamental principle of the teaching is not to expand the Order, but to truly save each individual, explicit proselytizing, or *otaske*, is considered as one of the three central practices (besides *gohōshi*, the sweeping of public places and *kangi*, the offering of donations to the organization), and the missionary record of a person is an important basis of promotion within the movement. The first Shinnyo-en temple abroad was opened in Hawaii in 1973, and since, temples have been established in California, Taiwan, France, Italy, and Belgium. Once a group has been formed, a *reinōsha*, spirit mediator, is sent from Japan to perform the 'sesshin training'. The purpose of this form of spirit mediation is to discover the karmic causes of problems of members and to obtain concrete guidance. Although every member can become a *reinōsha*, no foreigner has as yet reached this rank (which, according to some, is why Shinnyo-en has not attracted many Western members). In Europe, Shinnyo-en has less than two hundred members, most of whom are Japanese living in the West.

The dissemination of the teachings of Kofuku-no-Kagaku has occurred mostly through the books of Ryuho Okawa, some of which have become best-sellers in Japan. The most programmatic of these books are the 'Laws Trilogy': *The Laws of the Sun*, *The Laws of Gold*, and *The Laws of Eternity*, first published in 1986, but revised in 1994, the year of the campaign of world-wide mission. In the effort to spread the teachings throughout the world, most effort has been put in the translation of these books. But members are also encouraged to proselytize in a traditional way. In his 'Monthly Message' in September 1994, Okawa presented his 'Missionary Work Sutra':

The world is still in darkness
Deliver your fellow humans
From the fog hanging over the end of this century,
And from their spiritual darkness.
Let them know
That to be ignorant of the Truth is, in itself, sin.
Considering the efforts and pains of Bosatsu
In the Heavenly World,
People living on earth must be prepared to sweat,
And to use their wisdom.
Be courageous enough to tell others
The facts as they are,
And the truth as it is.
Convey to as many as possible
The Truth of the Dharma of Buddha (Monthly Message, Sept. 1994)

The mission in the West has mostly proceeded through the distribution of the books and video's of Ryuho Okawa, and through the establishment of offices in London and New York. The name of the movement in the West is translated as Institute for Research in Human Happiness (IRH). The number of members in Europe is less than 150 and consists mainly of Japanese expatriates.

Japan as the origin of a New Civilization

While Shinnyo-en has remained relatively free from nationalistic traits,[24] the writings of Ryuho Okawa are replete with references to the unique role and mission of Japan in the history of salvation. According to Okawa's creative re-writing of history, this special role of Japan is the culmination of the sequence of various civilizations which date back to that of 'Gonda-Ana', 735,000 years ago, or the coming together of the civilizations of the East and the West: 'The civilization that emerged in Greece moved westward to the United States and then to Japan. Likewise, the Oriental civilization, which originated in India, moved to China and came through Korea to Japan. Thus, both Eastern and Western civilizations have flowed into Japan. Looking at this stream of history, I am sure it is a historical necessity that a new, great civilization or culture emerges here in Japan. And the civilization originating in Japan in turn flows back to the countries that are her predecessors in history. Therefore, for the period of the next 100 to 150 years, Japan will be the center of a great civilization in the world' (Okawa 1995a:54–55). Before the beginning of this new civilization, prefigured for the year 2020, the world, according to Okawa, will go through chaos and devastation, marked by the downfall of Europe and America: 'Humankind will usher in a new civilization in the twenty-first

27

century after decades of extreme chaos and devastation. The new civilization will begin in this land in Asia. It will spread from Japan to Southeast Asia, Indonesia and Oceania. Some of the existing continents (Europe and America) will sink into the ocean, and a new continent of Mu will rise from beneath the Pacific Ocean to offer a stage for a new civilization. These future civilizations will only become possible if we let the sun of God's Truth rise here and now in Japan. When the world sinks into darkness, Japan will shine as the sun' (Okawa 1990:178–179). Linking worldly events with developments in the spiritual world, Okawa states that in the course of the second half of the twentieth century, many 'angels of light' have incarnated in Japan, thus making it into the sacred land from which the salvation of the world is to proceed, and that 'high spirits in heaven wish to make future Japan the center of the salvation movement' (Okawa 1995a:82). In the preface to *The Challenge of Religion*, the importance of Japan in our day is compared to that of Israel in the time of Jesus or India in the time of Shakyamuni: 'The wind of miracles originating in this land, Japan, has begun blowing in all directions of the world. And the impact it has on Japanese people is comparable to what happened to the people of Israel who first encountered Jesus Christ's teaching, or to those in India who first heard Shakyamuni's teaching. This is the greatest religious event that has ever taken place in history, and its shock wave is beginning to spread to all other nations in the world.' This unique role of Japan in the history of salvation is related, according to Okawa, to its economic success: 'Rather than saying that Japan is the source, it is more accurate to say that Japan is becoming the source for the new spiritual movement. Historical observation suggests that once a country becomes economically powerful, it prepares also to become a cultural leader. Accordingly, now that Japan has become a great economic power, we are in the process of becoming more culturally influential' (Okawa 1995a:105). This view of Japan as the most spiritually and economically advanced nation is presented as a reaction against the sense of inferiority which affected the Japanese during the first decades after the Second World War: 'The postwar period in Japan began with the idea that Japanese had nothing valuable since they lost the war. However, that period is over, and it is time to once again evaluate themselves correctly to determine their future course' (Okawa 1995a:105). As opposed to this, Okawa thus presents a kind of triumphalist nationalism which relates the economic successes of Japan to its spiritual mission and to the idea that it is called to 'lead the people of the world' (Okawa 1995c:52).

Conclusion

The new religions of Japan represent a complex mixture of universalistic and nationalistic attitudes, of concern with on the one hand the salvation of the world and on the other hand the preservation and the promotion of Japanese culture, values and ethnicity.

The universalism of these religions may be understood in the light of the opening of Japan to the world since the Meiji period, or as the religious expression of a wider tendency toward 'internationalization' and 'globalization' evident in Japanese society in the twentieth century. From the point of view of the religions themselves, it may be seen as logically following from the belief in one God, in the uniqueness of the founder, and in the imminent end of the world. Tenrikyo, Omotokyo, Sekai Kyusei Kyo and Mahikari emphasize that all people are children of the same God and should be saved. Since the respective founders of each of the new religions of Japan is believed to fulfill a unique role in the history of the salvation of the world, it is the responsibility of members to spread these teachings throughout the world. And since the world is about to come to an end, it is a matter of particular urgency. Many of the new religions of Japan are based on this-worldly or vitalistic, and therefore universally relevant conceptions of salvation in terms of health, harmony, happiness, wealth, etc., and have made the means of salvation accessible to all.

In spite of this universalistic orientation, many of the new Japanese religions continue to be characterized by latent or sometimes explicit forms of Japanese nationalism and ethnocentrism. Like the universalism of the new Japanese religions, their nationalism might be understood in its historical and social context as a conservative reaction against the loss of identity, tradition and culture in the face of a threat of wholesale Westernization.

The meaning of this nationalism may differ from one new religion to the next. In Tenrikyo, one of the oldest of the new Japanese religions, the seemingly nationalistic ideas were merely the outcome of the worldview of the foundress, Miki Nakayama, for whom the world coincided with the valley in which she lived. While her view of the Jiba as the center of the world may thus not be seen as nationalistic in the strict sense of the term, this idea has been used for nationalistic purposes in the history of the movement. In a movement as Omotokyo, on the other hand, the nationalism manifested here is of a more explicitly imperialistic type, coinciding with the imperialistic pretentions of Japan in the first half of the twentieth century. Unsurprisingly, the nationalism of movements which emerged after the Second World War such as Mahikari is of a more reactionary kind, attempting to hold on to the traditional symbols of the greatness of Japan, such as the emperor, or substituting for this symbol by the veneration of their own leader as God. The rapid economic recovery of Japan since the Second World War has however brought about a new self-confidence which has again fuelled the more triumphalistic kind of nationalism which may be found in Kofuku-no-Kagaku.

In spite of their universalistic teachings, the mission of the new religions outside of Japan seems to have been a matter of chance, rather than a conscious strategy. It was mostly after the Second World War, when Japan became a world economic power, that the new Japanese religions developed more explicit missionary activities abroad. The original mission was generally accomplished by members who happened to live in foreign countries and continued the normal proselytizing activities there. Once a sizable community is formed in a particular country, trained ministers or missionaries are sent from Japan to cater to the local needs. But very few have been the cases of missionaries being sent into foreign and virgin territory to spread the teachings, and convert local people to the faith. Apart from Mahikari and Soka Gakkai, the membership of the new Japanese religions discussed consists mainly of expatriate Japanese. And in most cases, little effort has been made to adapt the rituals, languages customs and leadership to non-Japanese contexts. All this seems to imply that, at this point in time, the universalism advocated in most of the new Japanese religions is part of its nationalist ideology, no more than a way of displaying the universal validity and relevance of an essentially Japanese religion. While every universalistic religion must struggle with the tension between its particular cultural and religious origins and its universal claims, a true universality is ultimately irreconcilable with the glorification of that particularity, which is what religious nationalism is about.

Notes

1 In the *Kojiki*, the Shinto creation myth, the creation of the world is recounted in terms of the creation of the islands of Japan. It is from the union between the two world-parents, Isanagi and Isanami, that the various Japanese islands emerged. According to the text, the first island was formed from the brine dripping from the sword of the God Isanagi after dipping it into the cosmic ocean. This island was called Ono-goro-jima, 'Spontaneously-congeal-island', and is identified with a small island near Ahaji. Besides explaining the origins of Japan, the main function of the myth is to establish the divine origin and the soteriological function of the emperor of Japan who is presented as a descendent of the sun-goddess Amaterasu, and a mediator between heaven and earth.

2 This was for example the case in the *Kokugaku* (National Studies) movement which started in the beginning of the nineteenth century and which used the Shinto creation myth to establish the idea of the grandure of Japan and the Japanese.

3 Here I do not consider the work of Zen masters such as Sokei-an, Senzaki and D.T. Suzuki whose efforts to spread Buddhism in America in the first half of the twentieth century was based on their own initiative, and not on the concerted effort of their respective schools.

4 This coincides also to a certain degree with a dwindling interest in Buddhism in Japan. At the latest (1996) Zen retreat of the FAS in Japan, only about a dozen people participated, while four times this number signed up for the same retreat in Europe.

5 I classify the new religions according to the following sociological criteria: The 'old new religions' are those with more than three generations of followers (these religions should strictly speaking no longer be called 'new'), the 'new

religions' are those with no more than three generation of followers, and the 'new new religions' are those whose founder is still alive.

6 The *Ofudesaki* is the basic scripture of Tenrikyo, based on the revelations which the foundress received and written down between the years 1869 and 1882.

7 Cfr. the book *The Missionary* (Tenri: Tenrikyo Overseas Mission Department, 1981) on the life and trials of Yoshizo Katayama, a missionary in Korea, China, and the United States.

8 P.L. Kyodan is another new Japanese religion which after the War changed its name from Hito no Michi for universalistic purposes. According to its Patriarch Tokuchika Miki, 'The teachings of PL are universal and should not remain the exclusive religion of a limited number of Japanese. It is my solemn duty and responsibility to propagate the PL doctrine throughout the globe. So words from a language (English) that I consider most universal are used to signify my conviction that what I teach is for the benefit of mankind.' Quoted in Marcus Bach, *The Power of Perfect Liberty*. Englewood Cliffs: Prentice Hall, 1971, p. 142.

9 This ritual is an adaptation of the Omoto ritual of *miteshiro* in which a rice ladle is used in stead of the palm of one's hand in order to transmit the Divine Light.

10 This was also already prominent in Omoto. Its own 'earthly paradises' are located in Kameohe and Ayabe, and it has organized exhibitions of its art not only in Japan, but also e.g. in New York.

11 J. Churchward, *The Lost Continent of Mu*. London: Neville Spearman, 1959. Other sources of Okada were Kiku Yamane's, *Authentic History of the World*, Yamane, 1964; and M. Nakazono's *Ancient World History*, Nakazono, 1977.

12 In *Dojo, Magic and Exorcism in Modern Japan* (Stanford: Stanford University Press, 1980, p. 80–83), Winston Davis points out how the myth of Mu has been used to feed the ethnocentrism of various groups and individuals. While Churchwood believed that the original civilization consisted of 'stalwart, young adventurers with milk-white skins, blue eyes, and light, flaxen hair', Okada insisted on the Japanese origin of all races.

13 This is represented in the emblem or main symbol of Mahikari which consists of a circle within a star, and within the circle 16 lines which proceed from the center.

14 *Kotodama* is in fact a Japanese form of pseudo-etymology, popular already in the eighteenth century, in which the 'spiritual meaning' of words or syllables is elaborated. In Mahikari, the word '*kotodama*' is used in a variety of ways. It may refer to the spiritual etymology practiced by the founder of the movement throughout his writings, but it is also used to refer to the spiritual or magical vibrations of words, and to refer to the language itself used in the prayers.

15 The source of these teachings are the so-called Takenouchi documents, an ancient collection of sacred texts preserved by a Shinto priestly family in the Ibaraki Prefecture. These teachings form part of the advanced course of Mahikari. They may also be found in the book of A.K. Tebecis, *Mahikari, Thank God for the Answers at Last*. Tokyo Yoko Shuppan, 1982.

16 This is information which is given to members during the advanced course, and which non-members can only have access to through hear-say from advanced members.

17 The loyalty to the emperor may be understood from the point of view of the strong Shinto influences within the movement, but also from the history of the new Japanese religions, where Onisaburo Deguchi the leader of Omotokyo, the

parent-religion of Mahikari, was accused of lese majeste, and thereupon became a fervent defender of the emperor system.

18 Words of Okada Mokichi in *Handbook of the Hakone Art Museum and the Atami Art Museum*, p. 3.

19 In *Sekai Kyuseikyo, World Messianity and what it Means*. Atami: SKK Headquarters, 1957, p. 30.

20 There are signs that this is changing, even in Japan. Soka Gakkai has taken the initiative to enter into dialogue with Christian members of the Nanzan Institute for Religion and Culture in the course of 1996, and the proceedings of these dialogues are about to be published in Japan.

21 The two sons of the founder who died in childhood are for example believed to have died in order to open the way to the spiritual world and to establish communication through the mediums of the movement, called *reinoshas*. The death of the wife of the founder is believed to have brought about an extension of this salvation throughout the world, and the death of the founder himself is believed to bring about universal salvation. These four figures are object of an intense devotion in the movement.

22 The death of other members of the founder's family is also believed to have a soteriological function. As such, the death of the two sons of the founder in infancy and at the age of fourteen is believed to have established the primary opening of the spiritual world.

23 In pamphlet of the movement, *In Pursuit of Truth*. About eight months before her death, the foundress had accompanied her husband to eight Western countries to try to spread the teaching in the West.

24 What stands in the way of a true universalism is here related to the cultural specificity of some of its beliefs and rituals which do not seem to appeal to people of a different culture. While Japan has a long tradition of spirit mediation and an age-old belief in the spiritual origin of diseases and misfortunes and in spirit-possession, such beliefs are relatively foreign to a Western scientific outlook. And even though Buddhism may be appealing to Westerners, the elaborate cosmology and esoteric ritualism developed in Shinnyo-en may be too alien for Western people to assimilate.

References

Clarke, P., and Somers, J. (1994) *Japanese New Religions in the West*, Kent: Japan Library.

Cornille, C. (1991) 'The Phoenix Flies West. The Dynamics of Inculturation of a New Japanese Religion in Northern Europe' in *Japanese Journal of Religious Studies* vol. 18, nrs 2–3, pp. 265–285.

Davis, W. (1980) *Dojo, Magic and Exorcism in Modern Japan*. Stanford: Stanford University Press.

Ellwood, R. (1982) *Tenrikyo: A Pilgrimage Faith*, Tenri: Yenri University Press.

Fields, R. (1992) *How the Swans Came to the Lake. A Narrative History of Buddhism in America*, Boston: Shambala.

Kouame, N. (1995) 'Tenri: Les Trois Visages d'une ville religieuse' in *Etudes Japonaises* 8, pp. 57–75.

Métraux, D. (1994) *The Soka Gakkai Revolution*, New York: University Press of America.

Nehring, A. (1992) *Rissho Kosei-kai. Eine neubuddhistische Religion in Japan*, Erlangen: Verlag der Ev.-Luth Mission.

Peel, S. (1985) *The Pure Land. Journal of Pure Land Buddhism*.

Reid, D. (1996) 'Internationalization in Japanese Religion' in Noriyoshi, T. and Reid, D., eds, *Religion in Japanese Culture*, Tokyo: Kodansha International, pp. 184–198.

Shupe, A. (1993) 'Soka Gakkai and the Slippery Slope from Militancy to Accomodation' in *Religion and Society in Modern Japan*, Mullins, M., Shimazono, S., and Swanson, P., eds, Berkeley: Asian Humanities Press.

Shimazono, S. (1993) 'The Expansion of Japan's New Religions into Foreign Cultures' in Mullins, M., Shimazono, S., Swanson, P., eds, *Religion & Society in Modern Japan*. Berkeley: Asian Humanities Press, pp. 273–300.

Snow, D. (1987) 'Organization, Ideology, and Mobilization. The Case of Nichiren Shoshu of America' in D. Bromley and P. Hammond, *The Future of New Religious Movements*. Macon: Mercer University Press, pp. 153–174.

Tadao U., Hardacre, H., Hirochika N., eds (1990) *Japanese Civilization in the Modern World*, Osaka: Senri Ethnological Studies.

Wilson, B. and Dobbelaere, K. (1994) *A Time to Chant. The Soka Gakkai Buddhists in Britain*, Oxford: Clarendon Press.

Young, R. (1988) 'From Gokyo-Dogen to Banko-Dokon. A Study of the Self-Universalization of Omoto' in *Japanese Journal of Religious Studies* vol. 15 no. 4, pp. 263–286.

Works by the New Japanese Religions

Tenrikyo

Fukaya, T. (1983) *The Truth of Origin*, Tenri: Tenrikyo Overseas Mission Department.

Inoue, A., Eynon, M. (1986) *A Study of the Ofudesaki*, Tenri: Tenri Jihosha.

Nakayama, Y. (1968) *Tenrikyo, Its Origin and Teaching*, Tenri: Tenrikyo Church Headquarters.

Nishiyama, T. (1981) *Introduction to the Teachings of Tenrikyo*. Tenri: Tenrikyo Overseas Mission Department.

Takano, T. (1981) *The Missionary*, Tenri: Tenrikyo Overseas Mission Department.

Tenrikyo (1966) *Tenrikyo, Its History and Teachings*, Tenri: Tenrikyo Overseas Mission Department.

—— (1986) *The Teachings and History of Tenrikyo*, Tenri: Tenrikyo Overseas Mission Department.

Yoshinori, M. (1973) *Tenrikyo: Some Misconceptions Corrected. Critique on H. van Straelen's 'The Religion of Divine Wisdom,'* Tenri: Tenrikyo Overseas Mission Department.

Sekai Kyusei Kyo

—— (1957) *Sekai Kyuseikyo, World Messianity and what it Means*, Atami: SKK Headquarters.

—— (1976) *Church of World Messianity, Question and Answer Series*. Los Angeles: Church of World Messianity.

—— (1984) *Foundation of Paradise*. From the Teachings of Meishu-sama. U.S.A.: Church of World Messianity.

—— (1986) *Sekai Kyusei Kyo, Introduction*, Atami: MOA Productions.

Mahikari

—— (1982) *Goseigen. The Holy Words* (trans.), Tujunga: Bishop of North American Region of Sekai Mahikari Bunmei Kyodan.
Tebecis, A.K. (1982) *Mahikari, Thank God for the Answers at Last,* Tokyo: Yoko Shuppan.

Nihonzan Myohoji

Fujii, N. (1975) *My Non Violence. An Autobiography of a Japanese Buddhist,* Tokyo: Japan Buddha Sangha.
—— (1980) *Buddhism for World Peace,* (Yumiko Miyazaki, trans.), Tokyo: Japan-Bharat Sarvodaya Mitrata Sangha.
—— (1984) *Itten Shikai Kaiki Myoho,* Tokyo: Japan-Bharat Sarvodaya Mitrata Sangha.
—— (1985) *Kill not Life,* Leverett: Nipponzan Myohoji New England Sangha.

Reiyukai

—— (1987) *The Reiyukai Movement: Buddhism as an Interreligious Philosophy,* Tokyo: The Reiyukai.

Rissho Kosei Kai

Niwano, N. (1968) *Travel to Infinity,* Tokyo, 1968.

Soka Gakkai

Causton, R. (1988) *Nichiren Shoshu Buddhism,* London: Rider.

Kofuku-no Kagaku

Okawa, R. (1990a) *The Laws of Gold. The Wisdom of Buddha that Inspires the New Civilization.* Tokyo: The Institute for Research in Human Happiness.
—— (1990b) *The Laws of the Sun. The Revelation of Buddha that Enlightens the New Age.* Tokyo: The Institute for Research in Human Happiness.
—— (1990c) *A Theory on the Creation of Utopia.* Tokyo: The Institute for Research in Human Happiness.
—— (1991) *The Rebirth of Buddha. Messages to his Beloved Disciples,* Tokyo: The Institute for Research in Human Happiness.
—— (1993) *The Challenge of Religion. The Wind of Miracles from Japan,* Tokyo: The Institute for Research in Human Happiness.
—— (1995a) *Buddha Speaks. Discourses with the Buddha Incarnate,* Tokyo: The Institute for Research in Human Happiness.
—— (1995b) *The Age of Choice in Religion,* Tokyo: The Institute for Research in Human Happiness.
—— (1995c) *Creating a New Japan,* Tokyo: IRH Press.

CHAPTER TWO

Spiritual Companies, Corporate Religions

Japanese Companies and Japanese New Religious Movements at Home and Abroad

Louella Matsunaga

In September 1997 one of the largest Japanese companies in the retail sector, Yaohan, was forced to file for bankruptcy at the initiative of its company union, after having postponed the payment of bonuses to its staff for the second time. Until this debacle, Yaohan had been widely viewed as a success story in the Japanese business world, and one that attracted a great deal of public attention because of the close involvement between Yaohan and the new religious movement Seicho no Ie, (literally 'the House of Growth'), a movement founded by Dr Masaharu Taniguchi in Japan in 1930. The bulk of the research for this paper was completed before Yaohan's demise, and it may be some time before a full assessment of the company's rise and fall is possible. However, this paper offers a preliminary overview of Yaohan's involvement with Seicho no Ie, and in this context seeks to address a number of broader questions concerning the relationship between Japanese new religious movements (NRMs) and Japanese corporations, both in Japan and abroad. These issues are addressed under several broad headings. Firstly, parallels between large Japanese corporations and Japanese NRMs are considered, while in the second section the influence of religion on the work ethic in Japan is examined. The third section of the paper focuses on the case of Yaohan and Seicho no Ie, and the role of Seicho no Ie in the development of Yaohan's management philosophy and in its overseas expansion. The fourth section of the paper examines the case of Yaohan and Seicho no Ie in the UK, while in the conclusion the wider implications of the Yaohan case are considered.

Large Corporations and NRMs in Japan

At first glance, large Japanese companies and Japanese NRMs seem to be two utterly different types of organisation. In terms of social status alone the contrast is striking: while on the one hand the large corporations are identified with the elite sector of Japanese society, with the graduates of Japan's top Universities competing for entry to the most prestigious of the large companies,[1] on the other hand Japan's NRMs have tended to suffer from a poor public image, attracting much negative attention from the media, and are widely associated with those on the margins of society, in particular those uprooted from their existing social networks in the course of Japan's urbanisation.[2] Recent scholarship has shown this depiction of Japanese NRMs to be misleading, particularly as far as the social composition of the movements is concerned, as the membership of those NRMs which have been studied tends to reflect a fair cross-section of Japanese society, and is by no means limited to an urban underclass.[3] However, in popular terms the image persists, and public concern in Japan over the activities of NRMs has been further fuelled by the Aum Shinrikyo incident of 1995,[4] and the ensuing trial of Asahara Shoko, the movement's leader.

Within the Japanese context, then, the images of the salaryman employee of a large corporation and the 'typical' follower of an NRM are so different as to be almost antithetical. Hardacre notes that 'large corporations in Japan typically screen prospective employees to eliminate members of the new religions' (Hardacre 1986: 192), and from my research it would seem that in at least some cases where employees of large companies are also members of NRMs this membership may be concealed. For example, a Japanese member of Sukyo Mahikari, a Japanese NRM active in the UK whose husband, also a member, works for a large Japanese company, told me that they kept their membership secret from the company as they feared it would endanger his career prospects. She compared their situation to that of the *kakure kirishitan*, or hidden Christians of the Tokugawa era.[5]

However, Hardacre argues that this apparent antagonism of large Japanese corporations to the NRMs derives not from their differences, but from their similarities. Hardacre suggests that such corporations are suspicious of anything which will tend to detract from total commitment to the company, and that NRMs may be seen as particularly problematic because their organisational structure in many ways parallels that of large companies, both in the rewards offered, and in the loyalty, and expenditure of time, demanded.[6] This makes them both a potential threat to large corporations in so far as employees who are members of NRMs may suffer from divided loyalties, and also attractive alternatives to those who are unable to join the salaryman elite. This includes both members of small and medium sized companies and women, who may be employed by large

36

companies, but do not enjoy the employment-related benefits offered to their male colleagues.[7] Hardacre explains:

> Much as a man rises through the ranks in a company, members of the new religions can win reward and recognition that might well be beyond their reach in secular society... For many members the new religions provide means to achieve prestige and recognition that parallel those available to men employed by large corporations.
>
> (Hardacre 1986: 192–3)

The parallel Hardacre draws here is reinforced by an examination of the organisational charts of any of the major Japanese NRMs, which show an elaborate hierarchy encompassing divisions with responsibilities for areas varying from property management and finance to religious affairs or care of pilgrims.[8] Within the formal organisation alone there would thus seem to be ample opportunity for recognition and promotion, in addition to opportunities offered to gain both prestige and spiritual rewards through, for example, recruiting new members.

Alongside the organisational similarities between NRMs and large companies in Japan, there is also a degree of overlap in the social roles played by the two types of organisation in so far as both may play an intermediary role between the individual and the state, providing a range of services concerned with their members' welfare as well as a social network linking members. Wilson (1991) argues that in Japan one of the most important roles of NRMs is that of mediator between the individual and the state, echoing Rajana's argument that NRMs in Japan 'help to integrate individuals who have few alternative means of participating in the larger society' (Rajana 1975: 197). Although Rajana may be overstating the atomisation of recruits to the NRMs in Japan, she does make the valuable point that major Japanese NRMs, such as Soka Gakkai (a Nichiren Buddhist movement), are able to help their members and articulate their interests in a wide range of secular domains through their activities in spheres including politics, education, and welfare. A number of the larger movements in Japan have their own schools, and even universities, and a few have even opened their own hospitals,[9] while Soka Gakkai established a successful political party, Komeito.[10] Komeito even enjoyed a brief spell in power as one of the partners in a coalition government formed in the wake of the political upheavals in Japan following the break up of the Liberal Democratic Party, before officially disbanding in 1994 to become part of the newly established New Frontier Party.

In addition to developing an organisational structure which appears to be modelled on that of large companies, many Japanese NRMs have adopted methods of spreading their message which owe much to secular marketing techniques. Several of the movements have large publishing wings dedicated to the production and distribution of their founder's works

– Kofuku no Kagaku, Agonshu and Seicho no Ie are three prominent examples, with Seicho no Ie indeed originating as a publishing enterprise.[11] Some movements have moved into more high-tech propagation methods: Agonshu, as noted by Reader (1991) uses a range of technologies to promote its teachings, including satellite TV, with further technological innovations in the pipeline. The founder of Agonshu, Kiriyama Seiyu, is enthusiastic about the potential of new technology, and has been considerably aided in the implementation of his ideas in this respect by his son-in-law, who was an employee of one of Japan's leading electronics corporations until he resigned in order to take up a full-time post within Agonshu.[12] In both this use of technology and in the adoption of a modern corporate type of organisation, it could be argued that Agonshu and other similar NRMs in Japan are examples of the process Wilson (1991) describes as the secularisation of religion, that is, the adoption of secular modes of organisation, propagation, and discourse in response to the increasing secularisation of society as a whole.

However, the secular-religious dynamic in Japan is far from simple. If Japanese NRMs appear to be secularised in many respects, and to resemble large corporations, conversely, when we examine large corporations in Japan they are not always as purely secular as might be assumed. In their statements of corporate mission, mottoes, and company songs, many of Japan's most prestigious corporations show concerns extending well beyond the material domain, and, as is explored in further detail below, are in many respects more reminiscent of the 'religio-economic'[13] corporations of the United States than of the American or Western European corporate mainstream. In a mirror image of the involvement of Japanese NRMs with the secular sphere, Nakamaki (1992) argues that the activities of large Japanese companies have extended into the ritual, religious and ethical spheres to such an extent that one may speak of *kaisha-kyō*, or the religion of 'companyism'. In this connection, Nakamaki (1992, 1995) cites the growing practice in the post war era of performing memorial rites for deceased company members at company monuments, concentrated in a few particularly sacred areas of Japan, such as Mount Koya.[14] These company memorial rites place the deceased company members in an analogous position vis-a-vis the company to that of ancestors vis-a-vis the household, or *ie*.[15] And since memorialisation of ancestors is one of the most important activities of both mainstream Buddhism and many of the NRMs in Japan,[16] the appropriation of this area by the company has particularly strong resonances. Nakamaki tells us that although priests from the Shingon sect of Buddhism perform company memorial services on Mount Koya, bereaved relatives who do not belong to the Shingon sect are reassured by being told that these services transcend sectarian divisions. Rather, it is argued by the priests that Mount Koya is a holy place for all Japan, and by company representatives that the rites are in any case organised not by a particular sect, but by the company. The company thus appears to take on the role not only of consumer, but of provider of religious services (Nakamaki 1992).

Nakamaki also draws our attention to the widespread practice of erecting shrines or small temples on company grounds, with at least one leading firm, Matsushita, employing its own full-time company priest (Nakamaki 1992). The erection of shrines on company premises has also been noted by Pye (1989) and Lewis (1986). Exploring the rites performed at a factory producing synthetic fibres in the Kansai area of Japan, Lewis notes that safety is a predominant theme, with special ceremonies performed to avert fire, a recurrent problem at the factory. Other rites of interest reported by Lewis include rites of purification; the groundbreaking ceremony (*jichinsai*) performed when new buildings are erected by the company, and also the New Year visit to the main company shrine for 'New Year Safety prayers, when departmental managers and company executives join with members of the factory safety company in prayer for "the safety and prosperity of our factory this year" (Lewis 1986: 263). It may be noted that most of the rites reported by Lewis, with the exception of rites to appease the spirits of the dead, fell under the Shinto umbrella, so that within the company, as within Japanese society as a whole, a division of labour was seen, with Buddhist priests concerned with the care of the dead, while Shinto dealt with purification and inaugural and New Year ceremonies.[17]

Another area where the concerns of Japanese companies stretch beyond the realm of economic activities is that of training: more specifically the training of new company employees. As has been widely noted (Rohlen 1970; Nakamaki 1992; Matsunaga 1995), these training programmes can be considered as rites of passage, marking the transition from the irresponsible, child-like status of student, to the status of adult and member of society.[18] The aim of such programmes goes beyond a straightforward process of technical job-related training to encompass the transmission of values and corporate culture, indeed, one of the aims of many of these induction training programmes is to transform the hearts and minds of the new recruits. As many as a quarter of such programmes[19] may include an explicit element of *seishin kyōiku*, or spiritual education, a heading which comprises a wide range of techniques, including military style training under the auspices of Japan's self-defence force; marathon running; unpaid service in the community; and, most interestingly in the context of this paper, activities organised by religious groups, both mainstream and NRMs. Some well documented cases include a bank which sends its trainees to practice meditation at a Zen temple (Rohlen 1973), and the provision of training programmes for companies by the NRM Ittoen (Reader 1995), while the role of Seicho no Ie in providing training for Yaohan employees is discussed further below.

Another parallel between NRMs and large companies in Japan lies in the role of the founder. In both types of organisation similar patterns are commonly found: an emphasis on the founder's role in establishing and developing the organisation; the preservation and promulgation of the founder's distinctive philosophy and teachings, both by oral dissemination and by the publication of texts by the organisation; and memorialisation of the founder, if dead, in monuments and ceremonies. Furthermore, many of the biographies produced of founders of both NRMs and large companies have a common narrative structure stressing the suffering undergone by the founder before he or she was able to establish the organisation. In this respect both types of organisation may be said to be representative of the wider phenomenon of the way in which leadership is legitimised in Japan: Davis notes that: 'part of the moral legitimation of leadership in Japan is the idea that the founder of an institution suffered in order to bring it into existence' (Davis 1992: 306, fn 27). Other similar biographies of founders may be found for other sorts of groups – one example drawn from the martial arts is the biography of Ueshiba Morihei, the founder of Aikido (Ueshiba 1991).

As far as NRMs are concerned, the structure of these narratives is well documented, with some characteristic variations, depending on the gender of the founder.[20] In both cases poverty and ill health, either of the founder or of his or her immediate family, are recurrent themes. In the narratives of male founders, they are often sent away from home at an early age, sometimes to be adopted by another family. The narratives of female founders often recount that they were forced into early and unhappy marriages, with more tragedy awaiting them in the shape of their children, with the death or serious illness of a child being another common theme. However, these accounts stress an acceptance of their position as wife and mother, and it is quite common to read depictions of the founder toiling tirelessly to support the drunk, ill or indigent husband to whom she had not wanted to get married in the first place. The sufferings of the founder often lead him or her to ascetic practices, and in many cases to increasing involvement with existing religious organisations. All this culminates in an episode of spiritual enlightenment, sometimes by spirit possession, some-times in a dream, in which the founder's mission is revealed, thus resulting in the establishment of the movement.

A recent example of such a narrative may be drawn from Reiha no Hikari, a movement established in 1954. The founder of this movement, Yoshio Hase, was born in 1914, the eldest son of eight children in a farming household in the Tokyo area. His early life was characterised by poverty and illness, with Yoshio himself being a sickly child. The movement teaches that both his poverty and his own illness had a spiritual significance: it was important for him to experience poverty and hardship in order to save others, and his sickness was a result of his small body having to harmonise divine energy. As an adult, Yoshio continued to suffer from ill health, eventually developing tuberculosis, which led to his being repatriated to Japan from China, where he had been serving with the Japanese army, in 1939. Given only a few months to live by the doctors who examined him in Japan, Yoshio embarked on a journey both spiritual and physical, travelling into the mountains of Shikoku where he hoped to put the existence of God to the test, explaining to his parents before he left that if God existed he, Yoshio, would surely be saved[21] through this journey. Eventually arriving at a mountain summit, exhausted, Yoshio lay down to sleep, feeling unable to move further. It was at this point that he heard the voice of God telling him to live, and that he was to be God's messenger. The next day he woke up, completely healed. Following this revelation, Yoshio continued to practice austerities for many years before receiving the further revelation that he should connect God and human beings. This then led to the establishment of the new religious movement Reiha no Hikari, which teaches that Yoshio Hase, to whom they refer as *Go-shugojin-sama*, was sent by God as a saviour, to connect people to God by means of the spiritual wave *(reiha)*.[22]

A very similar narrative structure, also featuring victory over poverty and illness may be seen both in the biographies of the Wada family, founders of Yaohan, discussed in further detail below, and also in the autobiography of the founder of Matsushita Electric, Matsushita Konosuke (born in 1894). Matsushita recounts how he and his family were plunged into poverty by his father's unsuccessful speculation on the commodity rice market, while not long afterwards the three eldest children of the family, including Konosuke's two brothers, died from a flu-like illness. Konosuke was then sent away from home to work as an apprentice while still only nine years old, and became the formal head of his family two years later, when his father died of pneumonia. However, the autobiography depicts Konosuke as continuing to work hard throughout all this misfortune, thus eventually succeeding in founding his own business, which in due course became one of Japan's leading companies.

But perhaps most the most interesting aspect of Matsushita's narrative lies not in the structural similarities between his biography and that of founders of NRMs – as has been noted, this kind of narrative, is, after all, fairly typical of biographies of founders of a wide range of institutions in Japan – but in the role Matsushita himself ascribes to his encounter with a new religious movement in the development of his distinctive management philosophy. In explaining the success of the company, Matsushita emphasises the importance of this philosophy, which he attributes in his autobiography to 'divine inspiration' (Matsushita 1988: 206). In a more detailed account elsewhere in the same autobiography, he describes how his thinking on business and management was transformed following a visit to the headquarters of a new religion, where he was very impressed by the scale of their construction projects and by the dedication of the workers, all unpaid volunteers. This religion was not named in Matsushita's autobiography, but was identified by Nakamaki (1992) as one of the oldest of Japan's NRMs, Tenrikyo, founded in 1838.

The visit is recalled by Matsushita in the following terms:

There was something to be learned from what I had seen – from the way it was apparently thriving, from the mountains of donated logs, from the energetic, dedicated way the members of the sect threw themselves into the construction work, from the sanctuary swept clean without a scrap of litter, from the pious mien of every worshipper, from the diligent students at the school who would later guide others toward understanding of the teachings of the sect, and from the way everything worked with clockwork-like smoothness. It was the epitome of skilful management...

The thought that what I had seen was a model of superior management filled me with excitement, and I began to think seriously about what true management ought to be like. It was both management for righteousness and righteous management... Even after returning home, I could not get the thought of religion on the one hand and management on the other off my mind. I stayed awake for a long time thinking about it. Religion was a holy pursuit aimed at guiding people out of suffering and toward happiness and peace of mind. My business, too, is sacred, I thought, in the sense that industry provides necessities that sustain and improve man's existence.

Indeed, the ultimate aim of production is to wipe out poverty and create prosperity... Eliminating poverty is a sacred task, the loftiest purpose in life. To achieve it we must work hard and produce a great abundance of goods; this is our mission and our enterprise. Production aimed at enriching the life of every person on earth is the sacred mission of the manufacturer.

(Matsushita 1988: 198–199)

Matsushita's account of this encounter with Tenrikyo and his thoughts on the interconnectedness of business and religion throws into clear relief the common ground between the NRMs and Japan's large companies. It seemed to Matsushita at the time, as it seemed to the Wada family where Seicho no Ie was concerned in a later generation, that the new religions, or at least Tenrikyo in this instance, had something to offer Japan's industrial world: a 'model of management', in Matsushita's own words, and also, perhaps, a key to motivating people to labour by articulating corporate goals in spiritual terms. The conclusion reached by Matsushita seems to have been that far from religion and business being antithetical, the two could be linked through the elaboration of a management philosophy. And for this, Tenrikyo provided the inspiration.

Later the same year, in May 1932, Matsushita called all his employees together to announce to them the new company mission. In this speech he briefly mentioned his visit to Tenrikyo, but, it would seem from his autobiography, without mentioning the movement's name, and then recapitulated his thoughts on the mission of manufacturers as stated above. He then went on to summarise this management vision with a striking image, which has resulted in his philosophy being commonly referred to in Japan as Matsushita's 'tap-water philosophy':

> This is what the entrepreneur and the manufacturer aims at: to make all products as inexhaustible and as cheap as tap water. When this is realized poverty will vanish from the earth. Only after there is a limitless supply of material goods as well as spiritual peace of mind will man achieve true happiness. I believe that here is the manufacturer's true mission and the mission of Matsushita Electric. I would like you all to keep in mind that the true mission of Matsushita Electric is to produce an inexhaustible supply of goods, thus creating peace and prosperity throughout the land.
>
> (Matsushita 1988: 203)

Noting that Matsushita Konosuke is commonly seen as the '*kami-sama*', literally, 'god',[23] of management in Japan, and that his ideas have been extremely influential in the Japanese business world, Nakamaki (1992) argues that Matsushita's 'tap-water philosophy' has furnished the creation myth of the mass production industry world, and that this is part of the process of sacralisation of management in Japan. However, Matsushita's philosophy is also worthy of further examination for the light it casts on the developing work ethic in Japan, and the role of religious belief and practice in the development of a distinctive corporate work ethic.

NRMs and the Work Ethic in Japan

Comparing Matsushita's tap-water philosophy with Weber's theory of the Protestant work ethic (Weber 1930), Nakamaki (1992) argues that the work ethic suggested by Matsushita is distinctive in that it does not depict labour as intrinsically virtuous. Rather, the virtue of hard work in the service of manufacturing lies in the potential of mass production to improve living standards, and lead to general prosperity. This contrasts not only with Weber's analysis of the role of the Protestant asceticism in the rise of capitalism in Europe, with its emphasis on the intrinsic virtue of frugality and hard work, and the righteousness of fulfilling one's social role in the world rather than withdrawing from it, but also with Bellah's application of Weber's thesis to Japan (Bellah 1957). Bellah finds an equivalent to the Protestant work ethic in the stress laid by the various Japanese mainstream religious traditions in the Tokugawa era on 'the importance of diligence and frugality' (Bellah 1957: 196) and in the development of distinctive forms of Japanese Buddhism, which, similarly to contemporary Confucianism, stressed the importance of fulfilling one's role in everyday life, in contrast to other monastic forms of Buddhism.[24]

Particularly important, according to Bellah, to the development of a distinctive work ethic in the Japanese context, were the interlinked ideals of filial piety and loyalty to one's superiors, both of which were seen as sacred duties. Transferred to the business context, these ideals had clear potential for creating an obedient and diligent workforce, although the early history of Japan's industrialisation, as well as more recent anthropological studies, indicates that the use of these ideals to motivate the workforce has long been a problematic area, subject to dispute and contestation.[25]

As evidence for the role in the establishment of capitalism in Japan of the Weberian principles of diligence and frugality, combined with Japanese notions of filial piety and loyalty to one's seniors, Bellah cites the example of Mitsubishi, founded in the Meiji era by a former samurai, Iwasaki. Mitsubishi's 'house-rules', quoted by Bellah, emphasise not only the importance of hard work and frugality, but also that of 'public service' and 'the national interest', making this enterprise fairly typical of the first generation of Japan's large companies, established at a time when the pursuit of profit was regarded with suspicion, and business activities were commonly justified in terms of their role in building Japan up as a wealthy nation state in order to preserve the country from the threat posed by the West.[26]

It is interesting, then, to observe in the Matsushita case, half a century later, a change of emphasis away from the importance of frugality and the enterprise as servant of the state, and towards prosperity, the alleviation of poverty, and the enterprise as servant of the consumer. However, other elements of the world view identified by Bellah as favourable to the development of capitalism remain in the Matsushita case, particularly the veneration of superiors, as can be seen in the extensive memorialisation of the founder in the company headquarters,[27] and also a retained emphasis on the importance of hard work, albeit now linked to somewhat altered goals.

The shifts evident in Matsushita's tap water philosophy as compared to earlier formulations of the work ethic in Japan in some respects parallel developments in the corporate sphere elsewhere, particularly in the emergence of 'the Gospel of Prosperity' in the United States. Matsushita's 'sacred mission' to create prosperity and eradicate poverty closely echoes statements by Henry Ford, founder of the Ford Motor Company, who is quoted as saying that the abolition of poverty 'is the only legitimate purpose of business... I want to abolish poverty from America.' (Bromley and Shupe 1981: 239). Ford was much influenced by harmonial philosophy and the ideas of positive thinking, in which health and material well being were thought to reflect a person's attitude and relationship with the greater cosmos. Prosperity, from this perspective, is dependent on a state of mind, something accessible to all, and which should be spread as widely as possible. It is seen as something good, to be celebrated, an outward sign of righteousness, as was also implied in the Calvinist ethic, but without the Calvinist strictures on the conspicuous enjoyment of wealth.

Other examples of corporations in the United States which combine a statement of transcendent mission with the idea of prosperity as a reward for right attitude include the Fuller Brush company, founded in the early 1900s by a convert to Christian Science, a movement itself influenced by harmonial philosophy; and, more recently, Mary Kay, Amway, and Herbalife, often grouped together as religio-economic corporations, owing to their mission statements, which stress the aims of these companies to transform the lives of their customers, their employees, and ultimately society itself (Bromley and Shupe 1981). In the latter cases in particular, the celebration of prosperity has moved increasingly towards the celebration of conspicuous consumption. Mary Kay, a cosmetics company, for example, rewards successful sales representatives with 'mink coats, diamond rings, gold pins, silver coffee services, and, the ultimate symbol of success, a pink Cadillac' (Bromley and Shupe 1981: 243). At the same time, a religious discourse is frequently employed by executives and rank and file employees alike to frame their activities, for example in the Amway case, with the goal of acquiring wealth legitimated with reference to quotes from the Bible (Bromley and Shupe 1981: 248).

In a further development, both Europe and the United States have in recent years seen the growth of businesses and training courses underpinned by New Age ideas, where, according to Heelas,

> the idea is to transform the values, experiences, and to some extent the practices of what it is to be at work. The New Age manager is imbued with 'new' qualities and virtues... to do with intrinsic wisdom, authentic creativity, self-responsibility, genuine energy, love, and so on. Trainings are held to effect this shift. Furthermore, work itself is typically seen to serve as a 'growth environment'. The significance of work is transformed in that it is conceived as providing the opportunity to 'work' on oneself. It becomes a spiritual discipline.
>
> (Heelas 1996: 90)

Specific examples cited by Heelas include business seminars organised by est, and the Bank of Credit and Commerce International, founded by a Sufi mystic and financier, which enjoyed considerable success for nearly twenty years before being forced to close amidst some scandal in 1991.

Taking an overview of these developments, there would thus seem to be a move over the course of the twentieth century from the asceticism of the

Protestant Work ethic to an increasingly positive valuation of wealth and an emphasis on prosperity, in business circles in the United States and Europe, as well as Japan, and it would further appear that in the American context this shift has in a number of cases been reinforced and legitimated in explicitly religious terms. More recently, there seems to be a further shift in some circles in the United States and Europe, with the spread of New Age ideas to a view of the work place as potentially an arena for personal as well as societal transformation. This suggests in turn an interesting possibility: are developments and innovations in the religious sphere providing a source of inspiration for the development of new management philosophies in the corporate sphere? That is, in the late twentieth century, are we still seeing a Weberian interplay between capitalism and religion, but with new forms and new motivations emerging? Turning back to Japan, then, we might ask, to what extent are twentieth century forms of religiosity in Japan influencing the corporate sphere? And, more specifically, do Japan's new religious movements have any role to play in the continuing evolution of the work ethic in the Japanese context?

We might note initially that both the positive valuation of prosperity and consumption and the emphasis on the transformation of self are echoed in both Japan's companies and Japan's new religions. Japanese corporate training programmes commonly emphasise the transformation of the *kokoro* – the heart, mind, or inner self of the employee. This concern with the *kokoro* is found even in companies that otherwise place little emphasis on explicitly religious concerns, and disavow any element of spiritual education in their training programmes.[28] Furthermore, ostensibly con-sultative activities in many companies in Japan have a strong element of self-reflection built into them. For example, in one in-company campaign in a large chain store, entitled 'TOUCH Heart',[29] where employees were asked to make suggestions as to how the company could improve itself, the suggestions all followed a highly predictable pattern, along the lines of, 'I do not smile enough at the customers, from now on I will try to always have a smiling face' (Matsunaga 1995: 326). Suggestions on improvements to conditions external to the employees, such as shoddy display units and poor quality merchandise, were conspicuous by their absence. Hardacre's comment for the new religions:

> the idea that circumstances can be changed by the power of diligently cultivated *kokoro* is pervasive... It is understood that the cultivated *kokoro* has the power also to change external persons and events
>
> (Hardacre 1986: 20)

could thus be equally well applied to the company context in Japan.

Another theme that receives strong emphasis in both the New Religious Movements and in the company context in Japan is that of gratitude, especially towards parents and social superiors. To be able to offer gratitude for any experience, even an unpleasant one on the grounds that it offers an opportunity for polishing one's spiritual being, is a key preoccupation of many of Japan's New Religious Movements (Hardacre 1986: 23–25). In the company context, the importance placed on gratitude in training programmes has been noted by Kondo (1990) and Matsunaga (1995). And in Matsushita Electric, 'gratitude for blessings' is one of the seven guiding principles of the company, and is referred to by Matsushita Konosuke as 'the most exalted of all virtues' (Matsushita 1988: 227).[30] Here a clear continuity can be traced with elements of religious orientation in the Tokugawa era identified by Bellah as favourable to the development of capitalism, particularly the stress on loyalty to superiors.

Finally, the notion that transformation of self leads to a transformation in the world beyond the self finds one expression within the NRMs in their well-documented stress on this-worldly benefits *(genze riyaku)*. For example, in Mahikari following the movement's teachings and prescribed practices are thought to help to eliminate spiritual impurities and establish a state of *ken-wa-fu* (health, harmony, and prosperity), while Toda Josei, the second president of Soka Gakkai, Japan's largest and best known NRM, famously described the *gohonzon*, or object of worship,[31] venerated by the movement as a 'machine that produces happiness *(kōfuku seizōki)* (cited in Arai 1996: 107). And turning to Seicho no Ie, the movement with which the remainder of this paper will be primarily concerned, the core of the movement's teaching is that we are all children of God, originally perfect, free from illness and misfortune. All illness and misfortune is therefore illusion, from which the movement aims to free its followers by teaching them to practice a form of meditation *(shinsōkan)* focusing on the true reality of existence *(jissō)*. Although the teachings of these movements show considerable variation in their detail, there thus seems to be a common message that both illness and poverty are symptoms of spiritual problems or wrong-thinking. Conversely, although most movements are wary of promising any automatic results, accounts abound of the followers who have achieved good health and prosperity through their spiritual practices. Here again, as in the 'Gospel of Prosperity' in the United States, prosperity becomes something God-given, to be celebrated, a sign of virtue.

In view of their concern with the consequences of spiritual practices in this world, it is perhaps unsurprising that Japanese NRMs do not seek to confine themselves to a narrowly defined religious sphere, but actively address a wide range of secular concerns, including problems of the workplace. It is common for Japanese NRMs to run seminars for their members on questions of business and management, for example the European and African division of Sukyo Mahikari organised a seminar in

April 1995 entitled 'Spiritual Economics'. Another forum in which issues concerning the workplace are addressed by the NRMs is in the magazines published the various movements,[32] as can be seen from a trawl through recent Japanese-language publications of two movements, Seicho no Ie and Kofuku no Kagaku. The Seicho no Ie magazines featured interviews with two owners of small businesses on the way in which Seicho no Ie had helped them in their work, and an interview with a factory worker explaining how Seicho no Ie had helped him find joy in his work (*Hikari no Sen*, May, June 1995); while the Kofuku no Kagaku magazine featured an article giving hints on how to become a member of the future top business elite, arguing that a heightened religious awareness and sensitivity to ethical issues would become essential to this goal in the future (*Hosokawa Tensyu*, '*Toppu o mezase!*' (Aim for the top!), in The Liberty, July 1995). Interestingly, the Kofuku no Kagaku article cites Matsushita Konosuke as an exemplar of right-thinking management leading to success, arguing that his notion of a mission to improve people's living standards through the production of a ceaseless flow of material goods (the 'tap water' philosophy referred to above), is an example of altruistic management, and that it was this attitude which enabled Matsushita Electric to become one of Japan's leading companies.

But perhaps the most prominent example of the involvement of NRMs with the corporate sphere in Japan is that of Seicho no Ie. Seicho no Ie, meaning the House of Growth, was founded in 1930 by Taniguchi Masaharu, and initially organised as a publishing company, publishing a magazine containing the thoughts of Taniguchi, before officially becoming a religious organisation in 1941. Briefly stated, the core of Seicho no Ie philosophy is the idea that there is a world of reality, or *jissō*, in which human beings are perfect, children of God, without sin; and a phenomenal world of our perceptions. All problems come from the illusion that is the phenomenal world: thus, illness, for example, is a reflection of a state of mind – in the real world there is no illness. It follows that if we can realise the world of reality, and cultivate a right state of mind, all our problems will be resolved. An outline of the early history of the movement produced by Seicho no Ie itself accounts for the early spread of the movement through the effect of Taniguchi's teachings, claiming that the first readers of Taniguchi's magazine found that their illnesses disappeared, their family relationships became harmonious, their mental abilities increased, and their business activities prospered.

Seicho no Ie draws on a number of elements in its belief system, not all of which are Japanese. In the brief synopsis given above there are evident links with some of the ideas of the Positive Thinking movement, and indeed Clarke (1994) traces a direct connection between the two through Fenwicke Holmes, founder of Religious Science, a New Thought, Positive Thinking movement, whose book, 'the Law of Mind in Action' Taniguchi is known to have read. Through this in turn, Clarke argues, a connection can be traced with the New Age movement, which was also influenced by New Thought. Other notions that receive strong stress in Seicho no Ie include the importance of sincerity and of gratitude, especially gratitude to one's parents, a notion which may be extended to employers in the business context.

Seicho no Ie's involvement with Japan's business world dates back to the early days of the movement's existence, when, during the Second World War, Seicho no Ie was active among medium and small sized enterprises in Japan as part of the drive to increase efficiency and productivity, and to support the war effort. McFarland writes:

> at the very time when the rapid production of large quantities of essential goods was required, Seicho no Ie was able to advance among small and medium-sized factories, there to be a spokesman for improved efficiency and to promise a reduction in accidents and sickness. It is said... that in one cotton-spinning company in Tokyo, placing a copy of the Seicho no Ie magazine in every room of the plant proved to be very effective in decreasing anti-war sentiment and activity.
>
> (McFarland 1967: 154)

In the post-war era, Seicho no Ie has established an entire subsidiary organisation called 'The Prosperity Association' devoted to questions of business and management. This group claims 3,500 companies as member organisations, including a number of large enterprises[33] as well as medium and small sized companies. The association claims that the majority of these try to implement Seicho no Ie principles in their management, and has published a number of accounts by the leaders of these enterprises of the ways in which the teachings of Seicho no Ie have helped them to achieve success in business. The aims of the Prosperity Association are to proclaim the principles of prosperity as taught by Seicho no Ie within the business community, based on faith in the spirit of the teachings of Taniguchi Masaharu as expounded in the movement's sacred text, 'The Truth of Life'; to promote the training of capable business people with a global vision; and, through activities on an individual company level, to develop a nation-wide movement aimed at achieving prosperity on a national level.[34] This is also linked by the association to the overall aim of achieving human enlightenment – so, as in the case of the Gospel of Prosperity in the United States, an explicit link is made between prosperity and spirituality.

However, as in the comments of Kofuku no Kagaku on the importance of altruistic management cited above, there is also a stress on the importance of business activities as a service to others. If true prosperity is a state of mind, that state of mind consists in not merely seeking profit, but in working for the sake of others. From this state of mind, according to Seicho no Ie teachings, prosperity will automatically flow. There is a continuity here with the early equation of business activities with service in Japan in the Meiji era – but now the notion of business as service to the state has altered to the idea of business as a service to other people: by implication, the consumers. This notion of service to others still takes its place within the wider frame of working for the good of the nation, but the nation itself is now placed within a yet wider frame of working for the good of the whole world, developing a 'global vision', in line with the increasing emphasis in Japanese society in recent years on internationalisation, or *kokusaika*.[35] And in line with recent shifts in the ways companies seek to create images of themselves which will appeal to the new generation of Japanese by placing more emphasis on the individual,[36] the Prosperity Association stresses the importance of developing each company's 'individuality', or 'personality' *(kosei)* as another part of their strategy for creating prosperity. This in turn is related back to religious faith, as explained in the following extract of a Seicho no Ie publication, 'Prosperity is in the Mind', by Katsumi Tokuhisa, (Tokuhisa was vice-chairman of Seicho no Ie at the time of Yaohan's expansion into Brazil, discussed further below, and partly responsible for encouraging this expansion):

> So, if we separate religious faith and business, saying that religion is religion and business is business, we won't be able to manifest our true strength. When, through the faith in God or Buddha, the whole personality starts to reveal itself through your business, this will give life to your faith, and the prosperity of the enterprise will come about.[37]
>
> (Tokuhisa 1991)

As part of their efforts to promote this philosophy, the Prosperity Association organises seminars, lectures, and research meetings, both in Japan and abroad. The roll-call of speakers at these events reads like a Who's Who of Japan's business elite – recent well-known speakers include executives from Matsushita Electric, Nissan, and Sanwa Bank. The association's members include the President of Kyocera, a large and prestigious ceramics company, and in 1995 was headed by Wada Kazuo of the retail chain Yaohan, at that time the jewel in Seicho no Ie's crown, and a company frequently cited in the movement's publications as a shining example of the practical business success that can be achieved through the implementation of Seicho no Ie principles.

Seicho no Ie and Yaohan

The relationship between Seicho no Ie and Yaohan is inextricably interwoven with the history of the founding family of Yaohan, the Wada family, as can be seen from a brief summary of the biographies of Wada

Katsu and her son Kazuo. Wada Katsu was the eldest daughter of Mr and Mrs Tajima, a couple who ran a small greengrocers business called Yaohan[38] in Odawara, a small town in Kanagawa prefecture, about 100 kilometres south-west of Tokyo. Born in 1906, a *hinoe uma*[39] year and therefore a particularly unpropitious year for women, her parents had difficulty in finding a husband for her, and decided that she should marry Wada Ryohei, one of the employees of their store. Katsu was very much opposed to this marriage, she wanted to become a teacher, not to carry on the family business, and she did not like the look of Wada Ryohei either. Eventually she made a bargain with her parents to consult a fortune teller, and to abide by the fortune teller's advice. In 1991 she recalled in a newspaper interview:

I was told that this man, Ryohei Wada, may have looked like a dull, rough pebble, but that he was special, and that in time he would shine like one of the diamonds on my fingers... But still I cried throughout the marriage ceremony.

(Japan Times, December 15th 1991)

The early years of their marriage were not happy. Katsu continued to dislike both her husband and the green-grocery business. Although she had initially thought of leaving her husband, she became pregnant shortly after their marriage and felt unable to leave. When this first son was still less than two years old, the Wada family moved to the hot spring resort town of Atami to establish their own business independently of Katsu's parents. Shortly afterwards, they had their second son, and then a daughter, while at the same time Katsu found herself having to work full time at the green-grocery store just to pay their bills and keep the business going. To make matters worse, her daughter Yoshie became ill and was hospitalised with pneumonia, and her husband, Ryohei, collapsed from overwork. Katsu worked harder than ever at the store, scarcely able to visit Yoshie, who died in hospital. Ryohei, however, recovered, and the couple went on to have three more sons, while the store gradually became more established. Katsu now put all her energies into saving as much as she could in order to send her five sons to University. Then, eleven years after her marriage she encountered Seicho no Ie.

Different versions exist of Katsu's encounter with Seicho no Ie. One published account (Enami 1994) links her interest in the movement with problems she was encountering in child rearing, while in the 1991 interview cited above, she is reported as saying that she was drawn to the movement on hearing of someone who had been cured of TB through their belief in Seicho no Ie. In any event, the initial impact of this encounter on the Wada family was largely confined to the domestic sphere, with Katsu making particular efforts, in accordance with Seicho no Ie teachings, to place her husband first within the family, and to offer him gratitude and respect.[40]

From this point onwards, relations between Katsu and Ryohei Wada slowly began to improve. However, the impact of Seicho no Ie on Yaohan as a company really began to be felt some years later, when the Wadas' eldest son, Kazuo, entered university, and from this point Katsu and Kazuo's biographies merge, and become part of the story of Yaohan itself.

Kazuo became involved with the communist party while at University, thus attracting the attention of the University authorities, who contacted his mother explaining that they planned to expel him from University. Distraught, Katsu pleaded for her son to be given another chance. She promised she would make him change his beliefs, and to this end enrolled him in a course at a Seicho no Ie training centre. Kazuo, who later became the managing director of the Yaohan group, emerged an enthusiastic convert, at the same time abandoning his dream to become a lawyer, and resolving to accept his role as successor to the store instead, in order to make his parents happy.[41] And in Kazuo's account of events, he also determined to transform Yaohan, still at that time a single small store, into a leading company.

The very next year however, disaster struck as a great fire swept through Atami, destroying the Wada family's house and shop. Kazuo, left in charge that day while his father was out buying vegetables and his mother attended the University entrance ceremony of one of his younger brothers, only managed to salvage the family's collection of the complete works of Taniguchi Masaharu from the flames. The Wadas then had to start their whole business again from scratch. This was in 1950, just at the beginning of the change in the Japanese retail sector from domination by small stores staffed largely by family members with few employees to the spread of chain stores on the American model. The Wada family not only succeeded in rebuilding the Yaohan store on a larger scale, but began to expand and to transform their business into one of the new chain stores.

From the 1960s, as the store expanded, Yaohan began to move towards a lifetime employment system, recruiting new graduates and providing them with induction training in line with the general pattern for large Japanese companies, but with a strong emphasis on spiritual training based on the principles of Seicho no Ie. Heung Wah Wong (1996) argues that the firm's success in this period stemmed in great measure from the efforts of their employees, who worked long hours for relatively low wages, a system which Wong argues they were led to accept through the use of Seicho no Ie ideals, particularly the notion of gratitude *(kansha)* to the customers expressed as service *(hōshi)*, an idea strongly stressed in the Yaohan training programme. This laid the Wadas open to the accusation of exploitation, and the suggestion that they were using religious ideals to manipulate the employees. In 1964, Yaohan's training programme came to the notice of Taniguchi Masaharu, the founder of Seicho no Ie, when a Yaohan employee contacted Taniguchi's wife, complaining that Yaohan was using Seicho no Ie to exploit its employees and line the pockets of the Wada family. Taniguchi then contacted the Wadas, suggesting that their approach could lead to a very serious misunderstanding.

The response of the Wadas was to formally extend the connection linking their family with Seicho no Ie as believers to the entire Yaohan company and its subsidiaries. Thenceforward, Yaohan was to be officially a Seicho no Ie company, with all its employees becoming members of Seicho no Ie, so that no 'misunderstandings' could occur. Employees who resisted this, some on the grounds that they did not wish to become members of a new religious movement, were told that they could seek jobs elsewhere. In the end, the majority complied. The following year, in the spring of 1965, Yaohan held a six day induction course for new company members at a Seicho no Ie training centre, during which Wada Kazuo is said to have received divine inspiration while practising *shinsōkan* meditation (the central practice of Seicho no Ie). This experience was interpreted by Wada as indicating the path Yaohan should follow, and was the source of the Yaohan declaration cited at the beginning of this paper, which states Yaohan's mission to 'render better service to people all over the world, and in so doing ... to become a model for other companies.'

However, more immediate pragmatic reasons prompted Yaohan to begin to implement this vision of expansion some four years later. By the end of the 1960s, competition in the retail sector had intensified, with the smaller chain-stores merging to form giant retail companies. In order for Yaohan to survive independently, Wada Kazuo suggested that they should expand overseas. Here he cited the example of Sony, who, by making a name for themselves abroad, had come to be recognised as a top-ranking company within Japan too. The country first targeted for Yaohan's overseas expansion was Brazil, apparently on the advice of the vice-chairman of Seicho no Ie, Tokuhisa Katsumi, whose comments on the relationship between business and religion are cited above. Tokuhisa had visited Brazil and told Wada that conditions there seemed similar to those in Japan during the era of high speed growth in the early 1960s. In addition, according to Heung Wah Wong (1996), Wada calculated that the strength of Seicho no Ie in Brazil would help Yaohan to establish itself. It seems that Wada anticipated that Seicho no Ie members in Brazil, who at that time were largely of Japanese descent, would provide a source of customers for the new venture, and also a source of employees who would readily fit in with Yaohan's corporate culture, as well as providing local 'know-how' (Enami 1994: 148). This latter point was important, as under Brazilian law two thirds of employees had to be Brazilian nationals. Recruitment procedures were weighted to favour those from a Seicho no Ie background, with a requirement that locally recruited staff had to have attended a number of Seicho no Ie seminars before their application could be considered. Seicho no Ie also seems to have been enthusiastic about the new venture: Tokuhisa himself welcomed Wada on his first exploratory trip to Brazil, and Seicho no Ie is credited by Enami (1994) with providing considerable help in the preparations for the opening of the first Yaohan store in Brazil,

However, Wada did not solely rely on the support of Seicho no Ie in Brazil, but also demanded a high degree of commitment on the part of those employees moving to Brazil from Japan. To this end, he elaborated ten rules to be adhered to by those posted to Brazil:

1. You should plan to live there forever.
2. All company members must be members of Seicho no Ie.
3. You should consider your working hours to be 24 hours a day.
4. Until the company is firmly established, the wives of company members should consider themselves as company members too.
5. Work must come first, and family a distant second.
6. As far as possible, do not give birth within two years of arriving in Brazil.
7. Your absolute priority must be company dividends and company profitability.
8. You must have the wholehearted approval of your parents and your brothers and sisters before you come.
9. You must have the character, intelligence, and competence to be leaders of the Brazilian people.
10. You must have a driving licence.

Additionally, you should bear in mind that you will be unable to return to Japan even in the case of the death of a member of your immediate family.

(Enami 1994: 141, author's translation)

Wada then asked for volunteers from within the company to go and establish a Brazilian branch. Of forty-eight who applied, twenty-eight were chosen, comprising ten different families. This group was given the name 'The Rising Sun Corps, Yaohan Brazil'.[42]

For a while, the Brazilian venture prospered, with the active co-operation of Seicho no Ie, and a total of four stores were opened by 1975. The Japanese staff appear to have adhered strictly to the rules laid down by Wada, with two of them remaining in Brazil in accordance with these rules, despite the deaths of immediate family members in Japan.[43] The Brazilian venture, however, eventually failed, owing to a combination of problems arising from the oil shock and from the high rate of inflation in Brazil, and by 1980 Yaohan no longer had any stores in Brazil.

Despite the failure of the Brazilian venture, Wada Kazuo was determined to continue the overseas expansion of the Yaohan group. Yaohan's Singapore store, established in 1974, prospered, and was followed first by additional branches in Singapore, and later by stores in the United States, Hong Kong, Malaysia, Brunei, Taiwan, Thailand, mainland China, Indonesia, Canada, and in 1993 the UK. In a highly unusual move for a Japanese company, the headquarters of Yaohan were moved to Hong Kong in 1989, and in the same year Wada Kazuo and his wife also took up residence in Hong Kong. By the mid 1990s Yaohan had become better known outside Japan than within Japan itself.

Throughout this overseas expansion, the emphasis on the spiritual side of Yaohan and on the company's links with Seicho no Ie, remained strong, although the way in which this was expressed underwent successive modifications. This spiritual aspect of Yaohan manifested itself in two principal ways: firstly in the way in which the policy of overseas expansion was explained and articulated by the group's chairman, Wada Kazuo; and secondly in the Seicho no Ie based training programmes offered to both Japanese and non-Japanese staff.

Wada Kazuo's accounts of the motivation behind opening various overseas branches have frequently been voiced in terms of spiritual as well as material considerations. For example, the opening of the Singapore branch was explained by Wada as an act of atonement to the people of Singapore for their sufferings at the hands of the Japanese during World War II. Similarly, in justifying his 1989 decision to move the headquarters of Yaohan International to Hong Kong, and to begin a vigorous programme of expansion in China in the wake of the Tienanmen Square incident and the imposition of international sanctions on China, Wada quoted the teachings of Taniguchi Masaharu, founder of Seicho no Ie. Explaining that the Chinese people were suffering from the imposition of sanctions, Wada argued that Yaohan's expansion into China at this time was his way of repaying the debt Japan owed China for China's magnanimity in not demanding reparations from Japan after World War II. Furthermore, by helping China, indirectly the whole world would benefit. In his book explaining 'Yaohan's Global Strategy' he writes:

> The management philosophy of Yaohan is exactly the same as the teachings of Seicho no Ie: 'Give and ye shall be given (sic). Contribute to the benefit of the whole mankind'
>
> As an enterprise steeped in these teachings, and also as a person who has been personally instructed by Mr Taniguchi: 'Don't forget the great debt of gratitude we owe China' I want to do my best for that country.
>
> (Wada 1992: 121)[44]

This stress on Seicho no Ie as the core of Yaohan's philosophy was also carried over to the training programmes provided for overseas staff. In addition to induction programmes for new staff, offered prior to the opening of each new branch, and repeated thereafter every three years or so, programmes were also offered to existing staff at the Yaohan education centre in Hong Kong, which opened in 1993. This centre ran four levels of course: a general course for general-grade staff lasting two days; an advanced course for middle management lasting three days; a four day course for Japanese staff; and a six day course designed to train instructors (May Wong 1994).

The conflation of Yaohan's management philosophy and the teachings of Seicho no Ie on these courses was not without problems, especially in the early years of Yaohan's overseas operations. When training courses were first begun in Singapore, they were led by the chairman's mother, Wada Katsu, who antagonised the Muslim recruits by her references to God in her lectures. The Muslims complained that their religion only permitted them to worship one God, Allah, and that they could not recognise Mrs Wada's God. This problem was eventually resolved by Mrs Wada dropping references to God, and substituting the term, 'the Creator', which remained the term used in Yaohan training materials. In all other respects, training materials remained very closely based on Seicho no Ie precepts. For example, Seicho no Ie teaches that human beings' real nature is perfect, but that our lack of clear vision prevents us from realising our perfection as children of God. This teaching was expressed in the English language training brochure issued to local staff at the London office in the following terms:

What is A Human Being?
You are the son (daughter) of the creator.
When you treat customers with a pleasant attitude and courtesy, they will be happy.
If we can keep customers happy, then the store will prosper.
When the store prospers, you will prosper too.
The point is to realise that you are the son of the creator, then happiness will come to you.
Say every day, 'I am the son of the creator.' 'I can do anything'. 'I am a happy person'.

(Yaohan training materials 1995)

Although data on this area is somewhat patchy, there is some evidence to suggest that the reactions to Yaohan's attempts at introducing spiritual training in its overseas branches varied from country to country. A 1990 article in the New York Times suggested that Yaohan had encountered labour problems in the United States 'reportedly because of its insistence that employees follow the company's rigid tenets' (New York Times, 19th February 1990), but did not explicitly mention the question of religion or of Seicho no Ie. In contrast, May Wong (1994) offers a very favourable assessment of Yaohan's training programme in Hong Kong, suggesting that the local Chinese staff were receptive both to the contents of the training (stress on filial piety, the notion of spiritual practices bringing you material, this-worldly benefits) and to its methods (learning by rote, group recitation of slogans), because of similarities in their own cultural background. Wong judges that the training programme helped the employees to feel 'incorporated in the corporate culture' (Wong 1994: 43), although she also suggests that the philosophy of Seicho no Ie was on the whole only selectively assimilated by the Chinese staff. Especially in the case of less well educated employees, she found that they tended to simply add the Seicho no Ie deity to a pre-existing pantheon of deities in popular local Taoist religions:

> They believed that these Gods would bless them with good fortune and good luck. They would not refuse any religions which could bring them good fortune and good luck.
>
> (Wong 1994: 41)

Heung Wah Wong (1996), on the other hand, offers a more critical interpretation of the situation in Hong Kong, reporting that local Chinese staff were largely excluded from Seicho no Ie activities, and arguing that this in turn reflected the differential value placed on Japanese and local employees by the company, with the local employees implicitly relegated to an inferior category not worthy of full inclusion in the activities lying at the symbolic heart of the company. He also queries the extent to which Seicho no Ie principles were accepted by the Japanese employees themselves, and reports that many of them would only attend Seicho no Ie activities if they knew Wada was going to be present, and were prevented from rejecting Seicho no Ie entirely largely by their dependence on Wada as head of the company.

The differing accounts of May Wong and Heung Wah Wong point to an ambivalence in the role of Seicho no Ie within the overseas branches of Yaohan: on the one hand large scale disinterest in Seicho no Ie on the part of the Japanese employees, but on the other the symbolic value of participation in Seicho no Ie activities or the Seicho no Ie based training programmes as symbolic of integration within an inner circle of full company members. Both these elements were also present in the London branch during its five year history as part of the Wada family group of companies.[45]

Yaohan and Seicho No Ie in the UK

Yaohan opened a store in North London in April 1992 to a fanfare of publicity. Wada Kazuo attended the opening ceremony, and was shown in a photograph in the Daily Mail leading members of the Japanese staff in prayer (Daily Mail, April 1992), while the Guardian began its piece on the new store, 'Kazuo Wada leads fellow executives in prayers at the opening yesterday of a £50 million shopping centre' (Guardian, April 1992). Within the company, trading began in an upbeat atmosphere, with considerable optimism for the future, and, initially, accompanied by a number of regular workplace rituals organised by the company. Chief among these were the morning meetings (*chōrei*),[46] one-hour long affairs held every morning, and involving all the one hundred or so employees. These comprised warming-up exercises followed by joint singing of the company song and joint recitation of the Yaohan declaration, after which everyone shouted the Yaohan slogan for that year,[47] punching their fists in the air. This would in turn be followed by general announcements and information, and the meeting concluded with thanks to everyone present.

Although the forgoing description does not differ significantly from a description of any Japanese company morning meeting, Yaohan did also introduce some exercises derived from Seicho no Ie into the meetings on special occasions, for example getting the staff to hold hands, look into each other's eyes, and repeat: 'You are a wonderful person, I am a wonderful person, let's do our best today'. Ritual practices with a more explicitly religious or spiritual content, such as *shinsōkan* meditation, or Seicho no Ie prayers, were not introduced to the British staff, although a *jissō* (the sacred object of Seicho no Ie was kept in the office, and the Japanese managers practised *shinsōkan* together with the appropriate prayers every morning in a private ceremony.

One manager I interviewed told me that in his opinion the local staff enjoyed the morning meetings, 'We had a laugh', and went along with what was asked of them, perhaps partly because activities such as doing exercises and singing the company song is part of the received image of Japanese management in this country. The Yaohan approach was therefore assimilated by its employees as part of its Japaneseness rather than as having a particular religious or spiritual underpinning. The meetings were, however, reduced in frequency from daily to weekly, and then monthly, and were finally dropped altogether. The manager attributed this to organisational problems rather than to any problems inherent in the meeting itself: it was difficult and expensive to arrange for all the employees to be present on site for one hour before work every morning, so meetings were made shorter and the numbers attending the meetings reduced from one hundred to only seven or eight. With these smaller numbers, people felt more self conscious about performing the activities referred to above, and the meetings were therefore ultimately dropped. However, another Yaohan employee offered a less positive interpretation of employee responses to these activities, saying that they viewed it as 'brainwashing' and 'a load of bollocks', and only conformed originally because they felt they had no choice, gradually resisting more as the numbers in the meetings dropped.

Local staff were not required to become members of the movement. Describing the induction programme run for new personnel prior to the opening of the London branch, the (British) personnel manager said that while he was aware that the attitudes and values conveyed on the course were 'very much Seicho no Ie', emphasising gratitude and respect for parents, and including exercises on smiling and laughing derived from Seicho no Ie, this connection was not made explicit to new local recruits. Seicho no Ie itself was not referred to on this course, and the lecturers, two senior Japanese from Yaohan international, were at pains to emphasise that what they were teaching was not a religion, nor was it specifically Japanese.

Senior British staff, however, were also subsequently sent on the training course for managers run at the Yaohan training centre in Hong Kong, where the Seicho no Ie elements were made more explicit. The first British manager to be sent on this course was from a mixed Muslim and Zoroastrian background, and freely admitted to experiencing a great deal of discomfort when required to participate in prayers, chanting, and meditation, although he claimed to have no problem with the Seicho no Ie philosophy, which he saw as 'no different from the core of many religions' and consisting of 'basically, positive thinking'. Some features of the prayers that he particularly disliked were the clapping and bowing – this is drawn from the Shinto tradition in Japan, where you clap and bow when greeting the *kami* on a visit to a shrine. He also reported differential acceptance of this among different nationalities, with particular discomfort among Muslim employees, and criticised the practice on the grounds that it emphasised the differences among the nationalities employed by Yaohan. He also reported problems with the practice of *shinsōkan*, finding it difficult to maintain the prescribed meditation position, a difficulty he attributed to 'dizzy spells'. To his annoyance, this was followed up by a string of faxes from head office to the London branch after his return from Hong Kong expressing concern about his health and a view that since illness is a state of mind he must be in need of spiritual purification. He commented,

'For them, in Seicho no Ie, illness is a state of mind. I find that really hard to take. I mean, if you come down with the plague, is that a state of mind?'

This manager's reaction seems to have been fairly typical of the reaction of British managers sent on the same course subsequently – a mixture of acceptance what was seen as the philosophical element of the course, with scepticism or outright rejection of the philosophical component. There was, however, one exception, a British manager who described the Hong Kong training course was a turning point, and who subsequently became an enthusiastic adherent of Seicho no Ie (he also became the butt of a certain amount of teasing by other local Yaohan staff, who said that he had been 'brainwashed'). This second manager recounted that before going on the training course he was very hot tempered, and impatient with his subordinates at work, but that after going on the course and practising *shinsōkan* meditation regularly he became able to control his temper, and his workplace relations improved dramatically. His description of his experience of the course was phrased very much in terms of an awakening:

> 'When I went to Hong Kong I just thought, "it's a trip to Hong Kong, what do I care?" But in Hong Kong they were so sincere and friendly, I couldn't have been looked after better if I'd been a member of the royal family. Their sincerity made me think, maybe there's something in this...
>
> On the second to last day the lecturer, Mr Sawa, was talking about "you choose your parents". I thought this was ridiculous. Then they asked, "does anyone not believe in God?", and I said, "Me". I went out that night and got drunk. I got back to the hotel room in a stinking mood, and rang my wife. I told her I was fed up with it, it's a load of rubbish. I went to bed and woke up at 5.00 a.m. with a stinking hangover. I had a big bottle of Perrier and a shower, but I couldn't get back to sleep. So I did some *shinsōkan* meditation and read the sutra until about 7.00 a.m., and went and had some breakfast. When I went into the course that morning I had a completely open mind, I felt as if my eyes had been opened. There's no explanation for this except that I'd done *shinsōkan* the night before...
>
> I don't consider myself a spiritual person, but when I was 16 I was interested in Taoism, the I-ching, and Buddhism. I drew my own conclusions from these things – the only reason we're here is to evolve as a human being.
>
> When I went to the course that day I remembered the truth I had seen twenty years before.'

It seems that for this employee the encounter with Seicho no Ie evoked a sense of recognition. Once his initial resistance had been overcome, he says he just knew that Seicho no Ie's teachings were true, he felt this deep within himself, and it reconnected him with the feeling of spirituality he had had in his twenties. The training programme also at first appeared to have been successful from Yaohan's point of view in this case, as it transformed his feelings about his relationship with the company. Reporting his reaction when, at the end of the course, the participants were told that they were now members of the Yaohan family, this manager said 'I totally felt that'. He also felt that he was now able to look at the company from a broader perspective and to understand better the management point of view, so that the training was beneficial to him, although it did not entail any material benefits in terms of pay or promotion. However, it is possible that this employee did nonetheless hope for some advancement as a result of attending the course. At the time when I spoke to him in 1995 he was very enthusiastic about a new business venture planned by Yaohan which he hoped to be placed in charge of. He also seemed to be positively viewed by the Japanese management, and was even interviewed by a Japanese language newspaper in the UK, with an article on him published in February 1995 under the title 'Our Company's Englishman' (Nichi-Ei Times, February 1995).

Unfortunately, this apparent success story of integration into Yaohan's corporate culture was short-lived: the following year Yaohan's sole British adherent of Seicho no Ie was dismissed, and was subsequently awarded £20,000 compensation by an industrial tribunal for 'unfair dismissal and racial discrimination' (The Guardian, February 1997). The Guardian went on to report that, 'the tribunal chairman in the Yaohan case said that [Mr A][48] had been ignored by his immediate boss, excluded from meeting held by Japanese executives and sacked without warning'. In a further twist to the story, when I contacted Yaohan for their comments on the case, and expressed surprise at this employee's dismissal, given his enthusiastic adoption of Seicho no Ie, one (British) source at the company who wished to remain anonymous admitted that the case had been badly handled by the company, but maintained that in fact this employee's conduct merited dismissal on a number of occasions, but that the Japanese management at Yaohan had failed to impose sanctions precisely because they were so impressed by his adherence to Seicho no Ie, eventually taking action without proper warning and thus laying themselves open to litigation. Whatever the truth of the matter, it would in any case seem that in the long term neither the interests of this employee nor those of the company were advanced by his membership of Seicho no Ie, which also signally failed to integrate him within the company.

If Yaohan UK thus largely failed to make much headway in its attempts to introduce the teachings of Seicho no Ie to its local managerial staff, it is also noteworthy that there also seemed to be a distinct lack of enthusiasm for Seicho no Ie among their Japanese employees, indeed the UK branch was reputedly rebuked by Yaohan's head office on the grounds that a number of the Japanese employees did not know how to perform *shinsōkan* properly. A member of Seicho no Ie in the UK who had met a number of Yaohan's Japanese staff told me that Yaohan UK's former managing director, Mr Tajima, a relative of Wada Katsu, was a keen believer, but the others were simply not very interested in Seicho no Ie. This opinion was borne out by Mr Tajima himself, who said that although Japanese staff had to attend Seicho no Ie ceremonies, there was no obligation on them to become believers, thus drawing a neat distinction between formal membership in accordance with company rules, and personal commitment. He added that he thought in most cases the Japanese staff had joined Yaohan not because of any interest in or affinity with Seicho no Ie teachings, but simply because it offered a good opportunity of an overseas posting.

It would seem that Yaohan's Japanese staff participated solely in internal company based Seicho no Ie events: the morning *shinsōkan* and prayers, and other such ceremonies as may be required. They showed no interest in spreading the teachings of Seicho no Ie more widely, or in establishing contacts with other members of the movement in the UK, and did not attend the meetings organised by Seicho no Ie in Yaohan except on special occasions when speakers were invited from Japan, and presumably head office would have been made aware of a poor turnout. On the Seicho no Ie side, there was a general feeling of disappointment among individual Japanese members in the UK at the lack of involvement in Seicho no Ie by Yaohan's Japanese staff. It was further reported to me that the wives of the Japanese employees of Yaohan, who are also supposed to be members of Seicho no Ie according to Yaohan rules, had never attended the Seicho no Ie meetings organised by Seicho no Ie's Japanese women members in the UK (by 1995 very few in number), thus putting paid to their hopes of resurrecting a Japanese-speaking women's section in the UK.

This sense of disappointment contrasts sharply with the enthusiasm with which Seicho no Ie initially greeted Yaohan's arrival in the UK. In 1992, Seicho no Ie was a relatively small and fragmented organisation in the UK, consisting of a Brazilian group who held regular meetings in Portuguese, and a much smaller Japanese group with a membership which tended to fluctuate owing to the short term residence in the UK of most of their members. The Japanese members in particular looked forward to placing their group on a firmer footing with the support of the Yaohan staff. This enthusiasm initially seemed to be encouraged by Wada Kazuo, who addressed a meeting of all the London members of Seicho no Ie on the occasion of his visit to London for the opening of the London branch in 1993. Wada opened his speech by stating that he looked forward to 'the wonderful expansion of Seicho no Ie in London from now on'.[49] This was backed up by the provision of a room in the Yaohan centre for Seicho no Ie to use for their meetings free of charge, and the dispatch of several guest speakers on Seicho no Ie from Yaohan Japan to address meetings held in the Yaohan centre. However, these provisions, together with the introduction of key local managerial staff to the teachings of Seicho no Ie proved to be as far as Yaohan's support extended, and even these were of questionable use. Seicho no Ie meetings were not publicised within the store, and staff rarely knew if, or where they were taking place. In addition, the Yaohan centre proved to be an inconvenient location for most Seicho no Ie members, so the meetings at Yaohan were very poorly attended, with the bulk of Seicho no Ie activities in London continuing in the same venues, attended by substantially the same group of people, as they had before Yaohan's arrival.

Looking back on the two years that elapsed between my initial research at Yaohan in 1995 and the bankruptcy of the Japanese parent company in 1997, a British manager explained that Seicho no Ie practice within the company had continued to decline, especially after the transfer of Mr Tajima, a member of the founding family, in 1995, and his replacement as head of Yaohan UK by a non family member, Mr Sakuma. After Mr Sakuma's arrival, it seems that practice of Seicho no Ie by the Japanese staff lapsed completely, with only Mr Sakuma continuing to pray by himself in the office in the morning. And although British managerial staff continued to be sent on Seicho no Ie training courses until March 1997, there was little reference to Seicho no Ie in everyday working life. The British manager to whom I spoke attributed this decline in Seicho no Ie based practices to the financial difficulties encountered by the company, which were already fairly evident to the managerial staff I interviewed in 1995. He explained:

> 'If the company had been a success [Seicho no Ie] would have been an excellent vehicle to keep everybody interested and positive, and to create a strong culture which creates loyalty... If we'd been a success I'm sure things would have been very different – we would still be doing the morning declaration and all that. But when a company is losing money, making people redundant, you can't say, "Yaohan grows with you"... it becomes an embarrassment.'

Although this manager seemed optimistic that Yaohan in the UK would survive despite its parent company's bankruptcy, he was dismissive of the prospects of Seicho no Ie continuing to play any role in the company, identifying Seicho no Ie as the concern of the founding family, who had been forced out of the picture with the company's bankruptcy. When asked to what extent he thought the Japanese staff had assimilated, or might seek to maintain, Seicho no Ie teachings, he commented that the bankruptcy of the company had been brought about through the action of the company union. Apparently, faced with huge debts, Wada Kazuo had negotiated a loan of $1.4 billion, more than enough to cover the company's liabilities. However, the loan was due to come through in October, and, when the employees in Japan found their bonus (an important part of company employees' total pay package in Japan) postponed for the second time in August due to the company's financial difficulties, the company union itself forced the company into liquidation rather than wait for the loan to come through. In view of these events, the manager asked me, how much importance do you think the employees attached to Seicho no Ie teachings?

Conclusion

It seems clear that Yaohan has failed in the aim stated in their company declaration, of producing a model for other companies, both Japanese and non-Japanese. But what are the wider implications of the Yaohan case? The involvement of Yaohan with Seicho no Ie, while unusual among Japan's large corporations, serves to highlight the potential affinities between NRMs and companies in Japan, as well as indicating what both partners in such an alliance might stand to gain – or lose. Yaohan's history shows the readiness with which the biography of a company founder can take on spiritual overtones, providing a close parallel with the biographies of founders of new religious movements, and appearing to give a divine stamp of approval to the founder's projects, elevating them into the realm of the unchallengeable. And yet the way in which Yaohan's demise eventually came about at the hands of its own staff, at the same time that Wada Kazuo had finally succeeded in putting a rescue package in place, suggests that the spiritual authority claimed in this way may not always be effective. Equally, the Yaohan case shows how a company can with relative ease introduce religious or quasi-religious activities, or appeal to a religious discourse, in the Japanese context, where the lines between religion and company may in any case often be blurred. Here the obvious comparison is with the United States, where, for different reasons, some companies have also appealed to a religious discourse to frame and justify their activities. Although in the United States company and religion are perhaps more clearly separate in their spheres of concern than is the case in Japan, the strength of the Bible belt has led many secular organisations, including some companies, to make use of biblical references, and seek legitimation from religious sources. In both cases, though for very different reasons, the use of a religious discourse in a corporate context may thus appear less shocking than it would in a Western European context, and would appear to have some cultural base for acceptance.

The Yaohan case also demonstrates the potential of NRMs to provide a coherent ideological underpinning for a modern corporation. Seicho no Ie teachings such as 'prosperity is in the mind' or 'give and it shall be given unto you' certainly proved to be inspirational for the Wada family, and, for a time, looked as if they might provide inspiration and motivation for ordinary Yaohan employees as well. However, the Yaohan case also throws into clear relief some of the pitfalls both of using the teachings of a particular religion as a base for corporate philosophy and, more broadly, of the new form of work ethic which the Seicho no Ie philosophy implies.

First of all, to rely on a particular religion, or philosophy, as the grounding for a corporate philosophy lays the company which does this open to the charges of religious discrimination, and of interfering with the employee's religious freedom. As we have seen, Yaohan ran into precisely such accusations during its history, both within Japan and elsewhere. Nor is the Yaohan experience an isolated case in this regard: for the United States, Rupert (1992) discusses a range of cases where religious or philosophical ideas have been used to underpin business training seminars, including both movements which fall under the 'New Age' umbrella and the so-called 'self religions' such as the human potential movement, est, or Scientology. Rupert states of the human potential seminars that 'the primary obstacle to the seminars' widespread use in business has to do with religious freedom' (Rupert 1992: 133). He cites the Pacific Bell fiasco in California in 1987 where the company was forced to abandon a training programme after vocal resistance from the employees, as well as various legal battles over this issue of which the following is an example:

> Soon after Steven Hiatt, an employee of Walker Chevrolet in Tacoma, Washington, refused to participate in 'New Age Thinking to Increase Dealership Profitability', he was fired from his job. Hiatt said that he refused to participate because the seminar stressed self-will rather than God's will.

(Rupert 1992: 133)

Furthermore, where the philosophy or religion adopted as the base for corporate culture reflects the personal predilections of the head of the corporation and is then imposed on the ordinary staff, there is a strong risk of the staff either resisting, or simply following the forms required of them with no real commitment, as appears to have happened in the Yaohan case. This risk may well be heightened if the religion involved is a movement with low social status, such as the NRMs in Japan, or the various self-religions in the United States. There is also the further risk that the company management may be accused of using the religion concerned to exploit, or even to brainwash its employees. It must therefore be questionable as to how effective such a base can be for a corporate culture, or whether it can survive the demise of the founder. It is possible that a philosophy which is less obviously denominational, such as Matsushita's tap-water philosophy, may have a wider appeal and may therefore prove more effective.

But more importantly the failure of Yaohan also highlights the vulnerability of the work ethic which was central to Yaohan's corporate philosophy: the idea that prosperity is a state of mind, something that flows from virtue, and is accessible to all those who follow the right path. As the Yaohan manager cited above so clearly stated, this is an ethic the credibility of which is dependent on success. When prosperity fails, the appeal of the philosophy is undermined. It is interesting to note in this regard that the increasing stress on links between prosperity and virtue, no longer balanced by the frugality of Weber's Protestant ascetics, but instead associated with consumption and the visible signs of wealth, has occurred in affluent countries such as the USA and Japan, and has been particularly evident in the relatively prosperous post-war era. The Yaohan case thus raises the intriguing question of what will become of the Gospel of Prosperity in the United States if the corporations that preach it, like Yaohan, fall on bad times.

Turning to the implications for NRMs of involvement in the corporate sphere, involvement with a corporate success story offers benefits in terms of positive publicity, as can be seen from the stress placed in the publications of Seicho no Ie's Prosperity Association in earlier years on the success of Yaohan as an exemplar of the implementation of Seicho no Ie principles. It may also offer financial benefits in terms of generous corporate donations, or large scale corporate membership. Yet once more, the pitfalls are very real. Charges of using the religion for corporate profit may rebound to the discredit of both parties, and, as argued above, if an NRM may hope for some increase in membership when its corporate protégé prospers, it also risks losing members when a company with which it is closely associated runs into difficulties.

In the overseas context, Yaohan and Seicho no Ie's hopes for expansion through mutual assistance have repeatedly come to nothing, boding ill for any groups hoping to further their overseas expansion through similar co-operative endeavours. In Brazil, Yaohan was forced to withdraw despite the active support of Seicho no Ie, while in England Yaohan's presence has failed to increase Seicho no Ie's membership or public profile. Seicho no Ie in the UK remains much as it was before Yaohan came: one of the smaller Japanese NRMs with a membership of less than a hundred, little known outside the Brazilian and Japanese communities in London. Of the other Japanese NRMs in the UK by far the largest is Soka Gakkai, with around 5,000 members, with Mahikari coming a distant second with around 350 members. Neither of these movements has any large scale company involvement in the UK, although, in common with most of the movements, they maintain an interest in the ways in which spirituality may inform the conduct of business, and count some business people among their members. There is thus little evidence that support from Japan's major companies is in any way significant in fostering the spread of Japanese NRMs in the UK.

Large Japanese companies in the UK, like their counterparts in Japan, prefer for the most part to distance themselves from Japan's New Religions. Yaohan was exceptional in this regard, all the more so since other Japanese companies in the UK seem also to have divested themselves of most of the quasi-religious functions so meticulously documented by Nakamaki and others for large companies in Japan. The training offered to local employees by other Japanese companies in the UK does not, as far as I was able to discover, have any ethical or spiritual component,[50] and the only religious rituals retained by any significant number of Japanese companies in the UK are those derived from Shinto – for example, ground-breaking ceremonies *(jichinsai)* for new factories or buildings. Even where such rituals do take place, they are on the whole performed by company personnel, without the aid of ritual specialists, and, as far as the British spectators are concerned, the religious aspect is played down.

Yaohan may therefore best be understood as an exception, a rare case of close co-operation between a large company and an NRM, an experiment which ultimately failed. And yet, as a failure, it is an interesting one, and as with the 'New Age' seminars documented by Rupert (1992), or the religio-economic corporations described by Bromley and Shupe (1981), it is indicative of a phenomenon of wider significance. Within the framework of religious pluralism of the late twentieth century, these cases demonstrate the continuing potential for the religious sphere to provide a source of inspiration for the secular sphere in highly developed post-modern societies, and also to provide a resource for large corporations in their attempts to unify and motivate their employees, and to create a distinctive corporate culture. That these attempts frequently fail or encounter difficulties, is perhaps not surprising. That the attempt is being made at all suggests that in the post-modern world the secular and religious spheres are far from disengaged, and that the relationship between the two is likely to continue to provide rich material for study.

Notes

1 More details on the social status of large companies in Japanese society and the contrast between large companies and small to medium sized companies, may be found in the extensive literature on Japanese companies, for example Clark 1979, Matsunaga, 1995.
2 For a recent articulation of this argument see Arai 1996: 109–110.
3 See Reader 1991: 201 for a summary of research relating to this issue.
4 In 1995, members of the NRM Aum Shinrikyo attacked the Tokyo Underground with Sarin gas, resulting in a number of deaths, and the injury of more than 5,000 people.
5 During the Tokugawa era (1603–1867) Christianity was outlawed in Japan (an edict outlawing Christianity was passed in 1612), and Christians who were unfortunate enough to be discovered were executed. Cut off from the rest of the Christian world, small groups of Christians continued to practise in secret, developing their own distinctive brand of Christianity. These are referred to as *kakure kirishitan*, or hidden Christians.
6 It is relevant to note here that where in England we differentiate between different categories of employee on the basis of time – full-time or part-time employees – in Japan the important distinction is on the basis of membership - *shain*, or company member, and those who are not company members. Membership of the company, expected to last from graduation until retirement for men, or from graduation until marriage or birth of the first child (or reaching age 30 or so) for women, represents an involvement that extends into all areas of the employee's life, especially for men, so that Japanese companies have been famously described as 'enveloping' their employees. (Nakane 1973)
7 For more details of gender-related differences in employment conditions in large companies in Japan, see Matsunaga 1995.
8 A number of these charts are reproduced in the *Shin Shūkyō Jiten* 1990.
9 Details are given in the *Shin Shūkyō Jiten* 1990. It should be noted that hospitals run by NRMs are also open to non-members.
10 Formal connections between Soka Gakkai and Komeito were severed in 1970, six years after the party's establishment, but informal links between the two organisations continued.
11 Seicho no Ie began as a publishing enterprise in 1930, publishing the thoughts of Taniguchi Masaharu in a magazine later re-issued as a series of books called *Seimei no Jissō* (Truth of Life). It was registered as an educational organisation *(kyōka dantai)* in 1936, only finally registering as a religious juridical person in 1949.

12 Information obtained by author during a visit to Agonshu headquarters in 1996.

13 Bromley and Shupe 1981.

14 These rites are, however, generally limited to either *shain* who have died in service, or, in the case of company members who have died after retirement, to those who held an executive rank (Nakamaki 1992).

15 See Nakane (1973) on the importance of the *ie* in Japanese society, and Hendry 1987: 22–25 for the importance of the ancestors in the *ie* system.

16 See, for example, Reader 1991.

17 Buddhism in Japan has tended to specialise in funerals and memorial rites because in Shinto death is seen as extremely polluting. These two religious traditions have therefore tended to co-exist under a division of labour succinctly resumed in the proverb 'Born Shinto, die Buddhist'. For more details on this, see Reader (1991).

18 'Adulthood' is a complex notion in Japanese, rendered by a number of different terms each conveying slightly different meanings. The notion referred to here is that of *shakaijin*, literally, member of society. For a full discussion of Japanese notions of adulthood see Matsunaga 1995.

19 Rohlen (1973) estimated that about one third of Japanese companies used *seishin kyōiku*, while a more recent estimate by Inohara (1990) gives the lower figure of one quarter. It is difficult to estimate with any precision how many companies in Japan use *seishin kyōiku* as for many Japanese people the term *seishin kyōiku* itself is redolent of old-fashioned, pre-war, right-wing ideas, and some companies who practice *seishin kyōiku* may be unwilling to admit to it because of possible negative publicity.

20 The gender-based variations in these narratives were explored in a paper presented by P. B. Clarke at postgraduate seminar, Department of Theology, King's College London October 1995 (unpublished).

21 The word used in the biography of the founder produced by the movement is *sukui*, which can mean help, succour, or salvation.

22 This narrative is drawn partly from material produced by Reiha no Hikari, and partly from interviews with Reiha no Hikari members in London. For other similar narratives see Ooms 1993 on Deguchi Nao, founder of Omoto-kyo, or Reader 1991 on Kiriyama Seiyu, founder of Agonshu.

23 It should be noted here that the resonances of the word *kami-sama* in Japanese are not the same as those of the word 'god' in English. In Japanese the line between human being and *kami-sama* are rather fluid: the survey on Japanese Religion produced by the Agency for Cultural Affairs notes that: 'The Shinto *kami* have never been conceived of as absolute or transcendent in relation to man and the world... On the contrary it has always been assumed that there is a significant continuity between the *kami* and man... the relationship between *kami* and man is well symbolised by the term *oya-ko*, an expression specifying the parent-child, or better, the ancestor-descendant relation' (Agency for Cultural Affairs 1972: 14–15). In everyday conversation, the word *kami-sama* is often used to denote someone worthy of particular respect: for example in the retail world it is commonly asserted that the customer is '*kami-sama*', in an exhortation that roughly corresponds in usage to the English saying 'the customer is always right'. It is in this latter sense that the term '*kami-sama* of management' is used to refer to Matsushita Konosuke.

24 Bellah cites particularly Nichiren-shu and Jodo Shinshu, especially as Jodo Shinshu developed under the leadership of Rennyo Shonin (1415–1499) (Bellah 1957).

25 For a historical view of the developing ideology of Japanese capitalism see Marshall 1967. A more recent account of the use of the household idiom in a modern Japanese enterprise is given in Kondo 1990.

26 The rallying cry of the time was '*fukoku kyōhei*' – rich country, strong army. See Marshall 1967 for a detailed analysis of the development of a distinctive management ideology in Meiji Japan.

27 See Nakamaki 1992 for a detailed description.

28 See Matsunaga 1995, for a detailed account of the importance of notions of *kokoro* in the recruitment and training of new employees in a Japanese chain store with a generally more secular orientation than Yaohan.

29 The name of the campaign, taken from the stores motto, was in English.

30 The complete list of guiding principles of Matsushita Electric is as follows:

   1. Service to the public
   2. Fairness and Honesty
   3. Teamwork for the Common Cause
   4. Untiring Effort for Improvement
   5. Courtesy and Humility
   6. Accord with Natural Laws
   7. Gratitude for Blessings

   (Matsushita 1988: 225–227)

31 The *gohonzon* is a mandala inscribed with the characters *namu myō hō renge kyō* – the title of the Lotus Sutra as rendered in Japanese.

32 These articles show a clear division along gender lines, with one common pattern being to produce a range of magazines, with one aimed principally at men another principally at women, and perhaps further magazines for younger readers. For example, Seicho no Ie produces *Hikari no Sen* (the line of light) aimed at older male members, and *Shiro Hato* (white dove) for women. Even where, as in the Kofuku no Kagaku case, a single magazine is produced, the articles within it are clearly gendered, by colour, design and layout, as well as by subject matter. In both cases, while the women's magazines or articles concentrate on how the movement's ideas may be applied to issues concerning the family, marital tensions, or children's education; the men's magazines or articles concentrate on the world of work.

33 Large enterprises are defined here as companies with 1,000 or more employees.

34 This summary of the aims of the Prosperity Association is based on internal Seicho no Ie documents, kindly supplied by Luiz Grasso of Seicho no Ie, London.

35 See Goodman 1990.

36 See Matsunaga 1995.

37 A section of the Portuguese language version of this text was kindly made available and translated by Luiz Grasso, the organiser of Seicho no Ie in London. The Japanese original was unavailable.

38 The name Yaohan is a combination of the first two Chinese characters of the word *yaoya*, meaning greengrocers, and the first character of Mr Tajima's given name, Hanjiro.

39 *Hinoe uma* years mark the conjunction of two different Chinese systems of naming years: the year of the horse, and the year of *hinoe*, meaning fire's elder brother. The two only coincide once every sixty years. Women born in such a year are thought to be difficult: strong tempered and possible husband-killers. The last time such a year occurred, in 1966, the birth rate in Japan dropped markedly.

40 Advising women who are encountering marital problems to tackle them by changing their attitude and behaviour towards their husbands is a standard

pattern in Seicho no Ie, at least in Japan, as can be seen from a survey of the women's magazine produced by the group, *Shiro Hato*. This advice seems to be proffered no matter what the women attribute their difficulties to, even where the wife places the blame on some aspect of her husband's behaviour, such as compulsive gambling.

41 In the *ie* system as enacted in legislation passed in the Meiji era, succession to the household, and therefore also to businesses based on the household, passed to the eldest son. Although this system was formally abolished in the post-war era, it remains a powerful social norm in Japan.

42 In Japanese, *Burajiru Yaohan hinomoto tai*. *Hinomoto* literally means 'origin of the sun': written with the same characters as *Nippon*, it is used as an alternative word for Japan. 'Rising sun' is therefore not a literal translation, but it is the translation which best captures the flavour of the word *hinomoto* in English.

43 One of these two was a younger brother of Wada Kazuo, who had been posted to Brazil. He refused to return to Japan when his father, Wada Ryohei, was dying in 1973, or to attend his funeral, on the grounds that this would be in breach of company regulations.

44 It would seem that these explanations may have been met with a degree of scepticism by local employees. One former employee of the Singapore branch expressed the opinion in an interview with me that Yaohan had expanded there for purely economic reasons, and dismissed any suggestions of this being a gesture of atonement, while for an equally sceptical view of Wada's comments on Yaohan's expansion into Hong Kong see Heung Wah Wong 1996.

45 At the time of writing, the London branch was not bankrupt, as it has a financial structure independent of the Japanese Yaohan. It therefore continued to exist in 1997, but independently of the Wada family.

46 The holding of *chōrei* is standard in Japan, although their content varies depending on the company concerned. For a detailed description of *chōrei* held in another large Japanese chain store without Yaohan's religious connections, see Matsunaga 1995.

47 This slogan changes every year: the 1995 slogan was 'Yaohan Renaissance, Bringing our Founding spirit into the Future'.

48 'Mr A' was identified in the Guardian article, but I am not identifying him here in view of the comments on the case given by a fellow employee below.

49 Taken from video of Wada's speech, my translation.

50 This finding is based on a telephone survey of the personnel managers of some of the leading manufacturing and financial companies in the UK, and was confirmed by Mari Sako, who has conducted extensive research on training programmes in Japanese manufacturing companies in the UK (personal communication).

References

Arai, K. (1996) 'New Religions' in N. Tamaru and D. Reid (eds.) *Religion in Japanese Culture: where living traditions meet a changing world*, Tokyo: Kodansha International.

Barker, E. (1995) *New Religious Movements: A practical introduction*, London: HMSO.

Barker, E. (ed.) (1982) *New Religious Movements: A perspective for understanding society*, New York and Toronto: Edwin Mellen Press.

Beasley, W. (ed.) (1975) *Modern Japan: aspects of history, literature, and society,* London: Allen and Unwin.
Bellah, R. (1957) *Tokugawa Religion: The Values of Pre-industrial Japan,* Glencoe, Illinois: Free Press.
Bethel, D.M. (1973) *Makiguchi the Value Creator: Revolutionary Japanese Educator and Founder of Soka Gakkai,* New York: Weatherhill.
Bremen, J. van and Martinez, D.P. (ed.) (1995) *Ceremony and Ritual in Japan: Religious Practices in an Industrialized Society,* London and New York: Routledge.
Bromley, D.G. and Shupe, A. (1981) 'Rebottling the Elixir: the Gospel of Prosperity in America's Religioeconomic corporations' in T. Robbins and D. Anthony (eds.) *In Gods we trust: new patterns of religious pluralism in America,* New Brunswick; London: Transaction Books.
Clark, R. (1979) *The Japanese Company,* New Haven: Yale University Press.
Clarke, P.B. (1994) 'Japanese "Old", "New" and "New, New" Religious Movements in Brazil', in P.B. Clarke and J. Somers (eds.) *Japanese New Religions in the West,* Folkestone: Japan Library.
Clarke, P.B. and Somers, J. (ed.) (1994) *Japanese New Religions in the West,* Folkestone: Japan Library.
Davis, W. (1980) *Dojo: Magic and Exorcism in Modern Japan,* Stanford Calif.: Stanford University Press.
—— (1992) *Japanese Religion and Society: Paradigms of Structure and Change,* Albany New York: State University of New York Press.
Dore, R. (1973) *British Factory, Japanese Factory: the Origins of Diversity in Industrial Relations,* Berkeley: University of California Press.
Dore, R. and Sako, M. (1989) *How the Japanese learn to work,* London: Routledge.
Enami, J. (1994) *Yaohan no chōsen,* Tokyo: Nihon kyobunsha.
Goodman, R. (1990) *Japan's "International Youth": The Emergence of a New Class of Schoolchildren,* Oxford: Clarendon Press.
Hardacre, H. (1986) *Kurozumikyo and the New Religions of Japan,* Princeton New Jersey: Princeton University Press.
Heelas, P. (1996) *The New Age Movement: The celebration of self and the sacralization of modernity,* Oxford: Blackwell.
Ikado, F. (1968) 'Trend and Problems of New Religions: Religion in Urban Society', in K. Morioka and W.H. Newell (eds.)*The Sociology of Japanese Religion,* Leiden: E. J. Brill.
Kitagawa, J. (1987) *On Understanding Japanese Religion,* Princeton New Jersey: Princeton University Press.
Kondo, D. (1990) *Crafting Selves: Power, Gender, and Discourses of Identity in a Japanese Workplace,* Chicago: University of Chicago Press.
Lewis, D.C. (1993) 'Religious Rites in a Japanese Factory', in M. Mullins, S. Shimazono, P. Swanson (ed.) *Religion and Society in Modern Japan: Selected Readings,* Berkeley, California: Asian Humanities Press.
Lewis, J.R. and Melton, J. Gordon (ed.) (1992) *Perspectives on the New Age,* Albany: State University of New York Press.
Marshall, B.K. (1967) *Captialism and Nationalism in Prewar Japan: the Ideology of the Business Elite 1868–1941,* Stanford: Stanford University Press.
Matsunaga, L. (1995) *Working in a Chain Store: a case study of a Japanese Company,* Ph.D Thesis, University of London.
Matsushita, K. (1988) *Quest for Prosperity: The life of a Japanese Industrialist,* Kyoto: PHP Institute.
Mc Farland, H. (1967) *The Rush Hour of the Gods,* New York: Macmillan.

71

Moeran, B. (1984) 'Individual, Group and *Seishin* : Japan's Internal Cultural Debate', in *Man* (N.S.) 19, 252–66.

Morioka, K. and Newell, W.H. (ed.) (1968) *The Sociology of Japanese Religion*, Leiden: E. J. Brill

Morita, A. (1987) *Made in Japan*, London: Collins.

Mullins, M., Shimazono, S. Swanson, P. (ed.) (1993) *Religion and Society in Modern Japan: Selected Readings*, Berkeley, California: Asian Humanities Press.

Nakamaki, H. (1992) *Mukashi Daimyō, Ima Kaisha: kigyō to shūkyō*, Kyoto: Tankosha.

—— (1995) 'Memorial monuments and memorial services of Japanese companies: Focusing on Mount Koya', in J. van Bremen and D.P. Martinez (eds.) *Ceremony and Ritual in Japan: Religious Practices in an Industrialized Society*, London and New York: Routledge.

Nakane, C. (1973) *Japanese Society*, Harmondsworth: Penguin

O'Neill, P.G. (1984) 'Organization and Authority in the Traditional Arts', in *Modern Asian Studies*, Vol. 18, No. 4.

Ooms, E. (1993) *Women and Millenarian Protest in Meiji Japan: Deguchi Nao and Omotokyo*, Ithaca, New York: Cornell University East Asia Program.

Pye, M. (1989) 'Woran glauben Japans Großindustrielle?' in P. Antes and D. Pahnke (ed.) *Die Religion von Oberschichten*, Marburg: Diagonal Verlag, 291–310.

Rajana, E. (1975) 'New Religions in Japan: an appraisal of two theories', in W. Beasley (ed.) *Modern Japan: aspects of history literature and society*, London: Allen and Unwin.

Reader, I. (1991) *Religion in Contemporary Japan*, London: Macmillan.

—— (1995) 'Cleaning floors and sweeping the mind: Cleaning as a ritual process', in J. van Bremen and D.P. Martinez (ed.) *Ceremony and Ritual in Japan: Religious Practices in an Industrialized Society*, London: Routledge.

Roberts, R.H. (ed.) (1995) *Religion and the Transformations of Capitalism: Comparative Approaches*, London: Routledge.

Robbins, T. and Anthony, D. (eds.) (1981) *In Gods we trust: New patterns of religious pluralism in America*, New Brunswick; London: Transaction Books.

Rohlen, T. (1970) 'Sponsorship of cultural continuity in Japan: a company training program', in *Journal of Asian and African Studies* 5:3:184–192.

—— (1973) 'Spiritual training in a Japanese bank', in *American Anthropologist* 75:5.

—— (1974) *For Harmony and Strength: Japanese white-collar organization in anthropological perspective*, Berkeley: University of California Press.

Rupert, G. (1992) 'Employing the New Age', in J.R. Lewis and J. Gordon Melton (ed.) *Perspectives on the New Age*, Albany: State University of New York Press.

Shimazono, S. (1993) 'The Expansion of Japan's New Religions into Foreign Cultures', in M. Mullins, S. Shimazono, P. Swanson (ed.) *Religion and Society in Modern Japan: Selected Readings*, Berkeley, California: Asian Humanities Press.

Sutherland, S, and Clarke, P.B. (eds.) (1991) *The Study of Religion, Traditional and New*, London: Routledge.

Tamaru, N. and Reid, D. (eds.) (1996) *Religion in Japanese Culture: where living traditions meet a changing world*, Tokyo: Kodansha International.

Thomsen, H. (1963) *The New Religions of Japan*, Rutland, Vt.: Charles E. Tuttle.

Tokuhisa, K. (1991) *A Prosperidad esta na mente*, Sao Paolo: Seicho no Ie do Brasil.

Ueshiba, K. (1991) 'The Life of Morihei Ueshiba', in M. Ueshiba, *Budo: Teachings of the Founder of Aikido*, Tokyo: Kodansha International

Wada, K. (1992) *Yaohan's Global Strategy: the 21st Century is the Era of Asia*, Hong Kong: Capital Communications Corporation Ltd.

Weber, M. (1930) *The Protestant Ethic and The Spirit of Capitalism*, London: Unwin.

Wilson, B. (1982) 'The New Religions: Preliminary Considerations' in E. Barker (ed.) *New Religious Movements: A perspective for understanding society*, New York and Toronto: Edwin Mellen Press.

—— (1991) "secularisation": Religion in the Modern World' in S. Sutherland and P.B. Clarke (eds.) *The Study of Religion, Traditional and New Religion*, London: Routledge.

Wilson, B. and Dobbelaere, K. (1994) *A Time to Chant: The Soka Gakkai Buddhists in Britain*, Oxford: Clarendon Press.

Wong, H.W. (1996) *An Anthropological study of a Japanese supermarket in Hong Kong*, D. Phil Thesis, University of Oxford.

Wong. M. (1994) 'Enhancing the Learning Capacity in a Japanese Organization in Hong Kong through Spiritual Education', in *The Learning Organization*, Vol. 1 No. 3, pp. 38–43.

Official Publications

Kaigai Keizai Jōhō Sentā (1995) *Zaiō nikkei kigyō no keiei jitsuno*

Agency for Cultural Affairs (1972) *Japanese Religion*, Tokyo: Kodansha International

Movement publications

Hikari no sen	May, June 1995
The Liberty	July 1995

General publications

Japan Times	December 15th 1991
New York Times	February 19th 1990
Daily Mail	April 1992
The Guardian	April 1992, February 1997
NichiEi Times	February 1995

CHAPTER THREE

Japanese Religion in Australia

Mahikari and Zen in a Multicultural Society[1]

Gary D. Bouma, Wendy Smith and Shiva Vasi

Australia's religious profile has been changed profoundly by immigration and conversion (Bouma 1994, 1995, 1997b). As a result Australia has become one of the most religiously diverse multicultural societies in the world. Japanese religions have come to Australia both by way of immigration and by way of conversion. This chapter focuses on Sukyo Mahikari and Zen Buddhism as examples of Japanese religions which have become established in Australia primarily as a result of conversion. For each of these religious groups a demographic background will be provided as well as a brief history and then a description of their life in Australia.

Multicultural Australia

Since the end of the Second World War the composition of Australian society has been radically changed by massive immigration. While at first immigration was limited to people from Northern Europe and North America, with the end of the 'White Australia Policy' immigration has included people from the Middle East and Asia. The 'number of annual arrivals' born in Asia increased from 1,800 in 1977, 25 per cent of all immigrants that year, to 6,000 in 1991, 50 per cent of migrants (Coughlan 1992: 3).

Comparing the religious profile depicted in the 1947 and 1991 censuses gives a picture of these changes. The 1947 census depicted a nation dominated by Anglicans (39 per cent) and mainline Protestants (23 per cent). Barely 0.5 per cent identified with non-Christian religious groups and there were 411 Buddhists. The 1991 census presents a very different picture. Anglicans at 23.9 per cent no longer dominated as Catholics had become the largest religious group at 27.3 per cent. Mainline Protestants (13 per cent) were just ahead of those declaring they have 'no religion' (12.9 per cent). In addition to these changes Muslims and Pentecostals are both at

0.9 per cent and Buddhists at 0.8 per cent. The growth of these three groups has been particularly dramatic over the past twenty years as migrants from the Middle East added substantial numbers to Australian Muslims and Asian migrants increased the presence of Buddhists. During this time Jews have maintained a steady 0.4 per cent of the population. Other groups just a bit smaller include Salvation Army and Jehovah's Witnesses at 0.4 per cent while the next larger groups are Lutherans at 1.5 per cent and Baptists at 1.7 per cent.

While much of the change in Australia's religious profile is due to immigration, some has been due to conversion. Conversion accounts for the rise of such groups as those declaring 'no religion', Pentecostal Christianity, Mahikari and Zen Buddhism. During the post-war period, and in particular since the 1970s, a variety of 'new religious' groups or 'new styles' of existing groups have attracted Australian members. Migration has also interacted with the conversion process. Migrants have strengthened some existing religious groups, especially Catholics and Muslims, and have brought to Australia religious groups not represented, or only minimally present before World War II, for example, strands of Indo-Chinese Buddhism. Some of these 'new to Australia' religious groups are present primarily because of migration and largely attract people from a particular migrant group. The Reformed Church in Australia is an example (Bouma 1989, 1995). Others of these 'new to Australia' religious groups come to Australia as a result of conversion attempts, or as a result of their appeal to people already in Australia. Pentecostal Christianity is an example of this process as are Mahikari and Zen Buddhism.

As these new to Australia religious groups have found their way in Australian society they have consciously and unconsciously made changes as has the society which now is more religiously diverse than before. The term 'religious settlement' has been used to describe the processes involved in the migration of a religion from one place to another (Bouma 1997a,b). As Mahikari and Zen have come to Australia they too have changed as has Australian society.

Japanese in Australia

Estimating the size of the Japanese proportion of Australian society is complicated by their small size (0.07 per cent in 1986) and the fact that the census only reports birthplace and not ethnic identification. Atsumi's profile of the Japanese resident in Australia based on the 1986 census reported 11,160 persons born in Japan (1992: 12). There were 3,593 Japanese in Australia in 1901, but that dropped to 330 in 1947,[2] climbed by about 2,000 per decade till 1981 (8,060) and then by 3,000 in the next 5 years. These figures under-represent the size of the Japanese ethnic group in Australia since it does not include the children of Japanese parents born in

Australia, nor does it include people of Japanese ancestry who were born in other countries (Atsumi 1992: 12). Price (n.d.: 2) applying a number of carefully devised criteria to the 1986 census, estimates the Japanese 'ancestry strength' at 12,307 and 'ethnic strength' at 15,000. A total of 12,411 persons resident in Australia claim to speak Japanese at home (Price n.d.: 2). Jones' analysis of the 1986 census revealed that of those in the 'Japanese Ancestry Group'(Jones 1991: 9–11) 92 per cent were first generation migrants and 78 per cent had resided in Australia less than 10 years. In general, Japanese Australians were more highly educated, earned higher incomes and were more likely to be found in managerial and professional occupations. Most (87 per cent) lived in 'major urban' areas while 12 per cent lived in 'other urban' areas (Jones 1991). According to Jones (1991: 88) Japanese in Australia identified with the following religious categories: Anglican (2.2 per cent), Catholic (3.1 per cent), Other Christian (4.6 per cent), Orthodox (0.1 per cent), non-Christian (27.8 per cent), non-theistic[3] (49.8 per cent) and not stated (12.3 per cent).

Religions originating in Japan, or coming to Australia from Japan, form a very small proportion of the population of Australia. It is possible to estimate the sizes of Japanese religions in Australia from the census and official statistics. In the 1991 census 1,478 Australians identified their religion as Zen Buddhists, 609 as Mahikari, 585 as Shinto and fifty as Tenrikyo. While fewer than ten people gave Soka Gakkai as their religion in the 1991 census, in 1995 the Australian District of Soka Gakkai claimed 1,350 members[4] of whom 66 per cent were Asian (Ward and Humphreys 1995: 413). Similarly in 1992 Tenrikyo claimed a total following of 240, 50 per cent Japanese (Ward and Humphreys 1995: 413). A study of Zen and Mahikari, Australia's two largest religious groups with Japanese origins, will provide a valuable picture of religious life in a multicultural society and the process of 'religious settlement' in the case of religious groups which have come to Australia primarily through conversion.

Sukyo Mahikari

Sukyo Mahikari – 'Supra-Religion True Light', henceforth referred to as Mahikari[5] – has been claimed to be the largest Japanese religion[6] in Australia (Shinbo 1992: 1). While in the 1991 census 609 Australians described their religion as Mahikari, official Mahikari records list about 2,000 adherents in Australia (Ward and Humphreys 1995: 375). Although the first Mahikari group was set up in Adelaide as a result of contact with three Japanese women in 1974, its existence in Australia is not dependent on a membership of Japanese immigrants, as is the case for other new religions such as Tenrikyo (Ward and Humphreys 1995: 377).

Mahikari grew under the leadership of Dr Andris Tebecis, a leading figure in the expansion of Mahikari outside Japan, who encountered

Mahikari while in Japan on a visiting professorship. He established the first Mahikari centre in Australia in 1977 in Canberra, which later became the site for the Australian headquarters. Mahikari now has centres in every capital city in Australia with membership including Australians of many ethnic origins, including Chinese who stand out as the largest single group in the centre in Melbourne. The Perth centre has an approximately equal distribution of people of European, Chinese and Indian origins. Ethnic Japanese are not a dominant presence. For instance, there were only three Japanese members at the Melbourne centre during my research. From my observations membership is not associated with a particular social class since members' occupations range from physicians, to bureaucrats, counsellors, business people, musicians, and those between jobs. Those involved in small businesses seemed the largest single group.[7]

In Japan, women constitute the majority of followers and devotees observed at temples and shrines, partly because Japanese men have little time away from their jobs for such activities until retirement. Moreover, women, as the unspoken custodians of the family's spiritual welfare, usually tend the family Buddhist altar and Shinto *kamidana* – household altar, literally 'god shelf'. Once their children are self-reliant, Japanese women have more time to spend on spiritual matters.

In Australia I observed more women than men attending the centres, called *dōjō*, literally 'training place', during office hours. But in the evenings, weekends, and at the monthly ceremonies, I observed a balanced presence of males and females partly because couples participate together. This pattern is characteristic of Mahikari membership in Japan as well. Mahikari places great emphasis on harmony within the family. Mahikari also attracts retired men and young single males as members. The Youth Corps movement provides special training within the movement for young people of both sexes.

What is Mahikari?[8]

Mahikari, often classified as one of the 'New New Religions', was established in Japan in the postwar era[9] by Okada Kotama (1901–1974) who received revelations from God in 1959, commanding him: 'The time of heaven has come. Rise. Thy name shall be Kotama. Exercise the art of purification. The world shall encounter severe times' (Okada Kotama 1982: 24).

In Japanese, Mahikari means 'True Light', a spiritual and purifying energy. It is similar to the Japanese 'ki' or the Chinese 'chi'[10] (McVeigh 1992a: 55–58), but is different in the sense that it has a divine aspect. It is the Divine Light of the Creator, Su God. People become members of Mahikari, or *kamikumite* – those who go 'hand-in-hand with God', after attending the three day Primary *Kenshū* – training course –and receiving an

Omitama – Divine locket, which enables the person to act as a channel through which they project the True Light from Su God. The *Omitama* is worn on the body of the *kamikumite* and is treated with great respect. It must not be allowed to become wet or touch the ground. That is why children do not become *kamikumite* until around the age of ten, when they are deemed to be able to take proper care of the *Omitama*. This process has been likened to an initiation (Hurbon 1991: 224).[11]

Members then have the ability to transmit the True Light following a procedure (see Davis 1980: 18–22) of praying to the Creator God which involves bowing to the *Goshintai* – sacred scroll containing the *Chon*, symbol of Su God – and then to their partner as an act of politeness. Then with their back to the *Goshintai*, the prayer of purification, *Amatsu Norigoto,* is recited and True Light is transmitted to the forehead of the other person through a raised palm of the hand. Light may then be transmitted to the back of the head and other parts of the body, a complete session taking about fifty minutes.[12] The practice of giving True Light and the attendance at group ceremonies, which magnify the transmission of Light from Su God, are the fundamental activities of Mahikari members.

Mahikari is open to people of all religions and viewpoints and does not attempt to convert people from their existing religious beliefs. Rather it intensifies their understanding of the major spiritual teachings of their religion, which are common to all religions. For instance, members explained to me that a Catholic priest would become a better Catholic priest by practicing Mahikari (see also Cornille 1994: 99). The non-coercive nature of the organisation is demonstrated by the fact that there is a significant dropout rate of those who have received the Primary *Kenshū*, a fact freely mentioned by senior members. Mahikari beliefs also reflect this openness by incorporating elements of the 'Five Major Religions': Buddhism, Taoism, Confucianism, Islam and Christianity. Symbols from these and other major religions can be seen in the architecture of the Main World Shrine – *Suza* or *Sekai So Honzan* – and the Mahikari Divine emblem, which incorporates the circle, the cross, the six-pointed star and the sixteen petalled crest, symbolic of the Japanese Imperial family who are the representatives of the Shinto gods on earth (Knecht 1995).

Studying Mahikari in Australia

I approached the central organisation in Canberra for permission to study Mahikari in Australia. Because there have been studies published in English focusing on Mahikari in both Japan and overseas by at least ten foreign researchers, I assumed that agreement for my research would not be difficult to obtain. However this was not to be the case. There were three areas of difficulty.

Firstly, the subjects of social science research often feel that their case has been misrepresented by researchers who come to study an organisation for a short period, and then try to fit the data they obtain into a preconceived theoretical model used in their discipline. This phenomenon can be understood in terms of the *emic* versus *etic* perspective in research. An *emic* perspective describes the way the members of the group studied perceive their own society, its practices and values. An *etic* perspective is an outsider's view, elucidating points about the society of which the members may not be aware, but which nevertheless are valid at another level of analysis. Members of an organisation who can read the reports written about their social world usually favour an *emic* perspective. In the case of religious movements, the perceptions of members and outsiders may be quite different, and as a spiritual dimension is involved, this difference can be quite distressing from a believer's point of view.

Secondly, incidents surrounding the demise of the Aum Shinrikyo group in Japan in 1995 (Shimazono, 1995: 411) have tarnished the image of Japanese new religious groups in general, even though their goals and practices are in no way similar to those of Aum. The fact that religious organisations were investigated by the Japanese authorities in 1995 in the context of proposed reforms to the Religious Corporation Law – *Shūkyō Hōjin Hō* – under which they are organised has understandably increased sensitivity to outside research. Thus, it seemed reasonable that in addition to securing ethical clearance from Monash University to engage in research on humans, I was required to obtain permission to conduct research on Mahikari in Australia from the head of the organisation, *Oshienushisama*.

Thirdly, people within Mahikari emphasise that the experience of receiving the transmission of True Light is the most important aspect in trying to understand Mahikari. Intellectual understanding alone is not sufficient. Therefore a condition of my conducting the research was that I should receive the True Light as many times as possible. This was an easy condition to comply with, as anthropological research involves participant observation and having respect for the beliefs and practices of the people studied. This is the methodology by which one attempts to grasp the *emic*, or people's own, view of their world. Thus I received the True Light about fifteen times in the Australian Mahikari centres and about ten times in the Japanese headquarters and other centres. In this way, I too experienced the 'experiences' that Mahikari members talk about – a painful toothache was alleviated and I was able to do without the prescription glasses I normally need for reading.

My questionnaire subject matter was approved and I was able to conduct interviews with six Mahikari members in the Melbourne centre, eight members of the Canberra centre and two visiting members from the Sydney and Brisbane centres. This sample included four members at the level of Centre chief or higher, five *dōshi* – ministers, and three other centre members with official rank. I decided to interview formally people with long experience or high rank in the organisation as they would be better qualified to answer some of the more technical questions. These were balanced with the many informal conversations which I had with members both in the *dōjō* and in their private homes.

Nine of the sixteen people I interviewed gave me the True Light, often just before or after the interview. As I interviewed several people per day and it is not the practice to receive True Light more than once per day, not all subjects gave me the True Light. Both in the Australian and Japanese centres it was usually arranged that I receive the True Light from *dōshi* – centre chiefs – or other people of high status in the organisation. Although the 'strength' of the True Light transmitted does not necessarily depend on rank or length of membership, but more on the sincerity of intent of the transmitter and the attitude of gratitude of the receiver, I interpreted this as an honour, as these people were very busy within the organisation. I also received True Light from ordinary members of the centres, and had the same experience of a feeling of heat in my body when receiving from them.

The appeal of Mahikari

While many people come to Mahikari centres for the first time with the aim of being healed of diseases, Mahikari members emphasise that the aim of giving the True Light is for purification, which incidentally may heal by purifing the environment, objects, or one's own spiritual attitude. True Light uplifts the spiritual, mental and physical realms. Healing in the physical realm is a by-product of this.

Mahikari teachings[13] also emphasise that the experience of True Light is best accompanied by the individual's grateful attitude, sincere self-reflection of faults, and feeling of apology to God for any past transgressions. When these go together, like 'the two wheels of a cart', there can be more effective change in the *sōnen* –innermost attitude – of the individual, which is the ultimate aim – spiritual elevation. Indeed, the extemporary prayers spoken by the leaders of ceremonies usually contain at least three elements, the expression of gratitude to Su God, sincere apology for mistakes and requests for continued blessings.

According to Mahikari teachings, 80 per cent of health and other human problems with emotional and mental states, relationships and even economic matters, are caused by attaching spirits. These may be deceased ancestors of the individual who remain unsatisfied in the after-death state, or resentful spirits who have been wronged by self or one's ancestors, or animal and elemental spirits that have been encountered. The afflictions caused by such spirits relate to the karma[14] of the individual. Giving True Light to purify and help these spirits has been called exorcism in the academic literature on Mahikari (Davis 1980, Young 1990, McVeigh 1995: 65).

However, this term is misleading in the sense that the aim is not to drive the spirits away in the classic sense of exorcism but to purify them, causing them to reflect on the error of their ways in causing harm to others, thus bringing them to a state of peace and happiness so that they voluntarily relinquish their interference with or hold on the human being. This process involves the procedure of *okiyome* in which a person receiving the True Light, usually in the first position, to the forehead, occasionally experiences 'spirit movement' – twitching, crying, dramatic body movements, speaking in strange voices or languages, and writing messages with finger movements on the floor. Only a few high ranking members of the organisation are qualified and allowed to conduct the 'spirit investigation', which involves questioning the manifesting spirit, trying to establish why it is interfering with the person and helping it to awaken and accept the beneficial power of the True Light, reflect on its mistakes and leave the person alone.

Spirit movement had been experienced by most of the sixteen members that I interviewed. Such experiences witnessed within the *dōjō* and the testimonies from Australian members are published in the monthly *Mahikari Australia and Asia Journal* give empirical status to this element of the Mahikari belief system, which has little precedent within the cultural background of Australians of Anglo-European origin. Members of Southeast Asian, Indian or African backgrounds are generationally much closer to small-scale, agriculture-based cultures where the belief in the influence of the spirit world on the living is an integral part of their cosmologies.[15]

Many examples of miracles experienced by Australians are documented (Tebecis 1982). In my own interviews I was told of a member's elderly father who had been deaf in one ear and came to hear clearly again after receiving the Primary Training. Another member described how four *kamikumite* were in an old car whose brakes seized up in the middle of six lanes of heavy traffic on a hilly road in Sydney. The car was rolling back, so they all jumped out and, reciting the *Amatsu Norigoto* prayer, they gave True Light to each wheel, successfully fixing the brake problem. A senior Australian member observed the materialisation of particles of gold on the pages of a book describing the life of *Sukuinushisama*.

Members are encouraged to share their experiences at special times within the structure of ceremonies and study groups. These testimonies can range from major miracles relating to health and safety to more minor convenient events, such as finding a good parking space. All these auspicious events come to be seen as Divine arrangements, the public sharing of which serves to reinforce the Mahikari world view among members that all of life is lived according to God's Plan, and that there are no coincidences. According to Shinbo (1992: 81–82) this public sharing is a crucial element in securing the long term commitment of recent converts to the organisation.[16]

Not all members experience dramatic miracle transformations after receiving the True Light. Some may even have experiences which involve discomfort, especially the 'cleansing' process which at times involves fever, chills, excessive elimination of body wastes, or financial misfortune. Unless these are understood within the Mahikari world view, members may feel discouraged and unable to interpret the cleansing experience as ultimately beneficial. The organisation addresses this problem with regular study groups and a system which organises members into groups functioning through the leadership of 'group carers'.

From individual miracles to universal ethical altruism

After the initial contact with Mahikari, the experience of personal miracles through the receiving of True Light, and the enthusiasm to join the organisation by receiving the Primary Training, it is important to transform this still rather individual, or family self-interest motivation into the wider world view of Mahikari in its Divine role to establish a new civilisation on earth. Nakamaki (1991: 217) writing about another new religion, the PL Kyodan, states: 'after the use of miracles as a point of contact, the next step was to teach people ethics for daily life'. He explains that since miracles in themselves are not sufficient to commit people to a religious faith in the long term, in many new religions, faith in miracles is linked to an ethical system. In Mahikari, the study of the teachings of the founder *Sukuinushisama* and the present leader, *Oshienushisama* – Great Teacher – are an integral part of ceremonies and regular group activities. For instance the monthly ceremony at each centre in Japan contains a tape recorded lecture from the teachings of *Oshienushisama*, followed by a lecture explaining the teachings by the centre chief (see McVeigh 1992c: 54–55). In Australia an English translation of *Oshienushisama's* teachings is transmitted by the centre chief. A constant theme in these teachings is that receiving the True Light helps one to change one's innermost attitude – *sonen*. Thus beyond the miraculous effects of the Light, is the aim of achieving an ethical way of life through the development of humility, gratitude and repentance in one's personality.

Although people may first come to Mahikari with the aim of solving personal health or other problems, the potential for altruistic concern to develop is made possible in the movement's other wings, youth education and the Mahikari Youth Corps,[17] the Yoko agriculture movement, the Yoko Health care program and the Yoko Civilisation Research Institute, which link into a general social awareness of contemporary problems in the environment, in contemporary social relationships and in the one-sided advance of technology and material culture. A strong theme expressed by Mahikari members is that it is not good to isolate oneself from the secular world. According to Mahikari teachings, this was not the case in the older religions of the previous Water Age, which emphasised solitary practices in lonely places. Since the new Fire Age began on 1st January 1962, mastery of the spiritual path can be attained in the context of everyday life experiences and it is here where the transmission of True Light is most needed.

Affiliation with Mahikari

In Australia, people become members of Mahikari through a variety of ways, but primarily through personal contacts. Mahikari members emphasise the importance of letting people experience the True Light and deciding for themselves, rather than trying to convince them with doctrine and reasoning. Tebecis' book, *Mahikari – Thank God for the Answers at Last*, has been very instrumental in attracting Australians to the movement. People report coming across it in public libraries or in the houses of friends.[18] Many of those who read it, say they found that its explanation of Mahikari thinking, or the many testimonies of personal miracles spoke to their immediate needs or seemed to express their hitherto unformulated understanding of things. An article on Mahikari in the alternative magazine, *Simply Living* was also mentioned as a first point of contact. Some read the article and went straight to the nearest centre to experience the True Light. Others encountered Mahikari and the True Light at its booth in the 1979 'Down to Earth' alternative festival.

At first, the media were interested in the book on Mahikari published by Tebecis, and this generated widespread publicity, but now membership has grown sufficiently for personal networks to be the main factor in recruiting new members. Members offer the benefits of True Light to family, friends, workmates and even strangers, preferring to offer the True Light and let the experience speak for itself. This may result in the person receiving the benefits and doing nothing more about it, or, if inspired to help others in the same way that he or she has benefited, deciding to become a Mahikari member by attending the three-day Primary Training and receiving the *Omitama*.

The atmosphere of the centres is very bright and positive (McVeigh 1992b: 103), and the attitude of members is very friendly, welcoming and sincere. The humility of senior members and their altruistic concern for individuals and humankind leaves a deep impression. As one informant commented, the personal qualities of Mahikari members themselves are a very strong reason for newcomers to decide to join Mahikari.

While affiliation is usually an individual process, in the case of some ethnic groups whose members have recently migrated to Australia, for instance the Chinese, the network of family ties has become the basis of affiliation. This accounts for the rapid rise in membership of ethnic Chinese in the Melbourne[19] and Perth centres, and in some centres in South Africa, where the members are predominantly of Indian ethnic origin. Once members of Mahikari however, there seemed to be little ethnic difference in the interpretation of teachings. For instance, members of Anglo-Australian cultural background would come to think about the importance of ancestors for the first time, but members of Chinese cultural background would need to 'unlearn' their traditional understanding of ancestors. The Mahikari teachings are straightforward and easy to understand, but in that they are believed to be universal, they have an absolute quality which does not necessitate or allow for cultural reinterpretation. In interviewing members of different ethnic backgrounds in Australia and in Singapore, I found a striking similarity in all their explanations of the teachings.

The organisation of Mahikari

Expanding movements face the problem of structuring their organisation to cope with growing numbers, geographical distance and the loss of the personal link with the founder. The problem of succession has already been experienced within the Mahikari movement (Inoue et al. 1996: 164, Cornille 1991: 268). Mahikari has made the transition to a global organisation with a clearly defined hierarchy of authority and a sophisticated communication system. To some outsiders these give the impression of a military organisation. A researcher of Mahikari in Western Europe noted that the wearing of uniforms, the marching practice and the emphasis on discipline in the Mahikari Youth Corps also impart a flavour of the military (Cornille 1991: 281). According to the observations of Tebecis however, 'In Australia, Mahikari Youth Corps activities do not seem to give a military impression'. This Corps is not compulsory for the younger members of Mahikaru and makes up only a small proportion of Mahikari youth.

Large *dōjō* in Japan have video camera monitoring systems installed to make sure that visitors are not neglected. The requirement that those visiting the *dōjō* sign in and sign out with the time of their arrival and departure impart a strict organisational atmosphere. This recording is overseen by receptionists in Japan, and although the registers are placed near the entrance of the Australian centres they are much more informal in mood. These organisational aspects are not unique to Mahikari but are typical of practices within mainstream Japanese society. For instance academic staff of a Japanese tertiary research institute were required to register the time of their arrival and departure with a receptionist, and the building was subject to video surveillance. However, such features may seem inappropriate in a religious context to Australians.

Mahikari centres are graded according to their size and importance, from *dai-, chū-, shō-* and *jun-dōjō* – large, medium, small and associate centres, followed by *okiyome-sho* – purification place – and *renraku-sho* –

communication place. This graded system of centres is common both to Japan and overseas. The largest centre, apart from the Main World Shrine and the Mahikari headquarters in Takayama, is the Kyoto *Daidōjō*, with a main hall of 340 *tatami* mats, which accommodated over 1,000 people at its New Year ceremony in 1996. Canberra, the largest centre in Australia, has the status of *chūdōjō*, and the Melbourne centre is an *okiyome-sho*. A feature of all these centres is the provision of a family room where parents can be with small children while receiving the True Light, or listening to lectures through the installed sound or video system. The homes of senior members who have inaugurated the *Goshintai* and who wish to make them available for this purpose, also serve as *Okiyome* Houses, which are open for several nights a week for people to drop in and receive the True Light, especially if they live far away from the centre. In 1996 there were four *Okiyome* Houses in Canberra and six in Melbourne.

Overseeing the *dōjō* are the Regional Headquarters – *shidōbu*, one for each prefecture in Japan, and one each for Europe/Africa, North America, Latin America, Asia and Australia/Oceania. The latter includes South Africa, Papua New Guinea, New Zealand, New Caledonia and Fiji. It is headed by the *Buchō*,[20] Tebecis, on behalf of *Oshienushisama* and his role includes both spiritual and managerial aspects. He visits centres in all the countries regularly, conducting the Primary Training and bestowing the *Omitama* on new members. He also administers the region, overseeing and recommending staff transfers and promotions in rank, and conducts the *Shidōbu* monthly ceremony as the spiritual representative of *Oshienush-isama*. Above the Regional Headquarters in the structure of the organisation is the Sukyo Mahikari Headquarters located in Takayama in a building opposite the Main World Shrine. Its role is to transmit spiritual guidance from *Oshienushisama* to the Regional Headquarters.

Roles within the movement are similarly ranked according to modern organisational principles[21] and are the same both in Japan and overseas. Below *Oshienushisama* herself are a few very senior members of Sukyo Mahikari Headquarters. In general the main ranks are *dōshi* – minister – and *dōjōchō* – centre chiefs). Centre chiefs below *Buchō* are spiritually in charge of the centre, are usually from the locality and rarely transferred. *Dōshi*[22] are the disciples of *Oshienushisama* who have undertaken a three-year training course, are of all nationalities and may be transferred, often at intervals of about three years, and across national boundaries. For instance, the present *dōshi* at the Melbourne centre is a South African, there are two Japanese *dōshi* serving in the Canberra Regional Headquarters and an Australian *dōshi* is posted to the International Division in Takayama.

Within the *dōjō* there are different group leaders, coordinators and other personnel who coordinate such groups as the Parents' Group, Educators' Group, Older Youth Group, Primary Students' Group, Kindergarten Group and so on. There are also various leadership roles relating to the Youth

Corps, Yoko agriculture and medicine. In these systems, spiritual elements and modern bureaucratic principles are combined. For instance, the appointment to a leadership role in one of these groups is officially made by *Oshienushisama* on the basis of the individual's spiritual qualities, yet the size of the group, its hierarchical structure and the communication and recording procedures mirror aspects of the large organisations found in modern society.

Mahikari centres

The decor of the centres was very similar in both Australia and Japan, except that in Japan, the floors were covered with *tatami* mats, in Australia, with carpet. There was a uniform style of simplicity, yet the effect was harmonious and attractive: a wide expanse of floor where people practise *okiyome*, using cushions, small pillows and blankets, with low cupboards at the back for people to leave their handbags and other personal belongings. The room is dominated by the *Goshinden* – altar. In larger *dōjō* it is a wooden structure reminiscent of a Shinto shrine, in smaller ones, an alcove decorated with gold as a backdrop to the *Goshintai* – literally 'body of God'–, a scroll on which is represented the cross with red vertical and blue horizontal lines, the circle with the sacred *Chon* symbol and the Chinese characters for Mahikari in beautiful calligraphy by *Sukuinushisama* (see McVeigh 1992a: 54). At one side of the *Goshintai*, the side further away from the entrance, is located a statue of *Izunome Omikamisama*, the deity who represents the physical manifestation of the earth on behalf of Su God. Similar prayers are presented consecutively to Su God facing the *Goshintai* and then to *Izunome-sama* during ceremonies. Apart from the altar which may or may not be shaped like a Shinto shrine, there is no attempt to express Japanese culture in the decor of the centres. Apart from the altar itself the only other items displayed on the walls are photographs of the Main World Shrine, a large chart of the *Okiyome* Zones, a diagram of the human body showing the key areas to which the True Light may be directed and notice boards and cupboards containing copies of the monthly journal and supplies of ancestral tablets for the ancestral altars, etc. There is always a beautifully arranged vase of fresh flowers near the *goshintai*.[23] Apart from the atmosphere of cleanliness and simplicity, there is no attempt to generate a 'Japanese' cultural atmosphere in the *dōjō* using cultural artefacts from Japan. Having visited *dōjō* in Australia, Japan, Malaysia and Singapore, the similarity in their style and atmosphere is striking. While the *Goshinden* was usually constructed using wood and was sometimes shaped in the style of a Japanese *Shinto* shrine, often it reflected local architectural styles.

In Australia, as in Japan, no shoes are worn in the centre. In Japanese interiors, the taking off of shoes signifies the ritual purity of the domestic space or shrine, as opposed to the impurity of the outside world (Ohnuki-Tierney 1984: 45, McVeigh 1992b: 106n). Thus there are special slippers to be worn only in the toilet in Japanese houses, as in the *dōjō*. In larger *dōjō* in both Japan and Australia there are taps near the entrance so that members can wash their hands after handling their shoes. This purification by water at the entrance of the holy area is similar to the practice of rinsing the mouth and hands before one enters a Shinto shrine.

To what extent is Mahikari a 'Japanese religion'?

Mahikari claims to be beyond religion – *su-kyo*.[24] According to the teachings, there are no 'religions' in the spirit realm. Religions, and the culture-based social boundaries that they give rise to, are the creations of human beings, not of Su God, who is the supreme deity transcending, or embodying simultaneously, all religiously specific deities. Yet the central beliefs of purification, and the importance of ancestors and spirits are derived from traditions embedded in Shinto, Japanese folk religion and Buddhism as practised in Japan. This does not mean that these beliefs are exclusively Japanese, but they are critical aspects of Japanese world views and everyday practices.

Purification

At the physical level, the centres were kept very clean. Cleaning the *dōjō* is one form of Divine service which members can perform, either individually or at the scheduled monthly *dōjō* cleaning session, usually the day before the monthly Thanksgiving Ceremony.

On the spiritual level, the transmission of True Light to the forehead purifies the soul of the recipient giving a spiritual uplift and purifies the attaching spirits which may be causing misfortune, thus pacifying and comforting them and helping them to leave the person in peace. Members also purify offerings of money using their hand to transfer True Light to the money in an envelope, before placing it in the offering box in front of the *Goshintai*. At the end of each morning's Opening Ceremony and before the evening Closing Ceremony, conducted daily in each *dōjō*, members rotate slowly counter-clockwise with raised hands, reciting the *Amatsu Norigoto*, the prayer of purification, in order to purify the *dōjō* and its surroundings.

Purification is a major element in all religions. Purification through confession, baptism and ablutions, the wearing of specially clean clothing, fasting and food taboos, visualisations and the recitation of mantras, all constitute aspects of a process of physical, mental or spiritual purification. In Mahikari there is emphasis on purifying the spiritual or the 'upstream' first, with the practice of *okiyome*, which leads to purification 'downstream' in terms of one's emotional well-being or physical health. Secondly,

Mahikari teachings explain that previous religions originated in the 'water age', where the method of purification was mainly by water. However since 1st January 1962, we have entered the Age of Fire and henceforth, purification will be by fire. The giving and receiving of True Light is one aspect of this, but the whole world will increasingly experience a tumultuous purification by fire.

Members also speak of major misfortunes they have experienced in life as *misogi* or *misogi harahi* – spiritual cleansing (Oshienushisama 1991). These could be related to ill-health, financial difficulties or relationship problems, indicating that purification is not just perceived in terms of the physical level of existence. Although sometimes very challenging and difficult, these are interpreted by members in a more positive light, as a form of cleansing. Similarly, after receiving True Light, many people experience a temporary cleansing, rather than an immediate feeling of well-being. These experiences may take the form of a dramatic increase in bodily discharges, or even losing one's wallet or other non-physical misfortune. In this way, the Mahikari teachings transform all of life's experiences into something of positive value, with a central theme of purification.

The concept of purity in the Mahikari teachings and its manifestations in the experiences of receiving True Light and in the environment of the *dōjō* were readily adopted by the Australian members. In all the Mahikari homes which I visited, shoes were taken off at the door. One informant described how her style of dress had become more formal and conservative since she joined Mahikari, and a male member explained how he had changed from scruffy hippy to business suit style, a change he could not have imagined of himself in the past. Yet another woman described how her speech had become more formal and polite without the slang and swear words of former days. Another story concerned a member's mother who had lived in a darkened, gloomy house for decades. On the very day that she made a substantial offering, her mother suddenly decided to renovate the house and it brightened up considerably. Whatever the reasons behind these occurrences, the fact that members explain them in terms of Mahikari teachings or other related phenomena shows their positive attitudes towards the concept of purity in the physical and spiritual realms.

Ancestors

In the Japanese Buddhist tradition, ancestors are remembered through the placing of a tablet – *ihai* – containing their posthumous names –*kaimyō* – in the family Buddhist altar – *butsudan*. A photo of the most recently deceased ancestor is placed above the altar, suspended from the ceiling. Offerings of food, candles, incense and water are made daily and gifts given to family members are often placed in front of the altar for a day or two.

Only those with the same surname are enshrined in the altar. Similarly, there is a common grave for the ashes of these members.[25]

Mahikari members are encouraged to inaugurate an ancestral altar, separate from the traditional Buddhist one, and the Divine teachings give clear guidance on how to go about this correctly. This may be much smaller but has similar name tablets and a shelf which slides out to receive daily offerings of food from the family meal in miniature vessels. A miniature baby bottle is filled with milk as an offering to family members who died in infancy. Cigarettes may also be offered. Unlike the offerings to a Buddhist altar, it is important that the food be accessible, for instance unpeeled fruit would be useless as an offering as the ancestor spirits would not be able to consume it. Most Australian Mahikari members who had received Intermediate training and above had inaugurated an ancestral altar in their homes in a special ceremony conducted by the centre chief. They had come to understand the importance of making offerings to the ancestors within the Mahikari world view, as a way of showing gratitude to their ancestors, helping them and preserving harmony in their daily lives. This was true for members of those ethnic groups who, before joining Mahikari, had no culturally based beliefs or even individual concern, regarding their relationship with their ancestors.

For members of Mahikari, the veneration of ancestors is a very important daily activity. It involves offering gratitude for the help from the past, showing respect through the daily offerings of food and other things. This process helps the ancestors who are also undergoing training in the spirit realm and it also avoids admonitions from ancestors towards the present generation, which sometimes occur when they do not receive sustenance.

Spirits

Spirits are people without physical bodies, who reside in the world of spirit. These include ancestor spirits. There are also animal spirits. Spirits may be resentful, attaching themselves to people in the physical world and interfering with their lives. They may be confused and seeking help, as do people in society. That is why Mahikari members emphasise that the *okiyome* is not a process of exorcism, driving troubled spirits away, but a process of purifying, helping and hence saving the spirits.

While belief in spirits is an integral part of the Mahikari world view, many of those I interviewed explained that we should not become too interested in spirits. Spirits do not always tell the truth and they can be very manipulative. That is why only *Buchō*, *dōjō* chiefs and *dōshi* are qualified and allowed to conduct spirit investigations, by questioning the spirits who manifest during *okiyome*. Spirits occasionally manifest to warn us that perhaps we are neglecting the needs of the ancestors, or they may be resentful due to suffering caused in the past. They can sometimes be identified during spirit investigations as ancestor spirits or animal spirits by the language, noises or bodily movements of the person experiencing the spirit movements.

The central rituals and beliefs of Mahikari, including the giving of True Light, give concrete expression to various themes typical of Japanese culture: a deep concern with purification (Kitagawa 1987: 261), including the distinction between pure and impure states of being; the reverence for ancestors demonstrated through ritual; and the influence of the spirit world on the living (Plutschow 1983).

Settlement

Bouma (1995, 1997a,b) uses the term 'religious settlement' to refer to the processes by which religions move from one place to another and become accepted parts of the religious mosaic of the new place.[26] Religious settlement involves change on the part of both the religion and the now socio-cultural context. What adjustments have been made to accommodate the local culture and circumstances of Australian Mahikari members? From my observations of ceremonies and everyday *dōjō* activities in both Japan and Australia, I conclude that very few adjustments were made, nor were they demanded. As overseas membership has never been based on a Japanese migrant presence, the use of English apart from specific prayers in Japanese as the language of ceremonies and communication within the *dōjō* was never an issue.[27] Such acts of mindfulness employed in patterns of speech and body postures as sitting in the kneeling Japanese style – *seiza*,[28] pausing momentarily to bow when one passes in front of the *Goshintai*, even when at the back of the *dōjō*, were all accepted by Australian members as a practical way of demonstrating the interrelated values of humility, reverence and gratitude. Often conversion to Eastern religions involves adopting distinctive styles of dress, diet and behaviour. For Western converts these aspects may constitute part of the appeal of the new religion and may come to dominate their daily lives and consciousness as members of an exotic group, perhaps even overshadowing the core spiritual elements. In the case of Mahikari however, no changes in dress or diet were required, although some changes in body movements, especially in the *dōjō*, patterns of speech and daily routines at home have come to be adopted. Thus, it would be difficult to identify Mahikari members as different from members of the prevailing society, without talking to them about their religious beliefs or visiting their homes. In general, the Mahikari non-ritual behavioural norms were performed in an unostentatious way within everyday life, devoid of spiritual egotism.

However, according to some senior members interviewed, religious settlement is an issue and a challenge: 'We have to make Mahikari accessible and differentiate what is custom and what is Divine teaching'. A *dōshi* said that they used to be very 'Japanese' in centres originally and that caused some reaction. So they tried to use fewer Japanese words, for instance referring to *Amatsu Norigoto* as the 'Divine World Prayer'. Another *dōshi* explained 'We try not to be too Japanese because we live in Australia. *Oshienushisama* wants us to be sensible and compatible with the local culture, but we won't change the teachings'. A centre chief said that they try not to make rules, but members observe the behaviour of senior members and follow their example. A representative of the Sydney *dōjō* said that there it was a lot more 'Australian' in mood. There is less bowing, as bowing is seen as 'Asian'.

Another Melbourne member said that he had never seen Mahikari as a specifically 'Japanese' religion any more than Roman Catholicism could be considered to be 'Italian'. Moreover, Japanese people do not necessarily understand the principles of Mahikari any better than non-Japanese, and in fact, may be burdened by Japanese cultural notions about ancestors and other aspects which they have to unlearn. *Dōshi* particularly emphasised that Mahikari is not trying to introduce 'Japanese culture' but 'Divine principles' which are universal. For instance, reverence for the other person as a child of God happens to be expressed well with the Japanese bow. People dress, speak and behave well out of respect. This is not necessarily Japanese.[29]

Finally they emphasised that people were encouraged to experience the True Light and, if they wish, make a decision to join even if they could not accept all the teachings. Later they would come to appreciate the significance of certain beliefs and practices. For instance, some Australians from all ethnic groups at first resisted the idea of the importance of ancestors, but after receiving more True Light, they came to accept the belief. In fact, it was not possible to fully understand the teachings without the experience of True Light. In the words of Tebecis: 'Australians are very open and practical. They ask, "Does it work?" If it does, they accept it.'

From my observations in the *dōjō* and from interviews, I conclude that the experiential, as opposed to doctrinal emphasis in Mahikari is a strong factor in attracting Australians to the movement. The experiences were palpable; they gave immediate meaning to the Mahikari system of beliefs. In an age where people are seeking concrete solutions to physical, emotional and spiritual malaise, the experience of True Light provided a powerful environment for both self-regeneration and altruistic help for others in a troubled world.

Zen Buddhism

Zen is a sect of the Mahayana school of Buddhism and is pre-dominantly practised in East-Asia. The origin of Zen is generally attributed to

Bodhidarma, an Indian Buddhist who brought Zen to China in 520 CE. The methods and techniques which are characteristic of Zen were evolved in China and through the centuries were further elaborated in Japan. Zen shares with other schools of Buddhism the attempt to realise enlightenment. Zen, however, utilises a unique method of body-mind training and holds out the remarkable promise that by following this method an experience of total enlightenment or *satori*, which was achieved by the Buddha, can be achieved in a single life time.

Zen Buddhism regards enlightenment as the most fundamental realisation possible for a human being. However, enlightenment is not a state of being which exists outside oneself, rather, according to Zen Buddhism, we are all enlightened from the start. In this sense there is no difference between us and the Buddha with regard to the substance, but our egoistic and relentless thoughts prevent us from seeing this. Through Zen practice we return to our original perfection and see beyond the false images of ourselves as sinful or incomplete. We wake up to our inherent purity and wholeness. The Zen approach to enlightenment is described as being independent of texts. Seated meditation – *zazen* – is the instrument of enlightenment and constitutes the basic practice of Zen. In fact the term Zen itself is the Japanese rendering of the Chinese term *Ch'an*, a rendering of the Sanskrit work *dhyana*, which means meditation. Zazen is practised everyday and during periods of intensive meditation, it is complemented by the master's *dharma* talks – *teisho*, interviews with the master – *dokusan-sanzen* – and work practice – *samu*.

Zen in Australia

Zen in Australia has emerged in the context of a sustained Buddhist presence. All the major traditions of Buddhism are well presented in Australia. In 1995 there were 150 separate Buddhist organisations representing the Travadin, Mahayana and Vajrayana schools of Buddhism (Ward & Humphreys 1995: 410).

Theravada Buddhism arrived in Australia in 1882 with the arrival of 275 Sri Lankan immigrants. In 1925 a few Australians, most of whom had been exposed to Buddhism in Burma, formed the first Theravadin group, the little circle of Dharma. Subsequently several groups were formed between 1938 and 1958. In 1971 a Sri Lankan monk, Somaloka, established the first Buddhist monastery in Australia. This was followed by a second Theravadin monastery, Wat Buddharangsee in 1974 and a third, Wat Buddha Dharma in 1978. Today there are over fifty Theravadin groups associated with monks from Sri Lanka, Laos, Burma and Thailand (Ward & Humphreys 1995: 410–411).

Mahayana Buddhism was first introduced to Australia in the mid nineteenth century with the arrival of Chinese immigrants. This phase ended with the end of Chinese immigration around 1901. Today there are fifty-five Mahayana groups in Australia but only a few are linked with the early Chinese expression. The majority of Mahayana groups represent Vietnamese groups, these have increased in number with the arrival of the Vietnamese refugees at the end of the Vietnam conflict in the mid-1970s. There are groups in Australia representing the Japanese Hongwanji school, the Korean Chogye sect, the Fo Kugan Shan sect from Taiwan and the Zen sect of Mahayana Buddhism. Soka Gakkai International Australia, another Japanese Mahayanist sect active in Australia, claimed 1,350 members in 1995 (Ward & Humphreys 1995: 411–413).

The Vajrayana tradition is represented in Australia by around thirty-two Tibetan groups and institutions. These are mostly situated in Melbourne which according to Croucher, by mid-1980s had 'more Tibetan Buddhists per head of the population than any other city in the Western world' (1989: 112). Teaching centres in Brisbane, Nambour, Adelaide, Sydney and Bendigo were established by Lama Yeshe between 1974 and 1984. The program these centres offer revolves around teachings given by a resident Tibetan Geshe. The Geshe also supervises the conduct of various rituals, confers initiation, counsels students and gives courses on Tibetan Buddhist texts. Over a period of years some of the Lamas from Lama Yeshe's centres in Australia have attracted their own students and branched out to separate centres. The largest Tibetan centre at present is Tara House which was founded in Melbourne in 1976 (Croucher 1989: 112).

Because of the different orientation of various Buddhist traditions and the varied cultural background, Buddhist groups in Australia have shown little support for organisational unity and remain fragmented. This is despite efforts that have been made to create some degree of unity, such as the formation of the Buddhist Federation of Australia, the Buddhist Council of Victoria, the Buddhist Council of New South Wales and the Buddhist Council of Brisbane (Ward & Humphreys 1995: 410).

According to the 1991 census of the 139,847 people who identified themselves as Buddhists, 1,488 said they were Zen Buddhists. Many Australians associate the presence of Buddhism in Australia with the increase in Asian immigration during the 1970s and 1980s. However, despite the considerable influence that these migrants from Asia have had, there are many national and ethnic strands in Buddhism in Australia. One of these strands which has been present for more than a hundred years consists of Australian converts to Buddhism including 12,000 Buddhists of non-Asian origin. Nearly all 1,500 followers of Zen Buddhism in Australia belong to this strand. Zen Buddhism has therefore been established in Australia as a result of conversion as opposed to being a religion brought to Australia through the migration of people who incidentally practised Zen.

Thus the two main defining characteristics of Zen in Australia are that it has been established through conversion and that it is an imported religion.

Zen came to Australia from Asia and the United States through a prolonged process of contact. The importation of Zen into Australian culture has involved a sectarian reformation of Zen. Historically, Buddhism has adapted itself many times to radically different cultures and it has been argued that the emergence of organised Zen in the West is no less important than the original diffusion of Buddhism to China in the first millennium. The predominance of social psychological perspectives in the analysis of new religious movements which define Zen as a cult movement and describes the popularity of Zen as resulting from a small group of marginal Australians responding to personal strain, obscures the broader historical and cross-cultural processes and ignores the origins of Zen completely (Finney 1991: 380). An account of Zen in Australia must include its institutional and organisational origins, and the impact of these on its subsequent development.

The transplantation of Zen in the west is not a simple case of religious importation. Rather, it resulted from religious schism and a sectarian reformation of Zen in Japan. Zen in the West may be understood as a 'conscious response to the decline of Zen Buddhism in Japan', or at least this was the motivation of early pioneers of Zen such as D.T. Suzuki, Nyogen Senzaki and Soyen Shaku, in the West. The institutional weakening of Zen practice in Japan together with competition from a variety of new and popular religions and the demand made by the Japanese living in the United States, led to a call to Zen Buddhist priests for increased missionary activities in the late Nineteenth Century. Although in Australia, unlike the United States, Zen was never exported in a missionary sense, nonetheless, Zen in Australia is not a reflection of the larger historical picture of established Zen in Japan. Rather, it was introduced by people who had challenged and changed Zen in Japan. Many Zen groups in Australia are affiliated with teachers who represent reformed sects of Zen such as Sanbo Kyodan – the Order of Three Treasures, a contemporary sect of Zen that was founded by Yasutani Hakuun Roshi in 1954 – or those who have adopted non traditional methods of teaching (Finney 1991: 387, 393).

Zen in Japan

A striking feature of Zen in Australia is the rigorousness of Zen practices which the Zen groups in Australia promote; also the high level of participation and the skill of Zen practitioners in performing chants, a variety of rituals and coping with the austerity of Zen practice, especially as is experienced during meditation. Australian Zen Buddhist groups report over half of their members are 'very active' in attending regular meditation sessions. This is in contrast with the kind of Zen practice encountered in most temples in Japan today where services relating to death, officiating funerals and performing regular memorial services for the dead are the foremost duties of the Zen clergy.

In Japan there is a lack of participation in central Zen practices at the level of lay people as well as the Zen clergy. The majority of the millions of members of Soto and Rinzai, the two main sects of Zen in Japan, are not ardent meditators. According to Pye (1973: 12) 'Most of them simply belong because their families are registered with these sects for funeral purposes. When one of these members dies, a monk will come to the family's house and read from the sutras at certain intervals. The ashes will be deposited in a temple cemetery.' Meditation, koan training, and manual Labor are the forms of religious practice that have most often been singled out by scholars as characteristic of the Zen school and today the Japanese school wishes to be known for promoting these practices. However, a vigorous practice of these fundamental aspects of Zen is not very visible in most Zen temples in Japan.

Zen institutions in Japan are of two kinds: the temples consisting of head temples and ordinary temples and monasteries. The principle activities of head temples are related to a year round schedule of ceremonies such as New Year's Assembly, Equinox Assembly, General offering, Emperor's Birthday service, Bon Festival, and Year-end Prayer assembly. Services relating to death, officiating funerals and performing regular memorial services for the dead continue to be the foremost duties of a typical Zen priest in Japan (Kraft 1988: 159–160). The centrality of these activities indicates the way in which Zen in Japan is distanced from the primary Buddhist pursuits. In many cases what keeps the temples going are the folk beliefs which are only distantly related to pure Buddhism. Closely related to the phenomenon of temples actively encouraging folk beliefs is the fact that Buddhist temples are business as well as religious institutions and priests have been quick to cash in on various religious 'booms' (Bocking 1987: 197).

Zen monasteries, the second type of Zen institutions in Japan, have preserved centuries' old forms of training and ancient ritual procedures are still observed. In monasteries monks and nuns lead a cloistered communal life in accordance with strict rules and schedules under the guidance of a teacher. The number of monasteries belonging to all twenty-two schools of Zen adds up to seventy-two which is very small when compared to more than 20,000 temples. Similarly, the number of monks in monastic training at any one time is never more than a thousand, even by the most generous estimates, which amounts to less than 5 per cent of the total Zen clergy. In the monastery they acquire the working knowledge of ritual procedures essential to their professional careers, as priests and become familiar with the classics of the Zen canon. Today all but a few monks are the sons, usually the eldest son, of temple priests, and they are expected to inherit the position held by their fathers. After college they undergo a minimum period of monastic training between six months and three years in order to qualify as the assistant priest in their home temples (Kraft 1988: 163, 165).[30]

The above description of the practice of Zen in Japan suggests that Japanese Zen, at least in its institutional dimension, is much more focussed on the practice of rites and rituals than the West would lead us to believe and by comparison Zen practice in Australia seems very rigorous. It should, however, be noted that Zen is present in the Japanese culture in a more general sense. Zen Buddhism in Japan has strongly influenced the Japanese approach to life as well as the Japanese arts and literature such as the tea ceremony, haiku poetry and garden design and most Japanese would claim an affinity with, and an understanding of these areas without necessarily linking them to Zen consciously. Therefore, despite a decline in Zen practice, the intellectual and artistic pursuits of contemporary Japan continue to reflect the influence of the Zen tradition, pointing to the fact that Zen in Japan has a very broad influence far beyond the monasteries.

The early history of Zen in Australia

Many of the Australians chosen for military intelligence and sent to Japan after the war were well-versed in Buddhism and the Japanese culture. The most notable of these figures was Les Oates who is probably the first Australian to receive formal Zen training in Japan. After his return to Australia he played a major role in forming the Buddhist society of Victoria. While Les Oates was training in Japan, another Australian, Len Henderson, also developed an interest in Zen. At the time the two men did not know each other, however, after the formation of the Buddhist Society of Victoria, Les Oates and Len Henderson were the driving force behind its operation for many years (Croucher 1989: 31). They would have founded a separate Zen group, however, in 1950s there were not enough people who were interested in joining a Zen group. In those days the interest in Zen was focused on books written by Zen masters especially D.T. Suzuki and the 'beat generation' writers such as Alan Watts, Gary Snyder and Allen Ginsberg. These works were largely based on the theoretical and cultural aspects of Zen. Very little emphasis was placed on the practice of Zen, and certainly there was nothing by way of instruction on how to perform meditation. With the exception of Suzuki they portrayed Zen as a disembodied spiritual experience readily accessible to Westerners and easily appropriated from the context of Buddhist tradition. Their writings, and Jack Kerouac's *The Dharma Bums* in particular, gave rise to the so called 'Zen boom'. Most members of the Buddhist societies of Victoria and New South Wales viewed the Beat phenomenon with horror and considered it very much out of alignment with anything remotely Buddhist (Croucher 1989: 69).

In the late 1950s some Australian artists began to take an interest in Zen. Among major painters Fred Williams, Sidney Nolan, Tony Tuckson and

Lawrence Daws have been at least indirectly influenced through Zen-inspired Chinese and Japanese landscape paintings. Similarly Australian pottery has since the 1950s been dominated by the Leach-Hamada tradition. Another influence of Zen has been observed among some Christians who have incorporated Zen Buddhist meditation practices into their lives as Christians. Occasionally, there are members of clergy from various Christian denominations who participate in Zen meditation retreats.

In describing the influence of Zen on Australian culture, one has to be careful not to overestimate its effect. As Croucher has rightly pointed out the effect of Zen runs deep if not wide. The same applies to the actual Zen practice. Zen groups in Australia do not have the broad constituency of Tibetan and Theravada Buddhism.

The history of organised Zen in Australia

Max Dunn, author of around fifteen books on psychology, aviation, drama and poetry was involved with the Buddhist Society of Victoria from the start and with the support of Les Oates and Len Henderson was elected as its president in 1955. His enthusiasm for Zen was apparent in his writings, in particular in 'The Jewel String of Dipankara' and 'Into the Radiance', which were published in a limited edition in late 1955 to celebrate his upcoming ordination as a Zen priest. After his ordination, Dunn got himself onto the ecclesiastical register and became the first ever officially appointed Buddhist chaplain at the Olympic games, a fact noted by the Melbourne press given that one out of every ten competitors were Buddhists. Dunn set up 'The Zen Institute of Australia' in a shop in Melbourne which contained a small library, study and a shrine as an adjunct to the Buddhist Society (Croucher 1989: 50–1). Apart from Max Dunn's Zen Institute, and a small Zen based community in Evelyn Central in north Queensland which was set up in 1971, there were no other attempts to establish formal Zen groups until the middle 1970s.

In the mid-seventies a small group of people in Sydney who practised Zen meditation wrote to several Zen teachers in the hope of getting some direction and waited for replies. Robert Aitken of the Diamond Sangha in Hawaii answered, encouraging them to continue. He visited the group for the first time in 1979 to hold a retreat, and then visited Australia annually until 1988. Robert Aitken is the first authorised teacher to transmit a Zen lineage to Australia. As such he ranks with Lama Yeshe and Phra Khantipalo who transmitted Tibetan and Theravada Buddhism to Australia, as the most influential 'patriarch' of recent Australian Buddhism (Croucher 1989: 90).

Aitken's first encounter with Zen took place in a prisoner of war camp in Kobe. After the war he began Zen practice in the United States and later practised in Japan under the guidance of various Zen teachers, among them Nakagawa Roshi, Yasutani Roshi and Yamada Koun Roshi. He established the Diamond Sangha in Hawaii in 1959. Since then the Sangha has grown and now has affiliate centres in California, Arizona and Australia. Aitken was recognised as a Zen teacher by Yamada Roshi and was given permission to teach in 1974.

Description of present Zen groups in Australia

In order to describe the present situation of Zen in Australia I conducted a telephone survey of Zen organisations in Australia and visited a number in Canberra, Sydney and Perth. What follows is based on this study.

Since the formation of the Sydney Zen Centre, Zen groups in Australia have proliferated. Currently there are 13 Zen groups, all specialising in orthodox Zen practices such as sitting meditation, walking meditation, chanting of sutras in Japanese and English, listening to dharma talks, full moon precept recitation and *sesshins* – retreats. The majority of the Zen groups incorporate the central practices of both Rinzai and Soto sects of Zen. The followers of the Rinzai sect seek enlightenment through meditative use of a *kōan*, a 'riddle' expressed in enigmatic or nonsensical language. In Soto Zen the emphasis is on *shikantaza* – just sitting –, mindfulness and serving others (Aitken 1982: 65). Students of Zen in Australia often have the option to do *kōan* practice, *shikantaza* or both. Zen groups facilitate the practice of Zen for their members in a variety of ways, such as organising regular meditation sessions and meditation retreats lead by Zen masters coming from overseas. They also provide venues, usually hired halls where practitioners can gather to perform various Zen activities. They emphasise various Zen rituals governing conduct in the meditation hall and the etiquette involved in taking formal meals together. Members learn these by close observation and imitation as well as direct instruction by senior members. All groups publish newsletters to keep members up to date and copies are exchanged between Zen groups in order to maintain contact.

A striking feature of Buddhism in Australia and Zen in particular is the simultaneous presence of many historical and cultural variants of the tradition. There are groups representing Japanese, Korean, Vietnamese and Chinese lineages of Zen. This is partly due the haphazard historical development of Zen in Australia. Zen was not brought to Australia in a systematic way. Rather it filtered into Australia slowly through Australians going to Asia, coming into contact with Zen and seeking to practice it upon their return to Australia. Others came to know Zen through an interest in its artistic manifestations. The Asian-Australian advocates of Zen Buddhism account for another strand of Zen Buddhists who are not involved with Zen Groups. These are mainly Vietnamese whose Buddhism represents a synthesis of Pure Land Buddhism and Zen. This synthesis is reflected in Australia in so far as several of their monks concentrate on the ceremonial functions while others come from more scholarly and meditative traditions.

Thich Nhat Hanh, the peace activist and author of several books, is probably the most highly regarded Zen teacher of any nationality active in the West today. He exemplifies the Vietnamese strand of Zen. Based at Plum village, a Zen community in France, he visited Australia in 1966 and again in 1986. His Australian talks, seminars and retreats attracted not only many Australians and Vietnamese Buddhists, but also a number of Catholics, who became favourably disposed towards his work through the writings of Thomas Merton. This visit facilitated the dialogue between Vietnamese and Anglo-Australian Buddhists in Australia and resulted in the purchase of a 100 acre property near Singleton in northern New South Wales, and the development of the Lotus Bud Sangha. Around half of the members of this centre at present are Chinese and Vietnamese Buddhists and the other half Anglo-Australians (Croucher 1989: 103). However the Lotus Buds Sangha is an exception in terms of the ethnic mix of its members as is the Zen Group of Canberra associated with Thich Kung Ba, a Vietnamese Buddhist abbot and a close friend of Thich Nhat Hanh.

The Zen groups in Australia are all affiliated with teachers who represent genuine Zen lineages. In Zen there are no self-declared teachers, and the permission to teach is handed down from master to student. Traditionally Zen masters have validated their doctrine by referring to the lineage which traces back through their own master, to their master's master and eventually back to Bodhidarma. The issue of affiliation is important in Zen because each lineage tends to emphasise different aspects of the teachings; forms of Zen practice passed down within the Zen tradition may be modified under the influence of a particular teacher. An advantage of the affiliation of the groups in Australia with established parent centres is that it allows Zen groups to draw legitimacy from their connection with authentic Zen traditions, as well as receiving guidance from authorised teachers. Despite these links with authorised teachers, it is important to note that Zen in Australia is different from the teacher-based Zen in Japan in that most Zen practitioners in Australia do not identify their daily and weekly practice with the presence of a teacher. Teachers are usually available only two or three times a year during meditation retreats. This represents a major shift in Zen practice in its transplantation to Australia, the transition from a monastic to a lay religion. The predominance of Sanbo Kyodan, a lay-based school of Zen, in Australia is evidence of this change.

For the most part regular members of Zen groups in Australia have been members a 'long time' and are employed 'full time', well educated, usually with at least some tertiary education, Anglo-Australians and from Christian backgrounds. While overall the genders are balanced, the groups vary in their gender composition. The age range is between 25 and 50. Most groups receive neutral to positive responses from their communities.

However, organised Zen groups represent only a minority of Zen Buddhists in Australia. While, in the 1991 census 1488 Australians declared themselves as Zen Buddhist, the number of Zen Buddhists who are members of Zen groups adds up to around 500 by the most generous estimates. The majority of Zen Buddhists therefore are not active in organised Zen.[31] Some prefer to practice in informal and small groups rather than becoming involved with Zen groups. Some people believe that groups consisting of more than just a few people become bureaucratic and dogmatic and therefore counter-productive to the goal of Zen practice.[32] In addition, Zen Buddhist concepts have a much wider appeal than is indicated by the number of Australians who identify themselves as Zen Buddhist. A further indication of this wide popularity is the sale of a total of 32,000 copies of two titles on Zen Buddhism, namely *The Way of Zen* and *Zen Flesh, Zen Bones,* in the period 1968–1988, a time when even very popular religious books were counted very successful if they sold a few thousand copies.

Religious settlement and Zen

Whenever a religion is transmitted to a new culture it is forced to redefine itself. New adherents seek to identify the essentials of the foreign religion and discard what they consider dispensable. This process of religious settlement (Bouma 1997a,b) is crucial if Zen is to maintain its vitality and relevance in the Australian context and not remain an exotic tradition. Zen underwent numerous changes as it settled in Australia, where already the influence of the peace movement, the Green movement and Western psychotherapy are becoming visible. Furthermore, in Japan the association of Zen with the Samurai tradition sanctioned it as a masculine ideal, but as a result of the influence of feminism this is changing. The Sydney Zen Group has taken the lead in this sense, as it has been holding meditation retreats for women only, as well as holding monthly discussion groups for men and women exclusively. Another change is the involvement of some groups with the Buddhist Peace Fellowship, an international organisation which applies a Buddhist perspective to contemporary peace, environmental and social action movements.

On the other hand the thoroughly ritualised mode of Zen practice in Japan is not maintained in its entirety by Zen groups in Australia. In Japan ritual etiquette controls every aspect of daily life in Zen monasteries where all activities from eating and bathing to sharpening razor blades are highly ritualised. Furthermore, each part of the day is marked off by a variety of sounding instruments, including various bells, wooden clappers and a large wooden drum in the shape of a fish. Zen groups in Australia have attempted to maintain most of these rituals, usually in modified and simplified form. For instance, rituals associated with entering and leaving the meditation hall, taking meals and interacting with the teacher are retained but simplified. The same applies to the physical lay out of the meditation halls. Following the Japanese example of simplicity, meditation halls – *dōjō* – are neat and sparsely furnished. The altar contains few images, if any, and a simple flower arrangement.

These changes pose a challenge for Zen practice, namely how to maintain a balance between retaining the tradition and changing it in such a way as to preserve its essence. However, to create such changes one needs to be a realised Zen Buddhist and hence in a position to do so. There are very few with the stature of Robert Aitken who would be in a position to make these changes. Therefore, Zen in Australia will only forge its identity as a number of authentic, home-grown teachers emerge. This process has just started with the appointment in 1996 of the first Australian Zen teacher to be resident in Australia. Another such appointment was made in 1997. The presence of several Australian senior monks who are already active in guiding Zen groups strengthens Zen in Australia also.

Although in the early days Australians interested in Zen were mainly attracted to its metaphysical and artistic aspects, this has changed substantially as the groups foster the practice of Zen. Despite the changes that have taken place, Zen groups in Australia maintain the core of Zen practice, namely meditation, without which we cannot speak of Zen training. The criteria for meditation as it is practised in Australia today are the same as those taught by the ancient *ch'an* masters. Although Zen groups in Australia do not have the broad constituency of some other Buddhist traditions, those who are involved have persevered in the face of difficulties, searching for ways to keep Zen vital in its new cultural context.

Comments

Two Australian religious groups originating in Japan have been described and located in their social context. Several comments can be made. Both groups offer the tangible, here and now, this-worldly rewards resulting from religious practices. In Mahikari, the True Light purifies, helps and heals the practitioner now and prepares them for the spirit life to come and the practitioners of Zen seek enlightenment as a realistic goal within this life. These rewards contrast with other groups which insist that the real pay-off comes only later, or in another life. This here and now aspect of these religious groups should make them very appealing in the current religious market place which, particularly in its New Age manifestations emphasises the immediacy and measurability of the benefits of religious practice and involvement. As religious groups compete for an increasingly free-floating religious consumer in Australia it may be that those which appear to offer more immediate benefits show higher rates of growth.

While both of these groups have come to Australia from Japan, neither has come in the same way as Islam or Hinduism which arrived here as the religions of migrants to Australia. Rather, both Mahikari and Zen have arrived in a more disembodied fashion. While this has made some aspects of 'religious settlement' (Bouma 1997) easier, these groups still are making both strategic and unintentional changes as they take their place in Australia's religious mosaic. These changes seem to be rather more substantial in the case of Zen than of Mahikari. In making these adjustments to different and changing demands of a new culture, or of the shifting expectations of the market each group will face discussions of what is 'core' to it and what is 'negotiable'.

While both Mahikari and Zen in Australia have primarily a Western clientele, there is some evidence that Mahikari appears to be appealing to some Chinese migrants to Australia and to the established Indian migrant communities in South Africa and Malaysia. It is likely that some 'new' religions like 'old' ones will appeal to some migrants for various reasons. As Australia becomes increasingly multicultural and Australians increasingly take a consumer orientation to choices about religious practice and meaning, those religious groups which grow by conversion are likely to reflect some of this diversity in their memberships. It is also possible that some religious groups will be particularly appealing to some migrant groups. This might lead to another category of relationship between migration and religion: a religion which, while neither of long standing in Australia nor popular in the migrant's homeland, appeals to those who have migrated to Australia. The mechanisms of this warrant further study.

The settlement of Mahikari and Zen in Australia has enriched Australia's cultural and religious life and contributed to the increasing diversity characteristic of this multicultural and religiously plural society.

Notes

1 The authors wish to thank Professor Peter Clarke and the Japanese New Religions Project at King's College London for a grant which made possible the original research on these groups conducted in order to prepare this chapter.
2 Japanese were completely banned from migration to Australia after World War II and at the end of the war those resident in Australia were repatriated to Japan. Only those born in Australia or who had Australian-born children were permitted to stay. Japanese war brides had a long fight to gain permission to migrate to Australia to join their husbands. About 500 finally did so in the early 1950s (Atsumi 1992: 14–17).
3 Unfortunately, Jones does not clarify how this code relates to the usual census categories. Given that the total for the Australian population for the category 'no religion' was 12 per cent and that the total for this table of first generation Australians was 13.8 per cent, I presume that by non-theist he means 'no

religion' and that those claiming to be Buddhists would be coded to non-Christian. However, it is possible that he coded Shinto 'no religion'.

4 Census figures and an organisation's claims of membership numbers often differ significantly. For some groups more identify themselves in the census than participate and for others more participate than identify themselves in the census. Moreover, rapid growth of new religions between census years can complicate the picture.

5 Sekai Mahikari Bunmei Kyodan – World True Light Civilisation Religious Body – was founded in 1959 by Okada Kotama, respectfully called *Sukuinushisama* – Lord Saviour, after he received Divine revelations and directives from God. After his death in 1974, succession became an issue and the organisation split into two although their beliefs and practices remain essentially the same. In Australia, centres belong to the Sukyo Mahikari group, which has its headquarters in Takayama, Japan and is led by the founder's daughter, Okada Keiju, respectfully called *Oshienushisama* – Great Teacher – by members. The other group, Sekai Mahikari Bunmei Kyodan, which kept the original name of the organisation, was led by a close associate of the founder, Sekiguchi Sakae, who died in 1995, and has its headquarters in Ise. It has also been the subject of academic study (Miyanaga 1984). Inoue et al. (1996: 140) list Sukyo Mahikari as having 497,723 members and 522 ministers. Sekai Mahikari Bunmei Kyodan is listed as having 99,954 members and 611 ministers (p. 163). Of the two groups, Sukyo Mahikari has experienced higher rates of growth both in Japan and internationally. In the US, according to Melton and Jones (1994:48) 'Mahikari has been one of the most successful groups in reaching a non-Japanese constituency'. Another source (Ward and Humphreys, 1995:375), mentions a world membership of 1 million for Sukyo Mahikari, of whom 300,000 are in Japan.

6 It should be noted that Mahikari teachings state that it is not a religion in the usual sense but embodies universal principles for people of any religion, belief or background.

7 This observation is based on interviews, talking with members in the *dōjō* and with senior members in the organisation. I was not given access to statistical data covering all members of the organisation, so generalisations based on participant observation must suffice.

8 The beliefs and practices of Mahikari have been extensively described in English language academic publications, especially in the work of Koepping, Cornille, McVeigh, Knecht, Hurbon, Young and Davis. It is not my intention to replicate their work, but only give an outline of the basic features of Mahikari so that the form in which it exists in Australia can be meaningfully discussed. Some aspects of the discussion in existing publications would seem to emphasise an overly *etic* approach, according to the *emic* perspective of a member of Mahikari, and attempt to fit the 'facts' about Mahikari into established paradigms within the social sciences. The work of Davis is especially notable in this regard. For a contrasting view from a member's perspective, see Tebecis (1982).

9 A New Religion has been defined as 'any religious movement originated by the people themselves independent of the tradition of established religions around and after the mid-nineteenth century in Japan' (Tsushima et al. 1974: 140n). It is difficult to create a definition which covers all newly emerging religious movements. Inoue (1991: 5–6) mentions the debate concerning the need to distinguish between a totally new religious movement and one which arises as a form of renewal within an established religion. According to Shimazono (1992,

as outlined in Reader 1993b: 235) the 'new New Religions' which emerged after World War II and particularly those which have showed dynamic growth in the 1970s and 1980s, are distinguished by a focus on immediate benefit in the here and now in their practices and beliefs and on the abilities demonstrated by the charismatic leaders of the movements (see Koepping, 1977:117–120). Thus the new New Religions offer tangible benefits and salvation in this world, as opposed to the other worldly focus of Buddhism. Importantly, in New Religions such as Mahikari, belief in the purifying power of God's light is linked to ethical systems in a very this-worldly context. New Religions teach that one's fate is not solely determined by the power of God or other transcendent beings, but that one can achieve salvation and happiness in this life by one's own efforts, such as changing one's attitude and daily behaviour (Shimazono, 1993:293). In the case of Mahikari it is recognised that the ability to change internally is greatly enhanced by receiving the True Light from the Creator God. Given their emphasis on spiritual matters in the here and now, New Religions are thus more acceptable to individuals operating within the world of competitive values typical of modern capitalist society (Reader 1993b:236). Shimazono also emphasises the importance of the spiritual status of the individual, as opposed to that of the family or the community as in the established religions or folk religion in Japan. In Mahikari this is represented by the belief in an individual's guardian spirit and individual spiritual advancement.

10 'Ki' is defined by McVeigh (1992a:55) as 'a vitality or essence underlying existence'. In systems of Chinese traditional medicine, the martial arts or such arts as calligraphy, this spiritual energy can be mobilised to create sublime results, sometimes defying the logic of the physical realm.

11 Within the Mahikari centres, the identification of those attending as *kamikumite* or *mikumite* – non-members – was very important so that non-members do not become neglected unknowingly. This fact and the *dōjō* of origin of members was recorded in a sheet at the entrance. Within the *dōjō*, new individuals were introduced as *kumite* or non-*kumite*. Non-*kumite* were made to feel very welcome and were offered the True Light as often as they wished without any obligation to join Mahikari. In some centres in Japan, non-members were required to wear a badge identifying them as such, a large badge with red and white circles in one, a yellow wool pom-pom in another. This was not required in the Australian *dōjō*. Obviously a non-member would not be able to transmit the True Light, but newcomers may not understand this. As a non-member I was welcome to participate in the *dōjō* morning opening ceremony. However when it came to the purification of the environment, when people stood in a large group and rotated on the spot around 360 degrees transmitting the True Light with raised hands, I attempted to copy them and was respectfully told to leave my hands at my sides.

12 This practice is also known as *okiyome* – purification, *tekazashi* –raising the hand, *Mahikari no Waza* – the practice of Mahikari. The transmission of True Light is the central feature of the Mahikari movement. The actual experience benefits both the giver and the receiver. If both are *kamikumite*, they take turns to give each other the True Light. Members emphasise that the experience of True Light is more important than any intellectual understanding of the teachings. Only with the experience of True Light will true understanding develop. In fact, members often undergo the primary training and receive the *Omitama* before they fully understand or accept all the teachings. But with continued experience of the True Light, they come to understand the significance of the teachings.

13 Mahikari teachings are contained in the collections of revelations from Su God, the *Goseigen* and the *Norigotoshu*, transmitted by the founder of Mahikari, *Sukuinushisama* – Okada Kotama. As with the Koran which is the word of Allah, transmitted through his prophet Mohamed, these teachings do not change and cannot be changed. After the death of the founder, there have been further revelations to his successor, *Oshienushisama*, some of which are given in her speeches which are broadcast at ceremonies in centres around the world, and published in translation in the monthly *Mahikari Australia and Asia Journal*.

14 For similar explanations of karma in other new religions (see Kisala 1994: 85) and of spirit possession in other contexts (see King 1987: 175 and Smith 1983: 31).

15 While living in Malaysia for nine years as a participant observer in Malay Muslim society, I observed that even those with tertiary education and professional occupations in modern organisations believed in the influences of the spirit realm on their health and their family fortunes, particularly when misfortune struck. These lawyers, politicians and university lecturers had roots in the village just one generation back. When elderly relatives became sick, they sought treatment for them with the most renowned shamanic healer as well as in the most modern, expensive American-style hospital.

16 However, I do not share Shinbo's view that this process of collective symbolic representation merely 'transforms arbitrary experiences into miracles' (p. 81).

17 The Mahikari Youth Corps – *Mahikari Tai* – are strikingly dressed in cream skirts or slacks and green blazers. These young people stand in line to greet those arriving at ceremonies and they aid in the seating arrangements for the crowd. Membership in the Corps is highly prized and it serves as a form of socialisation into the organisation's goals and a source of future spiritual leaders.

18 One informant described that he had been reading many religious books, 'looking for answers'. One day he was looking for something Japanese in the library and *Mahikari* was the only book with a Japanese name. 'I read the book – you read and it fits you perfectly. I put all the other books away. I had got what all the other books did not have. I was preparing myself to go to Japan, but I found that there was a centre in Melbourne. Each time I received the Light, people were so warm and friendly that you wanted to give back. It is about giving. The more you give, the more you receive' (interview, 16.12.1995).

19 So numerous are the Chinese members in the Melbourne centre that Wednesday mornings have become an informal meeting time for them. Shinbo (1992:1) estimated that about 40 per cent of the Melbourne centre members were Chinese at the time of his research, but this has since changed with more people of European background receiving primary *Kenshū* recently.

20 All the Regional leaders are directly appointed by *Oshienushisama*, as they are considered to be spiritual appointments. The Head of the Australia/Oceania Region told me that the management itself is conducted locally in an autonomous way.

21 Giddens (1989:745) defines organisation as 'A large group of individuals, involving a definite set of authority relations' and furthermore, a bureaucracy, as one type of modern organisation, is defined as 'A type of organisation marked by a clear hierarchy of authority, the existence of written rules of procedure, and staffed by full-time, salaried officials' (735). In the context of the need to organise a growing membership on a global scale, Sukyo Mahikari has developed a modern organisational structure, similar to the description of a

bureaucracy, with very efficient communication channels between the levels of the hierarchy. Although with a different theoretical point to make, the interplay between hierarchical relations and ritual in Sukyo Mahikari is a major theme in McVeigh (1992c).

22 The intensive *Doshi* training course is open to all nationalities and is conducted at the special Doshi Training Institute in Takayama in the Japanese language. There have been 30 classes of graduates so far, and *dōshi* identify themselves as 'of the class of 1987' for instance, and know of the graduation years of their fellow *dōshi*, much as members of Japanese companies identify themselves in terms of seniority or junior status by their year of recruitment. There is no notion of spiritual seniority among *dōshi* however. *Dōshi* must have the permission of their parents before undertaking the course. Mahikari emphasised family harmony and respect for ancestors. Thus it would be counterproductive if parents were strongly opposed to their child's wish to become a *doshi*. From thirty to fifty applicants are usually selected each year, from a field of several hundred. Selection is by interview, including interviews with parents, who are required to be members of Mahikari also. Foreign applicants are recommended by the Regional Headquarters chief. Male applicants should be no older than thirty-five, younger for females, and *dōshi* trainees are expected to be single because they must live in the 'bachelor' dormitory accommodation at the Training Institute and then be posted for practical training to any centre in the world for two years. The living conditions at the Training Institute are spartan, living expenses are provided by *Oshienushisama* and their personal income thereafter is minimal. About 10 per cent of each class are non-Japanese. Women slightly outnumber men as *dōshi* trainees, but they are required to resign from the role after marriage. It is considered not possible for them to be able to manage the duties of both *dōshi* and female family roles together. After marriage and motherhood, many remain active members of Mahikari centres and assume the role of *junkambu*. Male *dōshi* often remain unmarried until their late thirties or forties, and live a spartan existence in the *dōjō* itself, serving God twenty-four hours a day, giving Light to members, helping the centre chief, maintaining the centre and looking after the *Goshintai* along with rostered members who come to do *toneri* – sleeping overnight – at the centre), as the *Goshintai* is never left unaccompanied.

23 Arranging the flowers constitutes an important element of Divine service for members, usually women.

24 This view, common to many of the new religions in Japan, is related to the universalist nature of their teachings which explicitly combine the teachings of the major established religions. For instance, in the teachings of Seicho no Ie, it is stated 'In Absolute Truth, all religions are basically one and the same. This One Truth has appeared in different forms such as Christianity, Buddhism, Shinto and others according to differences in time, nationality and place. We have to know the Oneness of Truth. Through this understanding, people will be united regardless of differences in their religion. This is one of the *raisons d'etre* of Seicho no Ie' (Reader et al. 1993: 150).

25 See Smith (1974) for a detailed analysis of the role of ancestors in modern Japanese social life. Despite the changes in residence patterns and family structures created by modern urban lifestyles young professional Japanese still experience anxiety about how to organise the graves of their own and subsequent generations according to the norms of respect for ancestors. Ancestral graves may now be too far away for busy urban dwellers to visit. What if one has embraced a Buddhist sect as a matter of individual preference

and does not wish to be included in the grave of one's husband's family in the temple of a different sect? But then one's children will not be able to take care of two separate graves for their parents. Such dilemmas arise from the time pressures of modern living and from growing individualism in a post-modern society. In this context, Mahikari follows a traditional line in that the ancestors of the father's surname, and in the case of a married woman, the husband's surname, are venerated. If a female *kumite* is divorced she reverts to venerating the ancestors of her father's surname.

26 Some use the term 'indigenisation' to refer to this process, but it focuses more on the changes made by the migrating religion than the mutual changes required by the new socio-cultural environment as well.

27 See Nakamaki (1991: 233–244) for a discussion of the case of PL Kyodan in Brazil, which began with a membership of Japanese migrants and as it settled attracted the affiliation of Portuguese speaking Brazilians.

28 Although it is acceptable to sit in a chair when receiving *okiyome* or during ceremonies, and newcomers are always asked whether it will be difficult for them to sit on the floor, most people follow the norm if they are physically able to do so, or kneel using the support of one of the low stools which are supplied in the *dōjō*.

29 Perhaps it is true to say that Japanese culture is the foremost representative in the modern world of a culture which retains a high concentration of respect forms in behaviour and language. The combination of Japanese material progress, information technology and organisational forms, combined with the elements of universalist appeal in the Mahikari belief system may be one key to its growing presence overseas, on top of the experiences new members describe after receiving the True Light.

30 The decline in monasticism is not peculiar to Zen and there is a decline in the number of novices entering the monastic life in most branches of Buddhism and not just in Zen.

31 By way of comparison the proportion of those who identified themselves in the Census as Anglicans and who are active worshippers is much less than one-third (Bouma 1983: 20 and 1992: 95).

32 For practical reasons this paper only deals with organised Zen.

References

Aitken, R. (1982) *Taking the Path of Zen*, New York: North Point Press

Anderson, R. (1988) *Taiken: Personal Narrative and Japanese New Religions*, PhD. dissertation, Bloomington, In: University of Indiana.

Atsumi, R. (1992) 'A Demographic and Soci-Economic Profile of the Japanese Residents in Australia', pp. 11–31 in James Coughlan (ed) *The Diverse Asians: A Profile of Six Asian Communities in Australia*, Nathan, Qld: Centre for the Study of Australia-Asia Relations, Griffiths University.

Barker, E. (1995) 'The Scientific Study of Religion? You Must be Joking!', *Journal for the Scientific Study of Religion* 34(3): 287–310.

Batchelor, S. (1994) *The Awakening of the West – the Encounter of Buddhism with Western Culture*, Berkeley, California: Parallax Press.

Blacker, C. (1975) *The Catalpa Bow: a Study of Shamanistic Practices in Japan*, London: George Allen and Unwin.

—— (1971) 'Millenarian Aspects of the New Religions in Japan', pp. 563–600 in D.H. Shively, (ed.), Tradition and Modernization in Japanese Culture, Princeton: Princeton University Press.

107

Beyer, P. 1994, *Religion and Globalization*, London: Sage.

Bocking, B. (1987) 'The Japanese Religious Traditions in Today's World', in F. Whaling (ed.), *Religion In Today's World: The Religious Situation of the World From 1945 to the Present Day*, Edinburgh: T & T Clark Ltd.

Bouma, G.D. (1983) 'Australian Religiosity: Some Trends Since 1966', pp. 15–24 in Alan Black and Peter Glasner (eds) *Practice and Belief*. Sydney: Allen and Unwin.

—— (1989) 'Religion and Dutch Identity in Australia', pp. 34–45 in A. Ata (ed) *Religion and Ethnic Identity: An Australian Study, Vol 2.*, Melbourne: Spectrum.

—— (1992) *Religion: Meaning, Transcendence and Community in Australia*. Melbourne: Longman cheshire.

—— (1993) 'Religious Identification in Australia: 1981–1991', *People and Place*: 1, 2: 13–17.

—— (1994) *Mosques and Muslim Settlement in Australia*, Canberra: AGPS.

—— (1995) 'The Dutch in Australia: A Case of Successful Assimilation?' pp. 75–84 in Benoît Grüter and Jan Stracke (eds) *Dutch Australians Taking Stock*, Melbourne: DACA.

—— (1997a) 'The Settlement of Islam in Australia', *Social Compass* 44, 1: 71–82.

—— (ed.) (1997b) *Many Religions, All Australian: Religious Settlement, Identity and Cultural Diversity*, Melbourne: Christian Research Association.

Bucknell, R.S. (1992) 'The Buddhist Experience in Australia,' pp. 214–225 in N.C. Hable (ed.), *Religion and Multiculturalism in Australia: Essays in honour of Victor C. Hayes*, Adelaide: Australian Association for the Study of Religion.

Chinnery, T.E. (1971) *Religious Conflict and Compromise in a Japanese Village: A First Hand Observation of the Tenrikyo Church*, Vancouver, University of British Columbia, Publications in Anthropology, No. 5.

Cornille, C. (1991) 'The Phoenix Flies West: The Dynamics of the Inculturaltion of Mahikari in Western Europe', *Japanese Journal of Religious Studies*, 18(2–3): 265–286.

—— (1994) 'Jesus in Japan: Christian Syncretism in Mahikari', in P.B. Clarke and J. Somers (eds.), *Japanese New Religions in the West*, Kent: Japan Library/Curzon Press.

Coughlan, J. (ed) (1992) *The Diverse Asians: A Profile of Six Asian Communities in Australia*. Nathan, Qld: Centre for the Study of Australia-Asia Relations, Griffiths University.

Croucher, P. 1989 *A History of Buddhism in Australia 1848–1988*. Sydney: New South Wales University Press.

Davis, W. (1980) *Dōjō–Magic and Exorcism in Modern Japan*, Stanford: Stanford University Press.

Fields, R. (1992) *How the Swans Came to the Lake–a Narrative History of Buddhism in America*, Boston and London: Shambhala.

Finlay, S. (1995) 'Zen Buddhism in Australia: Patterns of Conversion and Commitment', a paper presented at the Postgraduate Conference, Anthropology and Sociology, Monash University. 29 November 1995.

Finney, H.C. (1991) 'American Zen's "Japan Connection": A Critical Case Study of Zen Buddhism's Diffusion to the West', *Sociological Analysis* 52: 379–396.

Hardacre, H. (1979) 'Sex-Role Norms and Values in Reiyukai', *Japanese Journal of Religious Studies*, 6(3): 445–459.

—— (1984) *Lay Buddhism in Contemporary Japan: Reiyukai Kyodan*, Princeton: Princeton University Press.

—— (1988) *Kurozumikyo and the New Religions in Japan*, Princeton: Princeton University Press.

Hurbon, L. (1986) 'New Religious Movements in the Caribbean', pp. 146–176 in J.A. Beckford (ed), *New Religious Movements and Rapid Social Change*, London: Sage.

—— (1991) 'Mahikari in the Caribbean', *Japanese Journal of Religious Studies* 18(2–3): 243–264.

Inoue Nobutaka (1985) *Umi o Wattata Nihon Shukyo* (Japanese Religions that have crossed the seas), Tokyo: Kobundo.

—— (ed) (1991) *New Religions*, Tokyo: Kokugakuin University.

Inoue Nobutaka, Komoto Mitsugi, Tsushima Michihito, Nakamaki Hirochita, and Nishiyama Shigeru (1991) *Shinshukyo jiten* [Encyclopedia of the New Religions] Tokyo: Kobundo.

Inoue Nobutaka, Komoto Mitsugi, Tsushima Michihito, Nakamaki Hirochita, and Nishiyama Shigeru (1996) *Shinshukyo: Kyodan-Jinbutsu Jiten* (Dictionary of the New Religions–Groups and Personalities), Tokyo: Kobundo.

King, S. (1987) *Passionate Journey–the Spiritual Autobiography of Satomi Myodo*, Boston: Shambala.

Kisala, R. (1994) 'Contemporary Karma–Interpretations of Karma in Tenrikyo and Rissho Koseikai', *Japanese Journal of Religious Studies* 21(1): 73–92.

Kitagawa, J.M. (1987) *On Understanding Japanese Religion*, Princeton: Princeton University Press.

Knecht, P. (1995) 'The Crux of the Cross: Mahikari's Core Symbol', *Japanese Journal of Religious Studies*, 22(3–4): 321–342.

Kobayashi S. (1960) 'Omoto, a Religion of Salvation', *Japanese Religions*, 2: 38–50.

Koepping, K-P. (1967) 'Sekai Mahikari Bunmei Kyodan, A Preliminary discussion on a recent religious movement in Japan', *Contemporary Religions in Japan*, 8: 101–134.

—— (1977) 'Ideologies and New Religious Movements: The Case of Shinrikyo and its doctrines in comparative perspective', *Japanese Journal of Religious Studies*, 4(2–3): 103–149.

Jones, F.L. (1991) *Ancestry Groups in Australia: A Descriptive Overview*. Canberra: Office of Multicultural Affairs.

Kraft, K. (ed.) (1988) *Zen: Tradition and Transition*. New York: Grove Press.

Lebra, T.S. (1986) 'Self-Reconstruction in Japanese Religious Psychotherapy', in T.S. Lebra W.P. Lebra (eds), *Japanese Culture and Behaviour*, Honolulu: University of Hawaii Press.

McVeigh, B. (1991a) *Gratitude, Obedience and Humility of Heart: the Cultural Construction of Belief in a Japanese New Religion*, PhD dissertation, Princeton University.

—— (1991b) 'Gratitude, Obedience and Humility of Heart: the Morality of Dependence in a New Religion', *Journal of Social Science* (International Christian University, Tokyo), 30(2): 107–125.

—— (1992a) 'The Vitalistic Conception of Salvation as Expressed in Sukyo Mahikari', *Japanese Journal of Religious Studies* 19(1): 41–68.

—— (1992b) 'The Master Metaphor of Purity: The Symbolism of Authority and Power in Sykyo Mahikari', *Japanese Religions* 17(2): 98–125.

—— (1992c) 'The Authorization of Ritual and the Ritualization of Authority: the Practice of Values in a Japanese New Religion', *Journal of Ritual Studies* 6(2): 39–58.

—— (1993) 'Building Belief through the Body: The Physical Embodiment of Morality and Doctrine in Sukyo Mahikari', *Japanese Religions* 18(2): 140–161.
—— (1995) 'Learning Morality Through Sentiment and the Senses: The Role of EmotionalExperience in Sukyo Mahikari', *Japanese Religions*, 20(1): 56–76.
Maeyama, T. (1983) 'Japanese Religions in Southern Brazil: Change and Syncretism', *Latin American Studies*, 6: 181–238.
Melton, J.G. and Constance Jones (1994) 'Japanese New Religions in the United States', in Clarke, Peter and Jeffrey Somers (eds.), *Japanese New Religions in the West*, Kent: Japan Library/Curzon Press.
Miller, A.S. (1995) 'A Rational Choice Model of Religious Behaviour in Japan, *Journal for the Scientific Study of Religion*, 34(2): 234–244.
Miyanaga, K. (1983) *Social Reproduction and Transcendence: An Analysis of the Sekai Mahikari Bunmei Kyodan, a Heterodox Religious Movement in Contemporary Japan*. PhD dissertation, University of British Columbia.
Nakamaki Hirochika (1984) 'The Structure and Transformation of Religion in Modern Japan: In Search of a Civilisation Studies Perspective' *Senri Ethnological Studies*, 16: 87–97.
—— (1986) *Shinsekai no Nihon Shukyo* [Japanese Religions in the New World], Tokyo: Heibonsha.
—— (1991) 'The Indigenization and Multinationalization of Japanese Religion– Perfect Liberty Kyodan in Brazil', *Japanese Journal of Religious Studies*, 18(2–3): 213–242.
—— (1994) 'The Japanese and Religion – a Consumer's Perspective', *Kansai Forum* pp. 26–29.
Okada, Kotama (1967) *Mioshieshu* (Collected Sacred Teachings), Tokyo.
—— (1982) *Goseigen* (Holy Words), Tujunga, California: Mahkari of America.
Okada Kotama (1988) *Yokoshi Norigotoshu* (Book of Prayers), Tujunga, California: Mahkari of America.
Ohnuki-Tierney, Emiko (1984) *Illness and culture in contemporary Japan–An anthropological view*, Cambridge: Cambridge University Press.
Oshienushisama (1991) '*Misogi Harahi* by God and the Path to Greater Happiness' *Mahikari Australia and Asia Journal* 9,1 (January).
Price, C.A. (n.d.) *Ethnic Groups in Australia*. Canberra: Australian Immigration Research Centre.
Plutschow, H. (1983) 'The fear of evil spirits in Japanese culture', *Transactions of the Asiatic Society of Japan*, 3rd.series, pp. 133–151
Pye, M. (1973) *Zen and Modern Japanese Religion*, London: Ward Lock Educational.
Rambo, L.R. (1993) *Understanding Religious Conversion*, New Haven: Yale University Press.
Reader, I. (1991) *Religion in Contemporary Japan*, Honolulu: University of Hawaii Press.
—— (1993a) 'The Rise of a Japanese "New New Religion" –Themes in the Development of Agonshu', *Japanese Journal of Religious Studies* 15(4): 235–262.
—— (1993b) 'Recent Japanese Publications on the New Religions in the Work of Shimazono Susumu', *Japanese Journal of Religious Studies* 20(2–3): 229–248.
Reader, Ian, Esben Andreasen and Finn Stefansson (eds.) (1993c) *Japanese Religions Past and Present*, Honolulu: University of Hawaii Press.
Richardson, J.T. (1991) 'Reflexivity and Objectivity in the Study of Controversial New Religions', *Religion* 21: 305–318.
Robertson, R. (1992) *Globalization–Social Theory and Global Culture*, London: Sage (see Ch 5. 'Japanese Globality and Japanese Religion' pp. 85–96).

Sered, S.S. (1994) *Priestess, Mother, Sacred Sister–Religions Dominated by Women*, New York: Oxford University Press.

Shibata Kentaro (1993) *Daiseishu–Great and Holy Master,* Tokyo: L.H. Shuppan.

Shimazono S. (1979) 'The Living Kami Idea in the New Religions of Japan, *Journal of Japanese Studies*, 6(3): 389–412.

—— (1982) 'Charisma and the Evolution of Religious Consciousness: the Rise of the Early New Religions of Japan', *Annual Review of the Social Sciences of Religion*, 6: 153–176

—— (1986a) 'Conversion Stories and their Popularization in Japan's New Religions', *Japanese Journal of Religious Studies*, 13(2–3): 157–175.

—— (1986b) 'The development of millennialistic thought in Japan's new religions: from Tenrikyo to Honmichi, pp. 146–176 in J.A. Beckford (ed), *New Religious Movements and Rapid Social Change*, London: Sage.

—— (1992) *Gendai Kyusai Shukyoron* [The Study of contemporary Salvationist Religions], Tokyo: Seikyusha.

—— (1993) 'The Expansion of Japan's New Religions into Foreign Cultures', pp. 273–300 in Mark Mullins, Shimazono Susumu and Paul Swanson (eds)., *Religion and Society in Modern Japan*, Berkeley, Asian Humanities Press.

—— (1995) 'In the Wake of Aum: the Formation and Transformation of a Universe of Belief', *Japanese Journal of Religious Studies*, 22(3–4): 381–415.

Shinbo Kuninori (1992) 'Religious Conversion and Social Integration: Japan's New Religious Movement in Australia', MA Thesis, Department of Japanese Studies, Monash University.

Shupe, A. (1991) 'Globalization versus religious nativism: Japan's Soka Gakkai in the world arena', pp. 183–199 in R. Robertson and W. Garrett (eds.), *Religion and the Global Order*, New York: Paragon House.

Smith, R.J. (1974) *Ancestor Worship in Contemporary Japan*, Stanford: Stanford University Press.

—— (1983) 'Ancestor Worship in Contemporary Japan', *Nanzan Bulletin* No. 7, pp. 30–40.

Spier, F. (1986) 'Introducing Agon-shu', *Japanese Religions*, 14 (2): 46–70.

Swyngedouw, J. (1978) 'Japanese Religiosity in an age of internationalization', *Japanese Journal of Religious Studies*, 5(2–3): 87–106.

Tebecis, A.K. (1977) 'On how little is known about altered states of consciousness', *Japanese Journal of Psychosomatic Medicine*, 17: 256–263.

—— (1978) 'Suggestions for Awakened Doctors to the Importance of Mahikari', Special lecture presented at the First International Congress on Spirit-Mind Medical Science, Tokyo, 16 October 1978. Proceedings, pp. 24–40.

—— (1982) *Mahikari–Thank God for the answers at last,* Tokyo: L.H. Yoko Shuppan.

—— (1988) *Sagashi motomete kotae wa kokoni: Mahikari*, Dickson, A.C.T.: Sunrise Press, Dai 5-han nihongoban.

Tsushima Michihito, Nishigama Shigeru, Shimazono Susumu and Shiramizu Hiroko (1979) 'The Vitalistic Conception of Salvation in Japanese New Religions: An Aspect of Modern Religious Consciousness', *Japanese Journal of Religious Studies*, 6(1–2): 139–161.

Ward, R. and Robert Humphreys (1995) *Religious Bodies in Australia: A Comprehensive Guide, third edition,* Melbourne: New Melbourne Press.

Weissbrod, L. (1983) 'Religion as National Identity in a Secular Society', *Review of Religious Research*, 24(3): 188–205.

Wilson, B. (1979) 'The New Religions: Some Preliminary Considerations', *Japanese Journal of Religious Studies*, 6(1–2): 193–216.

Yamada Yutaka (1985) *Religious Experiences of Members of the Church of World Messianity in California*, Melbourne: Japanese Studies Centre, Working Papers No. 6.

Yanagita, Kunio (1970) *About Our Ancestors–the Japanese Family System*, Tokyo: Japan Society for the Promotion of Science.

Yoko Civilisation Research Institute (1987) *Creating the Future of Mankind*, Proceedings of the First Yoko Civilisation International Conference, Tokyo: Yoko Civilisation Research Institute.

Yoko Civilisation Research Institute (1991) *What Does it Mean to be Human?* Proceedings of the Second Yoko Civilisation International Conference, Tokyo: Yoko Civilisation Research Institute.

Yoshihara Kazuo (1988), 'Dejiao: A Chinese Religion in Southeasst Asia', *Japanese Journal of Religious Studies*, 15(2–3): 199–221.

Young, R. (1990) 'Magic and Morality in Modern Japanese Exorcistic Technologies: A Study of Mahikari', *Journal of Religious Studies* 17(1): 29–49.

CHAPTER FOUR

The New Japanese Religions in Brazil

Some Remarks on the Church of World Messianity[1]

Ari Pedro Oro

This paper discusses aspects of the Church of World Messianity of Brazil (CWMB), or Sekai Kyusei-Kyo (SKK),[2] a Japanese religion settled in Brazil for more than forty years. The members and adepts of the CWMB are mostly middle class Catholics from different ethnic backgrounds.

In this article, I claim that there are a number of key factors which enable us to understand what appealed to people and made them stay linked to the CWMB; among these keys are the following: (a) the similarity of both these people's and the Church's religious conceptions and practices and (b) the re-evaluation of the meaning of life given by the CWMB, where people start to consider themselves useful and important to others, mostly because of the practice of the main healing ritual of this Church, *johrei*.

This text is the result of the fieldwork research made in the period from August 1995 to January 1996. The fieldwork took place in Rio Grande do Sul,[3] Brazil, and especially in its capital, Porto Alegre. The only temple of the CWMB in this state, called 'Diffusion House' (*Casa de Difusao*), is in Porto Alegre. The other places in the state where the fieldwork took place have 'Reunion Centers' (*Nucleos de Reuniao*) and 'Johrei' Centers' (*Nucleos de Johrei*). I adopted an anthropological methodology: above all, it consisted in the participant observance of the ritual and in the open interviews with the leaders, members and adepts of the Church. The total number of people I have interviewed is 40, 19 of these being men and 21 women, varying between 16 and 62 years of age.

I would like to present briefly some data on the Japanese immigration in Brazil and in Rio Grande do Sul, however, before treating the CWMB directly.

Data on the Japanese Immigration in Brazil and in Rio Grande Do Sul

Brazil today has the biggest Japanese community outside Japan. There are about 1.1 million people, 10 per cent of these being born in Japan and 90 per cent being descendants already of the fifth generation. The largest part of this Japanese-Brazilian community (70 per cent) is concentrated in the state of Sao Paulo, while 12 per cent is in the state of Parana and the other 18 per cent are scattered in the other Brazilian states (Takeuchi, 1994).

The official Japanese migration to Brazil began in 1908, when the first 781 Japanese immigrants arrived by boat at Santos, in the state of São Paulo. This migration can be divided in two stages: the first one being from 1908 to 1941 and the second one being from 1952 to 1965.

The first-stage immigrants, especially up to the year 1925, were for the most part integrated in the coffee and cotton farms in Sao Paulo's countryside, working there under contract. Since the perspective of economic growth was very small, understandably, these Japanese immigrants got rid of the 'bosses' and became independent farmers or autonomous workers in the city. These autonomous workers were to be found mainly in trade, the service industry or in industrial enterprises.

In the years from 1925 to 1941, we also observe in the state of Sao Paulo the formation of different Japanese colonial centers, similar to the ones existing in Japan. These centers helped to maintain the immigrants' original culture; on the other hand, these centers hindered their integration into Brazilian society.

In the first stage of the immigration, 190,000 Japanese came to Brazil. This immigration was interrupted during the years of World War II and then it restarted in 1952, continuing until 1965. Unlike the first immigrants, the people who arrived in Brazil in the fifties and sixties wanted to settle permanently in this country. In the second stage of the immigration, about 50,000 Japanese immigrants entered Brazil (Takeuchi, 1994).

The first families of Japanese immigrants arrived in the state of Rio Grande do Sul (RS) in the 1930s, coming from the state of Sao Paulo. These families settled near the big urban nucleus and planted fruits, flowers and vegetables. The official Japanese immigration in this state began in 1956, with the arrival of the first twenty-three immigrants at Rio Grande, in the south of the state. In the period 1955–1963, twenty-seven Japanese immigrants disembarked at the port of Rio Grande. Most of these immigrants were placed as agricultural partners and as leaseholders in the Brazilian and older Japanese rural properties settled in Porto Alegre's Metropolitan Area and in other important cities of the state (Flores, 1977).

Nowadays we cannot speak of a Japanese colony in RS. The *nisei* (second generation Japanese) are not numerically important in this state. The *nisei* are less than 30 thousand. The main activities of the *nisei* are

114

agriculture, above all the flower, fruit and vegetable growing, and commerce. The Japanese immigrants usually began their activities in the state of RS, and in all the rest of Brazil, as employees – and their descendants ended up being the bosses.

Presently in Brazil only 10 per cent of the Japanese and *nisei* dedicate themselves to agriculture. However, they are responsible for 70 per cent of the national production of potatoes, 45 per cent of the soybeans, 10 per cent of the coffee, 94 per cent of the tea and 50 per cent of the eggs. Most of the Japanese are employed in industries or self-employed. Because of their effort and work, the Japanese have achieved an enviable life standard in contemporary Brazilian society (Takeuchi, 1994).[4]

Most of the Japanese who arrived in Brazil were either Shinto or Buddhist. According to the informants in the present research, as the years went by, many of them were converted to Catholicism, specially their children, because the adhesion to this religion was understood as a means of integration into the Brazilian society.

I will now present a brief history of the Church of World Messianity of Brazil (CWMB), with special attention to the state of Rio Grande do Sul.

The Church of World Messianity of Brazil (Brief History)

The *Jornal Messianico* (Messianic Journal, June 1996) reports that the Church of World Messianity, or Sekai Kyusei-Kyo, began its activities in Brazil in June of 1955, in the second stage of the Japanese immigration. The activities began in the city of Curitiba, capital of the state of Parana, where the first image of the Divine Light and the photograph of Mokiti Okada (the Meishu-Sama) were put on an altar by ten pioneer members, guided by the Japanese Reverend Nobushiko Shoda and by the also Japanese minister Minoru Nakahashi. In July of 1965, the Church of World Messianity of Brazil was founded in Sao Paulo. Today it has 186 religious entities (churches, diffusion centers, meeting centers) scattered all over Brazil, mainly in Sao Paulo (71) and in Rio de Janeiro (39).[5] The Church's national headquarters are situated in Vila Mariana in Sao Paulo. It has about 300,000 members (missionaries) and about three million adepts (participants in the Church's services). With so many people, the Church of World Messianity of Brazil is the largest branch (in number of adepts) of the West – or, as the editorial of the Messianic Journal states: 'Brazil has become the bridge for diffusion of the faith in the West'. (*Jornal Messianico*, June 1995)

Recently, in November 1995, the Church of World Messianity of Brazil had what was probably the most important moment in its history in Brazil: the inauguration of the Sanctuary of the Holy Soil of Brazil, in Guarapiranga, Sao Paulo. This is its first Holy Soil in the West[6] and has been announced since 1985. Its fundamental stone was placed on

September 17, 1989, by Reverend Yasushi Matsumoto, the Church's World President, and by Reverend Tetsuo Watanabe, who is responsible for the Church in Brazil. The work took ten years, and was made mostly by the members themselves, as a collective enterprise (*mutirao*), in an area of 327 thousand square meters, by the Guarapiranga Reservoir. The building of the sanctuary, arrangement of the landscape and ecological park cost about 30 million dollars, mostly raised locally.

In the RS, the Church of Messianity started its work in January of 1973. The initiative came from the CWMB's own Headquarters, which sent the Minister Mikio Takase as the responsible for the diffusion and practice of the teachings of Meishu-Sama. In the state of RS, the Church of Messianity has nowadays about three thousand members – that is, people affiliated to the Church. About 160 people go through the Diffusion Center of Porto Alegre every day.

The administration of RS is linked to Curitiba, capital of the state of Parana, where the seat of the Regional Church of the Southern Area is found. This administration covers the states of Parana, Santa Catarina and Rio Grande do Sul. The Southern Area was inaugurated in February 15, 1986, and has today about 15 religious entities.

Only one Diffusion Center can be found in the RS, situated in Porto Alegre, at the Rua Marcilio Dias, 1419, at Azenha, a part of the city predominantly of the lower middle-class. It is a rented house that can accommodate up to 100 people for religious services. In April 1996, the Church will be opening a second Diffusion Center in Porto Alegre, which will also be a rented house, at the Rua Eca de Queiroz, 129, at Petropolis – a part of the city that is predominantly upper middle-class. This new house is three times as large as the first house. About one dozen Reunion Centers and *Johrei* Centers exist in other cities of the state of RS.

The CWMB of RS plans for the future are as follows: the acquisition of an area for the practice of Natural Agriculture (without the use of fertilizers or pesticides); the inauguration of the Korin Stores for the distribution and sales of natural products; and the acquisition of an area of fifteen hundred square meters for the construction of a Regional Church of Rio Grande Sul. All of this is a two-year project according to the Church's local directors.

Minister Paulo Roberto Leopoldino is responsible for the Church in RS. He is originally from the state of Rio de Janeiro and is not a descendant of Japanese; he has been a member of the Church for twenty years. There is only one assistant minister in RS, Mr. Ariovaldo Fernandes Lins, originally from the state of RS. The Church has a dozen co-ordinators (most of them being older women), and a dozen people can be seen dedicating themselves every day to the Church to the *johrei* administration.

The main rituals at the Diffusion Center in Porto Alegre are the following: two daily cults, one in the morning, at 8:30 a.m., and one in the evening, at 6:00 p.m.; the Monthly Cult of Gratitude, made the third

Saturday and Sunday of each month. Besides, there are the weddings, presentations (baptisms) and funerals.

I will now present the data resulting from fieldwork at CWMB of RS, specially at the Center of Diffusion of Porto Alegre.

A social profile of the members and adepts

The Japanese presence in the RS, as we have seen above, is small when compared to other Brazilian states. This fact is also observed at the Church of Messianity, which – though originally Japanese – has few *nisei* in RS. They are less than 3 per cent of all of the members, an average verified in Brazil according to 1988 data (Clarke, 1995).

The social profile of members, i.e., of those that can minister *johrei* because they possess the Ohikari (the medal of the Holy light), is predominantly white, i.e., of European descent (German, Italian, Spanish, Portuguese and Polish), female – women make up about 80 per cent of the total[7] –, middle class, urban, and who have completed a high-school education.[8] Only two out of the 40 individuals I interviewed had not completed high school, while thirteen of them had a University degree. Their ages varied mostly between 36 and 60 years old. Many of the women are retired, others are exclusively housewives, and others have professions such as school teachers, secretaries, psychologists, civil servants.

The male members of the CWMB have a similar social profile. They are also predominantly middle-class, have completed high school or hold a university degree, many of them are retired and others are self-employed or are public employees.

On the other hand, the Church adepts, many of whom show up only to receive the *johrei*, are of different social classes, although here too, there is a predominance of middle-class practitioners. Also, younger people, of both sexes, pass through the Diffusion Center of Porto Alegre with some regularity.

This data, resulting from research at the CWMB of RS, is similar to other researches in Brazil regarding the relation between social class and type of religious expression. Although this relation is not rigid, there is a tendency for the Japanese churches (CWMB, Seicho no Ie, Soka Gakkai) to attract mainly people from the middle classes in Brazil. The same seems to occur with *Espiritismo*.[9] People from the lower classes are more attracted to the Pentecostal churches[10] and by the Afro-Brazilian religions.[11] In these last two religions listed above obviously there are people of other social levels too. Catholicism was the religion of the Portuguese colonizers and remained hegemonic as the national religion, although not as the official religion until a few decades ago, when it had to compete with other churches established in this country. Catholicism is a religion that aims to have as many adepts as possible, regardless of their social origin. In practice, however, the Catholic discourse is much more compatible with the world view of the middle classes.

An exclusivist religion?

Only two of the forty people I interviewed have been members of CWMB of this religion since birth. Six of them stated that they did not follow any other religion before becoming members. The rest had been Catholic since childhood, twenty of them passing directly from Catholicism to the CWMD and ten of them moved between Catholicism and *Umbanda* or *Espiritismo* before going into CWMD. Finally, two were previously Seicho no Ie members.

Such figures reflect quite well the contemporary Brazilian religious scene characterized, on the one hand, by the reduction in the numbers of Catholic followers, confirmed by the official data[12] and, on the other hand, by the intense religious transit seen in this country. Faced with many possible religious options, people usually try out several different ones before adopting a particular religion.

The numbers given above show that half the people interviewed left Catholicism and went directly to CWMB. Most of them were not Catholic practitioners, but were in reality 'cultural Catholics', i.e. they identified themselves as Catholic because of the traditional Catholic culture of Brazil. One third of those who were interviewed had already been Espiritismo practitioners – which has a numbers of religious teachings, such as the reincarnation dogma, and some ritual practices, such as the mediunic pass, that closely resemble beliefs and practices found in the CWMB. Only two of those who were interviewed stated that they came from the Seicho no Ie, that is, they already had previous contact with a Japanese religion, or philosophy.

CWMB is not a conversionist sect, such as Pentecostalism, that is it does not have many emotionally appealing and dynamically strong rituals that lead to individuals actually dividing their life into before and after entry to the new religion. Nonetheless, the number of people who entered the CWMB and remained committed to it alone is high. In fact, 35 of the 40 people I interviewed stated that this was their situation. Only five of those interviewed belonged to Catholicism and the CWMB, visiting both religious spaces, this being in line with CWMB's own non-exclusivist discourse.

Why the Church of World Messianity?

Most members and adepts come to know and start going to the CWMB because of invitations made by their family and friends. As a matter of fact, this is common for other religions too in Brazil. The CWMB does not proselytise via electronic media (radio or television shows) or public preaching, as other religions do. The CWMB's message is made public by printed works (the Messianic Journal, a monthly publication, and books written by its founder) – a common way of diffusion for other new Japanese religions (Clarke, 1995) – and especially through personal contact with people who have affinity with the founder of the messianic doctrine.

According to the ethnographic findings, the majority of those who go to the Diffusion Center attend for a variety of personal reasons. About 50 per cent of them are distressed by problems of ill health; 15 per cent of them by financial problems (unemployment, business); 15 per cent by failure in their relationships, the search for a partner, loneliness; and 20 per cent because of existential anguish resulting from the loss of a meaning for life, personal dissatisfaction, etc.

All those who were interviewed said they remained in the CWMB because they found the solution to their troubles. Only a few stated they found the solution in some miraculous way. On the contrary, most said the solution came to them slowly, as they received *johrei* and were integrated to the Church.

Solutions to problems were followed by other positive developments which also strengthened their attachment to the movement.

For many *johrei* is considered something that 'gives harmony, will to live, peace, tranquillity, strength, power, energy, the possibility of rising one's self-spiritually'. The importance of *johrei* is such for the CWMB that it is unanimously considered the Church's 'spinal cord' and 'main pillar'.

Those interviewed also state that they found in the CWMB an attractive and **pleasant environment,** where they feel well. They are referring both to the physical space and to the people. The leaders of the Diffusion Center are greatly preoccupied with the aesthetic appeal to the Centre: they are concerned about growing flowers, and having flowers present in the Center, to create an agreeable environment. Everyone interviewed said that they felt most welcome. Besides, everyone felt that there existed a strong sense of mutual concern for the problems and sorrows of all the members. Everyone found support, love and friendship in the Church; one twenty-six-year-old man even stated that 'people here constitute one big family'.[13]

Those interviewed also found in the CWMB a **spiritual dimension** not evident in other religions. 'You can feel, you can live the spirituality here', 'The Church has a great capacity of making us leave aside the material things and of developing our spiritual side' and 'It is a church with very powerful spirituality' were some of the comments made.

Members emphasize that the CWMB is a church that knows how to harmonize the material side with the spiritual side. In other words, they underline the fact that the Church does not despise the body or the material concerns of everyday life, while at the same time valuing the spiritual aspects of existence.

Interviewers stressed repeatedly they had found **peace, security, tranquillity and harmony** after entering the CWMB. They also say that these aims had been extended to their families, where harmony and understanding rule, since 'the light of the *johrei* is contagious'.

Lastly, although these people explicitly state that they have not suffered any kind of 'brainwashing' by the Church and that all the changes in their life are gradual, they stress that as they receive *johrei* they observe changes in practically all aspects of their lives – a **life improvement,** as they say – that passes through the dimensions of health, love, finance, family, etc. Such changes are understood as 'a process of becoming more mature', as 'personal growth' or 'personal development'.

The meanings of *johrei*

Daily, from morning to night, there are people who can minister the *johrei* in the Diffusion Centers. This is an individual ritual that lasts 10 to 15 minutes, silently made, with one hand towards the person sitting in front of the person ministering the *johrei*, who wears on his chest the medal symbolizing the holy light or *Ohikari*. There is also common *johrei*, ministered by the reverends and minister at the monthly meetings.

In the followers' opinion the *johrei* is 'the foundation of our religion', 'a way of creating happiness', 'the spinal cord of the Church'. The analysis of the ethnographic data show that members and adepts give *johrei* the following meanings:

i) *Johrei* is **salvation**. The term 'salvation' refers to spiritual growth and to the physical improvement given by the *johrei*, since, according to the messianic doctrine, there is an inseparable relation between spirit and body. The spiritual rising and the purification of the organism, the spiritual growth and the improvement of the body's resistance to diseases occur the moment *johrei* is received. The number of accounts to be found in the pages of the Messianic Journal is truly impressive. Other numerous statements of this type are to be found in individual declarations, made every day in the temples of the Church, about the benefits people say they come to have because of *johrei*. Most of these benefits refer to healing. '*Johrei* is beneficial to the soul and to the body', 'It is medicine for the body and for the spirit', 'I see that I can cure when I am ministering, even if the person does not believe it. When I receive johrei I am being saved.' These are some of the statements I heard in my fieldwork.

ii) *Johrei* is **light**. *Johrei* is divine light for the spirit, it is a feeding light, it is food for the spirit. It is also a guiding light for people's paths. It is a healing light that makes the diseases go away and that produces miracles. In this sense, the members of the Church which possess the *Ohikari*, the medallion for the divine light, consider themselves 'God's instruments'. The divine light saves people through them.

iii) *Johrei* is **energy**. According to Reverend Leopoldino:

Johrei is positive energy that calms people; it is a tranquillizer for the spirit. *Johrei* takes away the tension and the negative fluids that people carry; it is a force from God to make people strong. The *johrei* is a power that overwhelms everything. Those who carry the *Ohikari* carry energy equivalent to a 100-watt lamp, against the common person's energy of a candle.

The local ministers of the CWMB also reproduce the members' and adepts' discourse on *johrei*, mentioned above. They emphasize other aspects, such as:

a) the CWMB carries out its mission – the practice of altruistic love –, making possible the spiritual elevation of all people, through *johrei*;
b) scientists are studying *johrei* and finding that it can heighten cells' resistance to sickness, acting on the cells that stimulate the immune system;
c) The *johrei* minister and receiver are led to the Alpha state by *johrei*, and such a state is responsible for the production of endorphin – the endorphin in turn giving people more resistance and energy. It should be noted here that this scientific explanation is intended to give greater legitimacy to the *johrei* ritual.

The social representations of Japan

All of the members know that the CWMB is a Japanese religion. Japan is a strong reference point among the members and adepts. The Church's followers usually have the following representations of Japan, its society and its culture:

1) Japan is a **chosen land** because Meishu-Sama, the Church's founder, was born there and 'everything started' there. Therefore, Japan is a holy land, although the followers always stress that Meishu-Sama said that his doctrine was universal.

2) Japan is a strong **economic power** having made an extraordinary economic comeback after World War II. One hears the following comments: 'A country where everything was lost and suddenly it became a world power.', 'It is the most [economically] developed country of the contemporary world.', 'It is a small country but it has huge potential.'.

3) The Japanese people and the Japanese culture have a **superior level of development and of evolution** in relation to the rest. Typical quotes are: 'These are very hardworking people; these people are role-models.', 'The people are mystical, spiritualized, orderly and serious.', 'They are many years ahead of us, for they emphasize the spiritual side and the discipline, while we (Brazilian) care much more about the material side and are

disorganized.' Finally, according to the followers, this is an ancient culture that holds much knowledge.

4) Lastly, and this is the most interesting aspect, many of the followers say they feel a link with Japanese culture because of past lives in Japan. With the belief in reincarnation, the followers are saying, in other words, that their spirit, in past lives, was incarnated in Japan. This explanation helps the followers explain why they are today in the CWMB and why they feel well there. 'I am very much related, I feel very kin, to anything that is Japanese because of past lives.' 'I have had past lives in Japan.' 'I have always felt strong ties to Japan because I have been incarnated there.' 'I feel myself very related to the Japanese. This comes from past lives.'

Analysis and Questions

I would like to provide some analysis here and ask some questions about the CWMB, based on the fieldwork in RS.

1. We have seen that the CWMB members have a considerable amount of free-time to dedicate themselves to the Church's activities, either because they are retired, or because they have jobs which leave them with a fairly large amount of spare time. I do not wish to reduce their religious participation by implying that they have little else to do, but I ask myself if many of them, women especially, who go every day to the Diffusion Center to 'attend the people' and 'to minister the *johrei*' or to 'take an Ikebana course', as they say, are not in search of an occupation? Besides, as the members establish a certain type of relationship among themselves and are linked by friendship, the Diffusion Centers function as privileged sites for social integration.

2. The CWMB allows people to participate at different levels, depending on the strength of their links with the Church. In that sense, people can take part only to minister and/or receive the *johrei*; they may also aim to understand in more depth the teachings of Meishu-Sama, studying the master's doctrine regarding the spiritual world (cult of ancestors), the cult of beauty, the arts, research and implementation of natural agriculture, etc. According to the members of the CWMB the way each individual chooses to participate is related to the karmic heritage of each one. However, the church stresses that the most appropriate procedure is to search for all these items, simultaneously, with no rush, in the so-called 'paradisiacal faith'. In any way, there is a relationship between the level of spiritual development and the degree of involvement in the church's internal hierarchy (adept, member, co-ordinator, missionary, salvation clergyman, minister, reverend, etc.). I observed, on the other hand, that this religious 'career' and the functions of each level of the hierarchy, are not rigid, nor clear, even to the CWMB leaders themselves. I ask myself therefore if the CWMB has not as yet attempted to structure its hierarchy or if it is going

122

through a process of redefining its hierarchy, functions and roles in this country?

3. The same observation holds for the rituals celebrated in the Diffusion Center that I have observed. There are daily rituals, as I have already mentioned, and an important monthly ritual (Gratitude Cult), besides the johrei ritual. The issue debated in recent months in this Church, in Brazil, concerned the Ancestral Cult and the possibility or otherwise of performing it here. The issue was finally settled by the CWM World-Wide President, Reverend Matsumoto, whose answer was recently published in the Messianic Journal: once the Sanctuary of the Holy Soil of Brazil was inaugurated, in Guarapiranga, this ritual could be celebrated there, on the 5, 15 and 25 of each month.[14] According to the followers of the CWMB, it is also possible to recite all the prayers said in the daily rituals in Portuguese. From now on Japanese will no longer be used.

4. There is a difference in the statements and discourses of the leaders, on the one hand, and of the members and adepts, on the other. The members and adepts center their speeches on the benefits of the *johrei* and on the curing diseases. The diseases themselves are understood as a spontaneous purification process of the body – to the extent that a member who gets ill, such as follower of Seicho no Ie, may say: 'I am getting purified'. The ministers, on the other side, tend to emphasize in their interviews 'Meishu-Sama's teachings', especially the cult for the ancestors, beauty as a form of bonding with God, and the benefits of the natural agriculture. Eating food produced through natural agriculture is seen as a way of purifying the body. This in its turn leads to spiritual development.

5. Although the CWMB is of oriental origin, many of its doctrinal elements and some of its ritual practices are similar to Brazilian religious representations and practices, such as Espiritismo, Camdomble and popular Catholicism. I suggest that these religions provide a range of elements for the understanding and greater acceptability of religions from other cultural origins.

After the inauguration of the Sanctuary of the Holy Soil of Brazil in Guarapiranga, both the Messianic Journal, and ministers made the point that now 'our ancestors are **situated** in Brazil. Before, they were in Japan, and Japan took care of them'. The term 'situated' also makes sense to Brazilian listeners as it is widely used by the Afro-Brazilian religions ('to situate an Orixa', for instance).

Moreover, the important ritual of *johrei*, is not completely strange to the Brazilian religious tradition, and for that reason it is easily absorbed. One of the rituals that attracts most people to Espiritismo, as well as to the Umbanda sessions, are the 'passes' – when the mediums, or the Umbanda entities (Caboclos and Pretos-Velhos), minister an individual 'pass' to people to eliminate their negative 'energies' and to give them positive forces, to protect them against the evils, coming from the world of the living or from the spirits. The concepts of 'vibration', 'fluids', 'energy', 'light', used in the CWMB (and also in the Seicho no Ie), are also found in the Brazilian religions mentioned.

We can also observe that the belief in reincarnation, preached by the CWMB, also exists in Espiritismo and about 60 per cent of the Brazilian Catholics. The CWMB, like Espiritismo, according to Mr. Lins, one of the CWMB reverends in Porto Alegre.

holds:

> ... that the succeeding reincarnations aim at change in personal feelings, transforming jealousy into altruism, materialism into spiritualism, to the point where a certain stage is reached – a stage in which we deserve to live in a paradisiacal world that has no sickness, no misery and no conflict, being only a real Paradise in which health, prosperity and harmony prevail.

We can see then that the success CWMB in Brazil is due to religious similarities and adaptations, and this is true of the success of other Japanese religions. It is important to note here that this is a two-way process: the Japanese religions in a certain way make their teachings, practices and language more 'native' so that they can be understood and accepted by Brazilians; the Brazilians, in turn, understand the Japanese religions based on pre-existing and native religious grounds. The result is that the adhesion of Brazilians to the new Japanese religions occurs with no cultural shocks nor conscience dilemmas.

6. In the CWMB, furthermore, every member receives the Ohikari, and is therefore able to minister the *johrei*. This fact makes people feel important, useful and valuable to themselves and towards others and many consequently attribute to themselves a personal mission that gives new meaning to their lives. It is thus possible for members to become actively involved in the activities of this Church. In other religions most of the followers have a passive role and only a few of them are chosen for an active role, which in turn might give them some personal satisfaction and prestige.

7. Another characteristic of the CWMB is the attention given to the individual. Not a single person passes unnoticed by a Diffusion Center, everyone is welcomed, there is always someone to listen to your problems and a hand to minister the *johrei*. In the same way, inside a Diffusion Center, the ambience is such that anyone who enters it has a feeling of peace and well-being. This last characteristic, though not stressed by the church, is an important factor in retaining members.

8. Lastly, although the CWMB is originally Japanese, few Japanese or *nisei*, at least in the state of RS, are members. Nowadays, some of these Japanese are Buddhist and most of them are Catholic.[15] It is important to remember, at this point, that their conversion to Catholicism was seen as 'a

necessary part of the process of Brazilianization' (Clarke, 1995: 121); it was a strategy for social integration and for the establishment of alliances with the Brazilians, through baptism. The CWMB followers are Brazilians who knowingly go into a Japanese church. So while *nisei* leave their parents' religion, converting to Catholicism, many Brazilians leave Catholicism and pick up on Japanese religions. This is not to say that many members of CWMB, especially those over 35, are not both Catholic and members of CWMB. This is also true of members of Seicho no Ie. The transition from isolationism to inculturation, or social integration, can be observed then for the Japanese and their descendants. At the same time, we can observe Brazilians adopting religions that given them status, self-esteem, and a sense of their own personal value besides other senses, because of the positive representations that the Brazilians have of these religions and of Japan.

Conclusion

The CWMB is one existing religious option among others in the contemporary Brazilian religious market. The CWMB came into Brazil around 1950; this was also the time when Brazilian religious diversity got under way. The Espiritismo and the Afro-Brazilian religions, which had been persecuted and discriminated until then, from that date on started to acquire greater visibility and expanding to all social classes. The evangelical churches, most of all the Pentecostal churches, rapidly increased in number, building more temples and attracting a growing number of followers. And in this same period, lastly, the new Oriental religions began to establish themselves in Brazil[16] within the middle class and the lower-middle class.

The CWMB is not a mass religion – it does not attract thousands of people to its temples by means of a rituals that aim to reach people's emotions, nor is it strong on proselytism. The CWMB is a religion that, because of its rituals' dynamics and its discourse, attracts people with considerable general knowledge and refinement, people who consider religion to be a fundamental part of their lives and who are also sensitive to modern problems (environment pollution, family disunion, humanity becoming a homogeneous mass, excessive rationalism, disregard for fundamental values and lack of spirituality). The rituals and the discourse that the CWMB makes available to these people agrees with their own personal expectations (psychological and spiritual).

The fulfilment of these personal expectations only happens because the religious rites and discourse promoted by the CWMB are meaningful to those people, that is, the Church's rites and doctrine are not incompatible with the culture of the Brazilian members nor are they incompatible with Brazilian (religious) culture. On the contrary, the Church's rites and doctrines seem to make sense to these followers' culture and to Brazilian culture in general; actually, as Clarke correctly states, it seems as though the success of this new Japanese religion is due to the fact that similar beliefs existed previously (Clarke, 1995).

The comments and analysis made here are the result of focused fieldwork research. I believe that these comments and this analysis indicate a general trend regarding the situation of CWMB in this country, even though it is not my purpose to generalize these research results to the rest of Brazil or to the other new Japanese religions brought into in this country.

Notes

1 I wish to thank Professor Peter B. Clarke of King's College, London University, for the incentive and support given for the research which resulted in this article.
2 Mokiti Okada, the Meishu-Sama, founded this church in Japan on January 1, 1935. This church, along with others such as Seicho-no-ie and Soka Gakkai, belongs to the category of 'new' Japanese religions (Clarke, 1994). According to Shimazono, we can divide the new Japanese religions into four periods: the first one is from 1800 to 1900; the second, from 1900 to 1925; the third, from 1925 to 1970; the fourth, from 1970 to the present-day. Seicho no Ie, Sekai Kyusei-Kyo, Perfect Liberty and other religions appeared in the third period, while in the fourth period the so called 'new new Japanese religions' appeared. (Shimazono, 1995).
3 The state of Rio Grande do Sul (RS) is located at the very south of Brazil; it is bordered by Uruguay and Argentina. The area of this state is approximately 280 000 square km and its population is 10 million inhabitants. Ethnically, it is the second 'whitest' state of Brazil. Porto Alegre, the capital of Rio Grande do Sul, has 1.5 million inhabitants.
4 According to the PINAD – National Research by Domestic Sample – report, made by the Brazilian Institute of Geography and Statistics, in 1988: 'The Brazilians of Asian descent (mostly Japanese) are today at the top of the pyramid in terms of rent, education and well-being. The average monthly income of the Brazilians, according to their ethnic origin, is: Asian = US$ 3396; European = US$ 1930; African = US$ 786. 27 out of a hundred Asian Brazilians are in the group that earns the highest rates, that is of those who receive more than US$ 6500 per month, while only ten in a hundred people of European origin are in this group. Those who have an Asian origin are also the ones who are most likely to be homeowners: 80 out of every 100 Asian (Japanese) descendants in the city of Curitiba, for example, own the homes they live in; the situation is similar in Sao Paulo, where we have 68 out of 100; and in Belo Horizonte, we have 88 out of 100. The Asian descendants have the highest number of academic degrees and diplomas, which are converted into the highest rates of pay, and so they end up having pleasant lives. The Japanese community differs from the other groups because of, among other virtues, their greater desire for saving than for consuming.
5 The CWMB had 144 religious entities in 1989, 53 in the state of Sao Paulo and 33 in the state of Rio de Janeiro. Therefore, about 58 per cent of all of these religious entities are located in these two states.
6 There are three Holy Soils in Japan: Hakone, Atami and Kyoto.
7 The predominance of women in this religion, as in other existing Brazilian religions, is due not only to a search, in the religious sphere, for the status and power denied to them in everyday life. It is also due to the fact that women who

are responsible for the maintenance of the house, the provision of food and the health of the family members, 'naturally' make incursions into the sacred space in search of solutions for the problems that affect themselves and their families.

8 This profile is similar to the one presented by Derrett, who states that the members of the SKK of Brazil are urban, middle-class, middle-aged, female and of European descent (In: P. Clarke, 1994 op.cit.). The social profile of the Brazilian Seicho no Ie member is similar to those of the CWMB.

According to P. Clarke, 'Seicho no Ie is one of the largest Japanese new religions in Brazil and maintains over two hundred shrines and around one thousand places of worship. Its membership is close to one million, a large per centage of whom are Brazilians of European descent.'(Clarke, 1994: 159).

9 The Kardecist *Espiritismo* is what I am referring to here, that is, to the school of spiritism founded by the French intellectual Allan Kardec. This is a religion which aspires to be philosophy and science; it arrived in Brazil in the last decades of the nineteenth century and it has grown specially among the middle classes in Brazilian society. Today, *Espiritismo* has about 7 million followers in Brazil (Prandi & Pierucci, 1994).

10 Brazilian Pentecostalism is originally from North-America and proceeded in 'three waves', according to the classification proposed by Paul Freston. The first wave is made up of the churches coming from the United States, namely the Assembly of God (*Assembleia de Deus*) – which arrived here in 1911 – and the *Congregacao Crista do Brasil* (1910). The emphasis is put on the virtues of the Holy Spirit, specially on the glossolalia. The second wave started in the 1950s and the most representative of these churches are the *Evangelho Quadrangular, Brasil para Cristo* and *Deus e Amor*. In this stage the enphasis is on the divine cure. The third wave began in the 70s; its main representative is the *Igreja Universal do Reino de Deus*, the enphasis being put on exorcism and on the media (Freston, 1994).

The different Pentecostal churches are estimated to have about 18 million followers in Brazil today. If to these we also add the historical Protestant churches, it would lead to a grand total of 25 million people – about 15 per cent of the Brazilian population. (For an analysis of the main reasons for the Pentecostal expansion in Latin America, see Oro, 1994.)

11 The so-called Afro-Brazilian religions are religions of an African origin, brought by slaves in the period from 1500 to 1888. They can be divided, in an ideal type form, into three different ritualistic forms: the *Umbanda*, where the gods worshipped are mainly the spirits of 'Preto-Velhos' (Old Black Slaves), 'Caboclos' (Indian Slaves) and 'Beiji'; the rituals of the *Linha Cruzada* or *Macumba* are concerned mainly with the 'Exus' and 'Pombagiras'; the cults of the *Candomble* are centered on the African 'orixas', this being considered the most African of these religions, deriving its mythological, axiological, linguistic and symbolic support from the traditions Jeje-Nago. These three tendencies are, to a certain extent, prevailing in all of Brazil, under different names, however, and with regional differences. None of these is actually a 'pure' form. About 50 million Brazilians – that is, about one third of the national population – attend nowadays, at least occasionally, the Afro-Brazilian religions' *terreiros*.

12 According to data of the Brazilian Institute of Geography and Statistics (IBGE), the per centage of those declaring themselves to be Catholic has decreased in the following manner: 1890: 98.9 per cent; 1940: 95.0 per cent; 1950: 93.5 per cent; 1970: 91.8 per cent; 1980: 88.4 per cent; 1990: 85 per cent; 1995: 75 per cent.

13 The quality of human relations, as well as a pleasant environment, are prime conditions for taking part in any religious group activity. According to R. Campiche, 'peu importe ce qui est propose au niveau de croyances, mais si l'ambiance n'est pas bonne, alors on quittera le groupe.' (Campiche, 1995: 78).

14 The Ancestral Cult is performed at least once a month, in all Seicho no Ie churches.

15 According to P. Clarke, the Japanese conversion to Catholicism began with the immigrants themselves. Many of the second and third generation descendants of these immigrants do not know anything about their own grandparents' and parents' religious beliefs and practices – although these descendants speak both Portuguese and Japanese. In Sao Paulo, besides Catholicism, many of the *nisei* are now involved in Pentecostalism, mainly the *Assembleia de Deus*. There is also a Japanese movement in *Umbanda* (Clarke, 1994).

16 It was from 1960 onwards that orientally-inspired religious movements started to penetrate Brazil, coming from the United States, particularly Moons' Unification Church, the Rajneesh Disciples and the Hare-Krishna, besides Seicho no Ie and the Church of World Messianity, which were already there. The numerous new Oriental religions, especially the Japanese ones, grew rapidly in the 1960s, not only in Brazil, but also in the rest of Latin America, Central America and the Caribbean (Clarke, 1995).

References

Campiche, R. (1995) *Quand les sectes affolent*. Geneve, Labor et Fides.

Clarke, P.B. (1994) 'Japanese "Old", "New" and "Newí, New" Religious Movements in Brazil' in: P. B. Clarke and J. Somers (eds): *Japanese New Religions in the West*,. Kent, Japan Library: 150–161.

—— (1995) 'The Cultural Impact of New Religions in Latin and Central America and the Caribbean with Special Reference to Japanese New Religions' in: *Journal of Latin American Cultural Studies*. V. 4, N. 1: 117–126.

Flores, M. (1977) 'Japoneses no Rio Grande do Sul' in: *Veritas*, Porto Alegre, PUCRS: 65–98.

Freston, P. (1994) 'Breve historia do pentecostalismo brasileiro' in *Nem anjos nem demonios*. Petropolis, Vozes: 67–162. *Jornal Messianico* (1995) N. 270, São Paulo, June.

Oro, A.P. (1994) 'Evaluation de l'emergence des sectes en Amerique Latine' in: *Studies in Religion*. Quebec, 23/2:211–225.

Prandi, Reginaldo & Pierucci, Antonio Flavio (1994) *Religiao e voto no Brasil*. Caxambu, ANPOCS.

Shimazono, S. (1995) 'New New Religons and This World: Religious Movements in Japan after the 1970s and their Beliefs about Salvation' in: *Social Compass*, V. 42(2):1913–205.

Takeuchi, K. (1994) 'Imigracao Niponica no Brasil' in: *Veritas*, Porto Alegre, PUCRS, N. 154:231–241.

CHAPTER FIVE

Modern Japanese Millenarian Movements

Their Changing Perception of Japan's Global Mission with Special Reference to the Church of World Messianity in Brazil

Peter B. Clarke

Various aspects of the millenarian theme in Japanese new religions have been discussed from different academic perspectives over the past thirty years including: Blacker, 1971; Yasumaru, 1977; Berthon, 1985; Shima-zono, 1986 and 1995; Miyata, 1988; Sponberg and Hardacre, 1988; Hardacre, 1990; Reader, 1991; Ooms, 1993; Yamashita, 1998; Kisala 1998. Several of these studies, for example Yasumaru's (1977), not only contain detailed life histories of those Japanese millenarian 'prophets' who fashioned and proclaimed this popular belief in the imminent arrival of a totally new, earthly existence, but also illustrate the overall importance of this theme to the cultural and social historian interested in the structure of popular Japanese thought in the modern period, and particularly from the beginning of the Meiji restoration (1868). As a concept millenarianism also performs many valuable functions.

Methodologically millenarianism can serve as a useful conceptual tool in that it can enable the researcher to grasp with greater clarity popular notions, in their ideal form, of the meaning and purpose of life, of what is considered to be of value and what is not, of self worth and self development, of the nature of morality, and to understand how people come to privilege one style of living and one set of principles over others. The study of millenarian thought also opens the door to a clearer understanding of the reasons for the different ways in which people respond to disruptive social change and how they interpret and explain various personal limitations and human and natural calamities, including earthquakes, defeat in war and great poverty.

Such study of this multifaceted belief also thows light on the nature of human motivation, on what drives people forward; millenarian belief has an extraordinary capacity to inspire people to concrete action, as we shall see in the Brazilian case. However, where its effects are concerned nothing is entirely predictable. The achievements of millenarian prophets, often self-educated, and their followers, are sometimes remarkable and suggest that such a belief can help unlock reservoirs of imagination and creativity that might otherwise remain dormant. By contrast, it can also induce extreme abandonment, passivity and resignation, characteristics of millenarianism in Melanesia studied by Worsely (1970), among others.

The belief in the imminence of an earthly paradise does not simply consist of a desire on the part of millenarians, as we will be seen, for material progress and fulfilment, but also for moral and 'spiritual' regeneration valued as the individual's, the community's and the nation's greatest resources and most effective means of bringing about fundamental change. From the perspective of the millenarians discussed here, and generally, to leave the transformation of the world to political ideologies and strategies would be misguided as these are dependent for their efficacy on being imbued by the power of the moral and the spiritual. Ontologically, the moral and spiritual exist on a level of reality that is indestructible, and function effectively as forms of individual and social psychology, constituting sources of permanently valid truths and explanations about destiny, relationships and the essentials of human happiness, in terms of the self and the community. Millenarians come to see themselves as destined to belong to an entirely new moral community, and this belief not only tends to greatly strengthen their motivation and single mindedness, but often gives rise to a strong aversion to what are seen as the political virtues of diplomacy, ambiguity, compromise and equivocation.

At the most general level millenarianism is an ideology of change that evolves and unfolds in response to the varying conceptions of human needs, and not only needs but also aspirations, desires and hopes. While some millenarian preoccupations are, as history shows us, enduring – the pursuit of authenticity, equality, harmony, meaningful work, and a world free of sickness and human want, for example – others are transitory and passing. The utopian dreams of one age or generation tend to become the commonplace aspirations, and sometimes expectations, of the next.

Examples of this evolution of millenarian belief can be found in all societies where it has been a force. Taking the West as a case in point one can see that with the growth of material affluence millenarian movements in that part of the world are now much more focused on the self-realisation of individuals through the maximum fulfilment of their capacities, whether intellectual, aesthetic or sexual, while a century ago the emphasis was markedly on collective values, the conservation of tradition and the satisfaction of material and physical needs. This change towards the development of the inner self, for some the Divine Self within, can be seen in such contemporary millenarian movements as the Rajneesh foundation, and is encapsulated in the 'intention' of the leader of the Sufi Order in the West, Pir Vilayat 'Inayat Khan, which states: 'We could build a wonderful world and we could all become beautiful people – and what is more we should. And we will' (Jervis, 1998: 245).

Millenarian movements not only throw light on the changing nature of human needs and aspirations, but also reveal a great deal about the mechanics of human motivation and the nature of the quest for human happiness. To refer to Ibn Khaldun, the medieval Muslim statesman, jurist and historian, millenarianism was from his historical perspective a most potent source of *asabiyya* or group solidarity (1967, Vol II: 196). At the same time, some of the communities brought together by such a persuasive and compelling belief and one that offers such hope of transcending human and physical limitations have been a reminder that there is but a very fine line between a world of complete happiness, harmony and self-fulfilment and one of anguish, exploitation and authoritarianism.

The possibility of the pursuit of happiness turning into its opposite notwithstanding, the millenarian dream of removing the frustrations of the human condition is too often wrongly mocked as naive and irrational. It has, on the contrary, done much to explore the complexities of life and the range of human possibilities, and its contribution to art, science, technology, and even to democracy, cannot be ignored. Moreover, as Arjomand (1984) has shown in the case of Iranian history, and as most anti colonial movements elsewhere have illustrated, it has been one of the few effective weapons at the disposal of the oppressed which the oppressor has greatly feared. It not only generates deep emotion, fervour, commitment, dedication and enthusiasm, but, like charisma, abhors bureaucracy and order, as many a reformer who has used it to mobilise mass support has discovered, and as Arjomand (1984) has shown in the case of Shi'ite Iran.

As for finding a general explanation of Japanese millenarianism, modernization cannot, any more than colonialism in relation to the phenomenon in other parts of the world, provide one of these. Looking at the incidence of millenarianism from a global and historical perspective the best one can say by way of evaluation of attempts to date at general explanations is that we still as yet see but through a glass darkly. Perhaps the most general comment that can be made about millenarianism would be to say that almost everywhere it functions at some level as an ideology of change. But given the complexity and diversity of the phenomenon the search should perhaps be for reasons rather than explanations of its origins and widespread appeal.

In many cultures millenarian hope appears to be central to the initial development of all new religion. Historically, as in the contemporary world, few if any new, alternative, movements of a religious, or for that matter, secular kind, have emerged in societies where the Judeo-Christian or Muslim traditions have had a serious impact that have not been in their early years intensely millenarian. The frequency and widespread nature of this belief has been witnessed nowhere more so than in the Islamic world in the form of Mahdism, the Islamic equivalent of millenarianism. With reference to Mahdism, Ibn Khaldun, already mentioned above, commented in his *Muqaddimah* or Introduction to History:

> It has been well known and generally accepted by all Muslims in every epoch, that at the end of time a man from the family of the prophet will without fail make his appearance, one who will strengthen the religion and make justice triumph... He will be called the Mahdi (God-guided one). Following him the Antichrist will appear together with all the subsequent signs of the Day of Judgement. After the Mahdi Isa (Jesus) will descend and kill the Antichrist... (1967: 156).

Though much will remain obscure regarding the moral, spiritual, social and psychological reasons for its frequency and prevalence, it is hoped that from a consideration of three movements that emerged at different critical junctures of modern Japanese history something can be glimpsed of the reasons for the recourse to millenarianism in nineteenth and twentieth century Japan, of its appeal in Brazil, and of the variation and difference in the global orientation and mission of modern Japanese new religions that have as their goal the creation of paradise on earth. The three movements examined are: Omotokyo (Religion of Great Origin), Tensho-Kotai-Jingu-Kyo (the religion of the grand shrine of *Amaterasu*), widely known as the Dancing Religion on account of its practice of self-less dancing (muga no mai), one of the two principal means it advocates for the attaining the Buddhist ideal of no self, the other being chanting, and Sekai Kyusei Kyo (The Church of World Messianity). In the case of Messianity the focus will be mainly on the Brazilian branch of this movement and its mission to create a global earthly paradise (*chijō-tengoku*) from its Brazilian base. Messianity is known in Brazil by its Portuguese name Igreja Messianica Mondial do Brasil (The Church of World Messianity of Brazil). Already this movement, also discussed in this volume by Ari Pedro Oro, has built in Brazil a *Solo Sagrado* or Holy Ground, meant to be a model of an earthly paradise. It has also plans to build a New Age City (*Cidade da Nova Era*).

Omotokyo has been chosen for study for two reasons in particular: firstly, it is one of the most thoroughgoing examples of modern Japanese millenarianism, and, secondly, it has exercised a considerable intellectual and moral influence on several other Japanese millenarian movements including Messianity, which went on to develop its own distinctive version of paradise on earth, and global orientation and mission. The strategic and tactical elements to millenarianism, are also addressed. The leadership of millenarian movements is constantly devising ways and means of ensuring the persistence and vitality of this belief on which so much good will and cooperation depends.

The movements discussed here often display considerable imagination and creativity not only in the way they grapple with the problem of motivation but also with the most acute and perplexing intellectual, existential and social problems. As will be seen below, Omotokyo, Tensho-Kotai-Jingu-Kyo and Messianity have offered explanations of and solutions to – perhaps greatly flawed from a political perspective – natural and human catastrophes and disorders such as famine, defeat in war, religious strife, the pains and pangs inflicted on the traditional way of life by modernization, and the breakdown in communications and relationships within and between local communities and families.

These movements were also preoccupied, in different ways, with the question of authenticity, with what was genuinely Japanese, as their country experienced large scale and deep levels of westernization, a process identified largely with technology, material progress and arrogance in its attitude to the non-empirical world of mystical and spiritual power. Millenarians in Japan were not alone in their pursuit of authenticity or in finding westernization problematic. Broadly the search for authenticity since the beginning of the Meiji era (1868) when the pace of modernization quickened dramatically, pushed forward internally by the state itself, and at the same time, greatly stimulated by increasing contacts with abroad, took one of two routes: the total rejection of modernity itself, and of its concomitant, westernization, as detrimental to the Japanese soul, to its culture and to its sense of its own destiny on the one hand, and on the other, the pursuit of modernization with a difference, of modernization that in form was clearly and distinctly Japanese (Waswo, 1996). To those who followed the second path the impact of modernization was seen as no more than catalytic in the sense that it helped to stimulate a Japanese variety of the modernization process that was in the air anyway and would have happened even without outside influence.

Thus, both the rejectionists and those who embraced modernization were able to appeal to tradition, interpreted flexibly, in support of their position: in the first case tradition was used to legitimate closure to the outside and to the new, in the second it allowed openness to new ways and new ideas in the name of fostering something that was essentially and from time immemorial, Japanese. Omotokyo was among those movements that followed the path of closure, as will be seen below. But first the meaning of the term millenarian, a controversial one in the Japanese context, needs to be unpacked.

Millenarianism in the Japanese Context

The obvious place to look for evidence of millenarianism in Japanese society is to the cult of Maitreya (*Miroku*) which entered Japan with Buddhism in the sixth century, and which greatly influenced the thinking of two of the movements discussed in this presentation, Omotokyo and Messianity. Those who question the value of the term millenarian in the Japanese context point out that there is no scriptural evidence in Japan, or indeed in Buddhist sources elsewhere in Asia (Nattier, 1988) for the belief in the expectation of Miroku as a future messiah combined with a detailed and concrete vision of the millennium. However, seen anthropologically as a datum of popular religion, the Maitreya cult, which is highly variable in the Asian context, clearly displays in parts of Japan several of the core characteristics of millenarianism. Miyata (1988: 183 ff), while supporting the view that the textual evidence for Miroku as a future messiah in a Judeo-Christian sense is missing, shows, nevertheless, that there have been popular or folk movements, some of them similar in their expectations to the Cargo Cults of Melanesia, in which Miroku has been perceived as a messianic figure, appearing from across the sea after disasters and famine, to provide an abundant harvest.

In particular Miyata (1988:184) has demonstrated the popularity of the Miroku cults in times of great hardship and famine in villages along the eastern coast of Japan particularly during the Edo or Tokugawa period (1600–1867). In special Miroku songs, accompanied by special dances that were meant to eliminate all the evil forces that afflicted them, devotees predicted the arrival of Miroku's ship, carrying a super-abundance of rice, to begin the *Miroku no yo* or Age of Miroku, an age of never ending plenty. There were various other ways in which devotees awaited the coming of Miroku, including self-mummification through fasting in which the individual in question entered a state of *nyūji* or suspended animation until the moment of the future Buddha's advent (Blacker, 1976: 89). A form of realised eschatology, this advent was believed by some to have already happened and when proclaimed often met with great popular response. Ito Ihei, founder of Fuji-ko, a lay association that practised self-mummification and whose worship centred on Mt Fuji, is but one example of this intense anticipation that was finally rewarded. A business man turned ascetic, Ito Ihei was informed through an oracle of the deity of Mt Fuji, Sangen Bosatsu, that the *Miroku no yo* had begun in 1773, and the result was the emergence of hundreds of new Fuji-ko communities in Tokyo and the surrounding rural areas (Miyata, 1988:185).

Millenarianism can also be found in the Buddhist ideas of the Three Ages and the notion of enlightenment or salvation in the present. These beliefs have been dominant themes in Japanese Buddhism at various times in its history. The idea of *Mappō* or Three Ages, culminating in *Mappō Shisō*, the Last Dharma Age, was to exercise considerable appeal in Japan in the later part of the Heian period (794–1185), and also in the Kamakura period (1185–1333) which immediately followed. As Marra states in relation to the late Heian period:

From the second half of the eleventh century the expression 'final age' (masse) occurs in many diaries, novels and works of history, often bringing with it a connotation of fear and inevitability (1988a: 51).

The thirteenth century also saw the emergence of Nichiren Buddhism founded by the uncompromising and militant monk and prophet, Nichiren Daishonin (1222–1282), son of a fisherman from southeastern Japan, who, in the words of Anesaki (1930: 202), 'deemed himself to be the man sent by Buddha to open the way for the transformed world, the messenger of Buddha, an incarnation of the Truth'. The idea of the present world as the location of paradise was central to Nichiren's mission, and like many founders of Japanese new religions in more recent times who also claim enlightenment, or are regarded by their followers as enlightened, including the founders of Omotokyo, Tensho-Kotai-Jingu-Kyo, Kofuku no Kagaku and Agonshu, to name but a few, he believed that Japan which, in an ideal sense, he took to mean the whole world, would be totally transformed in the light of the Scripture. Nichiren believed that Japan was the land where true Buddhism would prevail, and that all other lands would look to it for inspiration and guidance, a belief expressed in an interview with this writer in Kyoto in April 1997 by Kiryama Seiyu, the founder and present leader of Agonshu.

Nichiren, who identified himself as the *Jōgyō* or supreme leader of the boddhisattvas (enlightened, compassionate beings) of the earth, bitterly opposed the lack of faith found in theJodo Shu or Pure Land Tradition treachings, particularly its belief in the paradise of Amida Buddha which could not be realized for millions of years, denouncing its founder, Honen, for propagating the 'spirit of Hell' (Anesaki, 1930: 194). Nichiren held this tradition, and the Shingon and Zen traditions also, to be responsible for all the misfortunes and calamities – strife, famine, fear of foreign invasion – affecting Japan at the time, and preached that salvation would come from his religion alone which was based upon the Lotus Sutra.

Nichiren's strictures notwithstanding, that version of the Pure land Tradition known as True Pure Land or *Jodo Shinshu* school of Buddhism founded by Shinran (1173–1262) contained elements of millenarianism, including the possiblity of enlightenment in this world. Shinran stressed that faith was Amida's gift and arose and manifested itself when a person became aware of their own sinful state and the availability of Amida's compassion. This was the moment of 'transverse conversion', a conversion that came directly from Amida, and permitted the convert to cut off the five evil paths and pass over the sea of birth and death. According to Shinran those in whom faith had been awakened would see the end of karma at their death, and even in this world they would attain what was called 'profit in the present' or *genyaku*, the state of being equal to perfect enlightenment, thus assuring them of birth in the Pure Land and immediate enlightenment at their death.

Shinran was not the first to teach this. Prior to him the founders of the Shingon and Tendai schools of Buddhism in Japan, Kukai (774–835), commonly referred to as Kobo Daishi and Saicho (767–822), generally known by his posthumous title, Dengyo Daishi, respectively, taught *sokushinjōbutsu* or the attainment of enlightenment in this very body. A relevant extract from a legend about Kukai reads:

> *Sokushinjōbutsu* – means the people can attain Buddhahood in their lifetime. The human self becomes Buddha. In other words, man is capable of demonstrating what Buddha means with his own body. *Sokushinjōbutsu* thus means to become a Buddha as your are ... the Master (Kukai) held his hand in the right position, recited the holy words and let his mind enter Buddha. That moment he demonstrated with his own body *sokushinjōbutsu*... (Reader, Andreasen & Stefansson, 1993: 104–5).

The importance of the belief that enlightenment or paradise could be attained in this life lay in the fact that it seriously challenged the thinking that since it took Maitreya or Miroku five billion, six hundred and seventy million years to become a Buddha it would take an ordinary person infinitely longer. By comparison Kukai, Saicho and Shinran, like many of the contemporary founders of the new religions of Japan and elsewhere, offered a much swifter route to salvation and, moreover, there was no fear of retrogression in that once attained enlightenment could not be lost. As Marra comments on Shinran:

> (He) transformed the future oriented interpretation of the Jodo beliefs by the early patriarchs into a way of thinking *which assured human beings that ultimate salvation was reacheable in this life* (my italics) (1988b: 298).

Admittedly all of this does not constitute what, historically and theologically, might be called full blown millenarianism as interpreted by Cohn (1993). However, as in other cases where local ideals were blended with 'genuine' millenarianism from a Zoroastrian, Judeo-Christian source, such as early Daoist millenarian movements in China in the second century of the Common Era (Kohn, 1998), and the Cargo Cults of Papua New Guinea in the twentieth century (Worsley, 1970), these ideas have been blended with outside religious and secular ideas into a Japanese version of millenarianism.

In the teachings of the Japanese millenarian movements discussed here there is evidence of new assumptions about the historical process and about time that are broadly similar to those found in millenarian movements that derive directly from the Zoroastrian and through it the Judeo-Christian, and Islamic, traditions. Sociologically, moreover, they can be described as millenarian movements in the sense that they share the general features associated with such movements everywhere. These include the following in particular, as identified by Cohn (1970: 13): a belief that the joys of paradise are to be enjoyed by all the faithful as a collectivity; that this paradise is to be terrestrial in that it is to be enjoyed on earth and not in some other-worldly heaven; that it is imminent in the sense that it is to come both soon and suddenly; total in that it will utterly transform life on earth and bring perfection itself and not just improvement; miraculous in that it is to be accomplished by, or with the help of supernatural agencies. Not all of these conditions are always present in an ideal form in every millenarian movement, but all such movements display all of these characteristics to some degree and in most of them all of them are clearly enunciated.

One important distinction often made is that between pre- and post-millennialists and concerns the different ways in which the transformation of the world is envisaged. Those movements termed pre-millennial – a category in which I place all three movements examined here – emphasise the importance of human action alongside divine assistance in transforming the world and resemble the reformist sect or new religion as described by Wilson (1970). The notion of a pre-millennial movement is commonly thought of as presenting a dramatic, stormy, explosive vision of a new age, and as one disposed to use violent means to bring about this vision. Aum Shinrikyo is an example of this kind of pre-millennial movement. Pre-millennialism need not, however, be violent, and in the case, for example, of Messianity, there has never been any display of violence, a method that would be totally condemned if anyone were to consider such as strategy. Another example of active millenarianism of a non-violent kind is the Mahdiyyat movement which made peaceful means a sine qua non of establishing the New Jerusalem that would embrace both Muslims, Christians and Traditionalists in colonial Nigeria (Clarke, 1995a).

The post-millennial movement is one that waits patiently in a community of the perfect, usually situated away from the rest of society, for divine intervention to bring about the new world. I have suggested elsewhere that the Rastafarian movement is passive in this sense (Clarke, 1987) and, despite the vehemence of the rhetoric and the revolutionary implications of the symbols and rituals, violent action never has been a requirement in the case of any of those Japanese movements discussed here.

Omotokyo, Westernization and Japan's Global Mission

Omotokyo was esentially a product of westernization, a term synonymous with modernization, at the time it emerged in the 1890s. In the pre-World War II phase of its history it was driven by the search for Japanese authenticity, for the pure spirit of Japan, by the conviction that Japan was unique and self sufficient, and, therefore, by the belief that whatever good might be found in other cultures was essentially present in Japanese culture. It should be pointed out that Omotokyo's responded in this way not only to western culture but also to other civilizations, including Chinese civilization.

Initially Omotokyo was a movement of the economically deprived. Its principal founder was the impoverished peasant and mother of eleven children, Nao Deguchi (1837–1918), whose home life was made doubly uncertain and insecure by her husband's irresponsibility. Her distress and insecurity reached their lowest point when she was obliged to wander from homestead to homestead collecting rags in order to survive (Ooms, 1993).

Nao then began her movement in 1892 after spending a period of time with Konkokyo, an older Japanese new religion and also founded by a peasant, Bunjiro Kawate (1814–1883) in Okayama in 1859. No doubt influenced by Bunjiro's mystic encounter with the malevolent deity Ushitora no Konjin which radically changed his life, Nao was also to undergo a similar experience with this same kami which she used to legitimate her uncompromising hostility to the opening up of Japan to the outside world and its modernization by the Meiji emperors (1868–1912). However, she did not simply step back to the past to remain fixed therein, but was also a creative force, as Hardacre (1990) and Ooms (1993) show, reinventing tradition for the purpose of her campaign against what she saw as the abject surrender to foreign ways by the emperor, a surrender, she believed, that had dire consequences for the livelihood and moral life of the Japanese.

Her mission was to construct a model of a new and perfect world that would highlight the fatal flaws in the western model that government with the blessing of the emperor was constructing. The list of prohibitions that would be enforced in this new, perfect world, constitutes in itself a thesis against Meiji government initiatives and a complete rejection of modernity. Rather than a simple yearning for some Golden Age of Japanese history Nao's protest was more a plea for that as yet never realised condition: an equal, just and peaceful world. In her new world there would be no great and small, no high and low; the emperor would be on a par with everyone else. The feared and powerful deity, Ushitora no Konjin, or the Primary Being, traditionally thought of as the hot-tempered and destructive guardian of the Northeast direction, became in Nao's scripture or *Ofudesaki* (literally tip of the writing brush), a creator and protector, the one who would construct a divine kingdom on earth, radically different from that in process of being fashioned by the present emperor (Ofudesaki, 1974: 4–5).

As in the Marxist paradise, there would be no conflict and no war, and no need for a government or a police force, or even for laws, for all human beings would be pure in spirit, diligent in labour, honest and sincere. Secular knowledge, *chie*, and learning, *gaku*, would also be entirely unnecessary; only faith in Ushitora no Konjin's revelations would be of any value, and these revelations were to be found in the *Ofudesaki*. Thus, schools would be unnecessary, for all would be crystal clear and simple. Nor would there be a need for money as people would be self supporting, growing their own food, and living on a diet that would consist of grains, fruit, vegetables and fish only; there would be no meat.

The prohibition on money reflects the anxiety generated in communities where this commodity begins to take over as the principal means of exchange. This change can have a devastating effect on a society's morale giving rise to a sense of loss of control, powerlessness and helplessness, especially among those who have the most difficulty in obtaining money. Moreover, as Burridge (1971) pointed out, as money becomes the principal medium of exchange what is thought to be the source of virtue changes; this is no longer believed to reside in the nature of things, in the skills, industry and social and communal bonds necessary to survival in a subsistence economy, but becomes more a matter of choice.

Money, belonging as it does to complex, differentiated society, demands greater individual freedom of choice and, thereby, threatens group cohesion. From the perspective of those accustomed to and protective of the subsistence economy, the moral implications of such choice are increasing individualism, new criteria for establishing personal identity, and, consequently, a new way of determining the bonds and obligations between the individual and the community, indiscriminate opportunism and the emergence of a society based on greed and competition rather than on cooperation and collaboration. Ooms (1993: 99) illustrates the moral evil that money represented for Nao Deguchi by recounting a story about her refusal to accept a gift of money from her daughter Hisa. Instead, she offered the latter a lump of dirt, remarking:

> There is life because there is soil. You do not understand how much more important a single lump of dirt is than all the money in the world. Money is the source of the world's destruction.

The opposition to money as the new medium of exchange is usually not only moral; it can also be a form of economic protectionism. Nao's movement, for example, was not only concerned with safeguarding traditional sources of virtue, but also with protecting the local economy against the impact of Meiji reforms, including the reform of the land tax system which adversely affected peasant farmers. Followers were encouraged to live naturally, to use natural products for all necessities such as housing and clothing, to shun all forms of medicine considered western, including the vaccination of children. All of this would have lent support to the cause of local farmers, herbalists, tailors and so forth, as would the prohibition in the new kingdom on western style clothes, western hairstyles, the use of tobacco, gambling, and on eating 'fancy' cakes and sweets.

139

Deguchi Nao's pursuit of authenticity which contained an emphasis on simplicity and equality was also part of her campaign against modernization and westernization. To this end she outlawed all pomp and circumstance at festivals and ceremonials. Everyone would be equal, would live naturally and would live long, under the compassionate rule of Ushitora no Konjin, sentiments clearly also expressed in Messianity's account of how life would be in an earthly paradise. Simplicity and equality were also symbolic of the clarity and truth of her revelations, a role performed by nakedness in other contexts.

During Nao's time as its effective leader – though she was formally leader until her death in 1917 she was to all intents and purposes superseded in 1905 by her co-founder Deguchi Onisaburo (1871–1948) – both the tone and content of Omotokyo's teaching was unambiguously millenarian and hostile to the emperor. The introduction of the practice of carrying lanterns at noon and of walking on all fours through the streets were among the most potent symbolic acts employed by Nao not only to illustrate her total rejection of Meiji modernization and westernization, but also to display her profound resentment at the sight of a world turned upside down by this transformation.

Nao regularly described the world that was being created by the Meiji emperor in the most depressing and pessimistic language, one moment referring to it as a 'muddy tract of desolation' and at another, as a 'dark and devilish place' in which human beings were no more than monsters, the stronger preying on the weaker. Using powerful and vivid images to depict the present state of the world, she likened it to a 'dilapidated old house with rotted beams', a place 'on the brink of total extinction' (Ooms, 1993: 69).

There was, as was previously mentioned, the possibility of an alternative world, a model which Nao was determined to construct at Ayabe, her village situated to the Northwest of Kyoto. Ayabe would be the link between the unregenerate world and the new one to be created, an oasis of order, goodness and truth, and the source of the sacred in an otherwise chaotic and polluted wasteland, a model with the power to inspire others to imitate the way of life lived therein. Ayabe was intended both as bridge and mirror: as a bridge it provided the escape route from a state of absolute evil to absolute good, and, as a mirror, it reflected the future of wholeness and happiness (*Ofudesaki*, May 26, 1896).

In constructing her model of the future Nao's understanding of the nature of the historical process altered from a cyclical to a unilinear historical perspective. This is evident, Ooms suggests (1993: 97), in her belief in the total collapse of the world into degeneracy, followed by an endless future in a utopia described by her as a world of pines, *matsu no yo*, imagery that clearly emphasises qualities of durability, indestructibility and permanence, above all else. The divine agent, *Ushitora no konjin*, would be the principal agent of this total transformation and would communicate on

140

a personal level with his mediator. Although Nao's own term for this radical transformation was *tatekai-tatenaoshi*, meaning reconstruction, to Ooms (1993: 96–97) she had developed the concept far beyond its literal meaning to include the fundamental perspectives of millenarianism by investing it with the sense of: destruction or end of the present world and the beginning or establishment of the new world.

Nao's own description of paradise on earth supports Oom's interpretation of the extended meaning given by her to the term *tatekai-tatenaoshi*. For example, an entry in the *Ofudesaki* for December 6, 1897, using the imagery of the plum tree, the pine tree and the cherry blossom tree, begins in the past tense suggesting that the millennium had already begun and expressing with total clarity the central millenarian hope of radical and complete transformation:

> Now, an era has come when the plum will flourish, the cherry suffers blight, and the young shoots of the pine shall bloom... Thorough changes will occur which will turn this world upside-down. It will be better when the upper becomes the lower.

The plum blossom bursts forth instantaneously and at a difficult time of the year, February, a cold month, remains for some considerable time and, thus, symbolises endurance and the hope born of suffering. The cherry blossom, by contrast with the plum tree and the pine tree, though privileged by Nature, created as it was to bloom in Spring, not only soon disappeared, but was also without fruit, signifying impermanence and vanity. A later entry in her *Ofudesaki*, this time for January 1892, also makes it clear that Nao believed that the millennium had already arrived:

> The Greater World shall burst into full blossom like plum blossoms do – simultaneously. The time for Me, Ushitora no Konjin, to reign has come at last! This means the World opened like plum-blossoms shall be evergreen pine trees...

Like the cherry blossom, Omotokyo considered other religions – it singled out Buddhism, Christianity, Confucianism, Shinto and Taoism – to be symbolic of impermanence and powerlessness, a view shared by the founder of Messianity, and saw itself alone as capable of bringing into being this new, permanent, evergreen world, which it equated with Japan. Its millenarianism, as Berthon (1985) has shown, was founded on the hope of a strong, powerful, victorious and regenerated Japan. Nao even predicted a 'war of the world' after which Japan, the Land of the Kami, would encompass and incorporate the whole world, extending its own boundaries so that they would be commensurate with those of the earth.

This change in her interpretation of the historical process and of the concept of renewal notwithstanding, Nao was, as Ooms (1993: 34) describes her, 'a model of conventional morality, *tsūzoku dōtoku*, displaying to perfection the virtues of obedience, honesty and thriftiness'. Her view of women and their role in society was also traditional, and this influenced the manner in which she led her movement. Convinced that, as a woman, she possessed greater reserves of endurance and greater powers of perseverance than men (Yasumaru: 1977), yet believing that she needed male qualities to be an authentic leader Nao, after consultation with Ushitora no Konjin, decided to become the Transformed Male (*henjōnan-shi*). In this state she would consist of a female body and a male spirit, (Hardacre, 1990: 510ff; Ooms, 1993: 113ff), a state that conformed to the Lotus Sutra prescription that a female become male in order to achieve final enlightenment. On the other hand, the notion of a Transformed female (*henjōnyoshi*) – one who is male in body and female in spirit – developed by Nao and Onisaburo, seems to have been one of their own original constructions, presumably to ensure that Onisaburo possessed the requisite amount of the female virtues of endurance and perseverance.

Thus, in both cases having the nature, *shōrai* – it could also be translated as personality – of the other sex was 'proof' that each had the qualities to understand and guide those of the opposite sex. Also, in the case of Nao, Hardacre explains, 'assuming male gender was an elevation of status, allowing her greater authority, assertiveness and mobility than she could ever have enjoyed in the status to which she was born' (1990: 57). It gave her the authority to insist on her right to be heard and obeyed. Onisaburo, for his part, was able to turn to his advantage what was actually perceived as a fall in status – his becoming a female. As Hardacre comments, Onisaburo by becoming female was claiming 'superior lowliness', as this enabled him to identify himself with the female deity, Mizu, mother of the universe and inexhaustible source of love and kindness (1990:57).

Onisaburo's creativity and 'originality', and his optimism, were evident in a number of other areas including calligraphy, poetry, pottery, painting and the designing of new symbols to express and impart something of the sensation of living in an earthly paradise. His use of innovative colours and designs for his tea bowls, and especially for the tea bowl that came to be christened 'Paradise 28' are a case in point. To innovate in this way was not only to display creativity and hope, but also to convey a sense and spirit of authenticity.

The nature of the radical break with the traditional tea-bowl design and colour is best described by the widely respected Japanese art critic, the late Giichiro Kato (d.1974) whose fascination for and depiction of Onisaburo's tea bowl 'Paradise 28' reveals unmistakably why it should have constituted so expressive and persuasive a symbol of an earthly paradise in a Japanese context. Kato (1975) wrote of the originality, beauty and purity of the colours of Onisaburo Deguchi's tea bowls in general which 'surpassed in value those which we knew', and was stunned by 'Paradise 28' which he had great difficulty in naming. Onisaburo Deguchi's design and choice and use of colours in creating this tea bowl provided, Kato was convinced, a most potent symbol of paradise in that it broke with tradition and resulted in the creation of an object that deepened understanding and feelings in ways previously never imagined, the very stuff, I would imagine, of paradise on earth:

> This wonderful tea bowl ('Paradise 28') could not have escaped my notice... The day on which I discovered it I consulted the dictionary far into the night to find a suitable word to christen it. I finally made up 'scintillating bowl', Yowan: the character Yo signifies star light, shining of stars. Such compound words as 'brilliance', 'shiny bowl', 'beautiful bowl', 'excellent bowl', 'elegant bowl' could not satisfy me. I wished to find a genuine brilliance even in the name to be applied to such a bowl.
>
> ... On a white ground bright ultra-marine and crimson were daubed in mixture with the dominant colour of bluishgreen, but also yellow was there. They mixed with each other to turn into orange and purple in some places. To my surprise these colours were past the colour feeling we normally have: they were far brighter and more cheerful and genuine...

Deguchi Onisaburo is sometimes regarded as being less of a millenarian than Nao, and this may have been more a question of style than of substance. This notwithstanding, there can be little doubt about the strength of his desire to be accepted as a messiah. In his *reikai monogatari*, an account of his adventures in the spirit world, he claimed that he had been informed by the King of the underworld that he was to be the messiah of the two worlds. Moreover, he appears to have been one of the few founders (in his case co-founder) of a Japanese new religion to identify himself with Miroku, and to have claimed that he himself was in fact Miroku returned to earth to fulfil the prophecies contained in the sutras concerning the creation of a new terrestrial kingdom (Blacker, 1971: 596). Later Messianity, as we shall see, was to proclaim that the spirit of its founder, Mokichi Okada, had returned as Miroku in fulfilment of the prophecies of the sutras.

Claiming to be the Bodhisattva Miroku who had returned to establish a new terrestrial paradise, a claim that could very obviously be interpreted as a criticism of the imperial and political establishment, was not going to enhance Omotokyo's reputation for loyalty in the inner circles of government. The government struct out at Omotokyo in 1921 and 1935, destroying much of its property including its shrines, with explosives and imprisoning Onisaburo for lèse-majesté, or injurious affront to the sovereign. Such fierce reprisals as these have been interpreted as evidence of the revolutionary character of the movement's aims, both political and social (Ooms, 1993). But Deguchi Onisaburo was not a political radical. In the 1930s he joined forces with a number of conservative ideologues and went to Manchuria to set up the Red Swastika Association. He was also to assist in the establishment of the Federation of World Religions and take part in the Eperanto movement. In addition to its verbal abuse of the emperor and its symbolic assumption of his status and power what would have aroused the hostility of the government of the day was Omotokyo's ideological pursuit of a single, global language, esperanto, of a single world government and the ending of national parliaments, aims which it continues to pursue with conviction and energy.

Hardacre (1990) and Young (1988) are among those that have stressed the very limited character of Omotokyo radicalism. Hardacre (1990) while accepting that Omotokyo's millenarianism was unusual in pre-World War II Japan, believes that it was largely ineffective, especially in its critique of the place of women in Japanese society. It was ineffective in that it was indirect and largely symbolic – a ritual of rebellion – and left unquestioned the prevailing notions of the role of women. Moreover, even inside Omotokyo women were treated no differently from those in the rest of society. Hardacre concludes, therefore, that Omotokyo, instead of undermining the status quo regarding women, actually contributed to its maintenance (1990: 60). There is a parallel to this gap between rhetoric and practice in the African-Brazilian religion of Candomble in Bahia, Northeast Brazil, and in a number of other the new religions active in the West today (Puttick, 1997). To take the example of Candomble, in this movement those women who have gained authority and influence inside the movement and in the wider society as priestesses have done little, directly, to empower their female disciples (Clarke, 1993).

Young addresses the motives behind Onisaburo's use of imperial regalia and is persuaded that he adopted these, not for the purpose of opposing the existing government and the emperor, but to secure recognition from that 'sacred institution' of his own spiritual authority and that of his movement (1988:45). It has to be remembered, however, that Omotokyo's stance was oppositional not in the sense of wishing to destroy the imperial system but in wanting to restore it to its ideal state which, it believed, the Meiji government had undermined. Berthon (1985), as was previously noted, points to the strong element of nationalism and imperialism in Onisaburo's thinking illustrated by his symbolical redesigning of the map of the world in the image of Japan. The map which included Taiwan, then under Japanese occupation, showed Japan as consisting of five islands. Onisaburo then superimposed five continents upon these, fusing Europe and Asia into one. Japan, the model of the universe, was placed at the centre, Africa was situated on the island of Kyushu, Australia on Shikoku, Euro-Asia, his own construction, on Honshu, North America on Hokkaido and South America on Taiwan. Ushitora no Konjin, in his role as world saving *kami*, would ensure that these regions all converged on Japan.

Despite the conservative nature of the movement's cultural political orientation, Omotokyo's anti-government and anti-imperial rhetoric were exceptional, by any previous standards. It was, however, to be rivalled on both counts by Sayo Kitamura (1900–67), foundress of Tensho-Kotai-Jingu-Kyo, popularly known, as we saw above, as the Dancing Religion. Known as the Prophetess of Tabuse Sayo Kitamura was to concern herself with restoring Japan in the popular to the position of world laeder by turning military defeat in 1945 into spiritual victory.

The Millenarian Interpretation of Military Defeat as Spiritual Victory

Sayo Kitamura (1900–67) was from a peasant family from the village of Tabuse in Yamaguchi prefecture that belonged to the Jodo Shinshu or True Pure Land Tradition of Buddhism. Like Nao Deguchi she was luckless in marriage but determined to see it through to the end as the sixth bride of a man who, on his mother's orders, had previously divorced five women after using them as cheap labour. After possession (*kamigakari*) by a snake-deity who was to later reveal himself as Tensho-Kotai-Jingu, Sayo Kitamura began to practise Buddhist chants and cold-water austerities. In 1945 dressed as a man – she always dressed in this way in public – she announced that she had been called by this deity to save the world which was about to end. Known to her followers as Ogamisama, the great goddess, Sayo Kitamura frequently poured scorn – more precisely it was the spirit within her body, *Tensho*, another name for *Amaterasu*, the mythical ancestress of the Japanese imperial family – on the emperor of the day, Hirohito, denying his divine character:

> The present Emperor whose vocation it is to rule over the Nation, is packed in a box, nailed tight, and is given the role of an idiot. He is not a living God as hitherto believed by all (The Prophet of Tabuse, 1954: 26).

Though Japan was close to defeat, this kind of language was deeply shocking to many who heard it, including a local school teacher, Mr Hirai, who advised the prophetess to refrain from such utterances or risk endangering her life (The Prophet of Tabuse: 26). Sayo Kitamura was at this point interesting a considerable number of local people, mainly farmers, who not only admired her outspoken and uncompromising approach but were also impressed by her extraordinary abilities, including the unmatched speed at which she was capable of planting rice. This was the kind of 'miracle' that gave legitimacy and support to her charismatic claims among the villagers.

As in the case of Deguchi Nao, her criticism of the emperor was not directed at the imperial system as such, but at what was seen as the failure of the present incumbent to save the country from a defeat which many believed was close at hand.

Sayo Kitamura's son, known to followers as Wakagamisama, the present administrative head of the movement, spoke to this writer of his time as a soldier in Manchuria and of his mother's fear that he was either lost or dead, like many others, and of the depressing news that was reaching all parts of Japan, of the retreat or defeat of the Japanese army in various parts of the Far East.[1] Japanese cities, further, were experiencing heavy bombing and the endless demands made on the ordinary people to redouble their efforts to provide the military with supplies were making ordinary life intolerable. Demands for turpentine and castor oil, among other things, had to be met by digging up roots of pine trees for the former and by planting great quantities of castor beans around their homes for the latter.

The long hours spent on these laborious tasks forced people to neglect their rice fields, and responsibility for this lay with the emperor whose primary duty was 'to ensure the blessings of the deities for the new rice crop on behalf of the people.' (Ohnuki-Tierney, 1991: 200). Times of poor rice production and natural disaster, such as famine, increased the intensity of the already latent desire for renewal or *yonaoshi* which was generally understood as the restoration of things to their ideal state. The failure of the rich crop was one of a number of signs that the 'way of heaven' was not being followed, that the gods were unhappy with the emperor's performance and that he should, therefore, be removed from office to allow the situation to be returned to 'normal'.

Sayo Kitamura gave her full support to those who wanted to work on their rice fields. Pointing her finger at the corrupt who were making money out of the distress and hard labour of many and to the incompetence in the military and government, this self proclaimed saviour and redeemer of the Japanese people voiced the frustrations of many and informed her listeners that the divine spirit within her had revealed that no one was obliged to plant castor beans or pull up pine roots (The Prophet of Tabuse: 42).

Accounting for Japan's defeat in World War II, widely seen as the first ever foreign conquest of a special and divinely favoured nation, was Sayo Kitamura's main preoccupation. She proclaimed on the day (August 12th, 1945) that Japan surrendered unconditionally to the Allied Powers that God had chosen her as the True Redeemer to build his kingdom on earth, and to fight the most important of all wars which was the spiritual war against the evils of egotism which were the cause of all suffering and distress (Key to Heaven, 1960: 1–3).

Ogamisama was to develop a novel moral and religious explanation both for Japan's defeat and in support of her mission and this explanation formed part of a more general theory of the relative merits and efficacy of the various sources and kinds of power available to human beings, and of the different forms and levels of civilizations that had so far existed and would come to be. All in all an impressive ideology of change that gave followers the hope of accessing powers residing within the 'soul of Japan' with which to completely rebuild their broken worlds, reconstruct their Japanese identity on stronger foundations than ever before and give Japan itself the leading role in the new order of things that would be built on those highly effective and indestructible spiritual materials which it alone possessed in such abundance.

World War II, Sayo Kitamura was persuaded, was but an allegory and a necessary prelude to the real war to come between good and evil, a central theme of millenarianism. Her explanation of the country's defeat in this war enabled her followers to retain the notion of Japan as special. In a manner resembling biblical explanations of the disaster suffered by the Jewish people and their Hebrew forebears, she told her followers that Japan's defeat was not the result of the military superiority of the Allies, but God's victory for his purpose, which was to make Japan the dominant spiritual power on earth.

Instruments of war, no matter how sophisticated and powerful, were irrelevant to the success or failure of a nation. Japan, she insisted, had been defeated by 'mere bombs'. It was God's intention to turn defeat by such derisory and ineffective instruments of destruction made by simple humans into victory by making Japan the spiritual leader of the world. Bombs had a very limited use: the destruction of those who were unfit to live in God's world which was about to begin.

Her division of the historical process into divine time and human time made all of this easier to accept. Speaking shortly after the bombing of Horoshima she declared the End of the Human World which had lasted 2,605 years and the beginning of God's World which would endure for 2,300 years, and insisted that this was a sign that the 'defeat' of Japan was the sign that it was now ready to assume its role of spiritual pre-eminence in the world for which it had been destined:

> ... this does not mean loosing the war. No, absolutely not. Japan will become the spiritual leader of the world. However, the present Japanese are such maggot beggars that they are unworthy of this responsibility. Let the bombs and shells fall to exterminate the maggots in this country... (The Prophet of Tabuse: 57).

Sayo Kitamura's proclamation of the end of the old order or the 'maggot's world', as she described it, and the beginning of the New Era, of the New World, on Empire Day, February 11th 1945, was an unequivocal condemnation of the emperor, the government and the military. What Japan needed was an invincible leader who would carry on the real war – the spiritual war against evil – and not one played out with artificial and perishable weapons made by mere humans. Interpreting the unconditional surrender of Japan and turning its literal meaning on its head, she insisted:

This surrender does not mean the loss of the war. This is but the end of fighting between maggots. The war will be carried on by Me from now on against evil spirits... Pray and pray for this war can be won by prayer (The Prophet of Tabuse: 57–58).

Other Japanese new religions also saw the defeat of Japan as providential, including Mahikari which explained that 'Su-god made use of Americans in order to bring about a Great Purification of the land – Japan's defeat in World War II' (Davis, 1980: 258). Followers, however, did not always interpret her as meaning that the War would continue on in a spiritual or metaphorical sense. Sayo Kitamura devotees in Hawaii, on the United States mainland and in Brazil were, like many other Japanese immigrants in these lands, to take literally the pronouncement that the war had not been lost and retained for some time the position of being at war with Japan's enemies (See: Hamrin pp. 000). Many Japanese immigrants elsewhere, independently of the teachings of any religious organization, refused to acknowledge defeat. The staunchest of these nationalists were the Shindo-remmei who denounced the attempt to deny the fruits of victory to the emperor's loyal subjects in Brazil. These 'loyal subjects' came to be known as the Kachi-gumi or victory party and insisted – often by violent means including bombs – that what had actualy happened was the reverse of what the Allied Forces had announced. They also provided as proof of their claims doctored photographs, one purporting to show that MacArthur had surrendered to the imperial representative Shigemitsu on board the Missouri in Tokyo harbour, and another showing President Truman and naval officers bowing to the Emperor (Smith, 1979: 61).

Though Ogamisama's advent as the redeemer of the world and harbinger of the 'New Age' or 'Age of God', came earlier, as we have seen, paradise on earth actually began on New Years day 1946, and on February 5th of that same year there took place the symbolic burning of Buddhist sutras and of ancestral tablets, with the express intention of making a clean break with the failure and corruption of the past. Such symbolic burning of religious objects and the prohibition imposed on her followers were not the acts of a revolutionary. Nor were her verbal assaults on the emperor and her masculine demeanour and choice of language motivated by a personal ambition to create a new system of government in Japan, or by the desire to bring about gender equality. Instead, there was to be a new Japan in the sense of one that adhered more closely to its traditions and drew upon its most potent sources of power, the kami. It was a Japan that now had a leader who would ensure that the country received the blessings of the kami which the emperor had failed to secure.

There are several parallels here with Cohn's account (1970) of the millenarian protests of the Franciscan Spirituals of medieval Europe who believed that the popes, by neglecting their ritual duties through becoming over involved in political matters, had broken the vital spiritual link between heaven and earth and had, as a consequence, jeopardised the security of the world. Again, what they sought was not the overthrow of the papal system but an angelic pontiff, a pope dedicated to the fulfilment of his spiritual role, who would keep open the lines between the earthly and supernatural worlds, to ensure that the former was constantly sustained, maintained and directed in its purpose and aims by the latter.

The principal attractions for all in Ogamisama's New World or earthly paradise would be spiritual: it would be a world in which spiritual food and clothing only would be necessary and one in which there would be no need to work, and, echoing Deguchi Nao, one in which social position, honour and misfortune would be absent (The Prophet of Tabuse: 70).

Though, as already indicated, Sayo Kitamura intended to create a female centred world, this would not be a world of gender equality in the sense in which this is understood in the contemporary West. Women would be more important in this New Age of God than in the previous era, labelled the man-centred age, in which physical power ruled the world. Like Tensho, the god who possessed her, and who though female also displayed traditional characteristics, Sayo Kitamura instructed her women followers to be bold and assert themselves, like men. However, Himegamisama, her grand-daughter, appointed successor and current spiritual leader of the movement, explains that the prophetess was not a feminist in search of a Japan where women were treated on equal terms with men. On the contrary for she taught that women must first 'serve to establish their rights' and only those woman who were prepared to do so would have a voice later.[2]

Reflecting on their home life with Sayo Kitamura both Himegamisama and her mother, Ogamisama's daughter-in-law, described the foundress as a 'model' Japanese woman, carrying out the domestic tasks traditionally assigned to women and caring for her family with selflessness and devotion: 'At home she was really a kind mother and grandmother. She was so flexible and so gave a good example to everyone as a mother, wife and grandmother'.[3] However, like Nao Deguchi, her flexibility deserted her when it came to book learning and social climbing. She made her protests against such activities with great vehemence, dressing in the style and using the language of men to do so. This can be seen as her way of becoming a Transformed Male for the purpose of being heard and obeyed. She was God's radio, she would tell her listeners, making any other source of knowledge or learning an irrelevance (The Prophet of Tabuse, 1954).

The Omotokyo and Tensho-Kotai-Jingu-Kyo response to modernization and westernization and their orientation to the world outside Japan, share in common the pursuit of Japanese authenticity which included the dream of a world free of artificial forms and products, a world in which people and things would be as Nature designed and destined them to be. There is also evidence of a battle to be waged between the powers of good and evil, of personal communication with a deity who reveals the outcome of such a conflict and the future course of history, a course that will see the advent of a perfect world of complete happiness and bliss.

But amid the continuity of ideas, beliefs and symbols there is considerable variation between the two movements, and between these two movements and Messianity, as will be seen below. Before discussing Messianity it is worth remembering here that both Omotokyo and Tensho-Kotai-Jingu-Kyo have undergone changes in orientation since the end of World War II, and these changes have occurred in no small measure in response to the profound political, cultural and economic changes in Japan and globally since then. The millenarianism of Omotokyo, Tensho-Kotai-Jingu-Kyo, and Messianity, is a much different phenomenon now than during the life time of their founders; it is less strident and militant, and the object of its invective is no longer the emperor but the polluters of the environment, and paradoxically, strident nationalists, religious fundamentalists, and modern capitalism which, one leading member of Omotokyo, quoting an acquaintance who had predicted the collapse of Communism ten years before it had actually occurred, impressed upon me, 'is destroying itself and our world and opening up a tragic future for the next generation'[4]

Messianity in Japan and the Foundations of Paradise

The life of the founder of Messianity, Mokichi Okada (1882–1955) was fashioned by many diverse and unusual experiences. It began in adverse economic circumstances with his parents attempting to eke out a living from a wayside stall in the Asakusa district of Tokyo. Nor was Okada helped by his formal education which was limited and largely unproductive – like many millenarian prophets he was mostly self taught – or by his general health and personality. As described by Blacker (1971: 580), Okada was diffident, introspective, shy and prone to many illnesses, and reduced to total penury by the earthquake of 1923 which killed over 100,000 people in most of them inhabitants of Tokyo and nearby Yokohama. Other tragedies that deeply affected Okada included the failure of his small newspaper and° money lending business which collapsed when the Soko Bank with which he had financial dealings became insolvent in 1919. Around the same time his wife, who had already suffered the disappointment of one miscarriage and one stillborn child, died in childbirth (In Service to Man, 1980: 14–17). These crises which came when Okada was an unbeliever and led him in search of spiritual support to Omotokyo and the Salvation Army, among other religious organisations.

While acknowledging his membership of Omotokyo and his contacts with the Salvation Army, Messianity insists that Okada always remained an independent thinker who, by means of his own insights and divine

150

revelation, reached the conclusion that his universal salvific mission was too great to be confined to any one particular religion. It is clear that both these movements influenced Okada's understanding of his messianic role.

By 1926 he had already begun to see himself as a messiah, encouraged in this by his experience of almost continuous possession by the Bodhisattva (*bosatsu*) Kannon, who announced that she had chosen him as the vehicle for the salvation of the world by inaugurating a New Age in which there would be no more sickness (Blacker, 1971: 580). But it was not until 1928, while still a member of Omotokyo, that Okada established the *Dainihon Kannonkai* (The Great Japan Association for the worship of the Bodhisattva Kannon) for the purpose of communing with divine beings, and with the therapeutic aim of healing through the laying on of hands, a practice that came to be called *johrei*.

Although referred to as *Kannon-sama* or Lord Kannon, this Bodhisattva is widely regarded as female and widely associated with childbirth in Japan. The historian of Japanese Buddhist art and religion, Anesaki (1923: 17–18) writes of Kannon in much the same way as a Catholic author might write of Our Lady. This Boddhisattva, Anesaki tells us, is 'worshipped as the goddess of mercy'. He says of the last painting by the artist Kano Hogai (d.1888) of this figure that it expresses 'the inexhaustible love of Kannon, the Mother of All', and that it symbolises the 'love of a mother, a virgin mother of heavenly dignity, a pure maternal love', and exhibits 'a depth of tragic compassion' (1923: 18). Even the Hidden Christians (*Kakure Kirishitan*) continued to venerate Kannon whom they referred to as Maria Kannon, and in Brazil Bodhisattva Kannon is paired by some of the Japanese and Japanese-Brazilian communities to Nossa Senhora (Our Lady), in a manner similar to the way the African/Yoruba goddess Yemanja is paired by members of Candomble or African-Brazilian religion, with Mary the Mother of Jesus, and particularly in the form of Mary the Immaculate Conception.

This unambiguous depiction of Kannon as female, as a living and compassionate mother should not be allowed to obscure the fact that this Boddhisattva is a universal figure who can manifest anywhere, spread her blessings anywhere, and one who has the capacity to change into whatever form is necessary in order to come to a person's assistance.

Okada was the recipient of further revelations in 1931, this time from God (called by Messianity *Miroku-o-mitami*) and these occured while he was meditating on Mount Nokigiri (Saw Mountain). At this stage in his self-understanding and in the understanding of his role he took the name Meishu Sama which, although it may be taken to mean simply venerable founder or an equivalent title, according to one expert in Messianity theology, serves to indicate that he is both God and Man.[5] Other members, one a Japanese-Brazilian, who disclaimed the status of theologian, likened Okada's role to that of Jesus, perceiving him to be a divine saviour in human form. This informant also explained that since Messianity's image of God is an abstract one, Nature, they pray to Meishu-Sama who is both God and Man, and saviour, as Christians believe Jesus to be.[6]

Generally this comparison with Jesus as saviour is made by Brazilian members as frequently in Brazil non-Christian religions are interpreted through the medium of Catholic concepts and symbols. On the other hand, the belief in the second coming of Okada as the Messiah seems to be more widespread in Japan than Brazil. In a celebration ceremony that centred on the installation of the Great Miroku Scroll Meishu-sama's spirit was eternally housed as was the scroll in the Shunju-an, the Hall of Springs and Autumns, in the Messianity's Sacred Grounds, Heian-kyo, in Kyoto. This ceremony was performed, it is explained, in fulfilment of the prophecy *Miroku San-e* concerning the Second Coming of Meishu-sama, believed to be the final effort at saving the world through purification (The Completion of Miroku San-e: Dedication of the Great Miroku Scroll, 1995: 63).

Though exceptionally loyal, as already noted, Okada experienced further interference and restriction from government quarters during the period 1935–1945, over his healing activities which, since he had no recognised qualification or license to heal, were considered illegal. After the fall of the war time Japanese government healing or *jorei* became prominent again alongside the stress on communing with the spirits and the movement was renamed *Nihon Kannon Kyodan* (the Japan organization for the worship of Bodhisattva Kannon).

The post 1945 history of Messianity, though mostly free of government interference, has not always been smooth. The movement was to experience internal strife that led to a number of schisms beginning in 1950. This led to the adoption of yet another name *Sekai Meshiya Kyo* (Messianic Religion of the World). This new name plainly revealed the global ambitions of the movement, also clearly evident in the current name Sekai Kyusei Kyo or the Church of World Messianity. The most recent internal split which had lasted for more than a decade and divided the movement into three sections was healed in February 1998. At present and in accordance with Okada's mission objectives the movement is administratively and functionally divided into three principal units: the religious organization known as Sekai Kyusei Kyo or the Church of World Messianity, the Mokichi Okada Association (M.O.A), a philosophy and cultural organization, and Korin, which is concerned chiefly with the production, distribution and sale of naturally grown products.

Okada's Vision of Paradise on Earth

Okada considered two principles to be essential to the building of paradise on earth and these were: *johrei* and *shizen noho*, developed to foster the natural way of healing and food production respectively. By these means

Nature is permitted to use its fecund and high yielding properties to purify, cleanse, heal and restore health and wholeness, and supply the kind of unpolluted, energising foods that human beings require for health and wholeness. Clearly, this concept of Nature has been very strongly influenced by traditional Shinto ideas, and contains both an abstract and concrete meaning. It is both the concrete expression of the kami or gods, or, with the development of a more monotheistic perspective, of God, and also the medium or symbol of their spirit, or of the divine spirit. It also implies process, in the sense of the divine acting upon and shaping events, relationships and life courses.

The concept of *johrei* involves the idea – variants of which are also present in many other new religions, including Christian Science the Aladura or praying churches that emerged in western Africa just after World War I – that medicine is harmful. Evil which, on balance outweighs good, is inextricably linked to illness in Okada's philosophy in the following way: evil deeds create spiritual clouds which pollute the bloodstream leading to the accumulation of toxic substances in the physical body which in turn manifest themselves in sicknesses and misfortunes of various kinds. Evil acts performed in previous lives are particularly difficult to cure and these include cancer.

Through the practice of *johrei* as a method of spiritual healing in which the necessary divine, curative energy is transmitted to the sufferer through the hand of a member qualified to administer it, comes purification and healing. *Shizen noho* incorporates the idea that artificial means of food production, principally the use of chemical fertilisers are harmful, and hence the insistence on the absolute necessity of natural farming. As was mentioned previously, Nature and God are not always easily distinguishable in Messianity discourse, and Okada himself seems to have conflated the two concepts. God, it is often explained by members, cannot be imagined or visualised apart from Nature, a common Japanese view. In the mould of millenarian 'prophets' Okada made this point when proclaiming that a fundamental Truth had been forgotten with potentially disastrous consequences for human civilization:

> In its pure and unadorned state Nature is Truth. The sun always rises in the East and sinks in the West, and every man exists physically by eating sleeping and drinking. These are self-evident facts but human society has reached such a confused state it has lost sight of the utter simplicity of Nature and needs to be reminded that Truth is this simple.. Human sickness and crime, conflict and poverty are all caused by man's deviation from Truth. God intended that he should live under ideal conditions and these will be established when he attunes himself to the Laws of Nature (In Service to Man, 1980: 31–32).

According to Messianity's own account of the development of his thinking, the realisation of the absolute sanctity of Nature and of its all powerful essence came to Mokichi Okada after his failed attempt to raise the level of food production in Japan in the 1930s by using chemical fertilisers and the most modern farming techniques. He then became convinced that whatever contravened the orderly movement of Nature could never succeed, and reached the conclusion that all sickness, poverty and crime were ultimately the result of human beings having lost sight of the 'utter simplicity of Nature' (In Service to Man, 1980: 32).

Okada as Prophet of the New Age and World Saver

Though largely ignored in western accounts of the contemporary New Age Movement, Okada was, in reality, among the first of its modern 'prophets'. By the 1940s his thinking about the world had changed from a narrow, pre-World War II perspective which saw Japan as its cultural, political and spiritual centrepiece to a wider vision that focused on East-West co-operation and understanding, a perspective found in Indian new religions, among others, including Theosophy.

Among the most important of those outside influences already referred to which contributed to the development of Okada's millenarian vision were his exposure to Christianity through Omotokyo and the Salvation Army in Tokyo. He regularly gave donations to the latter in the 1920s toward its charitable works, and especially toward the welfare of discharged criminals and through his contacts with the movement came to know better the New Testament. Okada acknowledged his debt to the New Testament (In Service to Man, 1980: 17), and, drawing on this source, he described his mission as the fulfilment of the prophecy made by Jesus about the coming of the kingdom of heaven:

> I believe that in the Bible there are three especially important prophecies to be noted. These are the final judgement, the kingdom of heaven at hand (sic), and the second coming of Christ. Of the three, the judgement is directly performed by God when He is ready, and the second coming of Christ will be manifested by Him in His right time; these two need no explanations. But the second prophecy, that concerning the kingdom of heaven, must be fulfilled through the hand of man. This, of course, means that someday somebody will appear, make the plan and actually achieve the goal (Foundations of Paradise, 1984: 46).

This 'somebody' had to appeal to and unite East and West whose relationship so far had been guided by principles that on their own made for separation and conflict: *daijō* and *shōjō* (In Service to Man, 1984: 90–91).

Daijō is a horizontally, inclusive principle found largely in the liberal and more materialistic cultures of western civilization and *shōjō* a vertical, narrow and uncompromising principle, more in evidence in Oriental society. The new principle to bring both together and enable the creation of paradise on earth was *izunome*, symbolised by a cross:

> Up to today the East has stood for the vertical principle, and the West for the horizontal principle. This is why Orientals cherished the idea of ancestor reverence, the virtue of loyalty and filial piety. This is why they maintained a strict class system.
>
> In the West affection between husband and wife formed the keynote, expanding to love for one's fellow man and all humanity.
>
> The East adhering to the vertical and the West the horizontal, there has been little understanding between the two, which has often given rise to conflicts.
>
> However, the time is at hand for the vertical and the horizontal principles to merge and form the balanced cross, *izunome*. A happy unification of East and West will be the result. Only then can humanity enter the ideal state of true civilization and experience paradise on earth (In Service to Man, 1980: 91)

As proof of the universal nature of his mission Okada refused to be identified as Japanese and spoke of himself as a 'citizen of the world', and, moreover, he encouraged his followers to 'have a world consciousness', to shed old ways of self-identification and become 'New Age individuals' (Foundations of Paradise, 1984: 388).

He even claimed to be the recipient of a divine revelation of the coming New Age and predicted that it would culminate in a paradise on earth, and that the means to construct such a paradise – essentially the channelling of *johrei* and natural farming – were revealed to him personally and only to him. Through *johrei* intense divine activity would be transmitted throughout the universe enabling people to actively participate in the building of paradise on earth and thereby secure a place in it for themselves. Okada insisted that the time for constructing an earthly paradise was now, that the builder of the kingdom of heaven on earth 'was in our group', and that his mission was to fulfil the prophecy made by Jesus.

Motivated by the conviction of his own special status and calling, Okada set about building models of paradise on earth. Three were eventually constructed, one at the hot spring resort of Hakone close to Mount Fuji, which was begun in 1944, and is known as the Sacred Ground (or Soil) of the Divine Kingdom. Another was started in 1945 at the hot spring resort of Atami on the Izu peninsula, and was named the Sacred Ground of the Celestial Kingdom. A third was built on the outskirts of Kyoto, and was called the Sacred Ground of the Kingdom of Tranquillity. All three express the idea of paradise as a world from which evil, rooted in the mind, had

155

been eliminated, an interpretation, Okada believed, that was supported by the teachings of other great prophets:

> The end of the world prophesied by Jesus and founders of other new religions is nothing other than the end of the world of evil. What is going to come after that is the ideal world, paradise on earth, in which disease, poverty and conflict will be completely eradicated. It will be a world filled with truth, virtue and beauty, a world of Maitreya as prophesied by the Buddha (Foundations of Paradise: 28)

On other occasions he describes paradise on earth as '... a place where all who have reached a state of genuine happiness are unified in one world' (Foundations of Paradise: 243), and as 'a world of happy people, free from poverty, disease and conflict, with a most highly evolved civilization' (Foundations of Paradise: 241). Disease was identified as the primary cause of poverty, and disease itself was caused by wrong thinking (Foundations of Paradise: 242) reinforcing Blacker's point that in the case of the millenarianism of the *shinkō shūkyō* or newly arisen religions:

> '... the Enemy or Tyrant whose destruction is necessary before the millennium can come to pass is neither a specific hated race nor a specific class. It is simply and a little undramatically, "wrong thinking". To bring the earthly paradise into being we must simply learn to think aright...' (1971: 598)

Calligraphy, ceramics, horticulture, paintings, art and beautiful things generally, figure prominently in Okada's plans for acieving this and saving the world. Their use for this purpose distinguished what he termed 'old religion', essentially Japanese Buddhism, from 'new religion'. The main weakness of the former was its incapacity to transmit truth and virtue through beauty. He likewise distinguished civilizations. 'Old' civilizations were those without a soul, which treated only the symptoms of disease, failing to realise that all that exists has a soul and that the true cause of sickness was to be found 'on the inside' (Foundations of Paradise: 254).

Okada continued to develop his interests in art and horticulture after World War II and used them as a means of expressing ideas about the form and content of paradise on earth. This inspired the building of museums at both Hakone and Atami to house his valuable, varied and extensive art collection which includes the much admired, treasured and valuable jar from the Edo period with the wisteria pattern by Nonomura Ninsei.

Natural beauty in the form of flowers, like art, was an essential prerequisite of paradise. He illustrated what he believed was his unique vision of paradise on earth through the creation of a new kind of garden at Gora, Hakone, said to be different from anything ever seen before in Japan. Describing this garden, named the Shinsen-kyo, the Divine Garden, he claimed to have freed himself from tradition – in a similar way to Onisaburo Deguchi who believed his tea bowl 'Paradise 28', previously referred to, radically altered perceptions of tea bowl design – by developing a completely new way of structuring and understanding the purpose of a garden:

> This place is rich with rocks of fantastic shapes, which I have used to make unique arrangements as revealed to me by God. I have collected several varieties of trees and I have had them planted according to my inspired ideas. In designing cascades and small streams, I have enhanced all the natural materials. In other words, following God's Plan, in Shinsen-kyo I have harmoniously combined the beauty of Nature and the man-made beauty of natural gardening (Foundations of Paradise: 263).

In discussing the purpose of his new landscape forms, he emphasised that their primary objective was to stimulate in all who saw them that innate sense of beauty which every human being possessed. The effect would be to develop character and purify the spiritual body by dispelling spiritual clouds. The horticulturist, and the artist, in the broadest sense of the term, have a crucial role to play in this by appealing through their own soul to the souls of others (Foundations of Paradise: 254).

Okada meant by art more than fine paintings, fine music, fine literature and beautiful gardens. Art was everything that was based upon and in harmony with the conditions of truth, beauty and virtue. Spiritual healing or *johrei* is art, but illness is not art because the one who is ill is unbalanced, that is, not in a true state of being which is perfect health. *Johrei* restores this natural balance and in that sense is a form of art. In line with this tradition Okada imbued aesthetic forms with ethical importance, chiefly by insisting that things and the relationships between them must retain their natural or authentic shape and form, ensuring harmony everywhere and in everything. Plants must be grown naturally, that is in the proper location and soil, and facing in the direction that conforms to their nature or soul. He felt certain that all plants, all living things, have consciousness and 'perhaps', he said, 'they are exactly like us human beings' (The Foundations of Paradise: 273). Although they will attempt to adapt if wrongly planted, demonstrating that they have a soul that is struggling to express its true nature, the failure to allow Nature to operate unhindered results in disharmony and/or a state of 'impurity' in which 'unclean' or bad practice prevails.

As we have seen, Okada believed that these truths were being forgotten, with potentially tragic consequences. Greatly depressed by the climate of disease and poverty in Japan in the 1940s and 1950s he had lost hope in the old order. War in particular had unleashed huge amounts of what he termed 'animalistic power', the very stuff of future wars, and of conflict and crime. It was imperative to spread the practice of *johrei* to eliminate this 'animalistic' element of human nature if future catastrophes were to be avoided. Another, and most effective way of removing it, was by exposing people to beauty through the cultivation and distribution of flowers. He insisted that everywhere there were people there should be flowers, including in every goal and even in every prison cell, as this would do much to elevate people's consciousness and thereby alleviate considerably 'the negativities of today's world' (The Foundations of Paradise: 272).

Like millenarian prophets generally, Okada spoke in apocalyptic tones of a long dark period of suffering symbolised by night, in contrast to the New Age symbolised by day, 'a glorious day filled with Light...' and predicted that:

> A period of great destruction and then reconstruction such as mankind has never experienced before will come to pass (Foundations of Paradise: 401).

In the Age of Night water was the active 'ruling force' while the spirit of fire was less powerful. In the Age of Daylight the situation would be reversed with fire the dominant force turning darkness into light as it intensified, and creating what millenarians everywhere look for: a clearer distinction between good and evil, right and wrong. The turning of night into day would occur first in the spiritual realm and would then be projected in stages onto the spiritual world at large. There had already been two stages, the first in 1881 and the second in 1931. But before the projection that would turn night into day could take place on the physical plane a major catastrophe, interpreted as a cleansing action, would occur. Catastrophe, suffering and distress were in Okada's mind, along with good deeds, means of purification that led to the elimination of the above mentioned spiritual clouds that gave rise to every kind of sickness and misfortune.

This theodicy was constructed by Okada to explain the terrible suffering experienced by many Japanese, particularly in the immediate aftermath of the Second World War. Such suffering, he wrote, 'was nothing other than the purification of the clouds this country formed by invading other countries, exploiting other races, and killing many people' (Foundations of Paradise: 302).

Despite the use of traditional concepts, rituals and ideas, there is no nostalgia in his teachings for some past golden age. All that had happened in the past, including the evil, was given purpose and meaning by being interpreted as necessary to progress. Civilization must move forward and through the construction of models of paradise Okada believed that he was mapping out the route it should take and building confidence in the future. Again, like millenarian prophets everywhere, he saw nothing even remotely unrealistic about his mission:

... the realisation of paradise on earth is not mere idealism, for miraculous advancements toward our goal are actually being made. Also as part of our plan we have designed prototypes of the highest state of paradise on earth, have chosen places of tremendous scenic beauty in Atami and Hakone and have laid the groundwork. We are now engaged in the landscaping and construction of the buildings. When these are complete we will show the people of the world how sublimely beautiful and good the highest heaven is. Essentially paradise on earth can also be called a work of art... (Foundations of Paradise, 1984: 123).

With the stagnation of the movement in Japan, present day optimism regarding the success of Messianity's global mission centres on the movement abroad, and in particular on Thailand and Brazil, and it is to the crucial role of its activities in pursuit of paradise on earth in Brazil, and through Brazil, globally, that the focus of this presentation now shifts.

Brazil as Catalytic Converter

Messianity's millenarianism in Japan, we have seen, was given concrete expression in the construction of models of paradise on earth in Hakone, Atami and Kyoto and this path has been followed in Brazil where the movement has constructed its *Solo Sagrado* or Sacred Ground for Latin America at Guarapiranga in the state of Sao Paulo. It has plans for the construction of a New Age City further south in the state of Parana, which it refers to as the 'Noah's Ark of the twenty first century'. The stated purpose of both the *Solo Sagrado* and the New Age City is to lay the foundations of a New Era, of a new global civilization.

This mission represents a profound shift in Messianity's mission thinking and strategy in Brazil. Now one of the two largest Japanese new religions in Brazil, the other being Seicho no Ie (House of Growth), it was initially concerned with Japanese immigrants only. Japanese immigration to Brazil began in 1908, and today there are an estimated one million three hundred thousand people of Japanese descent in the country, the majority of whom live in the region of Greater Sao Paulo. Most of the early arrivals were agricultural labourers and came as family units of a kind, the Brazilian government insisting on at least three 'enchadas', hoes, in each group. Wages were low, illiteracy high, nutrition and medical facilities poor. Considerable numbers died, chiefly from malaria, and possibly in some cases from the heavy smoking of rope – cigarettes were unavailable (Handa, 1980:128) – and many others broke their contracts and fled from the colonia in which they were settled to build a better life for themselves and their families. Now 'free' they bought up inexpensive and poor quality land, set up agricultural co-operatives, and built settlements of which the school was the focal point. Religion consisted of emperor veneration and rudimentary ancestral rituals. There were few trained religious officials and anyone who could read with the requisite piety and gravitas presided at ceremonies and were known as 'bozos feitos na hora', monks created on the spot, or 'bozos substitutos', substitute monks (Maeyama, 1983).

Few of the first generation immigrants became Brazilian citizens and many regarded themselves as 'kimin' or unwanted people. Not only were they opposed to mixing with non-Japanese Brazilians but they also distanced themselves from the less insular and more modern, more educated outlook of the nisei or second generation immigrants, and the post World War II immigrants from Japan, referring to themselves as 'Meiji men' or real Japanese in contrast with these superficial ways of being Japanese.

A dramatic change ocurred after World War II as many issei, or first generation immigrants, also resigned themselves to remaining in Brazil, or, as they expressed it, to having their bones interred in their children's country (Smith, 1978: 59). Many felt ignored and neglected by Japan and had also come to feel that the Brazilian life style generally and personal relationships in particular were more relaxed than in Japan, and appreciated this. Many issei who returned to Japan after either shortly before or just after World War II with the intention of remaining there only to come back to Brazil within a matter of a few years unable to settle down to the more regimented life back home.

With the decision to remain in Brazil came the development of a more formal religious life among the Japanese. Now proper ancestral and burial rites in particular were demanded, and these replaced the veneration of the Emperor as the main religious concerns. By the 1950s when the new religions began to propagate their teachings among theJapanese immigrants substantial numbers of the latter, especially among the nisei and sansei, had become Catholics largely as a result of attending Catholic schools. Catholicism, on account of its schools, political influence, and wealth, was also associated with success, while the Japanese old and new religions which taught in Japanese and used Japanese in their rituals were cut off from the nisei and sansei, most of whom spoke little of the language of their parents. This, and the rise in the number of out-marriages among the nisei and sansei convinced most of the new religions including Messianity that if they were to have a future even in the Japanese community in Brazil they would have to adapt their teachings and practices and introduce Portuguese as the main language of communication and religious discourse. This strategy would also enable them to reach out to the wider society which since the 1940s had been undergoing a process of rapid industrialization and urbanization. Such outreach was essential, moreover, if these religions, many of which hoped to make the local branches pay for themselves and even become profitable concerns were to realize their millenarian dreams of constructing models of paradise on earth.

Modernization per se had few organised opponents in Brazil. What was strongly opposed was its social and economic effects, particularly over-urbanization, already mentioned, and the consequent chronic under-employment and unemployment, especially in Sao Paulo and Rio (Vasquez, 1998). The Japanese population was also migrating in ever increasing numbers to the towns in pursuit of education with a view to improving its chances in commerce, politics and the professions. The Japanese new religions, with much experience from Japan planned to offer healing, their most attractive feature, an ethic for daily living in a competitive and overpopulated environment, new forms of community, rites for reinforcing family links disrupted by migration, advice on bringing up children in an urban setting, and techniques for coping with stress and at the same time for preparing mentally to maximise the benefits to be derived from full involvement in life.

Messianity when it began its activities in Brazil in 1955, like most of the other Japanese new, and old, religions – the Pure Land, Zen, Shingon and Tendai schools of Buddhism all have temples in Brazil – was a small, ethnic religion, composed almost entirely of Japanese or Brazilians of Japanese descent. However, in a relatively short period of time beginning in the late 1960s, Messianity in Brazil was to experience phenomenal growth making its fortunes and influence there very different to those in the United States, both on the mainland and in Hawaii, where it has no more than five thousand members, and to those in Europe and Australia, where its membership is also low.

One major contributory factor to the difference in Messianity's fortunes in Brazil has been effectiveness of its policy of inculturation which accompanied the spectacular rise in its membership from just several thousand in the late 1960s, over ninety per cent of whom were either Japanese or of Japanese descent, to an estimated three hundred and twenty thousand by the late 1980s, over ninety per cent of whom were Brazilians of non Japanese origin (Clarke, 1995b). At the time of writing the membership is estimated at around three hundred and twenty thousand in Brazil, higher than Thailand where it has likewise made impressive gains the present membership standing at around 250,000.[7]

In Messianty's strategic plan to save the world the role of Brazil is perform the function of a catalytic converter. The conviction of the leadership is that Brazil, energised and directed by Messianity's teachings, its constructions such as the *Solo Sagrado* and the *New Age City*, its natural farms and the developing network for the distribution of organically produced foods, has already begun to act to convert people from activities that poison the world, especially in the area of food production and health care, to ones that conform with the Laws of Nature. By the year 2020, it is predicted, Brazil will be widely recognised as providing humanity as a whole with a prototype for survival, with the teachings and practices that will enable it to avoid self destruction and enjoy forever the good and harmonious life.

Fully committed to the notion of the geomancy of buildings and shrines, the construction of models of paradise on earth and of New Age Cities, is one of Messianity's principal means in Brazil of using its spiritual power to transform the surrounding society. The models built in Brazil will, it is believed, provide such compelling examples of modern living in conformity with the natural environment and with the all round potential of human beings, that eventually citizens throughout the country will demand the same standards and style of life from their government. The next and final stage of world transformation will begin when, with increasing contact, made not only possible but inevitable by the global revolution in communications and technology, this demand begins to spread from Brazil to the rest of the world. This in essence is how Messianity understands its global mission.

While the rapid progress made by Messianity in Brazil so far gives an indication of the mobilising and motivating power of millenarian belief, like charisma, the dynamism that this belief can generate is inclined to evaporate quickly. It is, thus, in constant need of stimulation and nourishment, especially where heavy financial commitments are involved, such as those incurred by the construction of a model of an earthly paradise and a New Age City. Messianity in Brazil, therefore, is constantly devising schemes to ensure that millenarian belief remains active and strong, and the most recent initiative for this purpose is the 'Flower for a Better World' campaign – flowers figure prominently as symbols of transformation in Messianity spirituality – which involves the making and the distribution of a flower to every Brazilian home by the year 2000, a massive operation, but one that is well underway. Millions of flowers have already been distributed and by April 1998 plans were well advanced for the distribution of ten million flowers in the month of September 1998 alone. However, it is Messianity's two major undertakings in Brazil in pursuit of its global mission, and the popular response to these initiatives, that I wish to focus on below.

Messianity's Brazilian Model of Paradise on Earth or *Solo Sagrado*

Messianity's magnificent *Solo Sagrado* at Guarapiranga in the state of Sao Paulo was inaugurated on November 9th 1995. This vast complex was largely the work of Brazilian members, who in their thousands volunteered their skills and labour, beginning in 1991, to built Messianity's Sacred

Ground for Latin America on 370,000 square metres of land surrounding the Guarapiranga dam which supplies Sao Paulo with its water.

In constructing the *Solo Sagrado* the natural forests, which form part of the Mata Atlantica, were preserved and extended by the plantation of four thousand more trees, as were the five lakes. Flowers abound, and among the most striking and numerous are the ten thousand square metres of azalea bushes. There is a computerised underground irrigation system at work preserving the quality of the water, and great care was taken to ensure that the sewage system did not pollute the dam. The electrical power supply, telephone circuit, and television sound circuit, are all located underground. There are no telegraph poles or wires, no pylons, nothing that might obscure or distract from the view of the perfectly laid out and meticulously cared for landscaped gardens, which are entirely free of weeds, and of the natural beauty of the surroundings that speak of life in paradise.

The design of the main temple and centre piece of the Sacred Grounds is based on that of Stonehenge and stands elevated on its own plaza in the centre of the gardens. The decision to use this model was inspired by a supernatural source which informed the president of Messianity in Brazil, the Reverend Tetsuo Watanabe, of its wishes in a dream. The choice of this model was also made to demonstrate the uniqueness of Messianity's mission; by choosing a symbol different from any associated with the major world religions, Messianity in Brazil; its president explained, was a way both of expressing this uniqueness and of avoiding rivalry and poor relationships with other religions.[8]

Circular in shape, the temple is supported by sixteen pillars, each eighteen metres in height, with a centrepiece in the form of a tower seventy one metres high which can be seen from the Avenida Paulista, the main street in Sao Paulo. The circular formation of the slender, unadorned pillars of this central place of worship, with its main altar and two side altars, one for the veneration of the ancestors and the other for the veneration of Meishu Sama, not only resembles a pre-Christian, solar temple, but is so structured and positioned as to secure the same effect as Stonehenge at the Winter solstice.

The *Solo Sagrado* is more than purely symbolic and ornamental. Training of staff, retreats and refresher courses take place there, and the monthly ceremony attracts thousands of members from all over Brazil. There are also numerous out buildings which serve as centres of Sangetsu, the special, and, as Messianity likes to stress, the essentially very natural and simple form of flower arranging developed by Mokichi Okada, calligraphy, and ceramics. The names of the pathways and assembly areas also speak of heaven on earth: there is paradise way, and a peace, harmony, friendship, hope, happiness and love plaza. All has been designed to enable the individual to feel in harmony with Nature and thereby grow spiritually.

An even more ambitious and more costly project than the Solo Sagrado is the construction of the previously mentioned New Age City or Cidade da Nova Era.

Daily Life in Messianity's New Age City

Messianity's attempt to realise the dream of building an earthly paradise by constructing a New Age city, clearly illustrates how reality imposes its will on idealism. The search is on for an ideal location and the basic infrastructure must be completed within ten years, Brazilian members were informed by the movements' third spiritual leader in November 1998.[9]

It is not intended that this New Age City should be a city standing apart from the rest of society, nor will its inhabitants be radically different from anyone else in terms of their attributes, needs and pursuits. Unlike the early followers of Omotokyo and Tensho-Kotai-Jingu-Kyo, they will require education and be subjected to laws; there will be crime and familiar kinds of punishment such as imprisonment; there will be a cash economy, a banking system run largely on traditional lines, and market forces will dictate economic policy; and the nuclear family will be the main building block of social and moral life. Most of the practices associated with living in society today will be retained.

However, there will soon be a fundamental difference between life in the New Age City and life as lived at present: there will be no sickness, no pollution, no poverty, no want, no disharmony, and every institution will function optimally and in an ideal way.

Messianity's response to questions concerning the form and content of education, political life, business and commercial life and legal and other activities in the New Age City, is prefaced by the comment that all has to be carried on within the existing law. It also insists that the New Age is not to be brought about by abandoning society to its fate and joining the community of the elect, or by ignoring it, or by circumventing or violating existing law. It is, however, convinced that where existing law is defective Natural Law, by and of itself, will triumph. But whatever its defects, existing law also leaves considerable scope for new initiatives and experiments in all spheres of life.[10]

Therefore, within the constraints of the law, Messianity's educational policy will be to introduce teaching on 'much more useful subjects' such as the Law of Nature and Art. In the area of health care, the current most widely practised form of medicine, allopathic, disease centred medicine, will likewise have to be respected. This notwithstanding, Messianity's four hundred doctors will simultaneously educate people to understand that true, effective medicine does not consist of taking remedies in the form of pills and other artificial treatments, but of allowing the body's organism to develop and heal according to the Law of Nature. Colds and other ailments, the inhabitants will learn, are forms of purification, and by taking artificial remedies the process of healing is impeded. In practice, among members, a dual approach is the most common response to healing. A survey of practices relating to healing showed that almost all the members of Messianity in Brazil would use *johrei* for a wide range of illnesses from influenza to cancer, and just over fifty per cent would use *johrei* only for all illnesses.[11]

Voluntarism will characterise Messianity's approach to politics also; there will be no attempt to impose the political programme of the City of the New Age. The normal system of democratic government in keeping with existing political arrangements will be respected and implemented: there will be elections for prefects, councillors and other officials. The hope is, however, that the effect of Messianity's education and training will be to inspire the people to elect representatives who implement policies in harmony with the Law of Nature.

Religious tolerance and co-operation will mark its dealings with other religions. There will be no Messianity version of sixteenth century Calvinist Geneva or of the 'cuius regio eius religio' principle endorsed at Augsburg (1555), making the religion of the 'principality' that of the ruler. To be intolerant and exclusive in these and other ways would, it is explained, be self defeating as all need to learn to live within the Law of Nature.[12]

A number of other comments on Messianty's attitude to other religions are worth making here before moving on to discuss the rest of its New Age City policies. Messianity is syncretistic in the sense that it is prepared, as we have seen, to adapt to other faiths, although the motivation for this is complex. In Brazil Messianity worship includes such prayers as the Our Father, and respect and veneration are given to Mary, the Mother of Jesus, while Jesus himself is held in the highest esteem. This is also the case across a range of Japanese new religions in Brazil, including Seicho no Ie, whose members often claim to have acquired a deeper understanding and devotion to Jesus than during their Catholic and/or Christian days. Even those who remain Catholics and/or Christians find the Jesus of the Japanese new religions of more significance and relevance than the one they had been brought up to believe in and worship.[13] Moreover, the emphasis on healing and ancestor veneration provide familiar and attractive parallels with that widely popular religion of African origin, Umbanda, and with Spiritism, particularly Kardecian Spiritism which has millions of paractitioners in Brazil.

Assimilation and adaptation are part of the temporary strategy of moving out beyond the Japanese communities to attract the non-Japanese population of Brazil, and not necessarily of a desire for religious integration. Certainly there are some signs that the stronger numerically, educationally and culturally a movement becomes the more it sheds its

Catholic and/or Christian rituals, prayers and beliefs for a less Christian and more obviously Japanese inspired cultural, philosophical, and humanistic approach. The tendency, once growth seems assured, is to prioritise Japanese ways of expressing and symbolising both the divine and the ideal or perfect world, Japanese approaches to the education of children and Japanese solutions to family problems and those of everyday life in general.

Thus, to the observer, syncretism can seem to be as much a device for expansion as it is a form of tolerance of religious differences, although this quality is not necessarily absent whatever the nature of the motivation. The course that relations will take between Messianity and other religions in the future cannot be easily predicted. Religious movements have a tendency to vary their approach to each other over time when they realise the effects on membership of being either too close or too distant to other traditions. The openness and eclecticism, or the intolerance and dogmatism that characterise their relationships at one stage of their history in a new environment are not necessarily to be understood as permanent features of these movements. The history of Catholic-non-Catholic relations in Brazil illustrates this point. Catholicism in pre-nineteenth century Brazil was more tolerant of and open to Candomble and/or African-Brazilian ritual than in the period c.1850–c.1960, and much less tolerant of Japanese religions in Brazil in the period c.1930–c.1960 than it is today.

While in the New Age City tolerance is to be the guiding principle of Messianity's attitude to other religions and other ways of life, there will be forms of exclusion, democratic ones, by which those that do not conform to the Law of Nature can be made to leave the New Age City. If actions are promoted that are destructive of the environment, then those responsible will be obliged by the majority to depart. This does not mean that all opposition to the Law of Nature will be outlawed. If an individual, religion or organization wishes to speak out against the principles of the Law of Nature that will be permitted. However, to act against those principles would be 'unlawful'.

Tolerance apart, a crucial test of the credibility of New Age City policies is its use of natural resources. The very construction of a New Age City itself makes great demands on natural as well as human resources and there is much concern in Brazil over the destruction of the forests. When asked about the building materials that will be used to construct the City of the New Age, Messianity's response is to trust that the Law of Nature will determine the kinds of the material to be used. Wood will be made use of but a limit will be imposed on the number of 'natural trees sacrificed'. Concrete will also be used so as to cut down on iron.[14]

Messianity's New Age City's social policy distinguishes it more than anything else from other millenarian movements, whether religious or secular. Violent crime and family breakdown are two of the most serious concerns in contemporary Brazil and Messianity's solution to these and other social and moral ills is to change the system of money lending. It sees its task as that of persuading the banking system and the multinationals to radically change their system of lending to allow the financially deprived agricultural worker to borrow without being obliged to purchase agrotoxic fertilisers as part of the requirement. The present arrangement has a twofold destructive effect with disastrous social and medical consequences: it is responsible for making the cost of borrowing prohibitive and for destroying the land. This not only gives rise to debt, bankruptcy, and poor quality food but also to the intractable problem in Brazil, and throughout the developing world, of overcrowded cities, as poor farmers, without the financial means to work the land, abandon it in ever increasing numbers and rush to the towns. Sao Paulo alone has an estimated four million people living in shanty towns or favellas, as they are known, and the growth rate of favellas in Rio since Brazil's economic boom began in the 1950s has been astronomical (Velasquez, 1998). Unemployed and penniless, some migrants are forced to take the paths of violence, drug peddling and prostitution in order to survive. The Messianity solution to violent crime concludes that by providing the conditions that would allow people to stay on the land society would virtually eradicate its three most threatening and serious problems: crime, insecurity and the breakdown of family life.

Messianity's idealism is tempered by realism. While members accept that these problems cannot be completely eradicated in one life time there is the hope that they can be reduced to humanly manageable proportions. Even life in its terrestrial paradise will never be entirely free of crime, whatever the banking system's lending arrangements, and this will necessitate some kind of penal system. On the question of retribution Messianity believes that there is no best way to punish crime; the real and lasting solution lies in reforming the criminal by creating an environment in which he and/or she is able both to receive and to offer love and gratitude.

Many of Messianity's attitudes to and ways of understanding and interpreting human nature will be very familiar to the visitor to the City of the New Age. For example, there will be competition at all levels of society on the grounds that this is natural. There will also be differentials in earnings, and men and women will have to perform different roles. Essentially the man will be the provider and the woman the nurturer with responsibility for the domestic sphere.

Much of the detail of the policies and the administrative framework of the New Age City still remain to be worked out. Millenarians commonly have a general vision of the perfect world which can be symbolised and expressed more easily through natural things – flowers, water, plants, shrubs and trees, and through fine arts such as ceramics, as in the case of Onisaburo Deguchi's tea bowl, 'Paradise 28' described above, than a detailed plan of action. Translating this dream into practice means introducing rules, bureaucracy and other 'profane' measures which engender routine and formalism, and diminish its dynamism and appeal.

Not only do present social and environmental conditions facilitate a millenarian approach but also from the perspective of Messianity's theology it is imperative that the movement continues to build paradise on earth. Its interpretation of the belief in reincarnation, to recapitulate, means that after death a person can only advance so far along the spiritual path before returning to earth, and this pattern is repeated. It is imperative, therefore, for believers to create a terrestrial paradise, otherwise on their return, they will find a situation worse than the one they left behind, and one in which it will be impossible to advance spiritually. Thus, the dire warning, intended no doubt to strengthen faith, by its president in Brazil: 'If we don't create a paradise here, it will be like returning to hell'.[15] Moreover, the state of life on earth impacts on the spiritual life in heaven, reinforcing the belief that there is no alternative to paradise on earth:

> People live in heaven as on earth; paradise is not simply a place where one sings and sleeps, but where we live the Law of Nature with happiness and without suffering.[16]

Apocalyptic gloom does feature in the discourse on the advent of the New Age in the Brazilian context, but in a more controlled way, than in the Japanese situations discussed above. The movement's Brazilian president Watanabe insists that there will be no Armageddon in the classical sense, no end of the world through nuclear war, but great illness and unhappiness, if the Law of Nature is not respected, particularly if there is failure to eliminate agrotoxic substances. There will be food to eat in plenty but, as was noted above, it will not be worth eating, and the quality of life as a whole will remain extremely low, thus defeating the whole purpose of living which is to evolve spiritually and in every aspect of one's being by living in accordance with Nature.[17]

The Response of Brazilian Members to Messianity's Millenarian Vision and Activities

So far we have examined the thoughts of the leadership of Messianity in Brazil on the construction of paradise on earth and I now wish to concentrate more on the 'naive theory' of Messianity's millenarianism: on the understanding, hopes, beliefs and dispositions of the 'ordinary' members, on what millenarianism means to them personally and collectively. This 'naive' theory can have a significant influence on the orientation of the movement as a whole by helping to ensure that Messianity in Brazil is not a mere satellite of the mother church in Japan but an integral and, at the same time, self-governing partner in a global movement.

The content and purpose of the millenarian faith and commitment of the 'ordinary' members of Messianity in Brazil were ascertained through interviews, questionnaires, and participant observation on many occasions at ceremonies, particularly in Salvador, Bahia, north-eastern Brazil, and in Sao Paulo, in the south of the country, where the majority of the members reside and where there are many more followers of Japanese descent. In Bahia, and the north-eastern region of Brazil as a whole, including Belem in the state of Para, Messianity has an estimated 20,000 active members and, to the best of my knowledge, apart from several of the pastors, known locally as reverendo, no more than a hundred are Japanese, or of Japanese origin.

There is considerable diversity of attitude and opinion among ordinary members depending on background, age, length of time in the movement, personal circumstances and other social, economic and psychological variables. These variables notwithstanding, there are basically two main types of member. Firstly, there is a minority that professes to uphold absolute standards; for whom the dividing line between good and evil is perfectly clear, and whose unswerving hope in the coming of a new world enables them to dispense with many of the practicalities and, as they would see them, the limitations, imposed by logic and reason. Then, there is the majority who are more prone to compromise, for whom gradualness is a virtue and not a sign of lack of faith, and who are not overly preoccupied with the timing of things. Not only is there diversity among members there is also change in their opinions and attitudes. Interviews carried out with the same person at different points in time show developments or alterations in that person's understanding of millenarian belief.

From whatever angle they are considered, including that of their own material conditions, the majority of the 'ordinary members' of Messianity in Brazil as a whole do not appear, if we go by the scholarly literature on this subject, to be the stuff of which millenarians are made. They do not display the kind of paranoia and rootlessness, or the debilitating anomie, often associated in scholarly discourse with those involved in such apparently escapist and unrealistic enterprises as millenarian movements. Nor are they starry-eyed visionaries and idealists either. Moreover, there is little in the general cultural, religious or spiritual background of this majority that can help to explain their later involvement in an intensely millenarian movement. Before joining Messianity most, 60 per cent of respondents, had been Catholics, some, around 15 per cent, were formerly either Protestant or Spiritualist, and 25 per cent did not belong to any religion.[18]

Those Messianity members who were formerly Christians appear to have been remarkably ignorant of, or unresponsive to, apocalyptic ideas and prophecies about the End of the World, such as those of Nostradamus, which have at various times played a large part in the thinking and recruitment strategy of several Japanese new religions including Kofuku no Kagaku, Agonshu, and Aum Shinrikyo (Kisala, 1998: 143–157). Furthermore, only a small minority expressed any interest in astrology, channelling, divination, out of the body or near death experiences, or Ufology. As to alternative religions, again only a minority had been involved in these. While Spiritualism was the most popular alternative, there was surprisingly little interest in the African Brazilian religions of Candomble and Umbanda. Likewise, few had experimented with alternative forms of medicine, apart from homeopathy practised by some 22 per cent.

A majority of members were perhaps a little unusual in that, prior to joining Messianity, they had developed an interest in things Japanese, and this was mostly in martial arts, or flower arranging, or Japanese cuisine. The Japanese origins of the movement were important for a majority, and more so for members in Sao Paulo than for those in Bahia. While the reasons given were variable most were based on the idea of Japan as uniquely favoured in terms of geography, history and spirituality. Also frequently expressed was the idea of the Japanese as endowed with the necessary personal attributes to transmit the divine message concerning the way ahead for this present age, and to efficiently establish the structures necessary to implement it across the world. Members spoke of Japan as a more spiritual country than Brazil, of its divinely arranged geographical location in the East, which made it a 'channel of the Light' for the world as a whole, and of its having been chosen by God to fulfil a special mission.[19]

The strongest attraction, initially, for a majority was *johrei* or spiritual healing. Most of the members came to know of this through a friend or through someone in the family, or through an acquaintance, in that order. Several other Japanese new religions in Brazil, including Perfect Liberty Kyodan, made their first breakthrough as healing movements. However, as has been shown in many cases, what at first attracts an individual to a movement does not necessarily remain for that person the principal or main pull. And where that initial appeal has been the promise of a reward of a physical kind, a process of spiritualisation of desire or want, as in NRMs generally, tends to occur.

Thus, healing comes to be explained as essentially to do with the 'inner', spiritual life and the development of the person; the purpose of the ritual, a movement comes to insist, is not to produce external improvements in the physical condition of the person. The new Japanese religion, Mahikari now makes it a condition, at least in Sao Paulo, of receiving *okiyome*, a similar though more complex healing ritual than johrei, that a client first be made fully aware by a competent person of its spiritual significance and intent. Messianity in contrast, continues to look for some form of all round, including physical, improvement from *johrei* and continues to sponsor medical research on its effects, including research into its effects on the immune system in relation to cancer (Ghoneum, n.d.).

When asked what initially attracted them to the movement about half of Messianity's members in Bahia gave *johrei* as the main reason, and while this continued to remain very important, 'spiritual growth'or 'the teachings', or the 'opportunity to save lives', replaced it as the most important attraction in time. Thus *johrei* remained the single most powerful attraction, but only alongside interests such as 'the teachings', 'caring for others', and the 'cult of the ancestors'. A small per centage only spoke, unsolicited, of the fulfilment of millennial dreams. Asked what she understood by the idea of a terrestrial paradise one female member in her middle thirties with one child, who combines her profession of occupational therapist with her role as an assistant minister in the movement, stressed that paradise on earth begins within each individual for 'God works only through individuals'.[20] A former Catholic, as were the majority, this informant found that the Catholic Church could not answer her questions about why she was born and her purpose in life. She also lamented over what she saw as the ever declining moral and social situation in Brazil and the developing world, the causes for this, and of her role in reversing it which Messianity had helped her to understand:

> I live because I am part of God's plan to construct a new world. The world is like a theatre in which everyone has a role, a specific function and mission. The world is everyday getting worse; there is more sickness, more conflict every day. It is more animal than human, and very far from God. It has left the way of truth, because of materialism and egoism. We cannot walk on the road at night for fear of being assaulted; we're full of medicines that don't cure and our food is poisoned with agrotoxic substances.[21]

Though the life of respondents was not marked by great poverty they, nevertheless, felt that they were victims of it. Some spoke of everyone's peace of mind, happiness and sense of integrity being diminished, and even threatened, in conditions where poverty and destitution for the majority were widespread. There was considerable pessimism generally among ordinary members about the present state of the world. Only two per cent described it as 'very good', while some ten per cent thought it was 'good'. Half replied that it was reasonable (razoavel), suggesting no more than tolerable. Seventeen per cent thought it was bad, and nineteen per cent very bad.[22]

Women, who accounted for seventy eight per cent of the respondents to this question, were on average more pessimistic than men, and the younger age groups, those under nineteen and between 20–29, were more pessimistic than those in the four older age groups: 30–39, 40–49, 50–59, and 60 years and over. The former accounted for the majority of the 17 per cent of the sample questioned that thought that the present situation of the world was bad, and of the nineteen per cent of those that believed it to be very bad.[23] Those who were pessimistic about the present state of the world and why it was no better than 'tolerable', or 'bad' or 'very bad', were almost unanimous in attributing this to egotism, giving it as the major reason for the desperate hunger, suffering, violence and above all poverty that were making it impossible for the majority to live as human beings with dignity and self respect. The solution to such egotism lay in radical self-transformation by the acquisition of the appropriate spiritual means. It was widely believed that moral and spiritual growth were greatly facilitated by improvements in others spheres; material deprivation, poverty, could undermine, it was pointed out, the attainement of this goal.

Poverty is a complex term that needs to be unpacked if it is to provide any useful insights into why Messianity members have come to see millenarian fervour and hope as the most effective means of eliminating it and of providing the conditions for self development. Of the different types of poverty the one most likely to give rise to millenarianism is structural poverty. This kind of poverty as Iliffe explains (1987: 4–5) is, or is perceived to be, massive in terms of scale, and long term, and is or appears to be occasioned by factors completely outside the control of those afflicted by it, such as drought, lack of access to fertile land or to employment, or severe disablement, whether this be physical, emotional or intellectual. Moreover, there are few safety nets available to those caught up in this type of poverty once their ingenuity, and emotional and physical resources have been drained in trying to combat it.

Structural poverty can be contrasted with conjunctural poverty (Iliffe, 1987: 6), a kind of poverty that affects those who are ordinarily self-sufficient people; it is temporary and brought on by some clearly identifiable crisis or other, such as bankruptcy, earthquake, famine, or war. This is a distinction that I have made use of to explain the incidence and pattern of millenarianism in parts of western Africa (Clarke, 1995a). The feeling that Brazil and the developing world are overburdened and overwhelmed with structural poverty, a burden to which no one appears to have a solution, or to be willing to devise a solution, at the national or international level, is widespread among ordinary members. There is, however, hope, and even evidence that it can be overcome for they have come to know that post Second World War Japan was also once in the same position, and yet managed to triumph over total devastation by virtue of character, reinforced by divine assistance.

Ordinary members did not focus exclusively on spiritual remedies for the resolution of chronic social ills. While they expressed a lack of confidence in political action as a means of effecting change, and this is general in Brazil, they did believe that it had a role to play in changing the world for the better.

Few members dismissed it as irrelevant, and, though no one thought that it could be effective on its own many felt that combined with an increase in spiritual awareness, it could make a useful contribution. There was also a degree of confidence and hope in scientific research as the means of making a difference to the present condition of the world. One third of the respondents gave this means high priority. Less than ten per cent of the respondents, however, were convinced that it constituted an indispensable means for bringing about the changes they considered necessary 'to save the world'.[24]

Messianity members are clearly not in any sense iconoclasts, machine breakers or anti-modern. Amidst some scepticism about the improvements that might be possible through technological advance, the importance of technology is widely recognised by members, over half of whom placed it second to an increase in spiritual awareness which, they believed, was the most effective means of changing the world.[25] Their notion of spiritual awareness also needs to be unpacked. While it contains the idea of individual improvement, it does not consist of something purely inner or personal, but often refers to the cultivation of unselfish, altruistic behaviour, love of neighbour, the pursuit of natural as opposed to material pleasures and rewards, self and world transformation through all of these means, and above all through living according to the Law of Nature.

The emphasis on spiritual awareness as the principal means of transforming the world notwithstanding, Messianity's response at the level of the ordinary member does not constitute a spiritual or religious response, in the usual understanding of these terms, to structural poverty. This movement neither defines itself as a religion in the widely accepted sense of the term, nor does it draw a clear line between religious and secular movements either. Humanists and people of no religion can participate in its activities and share its aims and objectives. There is no objection, we noted previously, to a non-member being the political leader of the City of the New Age.

It is this sense of itself as more than a religious movement that allows Messianity to work within the existing political process to transform it. Its laboratory of 'spiritual techniques' – *johrei*, sangetsu or the arranging and distribution of flowers, natural farming, and the construction of models of paradise on earth – all have a 'political' objective, in that they are intended to lead to a radical transformation in attitudes toward the environment, crime and punishment, educational policy and method, food production, banking, medicine and health care.

Thus, while there is a lack of confidence in the actual political process itself to effect change on a grand scale and tackle the problem of structural poverty, there is, at the same time, no rigid dichotomy between the spiritual and the political in Messianity's millenarianism. Participants in Messianity feel no more disenfranchised from the mainstream of power and its related activities than others, nor do they see the present world as being empty of all political and moral value. They are best characterised as reformers rather than revolutionaries.

Messianity's millenarianism does not, then, offer itself as an alternative to politics in the Brazilian context, not even in a symbolic sense. It is not so much the failure of politics as the desire for a more rounded and integrated approach to dealing with problems of a personal and social nature that attracts recruits to this movement. The conviction is widespread that most issues of an existential, moral and social kind are beyond the scope and competence of any one philosophy or institution to resolve single handedly. There is dissatisfaction with the increasing compartmentalisation of medicine, science and politics, and the view is general among members that political movements must draw on more than purely secular ideas and methods if they are to provide appropriate solutions to the complex issues of the contemporary world.

The major difference perceived to exist between Messianity's millenarian teachings and existing political ideologies lies in this: while the former draws upon the powers of the spiritual and natural worlds, both of which are seen as interdependent, and indispensable to personal growth and development, the latter restricts itself to and relies exclusively upon human and material resources which have patently failed when used on their own.

There are differences between the millenarians that belong to Messianity in Brazil and those who joined Omotokyo and Tensho-Kotai-Jingu-Kyo in their early years where the leadership and the majority of followers were from among the relatively deprived peasantry and the urban proletariat. Messianity members in Brazil also differ from those millenarians studied by Cohn (1970) whose research showed that in Medieval Europe revolutionary millenarianism drew its strength from people living on the margins of society, from:

> peasants without land or with too little land even for subsistence; journeymen and unskilled workers living under the continuous threat of unemployment; beggars and vagabonds – in fact from the amorphous mass who were not simply poor but who could find no recognised and assured place in society at all (1970: 282).

Not only are Messianity's members in Brazil not the kind of millenarians that constituted the bulk of its early membership and that of Omotokyo and Tensho-Kotai-Jingu-Kyo in Japan, or the same kind as those described above by Cohn, they could not be so. Messianity has not made a point of appealing to the marginalised and materially deprived and displaced, or to the peasantry or urban proletariat, nor has any other Japanese new religion in Brazil or overseas. While largely middle class in social composition Messianity and Japanese new religions generally do not display the political radicalism in the Brazilian context or elsewhere seen in other modern middle class movements including Liberation Theology. The latter, as

Martin (1990) points out, is a religion *for* the poor rather than *of* the poor. Folk Catholicism, and, increasingly, Pentecostalism, which make a causal link between an individual's moral failings and all personal misery, distress and ill fortune, including being raped and robbed, are the main religions of the poor in Brazil.

That is also something millenarian movements like the Jehovah Witnesses do in Brazil. If Messianity were to do so it would be a very different kind of movement from what it is at present. Its programme of constructing paradise on earth depends on a majority of members having certain aptitudes, competencies and skills. Moreover, its social welfare provisions are not as developed as its other activities which demand a degree of leisure and financial security. These include, as we have seen, sangetsu, calligraphy, and natural farming. Nor does Messianity operate in areas where the poor and the destitute are mostly found. This is not to suggest that the poor are purposely excluded or overlooked; there are programmes for schools in rural areas to learn natural farming and missionaries from Brazil have recently established centres in war torn Angola.

Conclusions

Commonly, the kinds of general explanation for the types of millenarianism discussed here, and millenarianism in general, are psychopathological, or come in one or other version of the anomic effects of rapid social change. The psychopathological explanation interprets millenarianism as a form of collective fantasising which attracts those that cannot cope. Different ages and different cultures use different labels for such people: melancholics, schizophrenics, hysterics and so on. While acknowledging that millenarianism – like religious fundamentalism whose literalism and strict and undeviating approach to scripture it lacks – can provide great emotional and intellectual security, such psychological explanations are usually of little value. They do not help us to see the potentially creative power of millenarian belief, or to understand why so many people from such different backgrounds and different ways of life, with so many different personal experiences, find in it such a compelling ideology of change in the sense of a meaningful way of surmounting what appear to be, humanly speaking, insuperable obstacles to the realisation of that irrepressible desire for self fulfilment.

As to explanations built on the analysis of the effects of rapid social change, it is clear that only certain kinds of change produce anomic effects. Change, even rapid change, is by no means always problematic in itself, and certainly not for all those affected by it. Social change to speak of that does not necessarily destroy or undermine confidence or create deep seated anxiety, or a yearning for the stability of the past. It can be a liberating experience. It is the nature of change, the course it takes and the manner of its implementation, that can be profoundly disturbing. For example, the kind of change that threatens to take away an individual's or community's power to manage and control what is happening to their world can be both bewildering and incapacitating. Lack of the means to effect radical change of a political, economic or social kind can also generate millenarian fervour, as in the case of those Tupi Guarani who went in search of The Land-Without-Evil to escape the strictures and limitations of the traditional political structures (Clastres, 1995). In either case millenarianism can enter in to provide a meaningful way out of the impasse.

But the degree to which millenarian belief takes hold of an individual must not be exaggerated. Most millenarians do not go around in a dream world, neglecting their everyday duties. As our Brazilian case study shows they behave outwardly like most others with a strong desire for personal development and wholeness. Collectively, the situation is somewhat different in that they manifest a high level of commitment to the the goal of creating a new kind of person and a new kind of moral community.

The millenarianism of Messianity, and Omotokyo and Tensho-Kotai-Jingu-Kyo has certainly served these moral and spiritual purposes. Falling back on Folk Shinto beliefs, practices and symbols, the founders of Omotokyo explained how the disastrous effects of the Meiji revolution which, they believed, was then destroying Japan would be overturned in the new world of permanence and universal equality brought into being by Ushitora no Konjin. Their country would again be master of its own destiny, and rule itself, uninfluenced from without, according to Japanese principles of authenticity and integrity, for all in this new world would be, as Onisaburo Deguchi's map made clear, within the 'boundaries' of Japan.

The millenarianism of Sayo Kitamura, foundress of Tensho-Kotai-Jingu-Kyo, also concerned itself with the provision of an intelligible explanation of how Japan would recover its real, authentic soul and thereby reassert its unique global significance. She spoke of the insignificance of Japan's defeat in World War II and, a fortiori, of the irrelevance and weakness of power based on modern technology and weapons of mass destruction. This defeat was even presented as an act of divine providence the purpose of which was to enable Japan fulfil its destiny as the most powerful nation on earth by drawing upon and using its inexhaustible and incomparably rich spiritual resources.

Messianity initially reacted in a similar way to modernity and military defeat before developing its own original interpretation of Japan's global role. Defeat was also seen as an opportunity, but this time not for Japan to rise to a position of pre-eminence either politically or spiritually, but for the cultures of East and West to join together to complement each other. Further, it was the occasion for the pursuit of a global understanding, not a national one, of the way to resolve the environmental, economic and social problems threatening the survival and development of human beings and of the planet, using Brazil as a catalytic converter for global purification and salvation in the twenty first century.

All three movements have waned in Japan in recent times as new forms of new religion have emerged in an attempt to provide for the contemporarty age what they once offered preceeding generations: an ideology of change and a way of explaining, predicting and even controlling events. On the other hand, Messianity's millenarian fervour seems undiminished in Brazil. There are complex reasons for these different trends, one of which is the greater problem the Japanese branch of the movement has in motivating second and third generation members, and the lack of enthusiasm for communal, group focused religion there. Another is that the model of living that is offered is perceived by many to be unattractive, unappealing and out of date. In the present Brazilian situation Messianity's dynamism and success can be attributed principally to the wide appeal of *johrei*, the environmental activities of the movement, in particular natural farming, and the careful policy of inculturation followed by the leadership.

Crucially important also to its success and dynamism are: its charismatic and effective leadership style which continues to be aware of the motivational value of millenarian belief, the movement's sense of itself as more than a religious movement, its reformist approach which offers members an active and meaningful role in the building of paradise on earth, and its new outward looking focus which gives Brazil – the global catalytic converter – the leading role in world transformation.

Notes

I am very grateful to those leaders and ordinary members of Omotokyo in Japan, to those of Tensho-Kotai-Jingu-Kyo in Japan and Hawaii and to those of Messianity in Japan, Brazil, Hawaii and the mainland of the United States, who so generously gave me their time and co-operation with my research. No suggestions were ever offered about what I should write, nor did I feel in any way under obligation to write from a particular perspective.

1 Interview at the Headquarters of Tensho-Kotai-Jingu-Kyo in Tabuse, Yama-guchi Prefecture, 23rd April 1997 with Wakagamisama, son of Ogamisama and the present administrative head of the movement, and his wife and their daughter, Himegamisama. The latter was appointed by Ogamisama to be her successor and is the present spiritual leader of Tensho-Kotai-Jingu-Kyo.
2 Ibid.
3 Ibid.
4 Interview on 21st April 1997 at the Kameoka Headquarters of Omotokyo with a senior member of the International Department.

5 Interview at Atami, 29th April, 1998 with members of the international department of Sekai Kyusei Kyo.
6 Ibid.
7 Ibid.
8 Interview on 5th September 1996 at the Brazilian headquarters of Messianity with Reverend Watanabe, Vice President of Sekai Kyusei Kyo and President of Messianity in Brazil, and several senior members of the Movement. Reverend Watanabe is responsible for the initiation and completion of Messianity's millenarian projects in Brazil, including the two discussed in this article: the Movement's Solo Sagrado, or Holy Ground, at Guarapiranga which serves as the Holy Ground for Latin America as a whole, and the New Age City.
9 Interview with Hidenari Hayashi, Vice President of Messianity in Brazil and Masahito Oro, General Co-ordinator of Messianity in Brazil, 3rd Dec. 1998.
10 Interview at Atami on 12th April 1997 with Reverend Watanabe.
11 These data are derived from questionnaires completed by Brazilian members in Sao Paulo and Bahia during the August and September 1996 and 1997 (henceforth Questionnaires). From 60 questionnaires delivered to members in Salvador Bahia and Sao Paulo, 55 were completed. I am most grateful to the Reverend Eduardo Takama of the Church of Messianity in Sao Paulo who kindly helped me in this part of my research and in other ways.
12 Interview at Atami on 12th April 1997 with Reverend Watanabe et. al.
13 Interviews with Brazilian members of Messianity in Sao Paulo and Bahia (August and September, 1996 and 1997). Interviews with members of other Japanese religions in Brazil including Seicho no Ie show that this kind of theological reinterpretation or reconstruction to be common among those who join Japanese new religions. It helps explain the point made to me on several occasions by Reverend Fujikura of the Church of Perfect Liberty Kyodan in Sao Paulo: 'there can be no successful religion in Brazil without Jesus'.
14 Interview at Atami on 12th April, 1997 with Reverend Tetsuo Watanabe et al.
15 Interview on 5th September 1996 with Reverend Tetsuo Watanabe et al. op.cit.
16 Ibid.
17 Ibid.
18 Questionnaires.
19 Ibid.
20 Interview on the twentieth August 1997 with an assistant minister at the Church of Messianity, Fazenda Garcia, Bahia, Brazil.
21 Ibid.
22 Questionnaires op.cit.
23 Ibid.
24 Ibid.
25 Ibid.

References

Anesaki, M. (1923), Buddhist Art, New York: Houghton Mifflin Company.
Arjomand, S.A. (1984) The Shadow of God and the Hidden Imam: Religion, Political Order and Societal Change in Shi'ite Iran from the Beginning to 1890, Chicago: Chicago University Press.
Berthon, Jean-Pierre, 1985, Espérance millenariste d'une nouvelle religion Japonaise, Paris: Cahiers d'etudes et de documents sur les religions du Japon, No. 6, Atelier Alpha Bleu.

Blacker, C. (1971), 'Millenarian Aspects of the New Religions in Japan', in Tradition and Modernisation in Japanese Culture, D.H. Shively (ed), Princeton: Princeton University Press.

Blacker, C. (1976), The Catalpa Bow, London: George Allen and Unwin Ltd, pp. 563–600.

Burridge, K. (1971), New Heaven, New Earth, Oxford: Basil Blackwell.

Campanella, T (1981), La Cité du Soleil, Paris: Vrin (Trans. A. Zevaes).

Clarke, P.B. (1987), Black Paradise. The Rastafarian Movement, Wellingborough, Northants: Aquarian Press.

Clarke, P.B. (1993), 'Why Women are priests and teachers in Bahian Candomble' in Puttick, E and Clarke, P.B (eds), Women as Teachers and Disciples in Traditional and New Religions, Lewiston, N.Y., Queenston, Ontario, Lampeter, Dyfed: Edwin Mellen Press.

Clarke, P.B. (1995a), Mahdism in West Africa. The Ijebu Mahdiyyat Movement, London: Luzac Oriental.

Clarke, P.B. 'The Cultural Impact of New Religions in Latin and Central America and the Caribbean with Special Reference to Japanese New Religions' in Journal of Latin American Cultural Studies, Vol. 4. No. 1 pp. 117–126.

Clarke, P.B. (ed) (1998), New Trends and Developments in the World of Islam, London: Luzac Oriental.

Clastres, H. (1995), The Land-Without-Evil, (translated from the French by Jaqueline Grenez Brovender), Urbana and Chicago: University of Illinois Press.

Cohn, N. (1970), The Pursuit of the Millennium, London: Paladin.

Cohn, N. (1993), Cosmos, Chaos and the World to Come. The Ancient Roots of Apocalyptic Faith, New Haven and London: Yale University Press.

Completion of Miroku San-e (1995): Atami: Sekai Kyusei Kyo Publishing Section.

Davis, W. (1980), Magic and Exorcism in Contemporary Japan, Standford: Standford University Press.

Foundations of Paradise (1984), Church of World Messianity, USA.

Ghoneum, M. (n.d), Nk Cell Immunomodulatory Function and Anti-Cancer Activity By Johrei (At the time of writing (1996?), the author of this paper was Associate Professor and Chief of Research at the Drew University of Medicine and Science, Los Angeles, California).

Giichiro, K. (1975) 'Yowan and Me' in Cahiers De La Ceramique Du Verre Et Des Arts Du Feu, Revue Trimestrielle, No. 57, Paris: Pejout, pp. 1–2.

Gray, J. (1998), False Dawn. The Delusions of Global Capitalism, London: Granta Books.

Groszos Ooms, E. (1993), Women and Millenarian Protest in Meiji Japan. Nao Deguchi and Omotokyo, Ithaca, New York: Cornell University East Asia Program.

Handa, T. (1980), Memorias De Um Immigrante Japones No Brazil' Sao Paulo: T.A. Queiroz, Editora, Centro De Estudos Nipo-Brasileiros.

Hardacre, H. (1990), 'Gender and the Millennium in Omotokyo, A Japanese New Religion', in (eds) Umesao, T et al., Japanese Civilisation in the Modern World VI, Osaka: National Museum of Ethnology.

Ibn Khaldun, Abd ar Rahman (1967), The Muqaddimmah. An Introduction to History, edited and abridged by N.J. Dawood (trans. from the Arabic by F. Rosenthal), London: Routledge and Kegan Paul, 1958, Vol. 2.

Iliffe, J. (1987), The African Poor. a history, Cambridge: Cambridge University Press.

In Service to Man (1980), Atami-shi: M. Okada International Association.

Jervis, J. (1998), 'The Sufi Order in the West and Pir Vilayat 'Inayat Khan: Space-Age Spirituality in Contemporary Euro-America' in Peter B Clarke (ed), New Trends and Developments in the World of Islam, London: Luzac Oriental, pp. 211–261.

Kisala, R. (1998), '1999 and Beyond: The Use of Nostradamus' Prophecies by Japanese New Religions', in Japanese Religions Vol. 23 Nos. 1&2.

Marra, M. (1988 a), 'The Development of Mappo Thought in Japan (I)' in Japanese Journal of Religious Studies, 15/1, pp. 25–54.

Marra, M. (1988 b), 'The Development of Mappo Thought in Japan (II)' in Japanese Journal of Religious Studies, 15/4, pp. 287–305.

Martin, D. (1990), Tongues of Fire. The Explosion of Pentecostalism in Latin America, Oxford: Basil Blackwell.

Maeyama, T. (1983), Japanese Religions in southern Brazil, Latin American Studies, 6, University of Tsukuba, Ibaraki, Japan, pp. 181–238.

Miyata, N. (1988), 'Types of Maitreya Beliefs in Japan' in (eds) A. Sponberg and H.Hardacre, Maitreya, The Future Buddha, Cambridge: Cambridge University Press. pp. 175–190.

Nattier, J. (1988), 'The Meaning of the Maitreya Myth: A Typological Analysis', in A. Sponberg and H. Hardacre (eds) Maitreya, The Future Buddha, Cambridge: Cambridge University Press pp. 23–47.

Ohnuki-Tierney, E. (1991), The Emperor of Japan as Deity (Kami): An Anthropology of the Imperial System in Historical Perspective, in Ethnology, 30 (3) pp. 199–215.

Puttick, E. (1997), Women in New Religions. In Search of Community, Spirituality and Spiritual Power, Houndsmill, Basingstoke and London: Macmillan.

Reader, I., Andreasen E. and Stefansson, F. (1993), Japanese Religions Past and Present, Folkstone: Japan Library.

Reader, I. (1991) Religion in Contemporary Japan, Houndmills, Basingstoke: Macmillan.

Shimazono, S. (1986), 'The Development of Millenaristic Thought in Japan's New Religions: From Tenrikyo to Honmichi' in J. Beckford (ed) New Religious Movements and Rapid Social Change, London: Sage Publications, pp. 55–86.

Shimazono, S. (1995) 'In the Wake of Aum: The Formation and Transformation of a Universe of Belief' in Japanese Journal of Religious Studies, Vol. 22, Nos. 3–4, pp. 381–415.

Sponberg, A. and Hardacre, H. (eds) (1988), Maitreya, the Future Buddha, Cambridge: Cambridge University Press.

Smith, R. (1979), 'The Ethnic Japanese in Brazil' in The Journal of Japanese Studies, Vol. 5 No. 1 pp. 53–70.

The Prophet of Tabuse (1954), Tabuse, Yamaguchi Prefecture: Tensho-Kotai-Jingu-Kyo Publications.

Vasquez, M. (1998), The Brazilian Popular Church and the Crisis of Modernity, Cambridge: Cambridge University Press.

Waswo, A. (1996) Modern Japanese Society, 1868–1964, Oxford: Oxford University Press.

Wilson, B.R. (1970), Religious Sects, London: Weidenfeld and Nicolson

Worsley, P. (1970). The Trumpet Shall Sound, St. Albans: Paladin.

Yamashita, A. (1998), 'The "Eschatology" of Japanese New and New New Religions: From Tenri-kyo to Kofuku no Kagaku' in Japanese Religions Vol. 23 Nos. 1&2, pp. 125–142.

Yasumaru, Y. (1977), Deguchi Nao, Tokyo: Asahi Shimbunsha

Young, R. Fox (1988), 'From *Gokyo-to Bankyo-dokon*: A Study in the Self-Universalization of Omoto' in Japanese Journal of Religious Studies, 15/4, pp. 263–286.

CHAPTER SIX

Adapt or Perish

The Story of Soka Gakkai in Germany

Sanda Ionescu

The ten people gathered in the living room on that November evening eyed each other with the nervousness of strangers. The serving of the *norimaki* helped to break the ice a little. 'Did you make them? They are delicious!' 'Where do you buy your seaweed from?' As they munched on their exquisite little rice and seaweed parcels, the conversation began to flow in a direction that concerned all present. 'So how many members are there in total in this town?' asked the senior man among the guests, 'And how often do you organise study meetings?'

Although he was genuinely interested and tried to sound friendly, there was something stentorian about his tone of voice, which seemed to intimidate the hosts, whose answers were barely audible. Visible relief therefore greeted his suggestion that they should start on the *Gongyō*. Guests and hosts sat down on the floor facing the carefully tended *Butsudan* and took out their prayer beads and prayer books, wrapped in delicate handkerchiefs or elegantly embroidered little pouches. The persistent rhythmic strains of 'Nam myoho renge kyō' soon enveloped the room, the candles were lit in front of the *Butsudan*, its doors now open to reveal the *Gohonzon* scroll inside. As the familiar Buddhist words resounded in the many different voices but in perfect harmony, as the brass bell was struck to mark the moments of silent prayer, the participants relaxed. *Gongyō* lasted one hour that evening and after that everybody seemed to feel they were among friends. Jokes and laughter flowed as readily as the wine and mingled easily with intimate revelations.

This would seem to be the description of a classical, though rather small, guest meeting of Soka Gakkai members. This particular one, however, did not take place in Japan – in fact, there was not a single Japanese face among those present. Instead, it took place in a little provincial town in the centre of Germany and was a guest meeting organised for the foreign participants at the annual conference of the Youth Divisions. A total of six nationalities were present. The language of communication was generally broken English, followed by some half-whispered, quick-fire German and French translations. Only one of those present had been to Japan for more than a brief visit and spoke Japanese (she had prepared the *norimaki*, too), but all had chanted the difficult Japanese Buddhist terms of the Lotus Sutra with confidence and remarkable speed. It could, in fact, with minor modifications, have been the meeting of a Soka Gakkai group anywhere in the world.

Attending a meeting like that raises question about the globalisation of ideologies and cultures. To what extent can a religion, which has arisen under specific historical and cultural circumstances, become relevant to people in entirely different social, cultural and temporal contexts? What is the exact proportion of universality to cultural specificity that a religion should have in order to gain a following beyond its national borders? And how much does a religion entering a foreign culture with proselytising intentions have to take into account the characteristics of the host culture? Although the issue is rarely as clear-cut as I seem to imply in the title of this paper – 'adapt or perish' – it remains true that a religion seeking to expand abroad will need to tread a fine line between failure to grasp the core elements of the host culture and over-adaptation, the danger of losing its 'authenticity'.

This paper then will look at the history of a specific Japanese new religion, Soka Gakkai, in Germany, and examine to what extent globalisation theory can be used to explain the processes going on there.

Typographical ink has flown copiously on the subject of 'globalisation'. It is one of those buzz words, like 'secularisation' in its heyday, which has members of the scholarly community, not to mention politicians, management consultants and development workers, up in arms and engaging in lively debates about its extent, nature or, indeed, its very existence.

So, is the world really shrinking and are we seeing, as a consequence thereof, the emergence of a cultural phenomenon which transcends nation-state boundaries and operates on a global scale? These transnational flows, or even the study of them, are not new; what *is* new, however, is the extent to which certain processes are being conceived and organised on a global level and the awareness of the interrelatedness of people and events around the world (Yearley, 1996:9).

In the past decade or so, social scientists have moved beyond the largely materialistic formulations of world-systems theory (this includes even the doyen of economic determinism, compare Wallerstein, 1974 to Wallerstein, 1991) and towards a more culture-centred approach to global integration, therefore I shall not dwell here on the critique of the purely economic and political theories surrounding the subject (cf. Robertson, 1991 and 1992; Smith, 1990; Bergesen, 1990).

The ambivalence of scholars on the subject reflects perhaps the multiple facets and ambiguity of globalisation itself, and it is often difficult to find common ground between the various orientations. I shall not attempt a thorough analysis or even listing of the ongoing debates, but shall content myself with enunciating some common themes, which have a bearing on this present paper.

Identity

Culture is losing its spatial referent, is becoming 'deterritorialised' (King, 1991; Beyer, 1994), as the flows of technology, capital, people and expertise between countries become ever more complex. This process, however, is anything but straightforward. The inherited, traditional cultural and personal identities have been corroded by the global system (Beyer, 1994), but no common model, acceptable to all societies, has yet emerged to take their place (Robertson, 1992). This leaves considerable leeway for diversity as regards direction and pace of development, and also encourages the creation and revitalisation of identities, as a means of gaining control over systemic power (Beyer, 1994). This is probably what Hannerz means when he suggests that world culture is characterised by the organisation of diversity rather than the replication of uniformity (Hannerz, 1990:237).

Identity is at best an ambivalent construct (Hall, 1991b), more easily defined as what one is *not* rather than what one is. Therefore, the presence of the other is important, almost obligatory, in order to have something to distinguish oneself from. This works best if the 'Other' is not too well-known, so that sweeping generalisations can be made and clichés can be resorted to, which serve to enhance the clichés and generalisations applied to one's own identity, the ignoring of difference, the assumption of agreement and homogeneity.

In the case of Soka Gakkai in Germany, this was reflected in the way both the Japanese and German members presented the other ethnic group. Although they knew many members of the other group personally, they were quite comfortable with stating: 'Well, there are of course exceptions, but *generally* the Japanese ... or the Germans...'

Another interesting way of looking at creating identity is through consumption. Whether deliberate or unconscious and taken for granted, consumption tells us more about the personal choices we make in the way we present ourselves to others or think about ourselves, and is certainly part of the more general strategy for the establishment or maintenance of selfhood, together with other practices of cultural self-constitution, such as: ethnicity, class, gender, religion (some of these being less open to individual choice) (Friedman, 1991). All ideas – religious, political, moral or aesthetic – must jostle to compete against each other in a world resembling a free market economy and strive after global hearing and recognition (Tenbruck, 1990:205). Some of them are organised with that aim in mind and I would argue that Soka Gakkai is one of them.

Globalisation of Conscience

Robertson (1991) talks about the globalisation of conscience, the increasing tendency for individuals, organisations or communities to locate themselves within a wider (global) context and feel themselves as part of a whole rather than as an isolated entity. However, this movement towards the global is nearly always accompanied by a rising concern not to 'be swallowed up whole' by the relentless globalisation process, but to maintain a separate local identity.

There is an ambiguous, one might say almost schizophrenic, position in regard to the outside culture. On the one hand, one may covet the 'Other', but, on the other hand, one may resent its prescriptive nature. One may be critical of certain aspects of one's own society and look to the external model as an improvement, yet at the same time one may wish to maintain one's identity, which includes the national identity, or at least the positive aspects thereof.

Beyer (1994) points out the paradoxical character of religion: that it can be both anti-systemic and pro-systemic at the same time, i.e., that it can further globalisation even while it opposes it. Religion has traditionally been linked to particular cultures, however, Beyer (1994) argues, it has always had its universalist strains. If one could avoid seeing the world system as predominantly economic or politic, then religion is a relatively independent force with strong globalistic tendencies. Not all religions react, in moments of crises, in the conservative way, looking inward and stipulating that no change is necessary or desirable. Some reorient themselves towards the global whole and learn to incorporate change as they go along.

Yearley (1996), in a somewhat different context, talks about 'working down to the global'. He says that the most common approach is to work *up* to the global from the national-level phenomena. He proposes, however (1996:17), approaching globalism from the angle of universalism. He makes no claims for universal validity of ideas, except for mathematics and logic and other sciences. He does mention moral right, however, as one contentious issue. For religious thinkers, this is one of the universal principles that religion should concern itself with. Religion deals with absolutes and absolutes may easily be claimed to be universal, at least by those pertaining to a certain religion.

The holistic world concerns of Soka Gakkai at times show striking similarities to the Green Movement ideology (see Galtung, 1990), which could explain why both appeal to the same category of people. The Green Movement is far more diffuse than Soka Gakkai, in fact it is a federation of movements who subscribe to some but not necessarily all of the policies listed by Galtung (1990:237–38). There is a correlation in the ideological universe in spite of that: the fact that the Green Movement is a reaction to the malfunctioning of the Western social formation, a reaction to the generally proclaimed and much lamented 'crisis'. To a certain extent, Soka Gakkai is that as well, it shows an alternative way for those who cannot or want not to be fully integrated in a society whose values they do not share.

Asymmetry

Hannerz (1992:261–267) believes that the distribution of culture within the world is achieved through a structure of asymmetrical, centre/periphery type of relationships. This view has been much criticised (by Wolff, 1991; Hall, 1991a and b; Massey & Jess, 1995; Abu-Lughod, 1991) for not conceding enough power of creative selection and adaptation to the periphery. The margin may be 'a space of weak power, but it is a space of power, nonetheless' (Hall, 1991a), since it appropriates foreign meanings by reinterpreting them and fitting them into the existing meaning system. Hannerz (1992:265) himself admits as much when he says that the influx of foreign culture does not occur in vacuum, but enters into interaction with already existing meanings. Furthermore, centres are difficult to locate with precision (Abou-El-Haj, 1991), and there is also an increasing pluralisation of centres (Boli-Bennett, 1980) or decentered centres (Hall, 1991). What is core in one context can become periphery in another. A Soka Gakkai related example might be the German branch (periphery in its relation with Japan, but core in its relation with the Austrian branch), while the Austrian branch itself serves as a core for the new periphery of Eastern Europe.

Appadurai (1990) casts strong doubts on the centre/periphery model, even when it attempts to accommodate the notion of multiple centres and peripheries, since he argues that the complexity of global flows is too great nowadays to allow the construction of a single model. Meanwhile, Smith (1990) is sceptical about the possibility of developing a global culture, since the existing culture areas (which he sees as an intermediate stage between national and global cultures) are accidental products of long-term historical circumstances, all the more powerful for being uninstitutionalised. A deliberate construction of a global ecumene, based often on the assumption that if the techno-economic frame is provided culture will follow suit, is, Smith (1990:180) believes, an example of economic determinism at its most wilful.

Closely related to the view of asymmetrical global flows is the idea that external forces or new cultures act in a unified manner upon the host culture (cf. Wallerstein, 1991), without examining at what levels this interaction takes place. In the case of Japanese religions in Germany, the interaction clearly involves two levels: the national and the local, since it would be wrong to see German society as perfectly homogeneous. Therefore, we will find a national strategy and its variations (urban vs. rural, east vs. west, north vs. south). We might also add the official relationship between Soka Gakkai and the German state as a third level of contact.

To return to the statement that an influx of culture occurs into an already existent system of meaning (Hannerz, 1992:265) – this presupposes, however, a strong system of meanings and values already in place in the host culture. How does this work, how can we talk about creative adaptation, when the host community cannot lay claim to a strong unity of background, shared history or even geographical proximity, as is the case of Soka Gakkai members in Germany? Most members may be German, but some grew up in the Democratic, some in the Federal Republic. As I pointed out above, there is considerable variation even within these units and the Soka Gakkai members come from an incredible diversity of backgrounds, social classes, professions and religions. When looking at the German Soka Gakkai, therefore, we require not only a redefinition of community itself – a form of organisation which aims to create an ideologically homogeneous group – but also considerable flexibility and reinvention of self in a constant interplay with both the society the community is enclosed in (Germany) and the one they have received their ideological nourishment from (Japanese Nichiren Buddhism).

The traditional understanding of the 'authentic community' as 'face-to-face interactions' comes under scrutiny by Young (1990). She sees this nostalgia for 'Gemeinschaft' as an illusory ideal, which wrongly identifies mediation with alienation. While not denying the specific value of face-to-face relations, proposing them for the organisation of a whole society is unrealistic and politically undesirable, since it would lead to boundedness, dichotomisation and exclusion. Rather, the author postulates the establishment of the 'unoppressive city', which remains open to unassimilated otherness.

It is indeed this last strategy that the German Soka Gakkai appears to have adopted, whether deliberately or under pressure is not always easy to tell. Although the local groups are certainly face-to-face type of communities, and there is some spontaneous interaction between them, most of the interaction is mediated by higher organisational authorities or by ideology, yet this is seldom perceived as alienation or constraint. The movement makes quite considerable demands on its members regarding commitment. Each of the geographical units (the local group, the district, the area, the *Bundesland* and the national level), as well as each of the divisions (Men, Women, Young Men, Young Women) has its own regular meetings, so that the schedule of an active Soka Gakkai members contains on average 2–3 events per week, as well as voluntary work at the national headquarters or the renovation of Villa Sachsen, intended to be the new main centre of activities in Germany. Members are thus constantly in touch, both with other members and with the national leadership. The community spirit is further strengthened by the monthly magazine *Forum*, prepared and

187

published by volunteer members and to which all members subscribe. Spring and summer are also punctuated by festivals, summer schools, excursions, exhibitions and training seminars for each division in Trets, France, always hugely popular and rapidly booked by German members.

Examples from Fieldwork

Nichiren Buddhism entered Germany in the 1960s. The story Soka Gakkai members like to tell contains certain mythologising aspects and goes as follows:

In 1961, about the time the Wall was built to separate the two Germanys, Ikeda, who was then the third president of Soka Gakkai, came to visit Germany and was so touched by this situation, that he decided to bring Buddhism to the split country, to alleviate the suffering. The first Japanese missionaries – or 'pioneers', as the present-say members prefer to call them – arrived soon after, most of them with no more than a little backpack on their shoulders and little command of the German language and even less knowledge of the German culture and society. At that time, the only possibility for a receiving a work permit that would enable one to stay longer in Germany was to work in certain sectors where there was a shortage of labour, so these pioneers found themselves working in the mines of the Ruhr area (the men) or in hospitals (the women), regardless of their professional qualifications. There was no more than a handful of these Japanese religious professionals in Germany – no more than 14–16 of them in all of Europe – but some of them have stayed on in the communities they helped to build.

The movement grew rather slowly till the mid-seventies, but now has an estimated 2000 members and is the largest Japanese new religion in Germany.[1] SGI-D (Soka Gakkai International – Deutschland) has taken on wholesale the organisational structure of the parent organisation in Japan, in spite of what seems at times a cumbersome and excessive system of divisions, branches and sections. Only about 5 per cent of members nowadays are Japanese. However, a disproportionately large number of these are in leadership positions, which is usually explained within the movement by the fact that most Japanese members have been practising longer than the Germans. The situation is beginning to change now and more and more Germans are being entrusted with leading roles not just at the local, but also at the national and *Bundesland* level. The Germans consider this a sign of 'indigenisation' of the movement and rate it very positively.

This take-over has not always been amicable or unproblematic. The new German local leaders were initially closely watched and occasionally told that they were stepping too far out of line and should do things in a certain way, 'as they have always been done in Japan'. A furious debate would ensue between the two camps – although there was also a minority of German members always willing to accept uncritically any Japanese suggestion 'because they know best'. This period was, however, mercifully short and I was told that German leaders have become more mature, while the Japanese are more willing to delegate responsibilities.

Some of the first generation of Japanese missionaries and even more of those who came a few years later, in the late 1960s and early 1970s, have adapted remarkably to German culture, speak German fluently, have often intermarried with Germans and tend to be on the 'German side' in disputes about further decentralisation or how things should be done. Others, on the other hand, are criticised by the German members for still not having learnt to speak German properly. One outspoken male informant told me:

'I'm sure they would have a lot to tell us, they have such a lot of experience, but they are still unable to communicate well in German, so they churn out the same tired old clichés...'

These are also the ones who tend to abide fairly strictly by the orders from above, i.e., from the Japanese headquarters, and have problems accepting the input of the German members.

One of the German women, who had been in leadership positions for quite a number of years now, described the process:

'We still have a lot to learn from them, but now gradually they are coming to accept that they too can learn from us, that it's an *exchange*. Because at first it was very much a case of "Hush, you don't know anything!". Everything came from above, like a parent with a child. But now we are all parents, from all continents.'

The initial strategy of Soka Gakkai expansion in Germany may be described as 'self-selective', i.e., the idea was that Soka Gakkai catered for certain needs and that people from any society who had those needs would find themselves attracted to the movement. These needs were defined as the same that led to the unprecedented success of Soka Gakkai in Japan in the 1950s and 1960s. Not quite integrated, non-intellectual, lower-class individuals, who felt let down by society, had made a mess of their professional or private life, did not feel central to anything within their society were attracted by the promise of immediate and practical benefits from chanting. The first Soka Gakkai members in the town where I was based during my fieldwork, for instance, were all recipients of social benefit at the time, largely unemployed, high-school dropouts or relatively poorly educated and quite often single parents. The proportion of single parents has remained the same, but the membership is now far more mainstream, educated (the initial members in many cases went back to study) and usually employed.

As Soka Gakkai became more sophisticated and experienced, it engaged in dialogue with its German members and established a new set of needs that it could then begin to cater to. This recent strategy might be called 'client-oriented'. More intellectual, middle-class and mainstream sections of society with an interest in the long-term benefits, especially those of a psychological nature, began to be attracted to Soka Gakkai and contributed to a change of emphasis. In the neighbouring town, for example, Soka Gakkai discussion meetings had evolved into highly sophisticated and complex psychological analyses (owing also to the fact that many of the members there were engaged in professions related to psychology or spiritual healing), which other members found rather far removed from the true meaning of Buddhism.

It is clear that Soka Gakkai acts as a sort of cultural broker, managing a flow of meaning between two very different socio-religious contexts and seeking to articulate its identity as a third culture in both local and global terms. But how precisely does it do that? And to what extent are there tensions, or even downright contradictions, between the globalising aims of a transnational religious organisation and the political and legal systems of individual nation-states? How well can a religion simultaneously satisfy its duties towards the community of members and humanity in general, as stated in its universalistic message? (Coleman, 1993:355).

Any discussion about a common or third culture, Featherstone (1991; 1993) postulates, must begin with a thorough examination of who does the defining, to what purpose and the parameters within which they are operating. I have tried to apply that to the specific case of Soka Gakkai in Germany.

Who does the defining?

Both German and Japanese members believe that they are defining the culture and the community. We start out immediately with two distinct definitions, but I believe that in the course of interaction a new, third definition develops, one made up of the interplay and compromises that the two sides have gone into. Nevertheless, it is quite clear that Soka Gakkai continues to maintain a somewhat asymmetrical core-periphery type of relationship with its German members, that initially the Japanese members were very reluctant to admit that they too could be learning something form those people they had been sent out to teach. This is changing now, although not fast enough for some German palates.

It is striking that, like in a marriage, it is the small things which almost lead to a breakdown of communication between the two sides. The German members were in full agreement with the Japanese members about the aims and meaning of Nichiren Buddhism, and they even accepted and found justification for the complicated organisational structure, but problems such as clothes worn at meetings, the correct position for chanting and the cleaning jobs for women proved far more difficult to accept and entailed intense negotiation on both sides. I will just refer to these three examples, which, though trivial, seem typical of the adjustment required from both Japanese and German members.

First of all, however, I must state quite clearly that most German members consider themselves fully aware of the differences between what is Buddhist and what is merely Japanese tradition in Soka Gakkai, and they scrupulously pointed out that it was the latter they disagree with, not Buddhism itself.

> 'When I first saw all these niggardly little details, I said to myself: "I don't know – I quite like this type of Buddhism, but do I want to take on board all this Japanese cultural baggage?" We are Buddhists, but we are German nevertheless. And we want to remain German.'

To return to the three examples I chose to illustrate this process of adaptation. Two of them are gender-specific, as they affected women only: the first of these, the matter of clothes, has been satisfactorily solved from the German point of view, but the second, the division of labour, is still a contentious issue.

Given the background of most of the first German members, those 'alternative' women were at first amused and then exasperated by the impeccably turned out Japanese women. They hastened to label them 'the pearl-hung faction'. Their concern was that they too would be expected to dress in similar fashion, while many of them were at the height of their punk or hippie experiments at the time. Although the neat Japanese women were, by all accounts, not openly judgmental of the more casual German way of dressing, a certain amount of role-model pressure must have been implied and the German women reacted quite strongly to that. They protested that external appearance had nothing to do with the Buddha inside or with their practice of Buddhism, and, if anything, tended to appear more dishevelled than usual at meetings. There was, however, only one seriously controversial incident, involving the wearing of skirts for the lesbian members in Hamburg. This tension petered out over the years, first, as the German members realised that they were not being forced to take on things they felt uncomfortable with, secondly, as the Japanese women themselves began to dress more casually.

The correct position for kneeling in front of the *Gohonzon* during chanting was also a sensitive issue, as many older and less flexible Western joints began to feel the strain of regular *Daimoku*. A female member, now over fifty, told me:

> 'I was perfectly happy to do that in earlier days, but now I have trouble with my arthritis and I don't see why I shouldn't use a stool. I mean, the pain doesn't help me to chant better, does it? Or bring me closer to Buddhahood? On the contrary, it hinders my concentration!'

191

At present, although most members do try to maintain a scrupulously correct position, there is considerable tolerance for those who cannot cope with that, e.g., older people and new members, and low stools or the edges of sofas or even chairs are regularly used.

Probably the most controversial and ongoing debate concerns the traditional division of labour among the gender and age-segregated groups. While few people minded the divisions per se, and most agreed that a higher number of activities scheduled for the Youth Divisions made sense, since older members generally had other commitments, such as work and family, there was considerable resentment over the gender division of labour. At all larger events, men were responsible for the general organisation, distribution of invitations, driving the guests around, while the women were relegated to the cleaning and catering functions. Some women deeply resented the cleaning itself:

> 'I don't understand why I have to clean [the *Kaikan*] for my personal development – I do the cleaning at home, don't I?'

Others emphasised that it was not the type of activity itself that they resented, but the fact that it was so strictly divided.

> 'If I'm a woman, but I am also a trained stonemason or carpenter or something, why shouldn't I use my skills? And if I were a man with no special skills, why shouldn't I clean?'

Things were beginning to change during my fieldwork, women being allowed to engage in a more varied set of activities after years of protest. One of my informants summed up the situation as follows:

> 'You must do something yourself, not wait for guidance from above. And if at first you don't succeed, you must be stubborn and simply continue hammering at the wall until you wear it out.'

What is the purpose?

Kōsen rufu[2] is the official purpose that both German and Japanese members will mention in the first breath when asked about the aim of Soka Gakkai or the reason for any of their activities. Underlying this may be hidden or semi-explicit agendas, and these are usually different for the Japanese and German members.

The Japanese members are concerned with building a reliable and efficient power structure of their organisation in Germany, which will continue to function (at least, in broad terms) much as they envisage, once they release the reins of leadership into German hands. Secondly, they are of course interested in gaining new members and also in keeping those they have already converted. Finally, there may be some incentive to create a financially self-supporting and viable branch of the movement in Germany, but this is a double-sided, potentially damaging tool, since it would give complete freedom of development (perhaps in unexpected directions) and a possible distancing due to increased independence from the Japanese headquarters.

The German members are concerned with maintaining their national and personal identity, avoiding a personality cult around the figure of the President, Daisaku Ikeda, and gaining access to the higher levels of leadership, while maintaining an effective grassroots approach.

The great number of changes that have taken place in the German Soka Gakkai in recent years, especially (I was informed) after the breakaway from the Nichiren Shoshu priesthood, are viewed by most German members as a promising beginning, but by no means quite enough. The decentralisation they envisage goes beyond the establishment of predominantly German leaders and adaptation to cultural sensitivities. The following strategy mapped out by a member of the Young Men's Division is typical:

> 'The future belongs to decentralisation. That's why we have to build up really strong local groups and encourage local initiative and autonomy. I think that after Ikeda's death there will be no single president, but a sort of confederation of country leaders. Strict hierarchy will disappear. This does not mean a descent into chaos, it's just the natural taking-over of power by the new generation. There won't be just one man or one group or one country setting down the law, but a great deal of co-operation and working out what is best for each individual case.'

A female leader summed up the German aspirations even more succinctly: 'There must be a German way of achieving *kōsen rufu*.'

Parameters

The limits within which both Japanese and German members are operating are delineated by the German state and its policy towards the new religions, but, just as importantly, these limits are likewise determined by the prevailing attitude among Germans towards religious commitment or towards foreign culture. The time frame within which they are operating is likewise significant, in two ways, namely diachronically (the fact that Soka Gakkai is a comparatively recent entry into German society – it has been around only for thirty years and visible perhaps in the last ten) and synchronically, the present point in time, with the more establishmentarist 1980s and 1990s having replaced the experimental and rebellious 1960s and 1970s. Furthermore, there are, as I mentioned above, the local variations which Soka Gakkai has learnt to live with: the rebellious North, the discouraged East, the diffuse urban community and the more inbred feuding of the rural community. Other problems which are perceived as still not fully solved include: gender roles and what, for lack of a better world, I shall call 'minority groups'. These include unmarried women, single mothers, homosexuals and lesbians and others, whose lives do not quite fit neatly into established patterns. Although there is no open disapproval or discrimination against these groups, some of them (and some who do not belong to these groups but are concerned about what they call the 'proper application of Buddhism') would like to see more active support and a greater understanding of their special needs.

> 'Buddhism has to learn to live with the realities of the German society. There *are* very many broken families here, many single mothers, and you can't present them with little booklets entitled "The Creative Family", all about women being the sunshine in the home and so on.'

One member drew my attention to the fact that local groups tend to form around members who share similar problems or life experiences, such as a town where single mothers predominate among the members, or another with single women, or Hamburg with lesbians, or another with people with nervous disorders, etc. She explained this through karma – it had obviously brought them together to try an solve their problems. The existence of these groups, however, could also be interpreted as an attempt to build up 'self-help groups', under conditions where they feel insufficiently taken into account by the central organisation. Indeed, the member who pointed these groups out to me, continued:

> 'Soka Gakkai still casts a blind eye over these people, still pretends they do not exist ... more needs to be done to understand how to apply Buddhism to the lives of people whose lives refuse to follow the prescribed patterns!'

Conclusions

I will now return to the questions I set myself at the beginning of this paper. The first of these was how a religion like Soka Gakkai, which arose under specific historical, geographical and social conditions (its period of expansion began in the era of post-war confusion and poverty in Japan and its success has been attributed to this fact by some authors, see Thomsen, 1963; McFarland, 1967; White, 1970), could become relevant to people who did not share the same language, history or cultural assumptions, such as the Germans. I think the answer lies in the fact that, while German members agree that there is a lot about Soka Gakkai which is tightly linked to the 1940s and 1950s Japan, they feel that those are inconsequential details, superfluous baggage which must either be thrown out or tailored to fit present-day requirements, which have changed in Japan as well. The essential part of Soka Gakkai, the Lotus Sutra and the teachings of Nichiren Daishonin, as revealed in the *Goshō*, are of lasting and universal value, and therefore likely to appeal to 'any human being who has ever reflected on the self and its relation to the world' (author's fieldnotes, 1996), regardless of historical or social circumstances.

The second question, strongly related to the first, concerned the proportion of universality and specificity that a religion should have in order to appeal beyond its national boundaries. The answer seems evident after the examples I gave above: members were willing to accept wholesale what they perceived as 'essential' to Soka Gakkai Buddhism: the teachings, the language of prayer, the organisational structure. It was the detail, the things which they felt belonged under the label 'Japanese custom' rather than 'Buddhism', which they objected to: the personality cult of Ikeda Daisaku, the gender segregation of work, clothes etc. Minor dissatisfaction with Soka Gakkai are perhaps raised to the status of major problems precisely because members have such high expectations of its universalistic message and believe it to be 'above' cultural traditions, historical or social specificity. Nichiren Buddhism as they see it is supposed to transcend both Japanese and German customs (or maintain only what is of value from either) and bring about a new world order and understanding.

Finally, can Soka Gakkai be accused of over-adaptation, of having lost its authenticity and specificity in its desire to gain German members? I think not. It is true that Soka Gakkai has changed a good deal in its around 30 years of existence in Germany. Long-time members are careful to point out that other religions, including Christianity, have needed much longer to adapt to foreign circumstances. The basis for change is now definitely in place, but German members feel quite a lot still remains to be done to make it a truly significant religion in their society, although they remain fairly critical of the latter as well.

However, as defined in its aims, Soka Gakkai has succeeded fairly well in Germany. It may not have as large a membership as in Italy, but the members it does have are generally long-term and thoroughly committed. There does seem to be a general concern for a good understanding of the doctrines, as well as regular practice. *Shakubuku* is not quite a top priority with German members, and many of them feel shy about discussing religious matters or even declaring their beliefs in front of people who have nothing to do with the movement, since they feel the German state and society in general is fairly hostile towards such commitment. However, the German members of Soka Gakkai seem genuinely interested not only in self-improvement and the immediate benefits of chanting, but also subscribe to the other key concerns proclaimed by Soka Gakkai International: social awareness, world peace, cultural exchange and so on. As Buddhists, they feel the interrelatedness of all things in the universe and therefore appreciate the global concerns of their religion. However, not many of them are personally involved in more than occasional study meeting discussions about the Third World. Perhaps the lasting legacy of Soka Gakkai in their lives is a curiosity and concern about other ways of living, thinking and understanding, a point where the reflexive self becomes a social self too.

Notes

1 There is some cause to suspect that Soka Gakkai underestimates its membership figures in Germany, probably so as not to appear a threat to the German authorities. The official figure has stagnated at 2000 for the past 6–7 years, although the movement also claims a net gain in members (offsetting the turnover rate) and that there were hardly any 'defections' to the Nichiren Shoshu faction after the split (Baumann, personal communication).
2 Lit. 'to widely declare and spread', it is usually glossed (on the Internet too, at the Soka Gakkai International home page) as securing world peace and happiness for all humankind through the propagation of true Buddhism.

References

Abu-Lughod, J. (1991) 'Going beyond the global babble' in King (ed.) *Culture, Globalization and the World System*. London: Macmillan.
Abou-El-Haj, B. (1991) 'Languages and models for cultural exchange' in King (ed.)*Culture, Globalization and the World System*. London: Macmillan.
Albrow, M. & King, E. (eds) (1990) *Globalization, Knowledge and Society*. London: Sage.
Appadurai, A. (ed.) (1986) *The Social Life of Things*. Cambridge:Cambridge University Press.
Bergesen, A. (ed.) (1980) *Studies of the Modern World-System*. New York: Academic Press.
Beyer, P. (1994) *Religion and Globalization*. London: Sage.
Bird et al. (1993) *Mapping the Futures. Local Cultures and Global Change*. London & New York: Routledge.
Boli-Bennett, J. (1980) 'Global Integration and the Universal Increase of State Dominance, 1910–1970' in Bergesen(ed.) *Studies of the Modern World-System*. New York: Academic Press.
Coleman, S. (1993) 'Conservative Protestantism and the world order: The Faith Movement in the United States and Sweden', *Sociology of Religion*, 54 (4):353–373.
Dhaouadi, M. (1990) 'An operational analysis of the phenomenon of the other underdevelopment in the Arab world and in the Third World' in Albrow & King (eds) *Globalization, Knowledge and Society*. London: Sage.
Featherstone, M. (1993) 'Global and local cultures' in Bird et al. *Mapping the Futures. Local Cultures and Global Change*. London & New York: Routledge.
—— (ed.) (1990) *Global Culture. Nationalism, Globalization and Modernity*. London: Sage.
Galtung, J. (1990) 'The Green Movement: A socio-historical exploration' in Albrow & King (eds) *Globalization, Knowledge and Society*. London: Sage.

Hall, S. (1991a) 'The local and the global: Globalization and ethnicity' in King, A. (ed.) *Culture, Globalization and the World System*. London: Macmillan.

—— (1991b) 'Old and new identities, old and new ethnicities' in King, A. (ed.) *Culture, Globalization and the World System*. London: Macmillan.

Hannerz, U. (1992) *Cultural Complexity*. New York: Columbia University Press.

Harvey, D. (1993) 'From space to place and back again: Reflections on the condition of postmodernity' in Bird et al. *Mapping the Futures. Local Cultures and Global Change*. London & New York: Routledge.

King, A. (ed.) (1991) *Culture, Globalization and the World System*. London: Macmillan.

Massey, D. (1993) 'Power-geometry and a progressive sense of place' in Bird et al. *Mapping the Futures. Local Cultures and Global Change*. London & New York: Routledge.

Massey, D. & Jess (eds.) (1995) *A Place in the World?* Open University and Oxford University Press.

Robertson, R. (1991) 'Social Theory, Cultural Relativity and the Problem of Globality' in King, A. (ed.) *Culture, Globalization and the World System*. London: Macmillan.

Wallerstein, I. (1974) *The Modern World System*. Vol. 1. New York: Academic Press.

—— (1991) 'The national and the universal: Can there be such a thing as world culture?' in King, A. (ed.) *Culture, Globalization and the World System*. London: Macmillan.

Wolff, J. (1991) 'The global and the specific: Reconciling conflicting theories of culture' in King, A. (ed.) *Culture, Globalization and the World System*. London: Macmillan.

Wuthnow, R. (1980) 'World Order and Religious Movements' in Bergesen (ed.) *Studies of the Modern World-System*. New York: Academic Press.

Yearley, S. (1996) *Sociology, Environmentalism, Globalization*. London: Sage.

Young, I.M. (1990) 'The ideal of community and the politics of difference' in Nicholson (ed.): *Feminism/Postmodernism*. London: Routledge.

CHAPTER SEVEN

Spirit First, Mind Follows, Body Belongs

Notions of Health, Illness and Disease in Sukyo Mahikari UK

Louella Matsunaga

This paper explores notions of health, illness, and disease, in one of the Japanese new religious movements (NRMs) which has succeeded in attracting a wide following outside Japan, Sukyo Mahikari. It begins with a consideration of healing and Japanese NRMs within the Japanese context, before focusing specifically on Sukyo Mahikari. Sukyo Mahikari teachings on health, illness and disease are then described, and the ways in which these teachings can be seen as closely interrelated with distinctively Japanese concepts of health and morality are examined.

Against this background, this paper goes on to ask how this movement has been able to expand with some success outside Japan, given a belief system which, on the face of it, appears to be strongly rooted in a distinctive Japanese worldview. This question is approached through an examination of how Sukyo Mahikari teachings on health, illness and disease have been received in the UK context, based on research conducted at the UK branch of Sukyo Mahikari over a period of around eighteen months. A combination of methodologies was used: firstly participant observation, including participation in the introductory or initiatory course followed by new members when they join the movement;[1] secondly 25 in-depth interviews with members; and thirdly a written questionnaire, distributed to the entire membership (approximately 350), from which I received 108 replies – around a 30 per cent response rate.

Healing and New Religious Movements in Japan

The topic of healing figures prominently in writing on Japanese New Religious Movements (NRMs), both in the texts produced by the movements themselves and in academic commentaries. Accounts of recovery from illness following the performance of prescribed practices are a recurrent theme in the testimonials produced by members of such movements for the

198

movements' own publications, and the biographies of their founders also commonly feature an episode of severe illness, afflicting either the founder or someone close to him/her. In this type of narrative, illness often plays the role of awakening the founder to his/her spiritual mission, and the eventual vanquishing of the illness is represented as furnishing proof of the divine inspiration and authenticity of the new movement.[2]

Academic commentators have noted the prominence of healing practices among Japan's NRMs, both in general outlines of the common features of Japanese NRMs (for example Thomsen 1963; McFarland 1967; Hardacre 1986; Reader 1991; Kitagawa 1987) and in ethnographies of particular movements (for example, Davis 1980; Hardacre 1984). However, it has also been pointed out that Japan's NRMs do not furnish the only ritual specialists concerned with illness. Kitagawa notes that the 'unusual spiritual powers in divination, sorcery, incantation, fortune-telling, and healing ... [attributed to the founders of these movements] ... are the very qualities which have been associated with the leaders of 'folk Shinto' and 'folk Buddhism' throughout the ages' (Kitagawa 1987:173), while Ohnuki-Tierney (1984) has provided a detailed description of the use of ritual specialists in Japan for the treatment of conditions ranging from gynaecological problems to tumours, with a number of mainstream Buddhist Temples and Shinto shrines specialising in particular conditions. In this sense, the healing activities of the NRMs in Japan are hardly new, and would seem to form a continuity with approaches to illness in Japan in which appeal to a religious specialist, whether from a NRM or a more mainstream movement, forms one of a plurality of health care systems[3] available to the sufferer.

Lock (1980) identifies four health care systems in Japan: the 'cosmopolitan' or 'Western' medical system, which will be referred to in this paper as bio-medicine; the 'East Asian medical system', based largely on Chinese medicine; the 'folk medical system' under which heading she includes shamanic healing and the use of talismans as well as moxibustion and massage; and the 'popular medical system', consisting of 'medical practice carried out among family members or friends without professional sources of advice' (Lock 1980: 15). To these four, Ohnuki-Tierney argues we should add 'religion-based medical care' (Ohnuki-Tierney 1984: 123). I would also suggest that the rise in popularity of alternative therapies imported from Europe and the United States in recent years has created another category of European/American based 'alternative medicine'.

However, it is important to recognise, as both Lock and Ohnuki-Tierney stress, that within the plurality of health-care systems available in Japan, the bio-medical system is dominant, and has been since the Meiji era (1868–1912). In early Meiji a system of licensing was introduced restricting medical practice, including the practice of Chinese style medicine, to those holding bio-medical degrees. Although some other types of health care also received official recognition, most notably acupuncture and massage, these were also subject to a licensing system and legal limits were imposed on their practice. Since World War II, the dominance of bio-medicine in Japan has increased further with the establishment of a universal health insurance system which covers health costs associated with bio-medicine, whereas in the case of alternative and East Asian therapies reimbursement is restricted to certain approved therapies, and further subject to the condition that such therapies are either prescribed and administered by a bio-medical practitioner, or that the patient is referred to an approved, licensed specialist by a bio-medical practitioner.

Similarly, although the consultation of religious specialists for health problems continues to be widespread, this tends to be in parallel with the use of bio-medicine, and is tolerated only in so far as the hegemony of bio-medicine is not challenged. Cases where individuals have rejected mainstream medical treatment in favour of a religious-based approach have attracted controversy in the media, and, in one celebrated case involving the NRM Sekai Kyusei Kyo (SKK), a movement well known in Japan for its critical stance on the use of medication, in the courts. This case involved the death of a 16 year old girl from kidney disease in 1968, following her decision to refuse medical treatment or medication, instead relying solely on *jōrei*, a kind of spiritual purification practised by the movement.[4] Although the courts cleared Sekai Kyusei Kyo of the charge of violating the Medical Practitioner's Law and acting in detriment to public welfare in the case brought against the movement by the girl's parents, they did, in the final judgement on the case, run up a warning flag against the intervention of NRMs in the treatment of illness in so far as this might run counter to mainstream bio-medical treatment, stating that: 'There is a possibility that the law may be violated and public welfare may be harmed by the undue promotion of a cure for disease other than that offered by ordinary medical treatment' (Oie, S. (ed.) 1984, my translation).[5]

There is insufficient evidence available to gauge the effect of cases such as this on NRMs in Japan, but in any event at present the approach of Japanese NRMs to matters of health and illness is marked by caution, and an avoidance of any suggestion of conflict with the medical establishment. The tendency is rather for Japanese NRMs to work alongside mainstream bio-medicine. The *Shinshūkyō jiten* (dictionary of new religions) devotes an entire section of its chapter on the social activities of Japanese NRMs to the involvement of these movements with mainstream medicine, and notes that, 'on the whole, the healing in New Religions and modern medicine are not in an antagonistic relationship: it would be more apt to describe their relationship as one of peaceful co-existence or complementarity' (Inoue 1990: 579, my translation).

Inoue also suggests that even where movements such as Sekai Kyusei Kyo, or indeed, Sukyo Mahikari,[6] are well known for their critical stance on taking medication, and appear to equate medicine with poison (often referred to in Japanese as *yakudokuron* – the medicine is poison thesis), what these movements are doing is criticising excessive reliance on medication, and stressing that medication can also have a poisonous or toxic aspect. It is important to note that such movements do not forbid their members to consult mainstream medical practitioners or to receive treatment, including in some cases medication, from these practitioners. Also, as McVeigh (1991) has pointed out, the concern of movements such as Sekai Kyusei Kyo or Mahikari with the potentially deleterious effects of medication mirrors widespread popular concern in Japan regarding the possibility of harmful side effects from medication *(yakugai)* (Ohnuki-Tierney 1984:102).

Inoue goes on to describe the involvement of Japanese NRMs with mainstream medicine in Japan, and notes that, despite the heavy capital investment required, a number have established clinics, laboratories, and even fully fledged hospitals. In addition to these high profile ventures, he also notes the involvement of many movements in ventures to promote health, for example the sale of special food by a number of groups including Agonshu, and the 'nature' (chemical free) farming engaged in by Sekai Kyusei Kyo.[7] As Inoue points out, this type of concern with the promotion of health as well as the healing of illness finds a ready echo in contemporary Japanese society, an observation which also holds true for much of Western Europe and America.

The *Shinshūkyō jiten* lists five hospitals established by NRMs in Japan: the Seventh Day Adventist hospital in Tokyo, whose beginnings can be traced back to the opening of a small clinic in 1927; the Tenrikyo Yorozu clinic in Tenri city, which began as a foundation concerned with medical treatment, counselling and welfare in 1935, eventually opening Tenri Hospital, which was designated as a hospital for clinical training in July 1968; Rissho Koseikai's Kōsei Hospital, opened in Tokyo in 1952; PL (Perfect Liberty) Hospital, established in Osaka in 1956 by PL Kyodan; and finally Ube First Hospital established by Shizen no Nami in Ube in Yamaguchi prefecture in western Japan in 1979. All these hospitals offer mainstream medical treatment along the same lines as secular institutions, although some also have special features associated with their parent organisation. Of these, a particularly interesting case is that of the Tenrikyo hospital, which offers alongside its mainstream medical treatment counselling by spiritual advisors, who try to diagnose, and help the patient to resolve, the underlying spiritual causes for their illness.

The Tenrikyo case is suggestive, in that it indicates that one way in which NRMs have achieved a complementary role to that of bio-medicine in Japan is through seeking to address the issue of the meaning of illness rather than the treatment of disease. That is, following the distinction made in medical anthropology, where disease is used to denote a biological disorder, and illness to denote the person's experience of that disorder, religious specialists attempt to place illness in a wider context of a system of beliefs where explanations for the occurrence of the illness, and why it should afflict this particular person at this particular time, may be sought. This diagnostic process may also lead to treatment, or recommendations as to how the illness may best be dealt with, and in some ways therefore follows a similar path to that of the biomedical practitioner, who also diagnoses, offers treatment, and may offer explanations of why and how the disease has occurred. However, there are some important differences, which allow biomedical practitioners and religious specialists to, in a sense, occupy a different conceptual space in their approach to the sick person. Notably, whereas explanations offered by biomedical practitioners tend to be located in an impersonal realm where the disease is treated as a separate entity, isolable from the person afflicted by it; in explanations offered by religious specialists; the sick person, and his or her experience is at the centre, and the social, moral, and spiritual contexts of the illness take on great importance in diagnosing, understanding, and possibly seeking to treat or at least deal with, the disorder.

The Tenri Journal of Religion, produced under the auspices of Tenrikyo, has published numerous articles exploring this difference in approach between biomedical practitioners and religious specialists, many of which are based on research conducted in Tenri Hospital. One of the more succinct statements of the relationship between the two is given by Hirasawa, summarising a sermon by the second leader, or Shinbashira of Tenrikyo not long after the opening of Tenri Hospital:

> The body is a thing lent from God the Parent, and the mind alone is at our command. Medical treatment has the function of repairing the body, a thing borrowed. Disease is a divine warning given to the body, a thing borrowed. (Hirasawa 1963: 19)

Thus, while it is the medical practitioner's task to repair the body, where possible, it is for the religious specialist, together with the person concerned, to interpret and respond to the 'divine warning' which constitutes the inner meaning of the disease.[8]

'Healing', as offered by religious specialists, therefore tends to take on far broader implications than the treatment of disease as offered by the biomedical practitioner. Indeed Yumiyama (1995) notes that many NRMs in Japan avoid the term 'healing' (*iyashi*) altogether:

> In most cases the words *sukui* or *kyūsai*, both meaning 'salvation', are preferred, even when the curing of sickness is involved ... religions often stress that the provisional cures effected by healing are but the entranceway to the profounder succour offered by true salvation.
> (Yumiyama 1995: 268–9)

202

Another way to look at this is that, for these movements, the healing of illness is only part of a wider process, in which all aspects of a person's life may be transformed. Thus not only the body, but also the person's relationships with those around them, their physical and social environment, their state of mind, their spiritual state, and the influence of actions in past lives may all be implicated. Therefore, to look at healing in NRMs is also to bring into question the worldviews of the movements and the role which notions of health, healing, illness and disease play within that context.[9]

Sukyo Mahikari: Background

This paper takes as its focus one of the best known NRMs in Japan, and one which also has a considerable overseas membership: Sukyo Mahikari. Sukyo is a word formed from two *kanji* (Chinese characters) which may be translated as 'revered teachings' but is more frequently rendered as 'supra-religion',[10] while Mahikari comes from two characters meaning 'true light'. The movement was founded in 1959 by Yoshikazu Okada, and, following a succession dispute on his death in 1974, split into two branches: Sukyo Mahikari, headed by Okada's adopted daughter, Keishu Okada; and Sekai Mahikari Bunmei Kyodan, headed by Sakae Sekiguchi, one of the founder's first followers.[11] Of the two, Sukyo Mahikari retained the majority of the followers at the time of the split, and continues to be by far the larger: in March 1996 Sukyo Mahikari claimed over 800,000 members, of whom around 150,000 were members of branches outside Japan. According to Sukyo Mahikari headquarters, the movement has now spread to seventy-five countries including Australia, Singapore, several African countries, the United States, Latin America, the Caribbean and a number of European countries. Most of the overseas missions listed by headquarters were established in the mid 1970s.

Within Europe, Sukyo Mahikari has one of the largest memberships of the Japanese NRMs, with an estimated 10,000 members,[12] second only to Soka Gakkai, the Nichiren Buddhist organisation, which claims 19,000 members.[13] Sukyo Mahikari is particularly strong in France, Belgium and Italy, and its European and African headquarters is located in Luxembourg. Smaller groups operate in various other European countries. Since the mid 1980s the movement has also been active in the Czech Republic and in Hungary, and has increased its activities in Eastern Europe generally since the end of the Cold War.

Sukyo Mahikari, henceforward referred to as Mahikari, describes itself as existing to 'establish a better world' and a 'spirit-centred civilisation',[14] while on an individual level, the movement aims to help people achieve health (*ken*), harmony (*wa*) and prosperity (*fu*). Both the global and the individual aims of the movement are thought to be advanced through the practice of giving and receiving light, *mahikari no waza*. (the art of true light). This practice is at the heart of Mahikari, and any person expressing an interest in Mahikari is likely to be first invited to receive light, on the basis that experiencing receiving light is essential to any understanding of the movement. In contrast to those Japanese NRMs which produce a large number of publications, and encourage or even require members to study these (for example, Kofuku no Kagaku or Seicho no Ie), Mahikari remains resolutely experientially based. The movement produces few publications, and many members appear sceptical as to how far the practice of Mahikari can, or should be, explained.

Mahikari no waza, also referred to as *okiyome*, meaning purification, can be described as the act of raising the hand over objects, people, oneself – anything – and, according to Mahikari belief, radiating 'true light' from the palm of the hand. Followers are enabled to radiate true light by receiving a sacred pendant, called *omitama*, following a three day introductory course to the movement.[15] *Omitama* must be treated with great care, and cannot be lent to anyone else, as it is viewed as a spiritual cord linking its wearer to God. Elaborate procedures exist for the wrapping of *omitama*,[16] and special provisions must be made both to wear it and to keep it in an appropriate place when it is not being worn. There are also prescribed procedures for removing it and replacing it, for example before and after a shower (it must never get wet). *Omitama* 'accidents', for example, dropping the *omitama*, are taken very seriously, and the *omitama* must be returned to the movement's headquarters for special treatment if such an accident occurs.[17]

When giving light to another person, prayers are first offered asking God's permission to give that person light, and then permission is asked of the person who is to receive. Then the person giving light sits or kneels opposite the person receiving, who is asked to close their eyes and place their hands together in prayer position with the left thumb over the right.[18] The person giving light then claps his or her hands three times and chants the prayer '*Amatsu Norigoto*' (this is always chanted in Japanese, as the words are thought to have special spiritual vibrations). After that, the person giving light raises their hand and gives light to a point in the forehead referred to as point 8, believed to be the site of the primary soul. This continues for about ten minutes, after which the person giving light says '*oshizumari*' (be still)[19] three times, at the same time bringing both hands down, sweeping the air on either side of the head and shoulders of the person receiving. The person receiving is then asked to open their eyes, and is then asked if s/he can see clearly. If s/he cannot see clearly the '*oshizumari*' procedure is repeated three more times. This is continued until s/he can see (inability to see clearly at this point is thought to indicate spirit disturbance, a notion which is explained in more detail below). The person receiving is then asked to turn round, and light is given to points at the back of the neck and the kidneys (important because of their role as one of the main purificatory organs of the body), and any other special points the person may request, or may be thought appropriate – new members are given a brief outline of what sorts of points are appropriate for different sorts of illnesses during the initial training. A full session generally lasts about 50 minutes, but if pressed for time point 8 only may be given. There are also cases where other points are given but not point 8 – for example in cases of mental problems or depression, and also in some cases of insomnia, because of the danger of a strong spirit reaction. It is also taught that one must never give oneself point 8 because of the possibility of spirit reactions.

For Mahikari, giving and receiving light is one of the main ways of achieving the overall goals of the movement. To give and to receive light is thought to raise levels of consciousness *(sōnen)*, and to make people more 'tuned in' with God. *Okiyome* therefore has a significance within the movement that goes far beyond notions of health or illness, rather it aims to effect a spiritual transformation. But accompanying this spiritual transformation there may be physical changes, and it is here that we become concerned with the notions of health, illness, and healing.

Notions of Health and Illness in Mahikari

The founder of Mahikari taught that the true state of the universe is one of health, harmony, and prosperity.[20] In the Mahikari worldview, health is the absence of disorder, and therefore implies the second quality, harmony. Illness, on the other hand, is a kind of purification, of either spiritual impurities, for example, wrong attitudes or wrong actions, or karmic impurities from previous lives; or physical impurities, that is, the accumulation of toxins in the body, which may originate from diet, environmental pollution, medication, or negative emotions such as anger. In the symptoms of illness, purification can be seen at work: as toxins melt they may be discharged for example through diarrhoea or vomiting, or through a runny nose or a cough. A fever is also often a sign that toxins are melting. Attaching spirits may also cause illnesses: this is when spirits attach to the sufferer, sometimes because that person harmed the spirit in a previous incarnation. Purification, or cleansing, is thought to take place not only on the level of individual illness but in all areas of life. For example, financial difficulties may be another form of cleansing, as may be difficulties in relationships. Cleansing also takes place in the natural world: rain, wind, and lightning are all thought to be forms of cleansing, as are events commonly termed natural disasters, such as earthquakes.[21] Mahikari teaches that the whole world is now undergoing a prolonged period of intense purification, referred to as the Baptism of Fire, and that events such as the Kobe Earthquake are a manifestation of this process.

205

Mahikari teaches that about 80 per cent of illnesses have spiritual causes, and 20 per cent physical or mental causes. In terms of the relationship between the movement and mainstream biomedicine, this means that Mahikari teachings are often critical of biomedicine on the basis that it treats symptoms, and does not address the causes of illness. Furthermore, mainstream medical treatment may suppress symptoms thought in Mahikari terms to be necessary purification – for example, fever or diarrhoea. And the use of medication is thought to be a contributory factor to the build up of toxins in the body.

However, this critical stance stops short of opposition to all biomedical treatment – indeed the movement encourages its members to consult biomedical doctors and to take medication where appropriate. Members are also encouraged to be grateful both to their doctors and for the medication they may receive. As to exactly when it is appropriate to seek such help, this is left largely up to the individual member, and the survey of members in the UK showed considerable variation in patterns of consultation of biomedical doctors and other healthcare specialists. In any case, in broad terms, the relationship of Mahikari with mainstream medicine is cooperative rather than confrontational, and follows similar lines to those described above for Japanese NRMs as a whole. Indeed, in 1989 the movement established the Yoko clinic as part of a health centre in Takayama city, the site of its main shrine. By 1994 this clinic, used by local people as well as movement members, had a paediatric department and a department of internal medicine, and nineteen beds for in-patients. A section on the clinic in a movement publication also featured prominently the various technological equipment available in the clinic, including X-ray equipment, and a CT scanner. The description of the clinic's objectives emphasised that it aimed for a holistic approach, treating both mind, or spirit,[22] and body; and also that as a religious organisation it had established this clinic to be of service to local society. Also along the lines of encouraging health (and not merely treating disease), the movement has established the Yoko Farm in Takayama city, where Mahikari principles are applied to farming (Sukyo Mahikari 1994).

But at the heart of the Mahikari approach to health lies the practice of giving and receiving *okiyome*. As pointed out above, this is a process thought to affect the whole person, and to be generally beneficial at all levels of being: physical, mental, and spiritual. One aspect of this may be to assist in the restoration of health by addressing the causes of illness. It is explained during the initial training for new members that the divine light radiated during *okiyome* causes accumulated toxins in the body of the person receiving light to melt and to be eliminated. This elimination may take various forms: frequently diarrhoea, vomiting, or a runny nose, and anyone receiving light for the first time is warned that this may happen. These, however, are merely the physical manifestations of a more far-reaching process, as *okiyome* is not thought to act primarily on a physical level, but on a spiritual level, with the spiritual level in turn affecting the mental and physical levels. This is explained using the metaphor of upstream and downstream. The spiritual world is upstream, with the mental and physical world downstream. Any impurities on a spiritual level will inevitably flow down to the mental and then the physical levels, while purification at a spiritual level will also have the effect of purifying the two lower levels. Purifying the mental or physical levels alone is ineffective, as the source of impurity remains. This is the principle of 'spirit first, mind follows, body belongs' (*reishu, shinjū, taizoku*). *Okiyome* is thought to be effective because it acts on the spiritual level, and this is also the reason why biomedical treatment, though sometimes necessary, is seen as insufficient: it treats the symptoms without addressing what Mahikari views as the cause. This is not a criticism directed solely at biomedicine: Mahikari also urges caution where 'natural healing' is concerned, suggesting that it may even be dangerous, because such healing relies on the individual's energy resources, which may become seriously depleted, whereas Mahikari teaches that *okiyome* is drawn from an external, divine, and inexhaustible source.

Two other important aspects of Mahikari teachings relating to health and illness concern spirit possession, referred to in Mahikari as 'attaching spirits', and the care of the ancestors. These are both complex areas of Mahikari cosmology which deserve a detailed treatment in their own right. Here I will only give a brief summary of these teachings in so far as they relate to notions of health and disease.

As stated above, Mahikari teaches that about 80 per cent of illness has a spiritual cause. This may be linked to attaching spirits, that is, spirits of the dead who attach themselves to a living person, and may then inflict various sorts of suffering on that person, which may affect any area of their life: including relationships, material prosperity, and health. These attaching spirits may be spirits of people whom the afflicted person has harmed in a previous lifetime; or they may be spirits from a family with whom the afflicted person's family has had some sort of conflict; or they could be spirits from the afflicted person's own family, perhaps because the correct ancestral rites for that spirit have not been observed by their family. The type of affliction is seen as being related to the original injury suffered by the spirit, for example a person with financial difficulties may have caused financial suffering to their attaching spirit in a previous lifetime, or one of their ancestors may have caused this suffering. For health related problems a similar pattern may apply, with the health problem related symbolically to the original injury suffered by the attaching spirit, for example a problem necessitating an operation, which involves cutting, may be linked to the 'sin of the sword', that is, the person undergoing the operation may be understood to have killed people in battle in a previous life, or one of his ancestors may have done so.

A symbolic topography of the body is also taught, and may be used to illuminate the causes of illnesses. Here back is related to front, and left to right, as spiritual is to physical.[23] An injury on the left side of the body may be a warning from God, as this is the spiritual side of the body.[24] Also, in a session of *okiyome*, after giving light to the seat of the main soul, believed to lie in the forehead, light is mainly radiated to the back of the body as this is the spiritual side, and, as explained above, it is the spiritual aspect which must be purified first, in order for the mental and physical aspects to follow.

A number of themes run through the way in which attaching spirits are viewed in Mahikari. Firstly, although these spirits may cause much distress, this is often thought to be because they themselves have suffered in the past, and may be continuing to suffer in the spirit world. They are seen as themselves in need of help and salvation, and it is for this reason that the imagery of exorcism is inappropriate. They are not evil spirits to be cast out, but spirits out of place, who have not succeeded in liberating themselves from the physical plane, and who may be very confused, possibly not even realising that their physical body is dead. By giving light to a person, any spirits attaching to that person will also be given light, and by this process the spirits too may achieve salvation, leaving this physical plane and moving to the astral world. Spirits may also be counselled and given Mahikari teachings *(mioshie)* during spirit investigations conducted by *dōshi* to identify attaching spirits.[25] This is not considered always to be necessary, as giving light to a person in any case has the effect of giving light to any spirit that may be attached to them: it is up to the *dōshi* to decide if and when a spirit investigation may be necessary.

Another important theme is that of responsibility. An illness or other misfortune may be ascribed to an attaching spirit, but the reason for that spirit attaching to that particular person lies in their own actions in past lives, or in the actions of their ancestors or close family (for example spouse). The illness or other misfortune is a means of purification, and also expiation. It therefore should be met with gratitude for having the opportunity for expiation and apology for past misdeeds.

The third important theme is that of continuity between ancestors and descendants. Ancestors and descendants are seen as spiritually linked: the misdeeds of the ancestors are visited on their descendants, and conversely, action taken to help the ancestors will have a beneficial effect on their descendants. This is another aspect of the upstream, downstream principle, with the ancestors upstream from the descendants, so that anything affecting the ancestors will flow downstream to their descendants. The same principle is also applied to the living: parents' spiritual state is believed to affect their children. This is particularly relevant in cases of children's illnesses, where the mother will generally receive light as well as the child, in the belief both that the child's illness may originate from the mother, and that for the mother to receive light will benefit the child.

Finally, and related to the above, there is a notion of mutual care between ancestors and descendants continuing after death. The descendants have a duty of care to their ancestors, and the ancestors, if properly cared for, will care for and watch over their descendants. However, if ancestors are not cared for properly they may remind their descendants of their duties by inflicting some sort of misfortune on them.

To summarise the Mahikari view of health and illness, then, health is seen as the natural, God-given state, from which humankind has departed through the accumulation of spiritual and physical impurities. Illness is one aspect of the process of elimination of these impurities: a process of purification, or cleansing, which takes place in all aspects of human existence, as well as on a societal and planetary level. Illness should be met with gratitude and apology, and seen as a way of expiating individual and ancestral karma. And although treatment of illnesses and accidents on a physical level may be necessary, it is also, and more importantly, necessary to respond on a spiritual level. This may be achieved through giving and receiving light to eliminate impurities and accumulated toxins, and also through changing one's attitude. It also implies a changed relationship with the spiritual world, particularly in areas such as care of the ancestors, and also in offering service and prayer to Su-God, according to prescribed Mahikari patterns.

This view of health and illness has a number of implications. Firstly it implies a moral system: McVeigh writes that in *okiyome*, 'one comes to expose the cause of and resolve a past moral/spiritual violation. It is a very obvious example of how sentiments and bodily states are mobilized to support social ideas' (McVeigh 1995: 65). This in turn raises the question of to what extent these social ideas are embedded in the Japanese cultural context: McVeigh argues forcefully that they are, writing of an 'ethnomorality', and, further, that 'Mahikari supports a set of normative ideas that are conspicuously congruent with mainstream Japanese society' (McVeigh 1995:59), specifically, a 'morality of dependency',[26] stressing the importance of gratitude and obedience, and, to a lesser extent, empathy and self-examination (McVeigh 1995: 59–63). The importance attached to the care of the ancestors and ideas concerning spirit possession also show clear continuities with practices and beliefs in other Japanese religions, both in the mainstream Buddhist sects (particularly as far as practices relating to the ancestors are concerned), and in the folk tradition, with its shamans and mediums,[27] as well as many of the other Japanese NRMs.

Helen Hardacre, writing on another Japanese NRM, Reiyukai, has argued that Reiyukai's explanations of illness and healing practices are closely tied to a particular world view in which harmony and care of the ancestors are stressed, and that Reiyukai healing may be effective in part because it offers an etiology of illness constructed of culturally familiar components, which is more readily understandable than explanations offered by biomedicine:

'This is so not because one is more or less true than the other, but because the ancestors are already connected in a world view that is real and intelligible to the individual in a way that germs and germ theory are not' (Hardacre 1984: 181). In addition, she points out that biomedical doctors in Japan may give explanations using a great deal of jargon, and English words which are unlikely to be understood by the patient. Other factors that she identifies as disposing people to seek help in Reiyukai are the support given by the group to the person receiving healing in Reiyukai as against the impersonal physician-patient relationship, and the high financial cost of medical treatment in Japan, although she also points out that it is not an either-or choice, and many Reiyukai members also use bio-medicine when they feel it necessary.

Much the same arguments could be made concerning the ways in which illness is explained in Mahikari: the explanations given can be seen as satisfying and readily comprehensible in the Japanese cultural context, and as providing an attractive alternative, or supplement, to the bio-medical mainstream. The importance of health/illness related teachings and practices in attracting new members to Mahikari in Japan may be seen in the high proportion of members who joined because of illness: Davis gives a figure of 52 per cent who joined for this reason in his 1980 study, and informal conversation with members in a Tokyo *dōjō* which I visited in 1996 suggested that this continues to be an important factor.

It could also be pointed out that Mahikari ideas of pollution and purification echo important elements of what might be termed folk beliefs concerning health and illness in Japan, and also of Shinto beliefs. Lock(1980) writes that in the *Kojiki*, human beings were thought of as basically good, and evil as something external which could be removed by purification. Illness might be caused by evil spirits, but also by contact with things thought of as polluting – she cites the examples of blood, corpses, and people with skin diseases. In either case, the treatment was to purify the sufferer, either through purification rituals where evil spirits were involved, or by treatments designed to purge the body of the pollution:

> the aim was to drive out the offending material. The medicine was required to be strong and to produce a visible and perhaps violent reaction inside the body, resulting in some form of expulsion.
>
> (Lock 1980:25)

The beliefs recorded in the Kojiki regarding disease causation and treatment later became a part of Shinto philosophy, as Shinto gradually became systematised, and remain influential in Japan today. Lock goes on to note that:

Avoidance of constipation and the practice of regular bathing and gargling are still central to concepts of health in Japan today – the body must undergo thorough and regular cleansing in order to avoid sickness.

(Lock 1980:25)

Although there are points of difference between Mahikari teachings and the beliefs described by Lock, there are also clear continuities, and it would seem that the idea of cleansing, or purification of the body as beneficial in the maintenance of health and resolution of illness are deeply rooted in Japanese society. Here again, as with beliefs concerning ancestors, and the 'ethnomorality' implied by Mahikari beliefs on the causation of disease, Mahikari teachings concerning health and illness seem profoundly embedded in the Japanese cultural matrix.

How, then, have these teachings been received by the overseas members of Mahikari? If we follow Hardacre's argument for Reiyukai, and suggest that part of the appeal of Mahikari teachings in Japan is that they provide a way of understanding and dealing with illness that makes sense in Japanese terms, how far can they retain any appeal outside Japan? At first glance, we might suspect that this is a movement with too strong a Japanese base to have much appeal overseas, but yet, as noted above, Mahikari has, comparatively speaking, quite a substantial overseas membership. How has this come about?

In the remainder of this paper I attempt to address this question through an investigation of the ways in which Mahikari teachings on health and illness are understood in the UK context.

Mahikari in the UK

The UK branch of Sukyo Mahikari, located in South London, has only been active since the early 1980s, and is still relatively small, serving an estimated 350 members or so nationwide. This makes it the second largest Japanese NRM in the UK, some way behind Soka Gakkai UK, whose membership is measured in the thousands,[28] and also far behind other major non-Japanese NRMs in the UK.[29] However, the movement estimates that a further 900 or so people receive light from members every month in the London centre or in the homes of members which are open for giving and receiving light.[30] These figures would seem to indicate that the influence of the movement, measured in terms of their core activity, extends beyond the actual membership figures, although it still lags considerably behind Soka Gakkai.

As far as the composition of the membership is concerned, the movement has an older membership on average than most NRMs in the UK, and could be described as predominantly middle-aged. A clear majority of the members (around 60 per cent) are aged between 30 and 49, while fewer

211

than 20 per cent are under 30. This contrasts both with Soka Gakkai UK, in which a little over half the respondents to Wilson and Dobbelaere's survey were under 30 (Wilson and Dobbelaere 1994), and also with many high profile non-Japanese NRMs – for example Eileen Barker calculated the average age of members of the Unification Church as between 22 and 23 (Barker 1984). On education, however, the overall picture is similar to Soka Gakkai in the UK, in that members have a relatively high level of education compared to the general population.[31] About half Mahikari members reported continuing their education past the age of 18, with another 14 per cent still in full time education. Many of these were mature students. On gender distribution, Mahikari is fairly typical of most religious organisations, both NRMs and more mainstream organisations in the preponderance of female members – a little over 60 per cent.[32] However, turning to ethnic composition and nationality, the movement is remarkable for being very mixed: nearly half of the questionnaire respondents were born outside the UK, of these, few were Japanese (around 5 per cent), with substantial minorities drawn from other European countries (14 per cent), the Chinese diaspora (10 per cent), and Africa and the Caribbean (8 per cent), as well as some members from India.[33]

About half the members of Mahikari in the UK are married, with another 10 per cent living as married. The per centage of single members is slightly lower than in Soka Gakkai at around a quarter, compared to about a third for Soka Gakkai. For those married or living with a partner, over half reported that their partner was also a member. And around 20 per cent of the total reported having another close relative in the movement – most commonly a parent or a brother or sister. So, despite the relatively short time that Mahikari has been active in the UK, some degree of family membership is emerging. This tendency is encouraged by the emphasis Mahikari places on family unity, and the policy of not allowing people to become members unless their family support this decision. However, with the exception of the 10–20 year old age group, most of whom were introduced to the movement by one or both parents, Mahikari in the UK is still largely a movement of first generation converts, most of whom are very recent converts, with a clear majority of the respondents to the questionnaire having joined since 1990.

As far as previous religiosity is concerned, around half the questionnaire respondents considered themselves as previously belonging to a religion, and most of these still felt they belonged to that religion, while several of the non-religious half added a comment on the questionnaire that they disliked religion and didn't consider Mahikari to be a religion. So here we have an interesting mix between those who feel their existing religious belief is accommodated, or even in some cases made more meaningful within Mahikari, and those who feel Mahikari is not a religion. There is also a contrast here with other NRMs where exclusive allegiance to the movement is demanded of members – in the Mahikari case, adherence to Mahikari does not necessarily displace previously held religious (or anti-religious) beliefs, although it may well lead to a reframing of those beliefs.

Around half the members also had experience of other spiritual practices, including spiritualism, yoga, TM (transcendental meditation) and Reiki. A smaller number expressed an interest in phenomena often associated with the New Age, such as divination (11.8 per cent), UFOs (22 per cent), astrology (24 per cent), or channelling (9.5 per cent). It is interesting to note that of the other spiritual practices respondents reported having tried, the largest categories after yoga, which many respondents said they did simply as a form of exercise, were Reiki (21 per cent of those having tried another spiritual practice) and Spiritualism (23 per cent), both of which offer a healing practice involving raising the hand over areas of the body which looks, at least superficially, very similar to Mahikari.

Looking at the occupations of Mahikari members in the UK, and comparing them with the findings of Wilson and Dobbelaere (1994) for Soka Gakkai, although both movements seem to draw their members largely from middle-class occupations, a much higher percentage of Soka Gakkai members are drawn from the Performing Arts, or Graphic Arts, both insignificant categories for Mahikari. In contrast, in Mahikari the largest single category was that of the caring professions, including, notably, alternative[34] therapists as well as mainstream medical personnel (see table 1).[35]

One of the most striking findings of the questionnaire was that as well as attracting a number of practitioners of alternative medicine, the movement

Table 1: A comparison of the occupational breakdown of the membership of Soka Gakkai International UK (SGIUK) and Sukyo Mahikari UK

	SGIUK	Sukyo Mahikari UK
caring professions	18.9%	37% (includes: 9% alternative therapists 7% other medical 14% teachers)
admin. and office staff	27.2%	26%
performing arts	13.6%	1%
public relations	6.5%	5%
graphic arts	10.8%	6%
industrial and service workers	10.4%	8%
none (students, housewives)	12.7%	17%

Soka Gakkai figures from Wilson and Dobbelaere 1994. Mahikari figures from author's questionnaire of Mahikari members 1996.

213

also has a very high proportion of members who have used some sort of alternative medicine – far higher than for the general population. Questionnaire results showed 72.4 per cent of Mahikari membership having tried some form of complementary medicine, as against an estimated figure for the UK as a whole of 26–30 per cent (Sharma 1995).

Putting this finding together with the high number of members with a previous interest in other non-mainstream spiritual practices, it would seem that a relatively high proportion of the UK membership of Mahikari has come to the movement from a background of interest in what might broadly be termed 'alternatives', or activities outside the mainstream, both in the domains of spirituality and healthcare. This background in many respects resembles Colin Campbell's notion of the 'cultic milieu', defined as 'the cultural underground' (Campbell 1972: 122) of society, which Campbell suggests characteristically combines elements of both mysticism and healing.[36] This is in some ways not a particularly surprising finding, as it is widely argued by sociologists of religion, including Campbell, that this type of milieu provides a particularly fertile recruiting ground for NRMs of all kinds. However, here I am concerned to probe one aspect of this milieu which seems of particular relevance to Mahikari, that is, the domain of alternative approaches to health and disease, and to ask why Mahikari in the UK should have such a high proportion of its membership involved in the alternative health network. In part, the answer lies in the history of the movement in this country.

The first attempt to introduce Mahikari to the UK was in 1971, when a member of the Mahikari youth group in Kyoto went to England in a solo missionary endeavour which seems to have been largely unsuccessful. The current UK movement can be dated back to 1982, when an elderly Japanese couple, Dr and Mrs Kinno, went to the UK to spread Mahikari. Dr Kinno had been head of a Mahikari centre in Japan, and also a professor at Tokushima University. However, according to the recollections of current members who joined at that time and knew the Kinnos, it was Mrs Kinno who played the major role in attracting members. The picture they give of her is of a very warm, energetic, charismatic woman, who spoke limited English, and dedicated herself simply to 'giving light' to as many people as possible. The recollection of these early members of their initial contacts with the movement is therefore highly experiential, with a more intellectual appreciation of the teachings of Mahikari only coming later, when the first *kenshū*, (introductory training course) for new members, was arranged.

This initial core of members seem to have met the movement via an informal network of friends and acquaintances involved in one way or another with the East West Centre, a building in East London which houses a range of alternative health practitioners and a macrobiotic centre.[37] Recalling their developing involvement with the movement, early members recounted initially knowing little or nothing of the movement beyond the experience of receiving light. But it seems that a number of them later began to frame their understanding of Mahikari in terms of their interests and experience in fields such as macrobiotics and alternative medicine – Mahikari was seen as providing something more, a dimension lacking in their current practice, or as a natural extension of what they were doing.

One member from these early days who has practised various kinds of alternative medicine, including shiatsu and acupuncture, as well as macrobiotics, pointed out what he saw as continuities between some of these practices and Mahikari: for example the importance of the idea of energy, which he connected with the energy meridians he had learned about in shiatsu and acupuncture, and also the parallels between *okiyome* points and acupuncture points. As far as macrobiotics and Mahikari were concerned, he noted that he had learned many of the ideas taught in Mahikari previously in macrobiotics, including teachings relating to karma – 'I heard about that in a lecture twenty years ago' – and also the idea of a forthcoming Baptism of Fire, which he related to macrobiotics teachings on the effect of the changing tilt of the earth on people's consciousness. Even *okiyome* was related by this member to the macrobiotics practice of palm healing, although he did feel that the *omitama* received by Mahikari members had a special role to play, commenting:

> 'Well, I think everyone has that ability, but now people are not in such good condition, they need *omitama* to help. But there's also something in me which feels it's a different kind of energy.'

Other members from this time also mentioned the links between Mahikari teachings and what they had previously learned in macrobiotics: for example another member from the East West Centre, when asked about the causes of ailments such as coughs and colds, concurred with most of the members interviewed that these were 'purifications of the body', but added 'I believed that with macrobiotics before anyway.'

Such perceived continuities were not only noted by those with a background in those areas of alternative medicine originating from Japan or China, where one might expect some common features to be present: Mahikari members with an interest in homeopathy, an alternative medical system of German origin which has been widely used throughout Western Europe since the nineteenth century, were just as likely to point out that Mahikari teachings on health and disease echoed much that they learned in homeopathy. For example, a practising homeopath who is also a member of Mahikari explained in answer to the question of what first attracted him to Mahikari:

> 'It fits in with other things I've been doing, like homeopathy. For example, when I had a discharge from the sinuses – that's something you would expect from a homeopathic remedy, it's an indication that

you've found the right remedy... I think Mahikari works maybe even at a higher level than homeopathy. Homeopathic remedies work on a higher energy level, on the vital force – it's a form of electromagnetic energy which seems to somehow harmonise with your vital force. It produces a reaction on the body or the mind – normally a sense of well-being, but also you often see discharge, the body getting rid of toxins. In *kenshū* also I've heard it mentioned that homeopathy is a way of opening up spiritual awareness.'

Indeed, the responses to the questionnaire indicate that of those members who have tried one or more of the complementary therapies, more have tried homeopathy (46.7 per cent) than have tried one of the therapies of Japanese or Chinese origin – 32.4 per cent each for acupuncture and shiatsu, and 18.1 per cent for macrobiotics. This would seem to reflect the general dominance of homeopathy among alternative therapies used in Western Europe.[38] Other popular therapies among the membership included reflexology, a practice developed in the United States, though based on Chinese medical thought, which had been tried by 38.1 per cent of Mahikari members; aromatherapy, (26.7 per cent) which uses aromatic oils to promote the health of body and mind, and which has been developed largely from work done in France; spiritual healing (25.7 per cent), and osteopathy (23.8 per cent).

In so far as Mahikari teachings on health and illness are felt by the movement's members to resonate with ideas with which they are already familiar from the field of alternative medicine, then, this resonance goes much further than a simple echoing of ideas already encountered in therapies of Japanese or Chinese origin. Rather, it would seem that certain of the Mahikari teachings are felt by the members to pick up more general themes which have become widespread in alternative approaches to health and illness. Of these one might single out in particular notions concerning the importance of the flow of energy; the idea that bodies accumulate toxins which need to be eliminated, and that many of the symptoms of illnesses are manifestations of this process of elimination of toxins, and are therefore beneficial, a sign that the body is healing itself; and finally the importance placed on a 'holistic' approach – that is, that the whole person needs to be treated, not simply their physical being. In fact, the expression 'be treated' is perhaps inappropriate, since another aspect of Mahikari teachings which finds a ready echo in alternative therapies is the idea that the person takes responsibility for themselves, and for their own condition. The sick role in this context is not the passive role of patient relating to doctor, but a very active process of identifying one's own problems, and of taking responsibility in seeking to resolve them or to come to terms with them. At issue is not simply the resolution of illness, but the restoration and maintenance of health, seen as a state of balance believed to be the natural condition of human beings.

It should be noted, however, that Mahikari has not been the only movement to attract attention in the East-West Centre, or in the alternative health network – the East-West centre is also mentioned by Wilson and Dobbelaere in their discussion of the ways in which UK members had encountered Soka Gakkai, as are other alternative health centres. Nor is this a phenomenon restricted to movements of Japanese origin: one of the interviewees in my research mentioned that est had 'swept' the Centre at one time, with large numbers of people from the Centre, himself included, attending one or more est seminars. So while it may be argued that while this milieu was receptive to Mahikari teachings, it was also receptive to other 'alternatives', and further that this in itself is a self-limiting factor, in so far as many different movements recruit members from the same, relatively small, section of the population.

Furthermore, Mahikari has not experienced a uniformly warm reception from people in the alternative health network: for example, attempts to introduce Mahikari in Boston in the United States, the home of the macrobiotics movement, have met with little success. Nor is the alternative health network the only means by which the movement has spread – within Europe the occupational composition of the movement varies across the different European countries, often reflecting to a great extent the circumstances of its introduction, in particular the personal networks of those individuals initially active in the movement in the country concerned.

Granted then, that Mahikari does not appeal to all those involved in the alternative health network, and that it may also appeal to many people with no interest in alternative medicine, it nonetheless seems reasonable to argue that Mahikari teachings have a particular resonance for those involved in alternative health practices. There is also compelling evidence that health-related concerns are a major source of attraction to the movement. This attraction seems to remain relatively constant across national boundaries: as noted above, Davis (1980) reported that 52 per cent of members in Osaka joined for reasons relating to illness, while in Europe Cornille writes of Mahikari in France and Belgium that the 'principal ... attraction is the promise of healing' (Cornille 1991: 273). For the UK, records kept in the Mahikari centre of the reasons given by non-members attending the centre for receiving light show that by far the most common reasons given relate to illness, pain or an interest in healing – this type of motivation accounted for 47 per cent of non-members attending the centre in 1996, with the next most common reason being curiosity (18 per cent) and looking for a spiritual path (15 per cent).[39] But if a concern with health, illness and healing remains a relatively constant factor, what of the ways in which the notions are interpreted across cultural and national boundaries? To what extent have Mahikari teachings on health and illness, as detailed above, been accepted by members outside Japan? In the remainder of this paper this question will be explored through looking at how members in the UK explain the causes and meaning of illness, and also at the ways in which they conceptualise the central practice of Mahikari: *okiyome*, or the giving and receiving of light.

Giving and Receiving Light: The Meanings of *Okiyome*

In all the countries where Mahikari is practised the experience of giving and receiving light is frequently connected by members to accounts of miraculous healing. In response to a question in the survey of UK members on whether or not members had experienced miracles since joining Mahikari, and if so, what sort of miracles, around 60 per cent reported having experienced miracles. Of these a large majority were related to healing – either the healing of others (60 per cent of miracles described), or change in the respondent's health (31.7 per cent), in either case related to the giving and receiving of light.

So how do Mahikari members in the UK understand 'light' and how does this relate to the issue of healing? The simplest explanation of light given by interviewees followed closely the explanation given in the introductory training course as outlined above: that it is divine light which comes from God, and that members are enabled to radiate this light by the *omitama*. Radiating this light to people, or come to that food, plants, or animals, will eliminate impurities that lead to illness and other sorts of misfortune, and restore us to our original state as created by God, of health, harmony, and prosperity.

Probing a little further in the interviews I conducted into how members explained what happened when they gave light I got a range of answers. Some simply said they couldn't explain how it worked, but it did, while others simply reiterated that God's light came out of their hand. But perhaps the most common explanation of light was as a kind of energy or vibration, with the *omitama* acting as a lens or a transistor. Some of the responses were:

'The pendant allows me to channel like a lens or a radio. I believe this is tuned in to Creator God. But to explain how it works – I don't know.'

'Everything you think and feel has a vibration. Giving light is you sitting down, consciously giving up your time to help someone else with no financial reward and no expectations of reward. This in itself gives you very pure energy. Light, cosmic energy is channelled somehow through the *omitama*.'

'We are like a transistor, transmitting waves from God.'

'Giving light is radiating positive energy. Because it's very strong and warm it detoxifies the toxins in the body.'

There were also some explanations framed in less secular language, for example:

> 'The *omitama* is like a mandala which gives you a direct link with Creator God. That light could be interpreted as God's love. But I think the quality of the light is down to the person giving it and the person receiving it.'

Other people referred to the notion of upstream and downstream, and also to the three bodies Mahikari teachings describe: spiritual, physical and astral, and explained that it is important that light is given to the spiritual aspect. However, it was striking that the majority of responses used a secular idiom to explain what light is and how it works, and that it was generally described as a sort of energy.

While this stress on the notion of energy echoes a discourse found in many alternative therapies, it also creates a link with mainstream scientific discourse, and is characteristic of the way in which Mahikari in the UK is presented to non-members in its introductory courses. This in turn reflects a concern on the part of the leadership both in Europe and Japan to establish the movement's credentials in terms acceptable to the scientific and medical mainstream, and to create a distinctively modern identity, distanced from the domain of the shaman or the medium, associated with pre-modern Japan.[40] The *dōshi* in the UK traced this concern back to the founder of the movement, commenting that 'the founder tried to explain things in scientific vocabulary, to make a bridge between science and spiritual things, and to make a difference with the many mediums then operating in Japan.' The *dōshi* added that it was necessary to make this difference especially as the idea of attaching spirits is commonly associated with mediums in Japan.

It is also noteworthy in this context that the Mahikari leadership appear to place great importance on their links with individuals employed in the fields of science and or medicine, and that testimonials by doctors or scientists who are members of Mahikari have in the past figured prominently in Mahikari journals produced for members. The movement has also organised seminars on themes related to medicine and science, and in introductory talks for non-members experiments are regularly performed to demonstrate the effects of light. For example, in a talk which I attended, a bottle of cheap wine was decanted into two other bottles, one of which was given light by a member during the talk. After the talk, we were invited to do a blind tasting to see if we could identify which had received the light. Most people present claimed to be able to detect a difference. Regardless of the validity or otherwise of these experiments, they are interesting in so far as they seek to demonstrate the effectiveness of Mahikari within the framework of mainstream scientific discourse – using notions such as that of an 'experiment' in 'controlled conditions' and 'objective evidence'.

In the UK one of the members frequently called upon to give introductory talks explaining Mahikari to non-members is a cell and molecular biologist working in the field of toxicology and cancer research. The relationship between science, medicine, and Mahikari is an area specifically dealt with in these talks, of which the following is a representative extract:

> Sometimes I am asked if I have any conflict between my practice of Mahikari and being a scientist. The answer is no.
>
> Science allows me the privileged opportunity to open small windows into nature to observe the intricate and complex interactions that exist in harmony and balance at the cellular and molecular levels within the human body and how disturbances in these physical interactions, step by step, can lead to the conditions we term 'diseases'. Mahikari, on the other hand, permits me to learn about, and then to understand through my experience, how many illnesses can be manifestations at the mental and physical levels of disturbances at the spiritual level. These spiritual impurities or disturbances manifest as the symptoms we observe in the clinic and the cell and molecular biology changes we observe in the laboratory.
>
> ... many doctors and therapists today are more ready to adopt a holistic approach to medicine. They try to treat a patient as a whole person, body and mind.

However, even treating the body and mind as a whole can still be inadequate in the treatment of chronic illnesses. In my opinion the reason why this is so is because science and medicine have neglected the most important aspect of health, the spiritual aspect.[41]

Understanding the Causes of Illness

In the talk referred to above, the 'spiritual aspect' of illness was explained in some detail, with reference to the accumulation of spiritual impurities, through, for example, negative attitudes; the idea of karma; and the importance of the ancestors and of attaching spirits. The importance of spiritual factors in the causation of illness was also emphasised by members whom I interviewed, but only for certain categories of illness. Members were asked what they thought caused three different types of illness: long term illnesses such as asthma, diabetes, or heart disease; very serious illnesses such as cancer or AIDS;[42] and minor illnesses such as coughs or colds. The last of these categories was widely understood as simply being purification in action, a sign of the body cleansing itself, and thus something to be welcomed, not treated or suppressed. As explained above, the symptoms commonly experienced with a cold, such as a runny nose, a cough or a temperature, are in any case typical examples given in Mahikari of reactions to receiving light, and are seen as signs that the light is working. For example, one interviewee explained that,

> 'If somebody has a cold and you give them light, you don't give them light to make them better, it might equally well make them worse, because they might purify more. That might be a good thing, but whether they'd see it that way is another matter.'

During the time I spent at the Mahikari centre, I would frequently hear members with the symptoms of a cold saying 'I'm having a cleansing', which is perhaps indicative of the extent to which this re-classification of minor 'illnesses' as 'cleansings', and not illnesses at all, is pervasive within the movement. Not all members, however, have adopted this terminology with equal enthusiasm. One commented, 'I say now I have got a cold or a cough, because it's alienating if you always talk in terms of "I'm having a cleansing" or "I'm having a purification".' Another member told me,

> 'At the moment I'm feeling negative about some of the people in Mahikari, the way people talk – "purifying" and so on – I want my language back! Also, the *dōshi* keeps telling us not to speak like this, we sound crazy, but we didn't pluck this out of thin air – I remember a senior *kumite* saying – you don't say you've got flu... But they don't recognise this comes from them.'

A member who admitted to being somewhat disillusioned with Mahikari further pointed out:

> 'Mahikari has a bit of a Catch 22 – if you do everything properly you get *ken-wa-fu* (health, harmony and prosperity), but if everything goes wrong, it's purification.'[43]

These comments notwithstanding, the view of disorders such as colds as constituting cleansings rather than illnesses per se is both widespread and relatively uncontroversial within the UK branch of the movement, with many members from the alternative health network drawing an explicit analogy here with ideas found in various forms of alternative medicine concerning the beneficial role of symptoms such as those associated with a cold in cleansing the body and eliminating toxins. Very few respondents gave spiritual reasons for such symptoms, a more common type of explanation was, 'we're daily producing toxins and eliminating them. It's like degreasing a motorbike engine.'

In contrast, for more serious illnesses, whether long-term, debilitating illnesses (chronic) or those which are more immediately life-threatening (acute) the explanation most favoured was that there were spiritual causes – 19 out of 25 respondents. However, many were quite vague as to what these spiritual causes were: four did not specify what this spiritual cause might be; while 'impurities' were cited by eight respondents. Only seven of the interviewees made specific reference to the role of attaching spirits. Other explanations favoured by many of the respondents (a number of whom offered several possible explanations) included the notion of karma (ten respondents); and also environmental factors (eleven respondents), including 'toxins', the overuse of medicine, diet, and pollution. Intervention by ancestors was mentioned directly by only six of the respondents as a possible cause for illness, although a number of those who discussed the importance of karma included in this the idea of family karma, and hence, implicitly, taking on the karma of one's ancestors.

So, although the explanations given by members in the UK of the causes of illness were broadly in line with the official teachings of the movement, there was a relative lack of emphasis on the role of the ancestors, and also on attaching spirits. On the other hand, the notion of karma was quite widely evoked, and appeared to be a familiar concept not only to to a number of those who participated in the interviews, but also to many of the members I met during the time I spent with the movement. Environmental concerns were also rated highly as a cause of illness, reflecting a widespread concern for the environment within the movement as a whole – action to improve the environment ran a close second to increased spiritual awareness, as actions considered most important in order to improve the world among questionnaire respondents.[44] There was also an emphasis on the role of *okiyome* in countering existing environmental damage, including food contamination. One woman, for example, explained: 'I used light to purify some beef my friend was going to throw out. If it's purified, there's no risk of mad cow disease.'

In part, the importance attached by members to environmental concerns, and the relatively ready acceptance of the idea of karma is explicable in terms of the general milieu from which Mahikari has spread in the UK: a fairly well educated, middle-class group of people many of whom had previous familiarity with non-European spiritual traditions, and also with the field of alternative medicine. In addition, the movement has a number of members from Buddhist or Hindu backgrounds for whom the idea of karma forms part of a familiar cultural lexicon. One Indian-born member told me:

'Fundamentally, Mahikari and Hinduism is the same teaching – how you should live your life, where you come from, where you will go after death... After seeing all this, I thought this is part of the same religion, just in Mahikari after receiving *omitama* you can radiate light, that is the special arrangement... You have to do karma – in Sanskrit it means deeds – to work, to make tea, this is karma. The question is, how do you do that? No one is without karma. You have to do it. The only question is how best to do it, That is what I am trying to learn.'

This member, although considering environmental factors to play an important role in the causation of illness also commented regarding very serious illnesses,

'It's your karma. However you die, whether accident or illness, it's karma.'

If ideas of karma find a receptive audience within Mahikari, composed of both those for whom it has been a familiar concept since childhood, and those who have encountered it as adults within an 'alternative' network, what then, of Mahikari teachings on attaching spirits and on the ancestors? As far as teachings on the ancestors are concerned, the *dōshi* in the UK explained that initially there were some doubts within the Mahikari organisation in Japan as to how far people in the USA or in Europe would be open to teachings regarding the veneration of ancestors which are closely linked to the ways in which ancestors are cared for in Japan, and therefore this area was not discussed much in Mahikari's overseas branches. Since then, the movement has found that there has been considerable interest in, and acceptance of, such practices in Europe and the United States, and there is consequently greater emphasis on this aspect of Mahikari in these countries than formerly.

Members in the UK are certainly encouraged to care for their ancestors in the way prescribed by the movement, along a pattern broadly following general mainstream Japanese practice, involving the consecration of an ancestral altar with ancestral tablets for ancestors in the male line, and regular offerings of food.[45] However, there is no compulsion to acquire such an altar, and in my survey I found that only just over 50 per cent of members in the UK had acquired an ancestral altar, although a somewhat higher figure of 69 per cent has been reported for Belgium in Cornille's 1991 study. The situation in some non-European Mahikari branches, however, approximates much more closely to the situation in Japan: teachings on the ancestors and on spirit possession are given considerable weight in the Caribbean, for example (Hurbon 1991), and also in Taiwan.[46]

Among the UK members, it seemed that the longer a person had been a member the more likely they were to have acquired an ancestral altar. 74 per cent of questionnaire respondents who had joined prior to 1990 had an ancestral altar, as compared to only 54 per cent of those joining between 1990 and 1993, while of the 21 who had joined since 1994 only one had acquired an ancestral altar as of summer 1996. Acquiring an ancestral altar involves some financial costs as well as special preparations, including the holding of a ceremony to inaugurate the altar, while the altar itself can only be placed in a location meeting certain preconditions. Its acquisition is therefore not something members undertake lightly, and it is unsurprising that there is generally a delay between taking *kenshū* and applying for an ancestral altar. Several members to whom I spoke told me that they would have liked to have an ancestral altar, but that their material circumstances made it impossible.

Echoing Hurbon's findings for Mahikari in the Caribbean (Hurbon 1991), a number of UK members from non-European backgrounds strongly endorsed Mahikari teachings on ancestors, even if they themselves felt unable currently to inaugurate one in view of the financial costs and requirements concerning its location. This was often explained in terms of a perceived link with their own traditions. For example a member from Mauritius, when asked why it was important to take care of the ancestors replied,

'They need looking after just like we do. They are confused, some of them, in turmoil ... [if] they feel they missed out on life, they will try to get back at you. In Mauritius, we have *la Fête des Morts*, when you acknowledge them ... give them offerings. Western people find it hard to accept that.'

Similar comments were made by a Jamaican-born British member who was critical of the patronising attitude towards black people that she had experienced in the Church of England, and was very interested in exploring her African heritage:

'In the culture I grew up in, we know the importance of the spirit. Growing up, if you dropped food on the floor you would say, "the ancestors are hungry" – this is very Caribbean, very African, there's always reference to the ancestors. So it was nothing new – it gave it form. I think I was looking for a sense of form.'

One of the clearest explanations of how ancestors might be involved in the causation of illness was given by a West African member who had suffered from breast cancer, which she believed had been cured through her practice of Mahikari:

'Maybe the ancestors have done something. Illness is sin and impurities. Maybe not your sin, your ancestor's sin. Spirits come and attach to you, so you have to purify yourself by giving light ... maybe for me, my husband's spirit attached to me, because he died of cancer, and I don't have cancer in my family. That's why I say it's spiritual disturbance.'

This kind of continuity was not only noted by members of African or Caribbean origin – the Indian member referred to earlier drew an analogy between Mahikari ancestral rites and the annual offerings of food and prayer made to ancestors by his people, the Maharati (people from Maharashtra state, India). So it would seem that Mahikari teachings on ancestors, although originating from a Japanese/Chinese[47] cultural matrix, have a wide resonance for people from a range of non-European cultural backgrounds.

On the other hand, several members from UK or European backgrounds with no tradition of ancestral veneration were either very non-committal or expressed reservations when asked about Mahikari teachings on ancestors. For example, one member commented,

'I don't have an ancestral altar. I don't disbelieve the idea. I've only been a member for a year and a half, so I have plenty of time... This is the part of Mahikari I haven't got terribly involved in... I don't want my life to change too drastically, too quickly. I don't believe I'll be punished for that.'

Other members expressed doubts about the applicability of these teachings in a European context, for example, another member who had joined recently said, 'There's something strange for me about this – it's normal in the Orient, but not in the West, so does this mean half the world's ancestors are suffering?' Along the same lines another member remarked, 'It's just a norm in the Far East. So is it very special, or just tradition? ... I've lost the strong sentiment that it will make a difference.'

However, it seems that with time many members from a European background, too, come round to the idea of having an ancestral altar. A majority of the long-standing members of all nationalities and ethnic groups have an ancestral altar, and appear to feel that it is important to care for the ancestors. And even members not brought up with a background of ancestor veneration, nonetheless often made sense of these ideas by relating them to other previously held beliefs. Again, a background in alternatives, including alternative medicine, may be a factor here. For example, a member who is also a practising homeopath suggested an explanatory framework linking homeopathy, ideas of karma, and Mahikari teachings on the ancestors. He discussed a case which is explained in *kenshū* of a girl who developed TB after two of her sisters had died from it. When the girl was brought to Okada, the founder of Mahikari, the root of the problem was identified as being the spirit of the first child to die, who was attaching to her sisters, causing them to suffer from the same illnesses.

'From a homeopathic point of view there are miasms – susceptibilities passed on from one generation to the next – often TB, gonorrhoea or syphilis. TB could get passed on as allergies – asthma or eczema – and the syphilitic miasm could be passed on as cancer or AIDS – or as bone deformities or destructive behaviour.

Then of course you can interpret it all in terms of ancestral karma ... that could be what in homeopathic terms we call a miasm, in Mahikari it's a spiritual disturbance.'

For others, a demonstration of the importance of caring for the ancestors was provided by their own experiences with their ancestral altar. For example, one member gave the following example of illness being caused by failure to care for the ancestors properly:

'You're meant to clean the altar. Once, I could see it was dirty, but I kept putting off cleaning it. I had a rash on my left hand. I often get rashes, but this wasn't the type of rash I usually get. They say if your ancestors are trying to tell you something you get a knock on the head or the eye. I hadn't had that, so I thought I was alright. But as soon as I cleaned the altar the rash cleared up. To me, this is because it wasn't a problem of not seeing the altar was dirty, but not doing anything about it – i.e. not using my hands to clean it up.'

This type of account, relating the consequences in members' lives of actions concerning the ancestral altar, its acquisition and subsequent care, was one I frequently encountered in conversations with members, often coupled with the statement that the person concerned had initially hesitated about getting an ancestral altar, but, having acquired one, had come to recognise its importance. Thus for many members, especially those from a European background who are unfamiliar with the idea of caring for the ancestors, there may be a gradual process involved, firstly deciding to have an altar, and only later beginning to develop their own accounts of how this altar and the care of the ancestors affects their lives. As these narratives follow a predictable pattern, and may often be repeated by members to each other, they will tend to influence other members to generate similar accounts, so that once having acquired an ancestral altar much that happens to the member concerned may be interpreted in a new light, in relation to the member's care for, or neglect of, the ancestors. However, at present the role of ancestors remains for most of the membership a relatively unemphasised aspect of health-illness related beliefs.

Attaching Spirits

Attaching spirits, (a category which overlaps with that of the ancestors, as attaching spirits may be the spirits of one's own ancestors), were also relatively under-emphasised as a possible cause of illness by members I interviewed. Most, as we have seen, preferred simply to refer to the vaguer notion of some kind of unspecified spiritual cause. This reticence can in part be explained by my status as non-member and academic researcher. When I asked the *dōshi* about this point he explained that in the past the movement had spoken freely about attaching spirits and that the result of this was that *Mahikari no Waza* had come to be seen by some as a kind of exorcism – he cited particularly in this regard the standard academic work on the movement, Davis's *Dōjō: Magic and Exorcism in Modern Japan* (1980). In order to discourage this, as he saw it, misinterpretation, he said that members were guided not to talk so much about attaching spirits to non-members. Instead, a detailed explanation of this area is given in the introductory course for new members.

There would appear to be a contrast between the situation in the UK and that in Japan here as for the issue of the care of the ancestors: an introductory leaflet on Mahikari distributed to non members in Japan in 1996 made prominent mention both of the problems which can be caused by attaching spirits, as well as the importance of caring for the ancestors. Also, on the many occasions on which I attended the London centre, or witnessed the giving of light at various Mahikari ceremonies, I never witnessed any dramatic, clearly recognisable spirit movements of the type described by Davis for Japan, and only overheard a spirit investigation being conducted on two occasions. Although members assure me that both spirit movements and spirit investigations do take place in the UK, again this aspect of Mahikari seems far less stressed in the UK than in Japan.

One result of the reluctance of the movement to elaborate to any great extent on beliefs relating to ancestors or to attaching spirits to non-members has been that some members have only come across these notions for the first time during *kenshū*,[48] and have not always been willing to accept them in the first instance. One long-standing member recalled:

'I didn't find out about attaching spirits until *kenshu*. I thought, "oh, I don't know about that." Also, at first I didn't want an ancestral altar. I thought, that's OK for Eastern people, but not for Westerners. But when I got to know more about it, I decided to have one.'

The ex-member I interviewed also commented on this issue,

'In *kenshū* they say about 80 per cent of illnesses are caused by possessing spirits. In the West it's a bit of a shocker... People might not bring it up because it's a bit controversial, they might think you wouldn't understand it, or would misinterpret it. I think it's basically true, however I can see it's worrying for a lot of people. My wife, for instance, [also an ex-member] doesn't like that.'

It appeared also that some of the members who had spoken freely to non-members about attaching spirits had encountered very negative reactions. One French member recalled:

'I made some mistakes at first, I went too quickly and – finished... One friend had a little boy with leukaemia, two years old. I didn't want to wait, I gave him light. I wanted to try it, I'm sure it doesn't harm, anyway. They were always wondering, "why us?" They are quite Catholic, the father is a doctor. They said they didn't mind trying, but I went too quickly, speaking about spirits. The grandfather died suddenly last year – I suggested there might be a connection, in which case it's easier to save through giving light.

They reacted very badly, they asked me to stop giving light. She was asking questions, I spoke too much, especially if I'm not sure. I suggested, for example, the grandfather was a surgeon, maybe there was an accident, someone he was unable to save. The logical victim is the youngest one, the child. Now I've decided not to speak about the spiritual aspect, to wait.'

As in the case of the ancestors, the reticence of some of the European members contrasted with comments made by some members of non-European origin, who stressed the continuities between Mahikari teachings on this and the beliefs current in the society in which they grew up. The member from Mauritius quoted earlier explained,

'I tried so hard, but I could never make it. I'm a musician, I have City and Guilds, I'm bilingual, but nothing ever works out for me. I can't keep a job down for more than two or three years. It's like being very unlucky, so much so that you feel there's someone else in you. I've been fighting to understand that all my life – Mahikari explained that for me.

In Mauritius, everyone believes in spiritualism... People used to say to me back home – you're so unlucky. I'm sure you've got a bad spirit. At the time I said, that's rubbish. Now Mahikari's explained it, understanding it helps. Mahikari explains how certain spirits can attach to you... I think I've got a bitter and confused spirit attached to me. I'm not saying I'm better now, but I understand it. If you don't understand it's frustrating, confusing. It drives you mad eventually if you let it.'

In this case the notion of attaching spirits was evoked to account for general difficulties that this member encountered in his life as a whole, and not as an explanation of illness. This overlap of theories of causation, with the same type of explanation being adduced for a range of apparently different problems, is consistent with the Mahikari world view that health is a reflection of a state of harmony, order, and that disorder may manifest itself in any one of a number of realms, including work, personal relationships and the financial sphere, as well as illness.[49]

One theme that emerged in this type of explanation of misfortune, whether illness related or not, which is also evident in the above account, was an emphasis on the importance of understanding the problem, whether or not it was actually resolved. Although many members did give accounts of what they saw as miraculous healings resulting from their practice of Mahikari, there was a widespread resistance among members I interviewed to equating Mahikari with 'healing' or 'treatment', partly on the grounds that it has a much broader significance, and partly on the grounds that it is not a process with any guaranteed outcomes. Some representative responses to my queries as to what treatment members would recommend for various illnesses included:

'That's difficult – Mahikari are not spiritual healers. Even if we give light to people with these illnesses, it doesn't mean they will be cured ... the purpose of giving light is not to cure.'

'Mahikari's not really about physical healing, it's about spiritual healing – there's no guarantee your condition will get better.'

'I wouldn't *treat* people as such. There are two sides: medication is important, but giving light is also important. But when I'm giving light I try not to focus on the condition, what I think should happen, because I don't know what should happen. It's up to God what the result is. You need to have care and compassion, but not the idea that this condition must go away. It's more the idea to purify spiritual impurities through giving light.'

Rather than something to be treated then, illness is seen as a learning process, and as this may stretch over more than one lifetime, it may not be possible, or even desirable, to resolve it in this lifetime. To continue to suffer from an illness, even while continuing to receive light is therefore not seen as a therapeutic failure, but rather as a sign of the continuation of the learning process, and the purification process, which, at the most basic level is what all illness is understood to be in Mahikari. One woman member who suffers from chronic eczema explained to me that 'if it (Mahikari) was a healing I would have left by now, because my eczema still isn't any better'. However she also went on to say

'Now I have eczema only on my face. This is symbolic. If (in a past life) I killed someone in an embarrassing way, or if I burned someone, this is appropriate compensation, perhaps, to be on the face because its visible and it embarrasses you. It reminds me to be humble – we need to have the attitude that we are very fortunate to be here. I think that broadly speaking, within the limits of our understanding, the ailments we have can be seen as symbolic of what we have to learn.'

Mahikari's approach to illness, then, consists not in giving light in the expectation that a cure will automatically follow. More important is the construction of a framework of meaning within which illness, as it is experienced by the individual, can be understood. As we have seen, different members may draw on the various elements of Mahikari in slightly different ways, with different emphases, and, through placing these in the context of their own background and beliefs, construct their own narratives within the terms of which they come to understand their illness whether or not it is resolved.

Conclusion

To return to the question posed at the beginning of the paper: how is it that a largely non-Japanese membership can find a discourse of illness developed by a Japanese movement, within a Japanese cultural context, meaningful for them in a very different setting? What is suggested by this study of Mahikari in the UK is that this transfer across cultural lines is possible to a large degree because the movement's teachings are not perceived as entirely alien: rather, many aspects of the teachings evoke a sense of recognition and familiarity among the members, although precisely what is recognised, and what is seen as familiar varies considerably depending on the background of the member concerned.

For members from an African or Afro-Caribbean background, for example, teachings relating to the ancestors or to attaching spirits may, as Hurbon (1991) has argued in his study of Mahikari in the Caribbean, echo ideas familiar from their own upbringing, and perhaps provide a dimension experienced by these members as absent in the Christian churches. On the other hand, some members from wholly European backgrounds may have some difficulty in accepting this area of Mahikari teachings, and may feel that this aspect of Mahikari is not for them. On the other hand, notions of karma, or re-incarnation may be readily accepted by these members, especially by those with a background in alternative approaches to spirituality/religiosity, where these notions have gained wide currency, and may no longer be seen as foreign.

As far as Mahikari teachings on health and illness are concerned, the idea of the body needing purification, although historically traceable to Shinto ideas on the maintenance of health and treatment of illness, finds a ready echo in many forms of alternative medicine. Similar parallels can be traced between ideas current in alternative medicine and Mahikari teachings in a number of other areas: particularly, the idea of illness as something involving the whole of the person, not just the body, and also the idea of taking individual responsibility for one's own health. Again, Mahikari teachings in these areas are seen by many of the members as forming a continuum with their existing knowledge. In some cases these continuities may be traceable to a common philosophical base, as many of the alternative therapies have a Chinese or Japanese origin, but this is not always so, as we have seen in the way in which members may also find continuities between Mahikari teachings and alternative therapies of European origin, notably homeopathy. Also, as noted above, Mahikari has striven to establish links with mainstream bio-medicine. These links have been made both at an institutional level, for example through the establishment of a medical clinic in Japan, and also through the selective adoption of a scientific-type discourse.

Turning to the ways in which meaning is ascribed to illness, although there are certain normative narratives which tend to recur, for example attributing illness to misdeeds in past lives, to neglect of the ancestors, or to attaching spirits, the ways in which individual narratives were constructed was variable, and depended to a great extent on the way in which that particular individual understood Mahikari teachings as applied to their own lives. McVeigh's notion of an 'ethnomorality' implied by theories of illness within Mahikari did not seem to be a stumbling block – in so far as elements of that ethnomorality such as the importance of descendants caring for their ancestors were perceived by individual members as unacceptable, or irrelevant to them, their own personal narrative could always be constructed along slightly different lines – perhaps by substituting the idea of karma for that of ancestors or attaching spirits, for example. On other aspects of the morality of Mahikari, offering gratitude and apology as a response to illness – gratitude for the opportunity to cleanse oneself, apology for whatever past misdeed may have brought this illness about – was an approach endorsed by almost all those I interviewed, and was very rarely identified as reflecting a particularly Japanese morality. Only one member, who had spent some time living and working in Japan, and was very familiar with Japanese society, identified the type of *sōnen*, or attitude, idealised within Mahikari as particularly Japanese, and queried why attitudes of gratitude and acceptance were positively valued, whereas emotions such as anger are largely negatively valued, or denied.

Readiness to accept Mahikari by its non-Japanese members does not seem to be dependent on a pre-existing knowledge of or sympathy towards things Japanese. Although 41 per cent of the UK membership did report a previous interest in various aspects of Japanese culture, a figure roughly comparable to Wilson and Dobbelaere's findings for Soka Gakkai UK,[50] there were also many who expressed fairly negative feelings towards Japan – in this context some pointed to historical factors, pointing out that their own antecedents, either as Chinese, or, in a few cases as relatives of British POWs of the Japanese, tended to make them, if anything, antagonistic to anything Japanese. But even setting this particular section of the membership aside, there were many others who were critical of aspects of the movement which they perceived as particularly Japanese. Which aspects were identified as Japanese varied, however, among members. A number pointed to teachings relating to gender, which in some cases were greeted with frank amusement;[51] others to the Mahikari-tai, the youth wing of Mahikari in the UK, which some saw as quasi-militaristic; while for others, as we have seen, teachings on the ancestors were seen as something specific to the 'Far East'. Again, what was identified as Japanese, and what was identified as of universal significance varied widely depending on the backgrounds of the member concerned.

The process by which Mahikari finds acceptance abroad is thus by no means a simple encounter between two distinct, isolable cultures: in this case Japanese on the one hand, and European on the other. Indeed, this study of Mahikari in the UK casts serious doubts on whether it is possible to speak of distinct, homogeneous cultures at all in this context. Looking at the UK side alone, it is impossible to understand the ways in which members relate to Mahikari without taking into consideration that the UK is a multi-ethnic, multi-cultural society, and consequently that any NRM entering the UK may present continuities with the beliefs of some sections of the UK population but not with others. Indeed, for some sections of the membership, Mahikari is seen as more in harmony with their own background and beliefs than is the religious mainstream in the UK, and many of the interviewees cited Mahikari's multi-cultural character as one of the main reasons they were attracted to the movement.

Furthermore, even among that section of the UK population with wholly European antecedents, many ideas originating outside Europe, such as karma, or re-incarnation, have become common currency in some circles. For these reasons, Mahikari is not, on the whole, seen as alien by its members, and its claims to universal significance and applicability are taken seriously by them. It is worth noting here that 77.3 per cent of questionnaire respondents stated that in their view it was not important that Mahikari originated in Japan – some adding comments such as,

> 'I don't really care whether it originated in Japan or not, it doesn't really matter. I wouldn't give a blind eye whether or not it was originated in Hawaii!'

or,

> 'I believe that Mahikari could have originated in Scunthorpe and I would still like it.'

Implicitly, this study also presents a challenge to the Nihonjinron-type view of Japan as a homogeneous cultural entity which is radically different from the rest of the world. It has been pointed out elsewhere[52] that Mahikari, in common with many Japanese NRMs, can be said to be syncretic, in so far as it incorporates beliefs relating to Jesus and Christianity in its teachings, alongside ideas derived from Buddhism and Shinto. However, it has been shown here that many beliefs present in Mahikari which appear to be closely intertwined with the Japanese cultural matrix from which the movement sprang, such as teachings relating to purification, the ancestors, and attaching spirits, have parallels in cultures and belief systems which are historically unrelated to Japan, and that the appeal of the movement outside Japan can be partly explained by these parallels. And, of course, the situation is further complicated by the exchange of information as well as people across national borders, which means that it is increasingly difficult to assign a particular 'culture' label to any one belief in any case.

It is perhaps a cliché of NRMs with an international presence that they present their teachings as being of universal applicability and significance, and in the case of Mahikari in particular it has been argued by Cornille that these apparent universalistic aspirations are underlaid by a profoundly nationalistic agenda (see Cornille, this volume). What I would like to argue here is that the question of what is Japanese and what is international is itself highly problematic in the Mahikari case, with the 'Japanese' element of Mahikari presenting a constantly moving target, defined differently depending on the perspective of the member concerned. In so far as Mahikari has enjoyed a degree of acceptance in the UK this must be understood in the context of the diversity of belief systems and cultural background of the people of present-day Britain, and in terms of the increasing permeability of cultural boundaries, as well as the implicit pluralism of the movement's own teachings.

Notes

1 I fulfilled all the requirements for becoming a member, attended all the relevant lectures, and attended monthly ceremonies and other special events as well as visiting the London centre and receiving light regularly. I did not, however, become a member – defined as receiving an *omitama* – and attended the introductory course on the understanding that this was for research purposes and that I did not intend to join. I am grateful to all the members of Mahikari who gave unstintingly of their time to help with this research. The interpretation offered, and any errors remaining, are mine alone.
2 For a more detailed exploration of the biographies of founders of NRMs in Japan, and the parallels between these and the biographies of founders of secular organisations such as large companies, see Matsunaga, this volume, pp. 40–41.
3 The term health care system is used here in the sense suggested by Kleinman: 'The health care system articulates illness as a cultural idiom, linking beliefs about disease causation, the experience of symptoms, specific patterns of illness behaviour, decisions concerning treatment alternatives, actual therapeutic practices and evaluations of therapeutic outcomes' (Kleinman 1986: 32).
4 *Jōrei* bears a close resemblance to the core practice of Mahikari, *okiyome*, described in further detail below.
5 I am grateful to Inaba Keishin, a doctoral student at the Centre for New Religious Movements at King's College, London, for his assistance in obtaining information on this case.
6 Sukyo Mahikari is not referred to directly by Inoue here, but as its philosophy is similar to that of Sekai Kyusei Kyo in many respects, Inoue's comments could just as well be applied to both movements.
7 Sekai Kyusei Kyo prefer to use the term 'nature farming' rather than 'natural farming' to translate the Japanese *shizen nōhō* in their English language material, in order to distinguish their practice from organic farming (The Society of Johrei: 1984).
8 It may be argued that the tendency of NRMs in Japan to have a complementary or cooperative relationship with mainstream medicine is the outcome in part of historical pressures: the societal dominance of bio-medicine, and the negative

publicity attracted by incidents where bio-medicine and the healing practices of NRMs are perceived to be in conflict as described above; and in part of the internal dynamics of NRMs. Stark and Bainbridge (1985), among others, have suggested that NRMs have a tendency to move away from claiming to be able to produce empirically verifiable results as they become more firmly established, and towards non-verifiable, supernaturalistic claims. The Tenrikyo case would seem to fit in rather neatly with this latter theory, as it is one of the oldest of the Japanese NRMs, and also the pioneer of cooperative ventures between bio-medicine and NRMs in Japan.

9   This is not only true of the Japanese case: McGuire (1988), in her Study of Ritual Healing in Suburban America, notes that in the groups she studied, too, that notions of health and healing were only one aspect of a larger, inter-related system of beliefs.

10 *Kanji* commonly have several related meanings, which makes a range of translations possible. 'Revered teachings' is the translation preferred by the *dōshi* (minister) of the London branch of Sukyo Mahikari, but as *sū* can mean above as well as revered, and *kyō* is also the *kanji* used in the word *shūkyō*, religion, *sūkyō* is commonly glossed as supra-religion, referring, as McVeigh explains, to 'a way of thinking transcending all religions, science and ideologies' (McVeigh 1991:390).

11 For more details on this dispute see McVeigh 1991: 22–23).

12 Figures for Mahikari supplied by the UK branch of Mahikari, June 1997. The overall membership figure given is the same as that in Cornille's unofficial estimate of European membership in 1991 (Cornille 1991:270).

13 'What is Soka Gakkai?' http://www.sokagakkai.

14 Quotes taken from Mahikari USA home page on the internet, and from internally produced Mahikari documents.

15 There are, at present, a number of requirements which must be fulfilled before one can attend this course. In the UK the main requirements are that one must have received light at least twenty times before embarking on the course, and that one's family must support membership.

16 At least, elaborate from my point of view, as they involve a number of layers of wrapping and the use of a special bag and a further pocket to contain the omitama which is sewn into the underclothes. However, long-standing members maintain that the procedures involved appear to them to be quite simple.

17 For more detail concerning rituals surrounding the care of the *omitama* see McVeigh 1991:171–176.

18 Mahikari teaches that the left side is the spiritual side of the body. The symbolic topography of the body in Mahikari is discussed further below.

19 The preferred translation of UK members is 'calm down'.

20 This echoes the teaching of another Japanese NRM, Seicho no Ie, that the true condition of human beings is health. However, where Seicho no Ie see illness as an illusion generated by the human mind, Mahikari views illness as purification, as described below.

21 The equivalent Japanese expression translated by 'cleansing' in Mahikari is *misogi harahi*.

22 The word used in Japanese was *kokoro*, which can mean both mind and spirit.

23 The left side is also associated with fire, and the right side with water. The opposition of fire and water is another important element of Mahikari symbolism: for a detailed description see Knecht 1995.

24 The left side is also sacred in Shinto (McVeigh 1993: 149).

25 See Davis 1980: 58–59 for a description of one such spirit investigation.

26 See Doi 1973 for an influential, if populist, account of the importance of the notion of dependency *(amae)* in Japanese society.
27 See Blacker 1975.
28 Wilson and Dobbelaere report that Soka Gakkai claimed a membership of about 5,000 in the UK in 1990 (Wilson and Dobbelaere 1994).
29 See Clarke 1987 and Barker 1989 for an overview of membership of NRMs in the UK.
30 Records are kept of all visitors to the centre who receive light, and also of visitors to most private houses where light is given. This figure is an approximate estimate based on these records.
31 Directly comparable figures for the general population are not available, but some indication of the comparative levels of education for the population as a whole may be gained from the General Household Survey of 1994, which shows less than 20 per cent of the adult population of the UK have educational qualifications going beyond A level (Office of Population Censuses and Surveys 1996: 42).
32 Puttick (1997) notes that 'in general, research shows a predominance of women in religion, including NRMs, although 'the proportions of women to men vary between individual movements and in some, such as the Unification Church and ISCKON, men are in the majority' (Puttick 1997: 28–29).
33 These figures probably underestimate the levels of ethnic minority membership within the movement, as they do not include British-born members from ethnic minorities.
34 There is a lively debate as to whether the term 'alternative' or 'complementary' is more appropriate for approaches to health-care falling outside the bio-medical mainstream. I have opted for the term 'alternative' here, in recognition of the alternative etiology of illness offered by many of these therapies. However, I recognise that many people using 'alternative' therapies use them alongside bio-medicine, and may see the relationship of these therapies and bio-medicine as one of complementarity rather than opposition.
35 The Mahikari results show interesting similarities with Rose's findings for the occupations of New Age participants, where there is a also a high proportion (indeed somewhat higher than that found in Mahikari) of people employed in the caring professions, and particularly in alternative therapies (Rose 1996: 135).
36 It should be noted, however, that the term 'cultic milieu' would be rejected by those involved because of the negative connotations of the term 'cult' in popular usage.
37 Macrobiotics is a diet-based approach to the restoration and maintenance of health which was founded by George Ohsawa, a Japanese immigrant to the United States, and has subsequently been promoted energetically in the United States and Western Europe by another Japanese-born American, Michio Kushi.
38 See Sharma 1995: 16–17.
39 Non members receiving light for the first time at the centre are asked why they wish to receive light, and a record is kept of these responses. These figures are based on records from January to December 1996.
40 A similar use of scientific discourse can also be seen in a number of non-Japanese NRMs, one notable example being that of Scientology, of which Wilson writes, 'it constitutes a religious system set forth in the terms of scientific discourse' (Wilson 1990: 275). Wilson argues that this use of scientific language is symptomatic of the increasing secularisation of religion.

41 From text of 'Sukyo Mahikari: True Light and Spiritual Principles for the Twenty-First Century', a presentation by Dr Sidney Chang, February 1996. I am grateful to Dr Chang for his permission to reproduce this portion of his presentation.

42 These categories roughly correspond to the division between chronic and acute illnesses, though I avoided using these terms.

43 As implied by this last comment, the term purification, or cleansing, can be used to describe, and account for, any sort of problem that a member is experiencing. So in addition to physical cleansings, members also talk about other sorts of cleansings, for example financial cleansings, as previously noted.

44 Environmental action was rated as important by nearly 85 per cent of respondents, while over 90 per cent believed increased spiritual awareness was important. Improved social welfare and overseas aid were seen as important by about a quarter of respondents, while science and politics lagged behind with around 20 per cent, and improvements in technology were rated as important by only around 13 per cent of respondents (multiple answers possible).

45 The Mahikari ancestral altar is similar in many respects to the *butsudan* familiar in Japan's religious mainstream, but there are some distinctive features in its lay-out, and the way in which the ancestors must be cared for. For a detailed description see McVeigh 1991: 69–75.

46 I am indebted to Yu-shuang Yao, a doctoral student at the Centre for New Religious Movements, King's College, London, for information about Mahikari in Taiwan.

47 Japanese beliefs and practices concerning the ancestors have been influenced historically by Chinese beliefs and practices. For a full discussion of the history and development of ancestor veneration in Japan see Smith 1974.

48 This is probably particularly true of those who joined in the early days of Mahikari in the UK, when there was less preparation for *kenshū* than there is now – the movement has since established pre-*kenshū* seminars and courses.

49 A similar overlap was found by McGuire (1988) in her study of ritual healing in the United States, where she found that in a number of the groups she looked at the notion of healing was extended to a range of problems besides physical illness, including problems related to the family, the workplace, or interpersonal relationships, and, indeed, to society as a whole.

50 Wilson and Dobbelaere found that 45 per cent of the membership of Soka Gakkai UK had a previous interest in Japan, with the largest category being 'aesthetic interests' – i.e. art, design, theatre, and film (Wilson and Dobbelaere 1994: 94). For Mahikari, too, 'aesthetic interests' was the largest category (53 per cent of those with a previous interest in Japan), but was closely followed by martial arts (41.5 per cent) – an interesting finding in view of the importance attached to notions of energy and the flow of energy in the martial arts, notions which, as we have seen, are also central in Mahikari.

51 An example cited by more than one person was taken from one of the founder's teachings as reproduced in an English language Mahikari journal, in which wives were exhorted to kneel at the doorway and bow to their husbands to greet them on their return home. Although this would be unexceptional (if somewhat conservative) in Japan, it provoked a mixture of hilarity and incredulity among the European members who heard it.

52 See, for example, Cornille (1994).

References

Barker, E. (1984) *The Making of a Moonie: Choice or Brainwashing?* Oxford: Basil Blackwell.

—— (1989) *New Religious Movements: A practical introduction,* London: HMSO.

Barker, E. (ed.) (1982) *New Religious Movements: A perspective for understanding society,* New York and Toronto: Edwin Mellen Press.

Blacker, C. (1975) *The Catalpa Bow: A Study of Shamanistic Practices in Japan,* London: Allen and Unwin.

Campbell, C. (1972) 'The Cult, the Cultic Milieu and Secularization', in Michael Hill (ed.) *Sociological Yearbook of Religion in Britain,* London: SCM Press.

Clarke, P.B. (1987) 'New Religions in Britain and Western Europe: In Decline?' in P.B. Clarke (ed.) *The New Evangelists: Recruitment, Methods and Aims of New Religious Movements,* London: Ethnographica.

Clarke, P.B. & Somers, J. (eds.) (1994) *Japanese New Religions in the West,* Folkestone, Kent: The Japan Library.

Cornille, D.C. (1991) 'The Phoenix Flies West: The dynamics of Mahikari in Western Europe', in *Japanese Journal of Religious Studies* 18/2–3.

—— (1994) 'Jesus in Japan: Christian Syncretism in Mahikari' in P.B. Clarke and J. Somers (eds.) *Japanese New Religions in the West,* Folkestone, Kent: The Japan Library.

Currer, C. & Stacey, M. (eds.) (1986) *Concepts of Health, Illness and Disease: A Comparative Perspective,* Oxford, Berg.

Davis, W. (1980) *Dojo: Magic and Exorcism in Modern Japan,* Stanford Calif.: Stanford University Press.

Doi, T. (1973) *The Anatomy of Dependence,* Tokyo: Kodansha.

Hardacre, H. (1984) *Lay Buddhism in Contemporary Japan: Reiyukai Kyodan,* Princeton: Princeton University Press.

—— (1986) *Kurozumikyo and the New Religions of Japan,* Princeton : Princeton University Press.

Hirasawa, H. (1963) 'Tenrikyo followers' views of disease seen from patients with malignant tumours', in *Tenri Journal of Religion* 9.

Hurbon, L. (1991) 'Mahikari in the Caribbean', in *Japanese Journal of Religious Studies* 18.

Ikado, F. (1968) 'Trend and Problems of New Religions: Religion in Urban Society', in K. Morioka and W. H. Newell (ed.) *The Sociology of Japanese Religion,* Leiden: E. J. Brill.

Inoue, N., Komoto, M., Tsushima, M., Nakamaki, H. Nishiyama, S. (eds.) (1990) *Shinshūkyō jiten,* Tokyo: Kobundo.

Kitagawa, J. (1987) *On Understanding Japanese Religion,* Princeton : Princeton University Press.

Kleinman, A. (1986) 'Concepts and a Model for the Comparison of Medical Systems as Cultural Systems', in C. Currer and M. Stacey (eds.) *Concepts of Health, Illness and Disease: a Comparative Perspective,* Oxford: Berg.

Knecht, P. (1995) 'The Crux of the Cross: Mahikari's Core Symbol' in *Japanese Journal of Religious Studies* 22 (3–4).

Lewis, J.R. and Melton, J. Gordon (ed.) (1992) *Perspectives on the New Age,* Albany: State University of New York Press.

Lock, M. (1980) *East Asian Medicine in Urban Japan,* Berkeley: University of California Press.

Mc Farland, H. (1967) *The Rush Hour of the Gods,* New York: Macmillan.

McGuire, M. (with the assistance of Debra Kantor) (1988) *Ritual Healing in Suburban America*, New Brunswick: Rutgers University Press.
Mc Veigh, B. (1991) *Gratitude, Obedience and Humility of Heart: the cultural construction of belief in a Japanese New Religion*, Ph.D Thesis, Princeton University.
—— (1992) (a). 'The Master Metaphor of Purity: the symbolism of Authority and Power in Sukyo Mahikari', in *Japanese Religions*, 98–125.
—— (1992) (b). 'The Vitalistic Conception of Salvation as Expressed in Sukyo Mahikari', in *Japanese Journal of Religious Studies*, 19/1.
—— (1995) 'Learning Morality through Sentiment and the Senses: the role of emotional experience in Sukyo Mahikari' in *Japanese Religions*, 20 (1) pp. 56–76.
Mullins, M., Shimazono, S. Swanson, P. (ed.) (1993) *Religion and Society in Modern Japan: Selected Readings,* Berkeley, California: Asian Humanities Press.
Ohnuki-Tierney, E. (1984) *Illness and Culture in Contemporary Japan*, Cambridge: Cambridge University Press.
Oie, S. (ed.) (1984) *Shūkyō Kankei Hanrei Shūsei 3* Tokyo: Daiichi Shobo.
Puttick, E. (1997) *Women in New Religions: In Search of Community, Sexuality and Spiritual Power,* London: Macmillan.
Reader, I. (1991) *Religion in Contemporary Japan*, London: Macmillan.
Rose, S. (1996) *Transforming the World: an examination of the roles played by spirituality and healing in the New Age movement*, Ph.D. Thesis, Lancaster University.
Sharma, U. (1995) *Complementary Medicine Today: Practitioners and Patients,* (Revised Edition) London: Routledge.
Shibata, K. (1993) *Daiseishu: Great and Holy master*, Tokyo: L.H. Yoko Shuppan.
Shimazono, S. (1993) 'The Expansion of Japan's New Religions into Foreign Cultures', in M. Mullins, S. Shimazono, P. Swanson (ed.) *Religion and Society in Modern Japan: Selected Readings*, Berkeley, California: Asian Humanities Press.
Smith, R.J. (1974) *Ancestor Worship in Contemporary Japan,*Stanford, Stanford University Press.
Spickard, J.V. (1995) 'Body, Nature and Culture in Spiritual Healing', in H. Johannessen, S. Olesen, J. Andersen (eds.) *Studies in Alternative Therapy 2: Body and Nature*, Gylling, Denmark: INRAT and Odense University Press: 65–81.
Stark, R. and Bainbridge, W.S. (1985) *The Future of Religion: Secularization, Revival and Cult Formation*, Berkeley: University of California Press.
Tebecis, A.K. (1982) *Mahikari. Thank God for the Answers at Last,*Tokyo: Yoko Shuppan.
Thomsen, H. (1963) *The New Religions of Japan*, Rutland, Vt.: Charles E. Tuttle.
Wallis, R. (1977) *The Road to Total Freedom: A Sociological Analysis of Scientology*, New York: Columbia University Press.
Wilson, B. (1990) *The Social Dimensions of Sectarianism: Sects and New Religious Movements in Contemporary Society,* Oxford: Clarendon Press.
Wilson, B. & Dobbelaere, K. (1994) *A Time to Chant: The Soka Gakkai Buddhists in Britain*, Oxford: Clarendon Press.
Young, R. (1990) 'Magic and Morality in Modern Japanese Exorcistic Technologies: a study of Mahikari' in*Japanese Journal of Religious Studies* 17.
Yumiyama, T. (1995) 'Varieties of Healing in Present-Day Japan' in *Japanese Journal of Religious Studies* 22, 3–4.

Movement Publications

Society of Johrei (1984) *Johrei: Divine Light of Salvation*, Kyoto: Society of Johrei.
Sukyo Mahikari (1994) *Sukyo Mahikari*, Tokyo: Mainichi group.

Government Publications

Office of Population Censuses and Surveys, Social Survey Division (1996) *Living in Britain: Results from the 1994 General Household Survey*, London: HMSO.

CHAPTER EIGHT

Illness and Salvation in Tensho-Kotai-Jingu-Kyo — The Dancing Religion of Hawaii

Tina Hamrin

From Japan To Hawai'i

In 1868, after a long period of isolation, Japan opened up to the outside world. The country was dependent on its agricultural products, and the amendments to the system of taxation in 1873 raised problems for the people tilling the land. Many were starving and could not find work in rural southwest Japan. Meanwhile the big plantations in Hawai'i could not get enough workers. In the early 1880s the Hawaiian king David Kalakaua sailed round the world and was the first king to enter Japan during the Meiji era. An agreement was made between the king and the Japanese government, and later a contract system developed. Between 1886 and 1899 circa 90,000 Japanese workers arrived in Hawai'i (Odo and Sinoto 1985: 49).

Hawai'i became American territory in 1898. Under the Organic Act applied to the islands in 1900, the contract system was abolished. The Japanese plantation workers were free, either to go home or to start new lives as Americans. Many stayed, and when coffee prices fell on the world market, the plantation owners left their fields. This was an opportunity for the Japanese, who moved in as the Portuguese moved out.

Kona on the Big Island Hawai'i became more and more Japanese in the beginning of the present century and most of the villagers in the places belonging to the Kona coffee belt, that runs along the upland slopes of Mauna Loa and Mt. Hualalai, from Honaunau to Honokohau, depended soley on faith healers for their medical care. 'In early 1895 when Dr. Hayashi opened his medical practice in Holualoa, he was astonished to see the poor socio-economic as well as unsanitary living conditions of the Japanese immigrants there' (Nakano 1990: 47).

This study is about people between 65 and 87 years old, all in poor health. Their parents came over to Hawai'i from Japan between 1885–1924 and those that did not arrive as children were born in plantation camps or in shacks on rocky lava soil, next to the coffee fields. Between 1900–1908 approximately 75,000 immigrants arrived from Japan and between 1908–1924 circa 60,000 came in (Odo and Sinoto 1985: 49). In Kona, the second generation immigrants grew up harvesting coffee and life was tough. The coffee farmers in the area worked hard in the hot sun on the few acres that they could lease from *haole* (Caucasian) landholders. The coffee prices went up and down on the World Market and by 1910 only Japanese coffee farms had survived (Kona Coffee 1993: 8).

When the farmers became ill they went to *ōdaishisan* (a corrupted form of *Odaishi-sama*), with the power of the great master himself, Kōbō Daishi, or to faith healers like Hawaiian *kahunas*.[1] The Japanese immigrants prefered Japanese healers, though, and with the help of *omamori* (amulet) some Japanese women knew how to exorcise evil spirits. They had learned from old relatives, sometimes with a Shugendo background. Curing illness with the help of exorcism, with specific amulets and magical formulas, were preeminently the domain of the *ōdaishisan*.

In 1952 Hawaiian Japanese newspapers proclaimed: 'Mrs. Sayo Kitamura, Dancing goddess, arrives'. Sayo Kitamura, or Ogamisama, was welcomed on Hawai'i as a new faith healer. Her followers learnt how to perform the ecstasy dance and to achieve an altered state of consciousness with a healing effect. Part of her divine mission was to establish a bridge to the world on Hawai'i. The charismatic, masculine, stocky woman from the Yamaguchi prefecture in the South-West of Japan, had a stentorian voice and could enchant the listener with her sermon.

The Dancing Religion in the Beginning

In the beginning of the 1940's, Sayo Kitamura was a farmer's wife, worked hard in the fields and never got enough sleep. In July 1942 a barn on the Kitamura family was burnt down and Sayo saw herself as the cause of the accident. Serving the *kami* of the ancestors had for her been the most important thing in life, so she was deeply disturbed by the fire. She blamed herself for having destroyed the ancestor's property and disturbing the neighbours. After praying and praying for forgiveness, she still suffered torments of conscience day after day. She went to a well-known healer in a nearby village, who gave her an explanation (the fire was caused by a jealous arsonist) and some advice for the future. In her diary two days later, and then thirteen days later, we can read, 'Got up at 2.00 a. m. and took cold bath of penance and prayed ... each time I take a cold bath of penance, I feel as if My body and soul have been purified and that I have come nearer to God. My mind is filled only with the eagerness of praying to purify Myself and I have no worldly cares' (Tensho-kotai-jingu-kyo 1954: 15).

In March 1944 the healer living nearby had a divine message for Sayo Kitamura: 'All the Angels of Heaven and Earth will descend upon You and You will become a living God on earth.' (Ibid.: 16). After that she began to receive inspiration from an Almighty *kami* given the name Tensho-kotai-jin and became the mouthpiece of this deity who possessed her. What the entity inside commanded her to say flabbergasted people and was often taken as a sign of madness or insanity. She was not enable to act in accordance with her own intentions but had involuntarily to obey the dictates of the one in her body. Otherwise she got headaches, stomach pains and suffered attacks of diarrhoea.

According to Sayo Kitamura's life history, what started with animal spirit possession, which is quite common in South-West Japan, became something else when the snake spirit transformed itself into two beings, that of Kotai-jin (a *kami* connected to Shinto shrines) and Amaterasu (the Sun goddess, here as *Tenshō*, meaning heavenly) who united in the body of this chosen woman as 'The Almighty God of Heaven'.

In the middle of autumn 1944 she was led by the divinity inside her to a mountain on her property at 02.00 a. m. Sayo Kitamura rode her bicycle to the foot of the mountain, about two miles from her house, and climbed the hill. At the top she commenced a prayer that was given to her as the only prayer that was in accordance with God's will: NA-MYŌ-HŌ-REN-GE-KYŌ.[2]

In *The Prophet of Tabuse,* the already cited account of her life, is written: 'Her prayer "Na-myō-hō-ren-ge-kyō", sometimes drawn out and some-times brief, was chanted with natural rhythm and reverberated among the surrounding mountains'. When she finished praying, She lay on the ground, face upward, and watched the dawn breaking. After a pause, She resumed Her prayer. Once celestial lotus flowers in full bloom showered down from Heaven as the reddish sun ascended amongst the blossoms. Angels in full costume were dancing before Her ... this is a dance of Angels, the One in Her body said. While She was watching the dance in admiration, She was in a celestial bliss and felt as if She had also become a dancing Angel' (Ibid.: 29–30).

In July 1945 Sayo Kitamura gave her first public sermon and her religious group was called *Odori Shūkyō,* the Dancing Religion, by out-siders. The dance was something given to the foundress as a way to restore peace. 'You have been appointed to perform a Salvation Dance when the present world is on the verge of collapse', the divinity inside Sayo Kitamura told her (Ibid.: 46).

To her followers Ogamisama said, 'I will establish true peace on this earth... World peace advocated by politicians is nothing but a camouflage of national interest based on selfishness... Peace can be brought only by practicing God's teaching' (Tensho-Kotai-Jingu-Kyo 1960: 1–2).

The Japanese Immigrant Community in Kona

Among the Japanese immigrants, disease was a sign of pollution in the form of spirit possession, and therefore dangerous to the whole neighbourhood. Some families were suspected of being carriers of evil dog spirits (*inu-gami*), other people were accused of enviousness and they sent their envy as an evil spirit (*ikiryō*) on the victim. This was a relic of witchcraft that still exists in certain areas of South-West Japan, such as Shikoku and Yamaguchi (cf. Smith 1985: 40 and Yoshida 1988: 85–104).

Relationships between the members of the Dancing Religion and the rest of the local Japanese community were not very good. In the mountain villages of Kona, religion was either Soto Zen or Jodo Shinshu – the *shin shūkyō* that came with the dancing foundress was very controversial. The new religion turned everything that had to do with funeral rites and ancestor worship upside down. This was very offensive to other Japanese Americans in Kona, and the newspapers wrote about the 'ashes issue'. The members wanted their dead relative's ashes returned from the Buddhist temple.

Since the converts were urged to get rid of all religious symbols including the ancestral altars, the *juzus* and the sutra books, many Zen and Shin Buddhists thought of them as insane, especially when they left the graveyards unattended. 'Members destroyed religious paraphernalia together with ancestral funerary tablets, cast the ashes of deceased family members in the ocean instead of placing them in graves, denied any concourse with other religions, and refused to participate in neighborhood funerary associations' (Nishiyama och Fujii 1991: 145)

Before 1988, when the ex-leader of the Dancing Religion in Kona was still alive, he gave the group a millennialistic, nationalistic and extremely odd profile. The leader of the Kona branch had been a language school teacher and took a strong pro-Japanese stand during the Second World War. He established the *katta-gumi* group Hisshō-kai ('Sure-of-victory-club') and refused to accept Japan's position at the end of the war.[3] In fact, the pro-Japanese group became Tensho-Kotai-Jingu-Kyo after the arrival of Ogamisama. (The Hisshō-kai sign outside the house of the leader was taken away and replaced by a new sign saying: Tensho-Kotai-Jingu-Kyo.)

Through the ecstasy dance, *muga-no-mai,* the members of Tensho-Kotai-Jingu-Kyo planned to gain spiritual dominion over the world. All human beings would sooner or later become followers of Ogamisama, and their souls would be purified and belong to the domain of The Great Goddess. Thanks to the dance and the formula *na-myō-hō-ren-ge-kyō,* evil spirits were pacified and saved. According to the teaching, hatred, jealousy, envy, and other emotional antipathies produced evil spirits and the members used to find a suprahuman explanation for any undeserved misfortune, illness or death. But in Tensho-Kotai-Jingu-Kyo they had a cure-all, this was promised by Ogamisama. In Kona, the struggle to establish God's Kingdom on earth was based on the work of a small, quite secluded, group of coffee-planters, led by a Japanese language school teacher. The group members looked upon agriculture as the socio-economic basis of society. As *nōhonshugi* they supported traditional values of rural life and included physiocratic theories in their politics.[4] In the area of the coffee belt, this aspiration was very realistic and in no way 'utopian'. But it was accompanied with a millenarian ideology that justified withdrawal from the wider society, so that members of the Dancing Religion could continue being outsiders in the Japanese American community on Hawai'i. Their agrarianist views were part of a broader nationalist ideology and a manifestation of the traditional Japanese spirit. Unfortunately, it all went wrong when the converts turned the funeral rites upside down and the group's policy became too controversial (Adams 1992). Then millenialism became the solution and their salvation. Thanks to Ogamisama the Japanese surrender did not mean the loss of the war: the war was carried on perpetually by the dancing goddess against evil spirits.

Health/Bad Health and Possession Spirits

The main thread in the soteriological process is health, or lack of it. What is health? Is health absence of disease or can there be health despite disease, is healthy behaviour when health is seen as 'the healthy life', is it physical fitness, energy and vitality, or is it social relationships with other people, a psycho-social well-being? Should we consider health as function – 'health defined by being able to do things, with less stress upon a description of feelings' (Blaxter 1995: 31). What do people mean when they talk of "health"? Among older people the idea of health as function is more likely to be expressed since it is later in life that health may be seen as a generally restricting factor, and the younger ones often take the ability to cope with the tasks of life for granted.

Ogamisama had been ill, psychologically and physically, and was suffering from very high blood pressure during her missionary trips around the world. As for many other healers, it seems to be a connection between the problems overcome and the status of the performer. When the apparent trauma which is mastered is considered to have been extremely grave then authority and power of the healer become great. Sayo Kitamura's ability to contain and control the causes of disorder, after her severe personal crisis, remained an essential requirement for her appeal. In 1944 she became possessed by *tōbyo*, the previously mentioned snake spirit. The super-natural being in her stomach demanded absolute obedience. Whenever she failed to perform what was commanded, the snake spirit caused acute pains in her stomach or head. She thus ceased to be herself, falling under complete control of the one in the abdomen, although she was well aware of the duality of her ego. Unlike some people labelled as schizophrenic, she did not totally identify herself with the supernatural, but only communicated with it. Obviously, it is this sense of personal identity that successful prophets manage to maintain.

According to Tensho-Kotai-Jingu-Kyo publications, Sayo Kitamura became possessed already in 1942 but it was not until 1944–45 that she began to deliver her sermons in the streets. The possessing *kami* called himself different names but in 1945 the internal voice told Sayo Kitamura that he would lead her as the *shidō-gami* ('guiding god'), because since birth she had been predestined to save the world. The influences on the would-be messiah were many. As Noboru points out: 'In Japan, the cult of Maitreya merged with traditional concepts of messianism and millenarianism; conversely, these native concepts were expressed through Buddhist millenarianism and messianic movements' (1988: 175).

The guiding god went through a metamorphosis on the night between the 11 and 12 of August 1945. All the different possession spirits that harassed Sayo Kitamura ever since one of the barns on her mother-in-law was burnt down, were interpreted as a kind of ordeal that The Almighty *kami* created to test her, since she was the chosen one. In her own words spoken in a sermon: 'Half an hour after midnight, God bestowed upon me the all-seeing spiritual vision by which I could view the world at a glance... When the mighty sword surrendered, it signified the death knell of the world of the devil. It also meant the dawn of a new age of God' (Ogamisama's sermon 1965: 14) The holy shrine of The Absolute God was the *hara* of Sayo Kitamura. According to Lebra: 'The meaning of the Japanese word hara is diffuse. It means stomach, belly, abdomen, womb. It can also mean guts in both the literal and the figurative sense. In the most abstract sense, it implies the spiritual center of the body' (1967: 40). It was as the mouthpiece of The Almighty God that she became a living goddess, an *ikigami*. In 1945, after the war, she told everyone in the surrounding areas that she was their new leader. Believing she was an *ikigami* Sayo Kitamura started to display symptoms of megalomania, according to people in the neighborhood. As Jabbour says: 'Following this phenomenon her street-side sermons became more frequent and her condemnation of hypocricy, dishonesty, and weakness more blunt and disarming. She was constantly warned by the police of preaching disloyalty and many people began to call her *baka* (insane)' (1958: 26). The heavily built woman shouted at people and told them that they were maggots and hypocrites. In accordance with notes by Lindholm: 'The social attribution of insanity and evil to the ecstatic practitioner is countered by the community's own claim for its leader's absolute deification. This dichotomy is lived out within the soul of the leader him[her-]self, and within the group, who affirm ever more extravagant claims to offset doubts and opprobrium, and who often repudiate completely the larger society that has treated them with such contempt. Furthermore, as in medieval millenaristic movements, charismatic involvement is defiantly affirmed as a whole way of being for the devotees, absolutely opposed in its negation of the self to the selfishness of the ordinary world' (1993: 170).

In Hawai'i, Ogamisama was, as previously mentioned, welcomed as a new faith healer. Her followers learned how to dance the ecstacy dance and they were all agents of her divine mission: to create peace and harmony in the world. According to *The Prophet of Tabuse*, Kona was an 'abutment' on the bridge to the world:[5]

> On August 14, 1952, Ogamisama went to Kona... The Kona district is formed entirely of lava and only rain water is available for use. Yet Ogamisama withstood all these ordeals and moved about from one place to another in the desolate mountainous region... About forty pious people came from houses that dotted a vast expanse of coffee fields and assembled at the hall to listen earnestly to Her sermons... These pious people observed their religious practice so well that an excellent branch hall was established in Kona during Ogamisama's one week stay (Tensho-Kotai-Jingu-Kyo 1954: 174).

In some places in Kona, families were accused of being *inu-gami-mochi*, 'dog spirit-holders'. My informants thought they knew exactly if someone was 'contagious' or not. How come people were so sure about who was an evil spirit carrier, and who was not? One plausible explanation is, as Yoshida points out: 'Animal-spirit-holding cleavages in village society are generally traditional and well defined because the holders inherit their status lineally within households' (1984: 86).

According to the members of the Dancing Religon one of the most important things Ogamisama taught them was *akurei-saido*, redemption of evil spirits. The dance is an important ritual considered to secure this for believers and the amelioration of ill fortune. The 'unseen inhabitants'/ 'bodyless beings' of Hawai'i that some Japanese Americans fear, bear a strong relationship to the spirit population described in Japanese folk traditions, at least in name. Every living person has both a body and a soul, *ikimitama*, capable of detaching itself from the body. The ancient Japanese held the notion of a dual soul, consisting of a free soul and a bodily soul. Among the Japananese in Hawai'i the expression *tama-geru* is used when someone is frightened and this is a colloquial form of *tama kieru* which, according to Taryo Obayashi's etymological presentation, means the loss or disappearance of one's soul (1991). Departure of the soul from the body of a living person, *tama sakaru*, was often described in literature during the Heian period. There is always a risk when the two concepts 'soul' and 'spirit' become mixed, but perhaps *rei* can be seen as both a free soul and an evil spirit. The malevolent *ikiryō* is in any case another form of the spirit or soul of the living, thought to be capable of doing great harm to enemies and rivals.

Ikiryō plays an important role in the Dancing Religion. My informants often told me about periods of illness, when they had gone to see their leader to find out why they were sick. Through 'spiritual contact' with Ogamisama he could immediately tell a person the reason why, since he saw the *ikiryō* of someone who was jealous or envious of the victim. The free soul or evil spirit looked exactly like the person to whom the soul belonged and the leader could describe the *ikiryō* to the possesed person, and thereby identify the cause of illness. *Ikiryō* can be avoided or sent back to its original location by concentrated prayer, and the magic formula *na-myō-hō-renge-kyō* will force a possessing spirit out. Then the possesing free soul or evil spirit leaves through 'the *gasshō*'. A kind of *mudra* used in salutation and during prayer, the palms are kept together in front of the chest. In other words a possessing element leaves through the finger-tips.

In the Dancing Religion, ancestral spirits are often defined as malignant. They contrive to make their descendants suffer because they themselves have not been redeemed. According to Sayo Kitamura's teaching, if a person remains engrossed in this world and becomes an unsaved soul, he will become an obstacle for the so called phenomenal world. Even after death he becomes an obstacle to the world in the formless form of an unreedemed spirit. Unredeemed ancestors are therefore always bringing misfortune; it is a matter of the moral status of spirits and souls. Kerner comments: 'The redeemed spirits reside in heaven, returning only infrequently to earth to give a bit of assistance to particularly devout doshi [members]. The unredeemed spirits, the akurei, are forced to linger near the earth, causing sickness and misfortune through their attachment to living people' (1979: 93). In the state of *muga* ('egolessness') a believer can redeem evil spirits, this state of selflessness is what the ideal human being exemplifies. According to the informants, Sayo Kitamura was a redeemer like Buddha and Jesus Christ, and the official theology describes her as the incarnation of God in the physical world.

It is through a holy prayer, named Oinori, that members put themselves in a *muga* state before they start dancing the so called trance dance. The prayer ends with *na-myō-hō-renge-kyō*, 'repeated indefinitely', and the formula represents the fact that Ogamisama is a living embodiment of God's teaching. The followers have been instructed that the words are untranslatable, reflecting in their sounds a transforming influence of evil or negative unredeemed spirits.

The prayer is repeated and becomes vociferous, while developing a sing-song rhythm it tends to induce a hypnotic frenzy. After the recitation of *na-myō-hō-renge-kyō* comes the 'ecstacy dance'. This ceremony is supposed to endow the participant with the divine power of supernatural insight into the secrets of the universe. When the follower is in this emotional state his prayers have the power to redeem instantly all evil spirits including malignant spirits of living persons. Sayo Kitamura asserts that the efficacy of these prayers of ecstacy carry into daily life and activities, miraculously preventing regret, agony, sickness and worry. According to the members they sometimes 'speak in tongues' during the times of spiritual ecstasy activated by dancing. Phrases in Chinese, English, or other languages are uttered, believed to be the words of souls which have entered the speakers' bodies to express gratitude for having been saved. Upon recovering from this altered state of consciousness, the subjects state that they were unable to recall having said anything while participating in the ecstacy dance.

The Ego-Less Dance in a Physiological Perspective

During the dance my informants went into something like controlled ecstacy. I prefer to call it hypnagogia. How can one describe hypnagogia without being too much of a reductionist? Using psychological and sociological models, when analyzing altered states of consciousness, is generally considered acceptable and unproblematic, but why do historians of religions usually react negatively when physiological explanations are being used? Is one reductionistic interpretation more reductionistic than another? I have found the thought model of Roland Fischer very helpful in my attempts to understand this phenomenon (cf. Fischer 1971, 1972a, 1972b, 1975).

When a person is in a relaxed and positive mood, through electro-encephalographic (EEG) investigations associated with alpha waves (8–14 Hz), we have a state of consciousness that can be called normal. This consciousness, Fischer divides in two sectors: 'ergotropic arousal' (associated with beta waves, 15–25 Hz) and 'trophotropic arousal' (associated with theta waves, 4–7 Hz). The ergotropic version is 'hyper' and activated by stress hormones stimulating the sympatic nervous system. At the end of the scale you can find ecstacy, when someone goes into raptures, but not the kind of ecstacy I found in Hawai'i. 'Hypo' is the label I attach to what I saw and experienced, since the ecstacy was rather on the low side.

Trophotropic arousal is a kind of 'very relaxed' wakefulness. This type of arousal reduces the sensitivity to external stimuli and screens off the outer world. It has the opposit function to the hyper, ergotropic arousal. The 'hypoversion' aims at the inside. It is there to turn our attention inwards, towards the interior of ourselves, away from the world. Trophotropic hormones have a soothing effect, almost like a sedative it is antipsychotic. A yogi in *samadhi* knows how to use those hormones to reach his peak, a calm and steady culmination.

The 'normal-I' is separated from the world around. Everything not being 'I' is something else, like a 'not-I', outside me; something I relate to temporally and spatially. During the *muga-no-mai* the dancers avoid themselves, and then the surrounding becomes blurred and indistinct. The seperated ego starts drifting towards everything 'non-ego' and amalgamates with it. You and the world become more and more a part of me, the I and the world is a confluence, they flow together; the subject-object relation dissolves.

After the dance none of my informants felt the pains they had felt before. The dance had been a pain killer. Hypnagogia has at least three functions. First, it has a hypometabolic function in that it acts as an anxiety-reducer, periodically drawing a person away from the tension-producing activities of the sympathetic system. Many reports emphasize the lack of affect and the sense of 'detached involvement' which is experienced by the hypnagogic subject. Second, it serves a trophotropic function by providing the individual with opportunities to conserve and maintain physical and psychic energy, and restore, regenerate and energize himself. Third, the psychological characteristics of hypnagogia are exactly those which might promote personal growth and development. It is obvious that an induced state of relaxation and detachment from the realities of the immediate environment would themselves have therapeutic consequences, as is appreciated by techniques for progressive relaxation and autogenic training.

Painlessness is a concrete proof of salvation. All my informants claimed that their illness had been cured or that they had undergone rejuvenation through conversion. An old lady that seemed to be anything but well, prefered to describe her situation in terms of symbolic salvation, instead of a failure in concrete salvation. If concrete salvation means that through some 'miracle', often during the dance, some disturbance of the identity system was demonstrably brought to an end, then a symbolic salvation is a transformation on another level. At least it enables the convert to experience events meaningfully.

The trance experienced by members of Tensho-Kotai-Jingu-Kyo, I call an altered state of consciousness (ASC), following Charles Tart and Arnold Ludwig. Tart states:'An altered state of consciousness for a given individual is one in which he clearly feels a qualitative shift in his pattern of mental functioning, that is, he feels not just a quantitative shift (more or less alert, more or less visual imagery, sharper or duller, etc.), but also that some quality or qualities of his mental processes are different' (1969: 1–2). And according to Ludwig ASC is 'any mental state(s), induced by various physiological, psychological, or pharmacological manoeuvres or agents, which can be recognized subjectively by the individual himself (or by an objective observer of the individual) as representing a sufficient deviation in subjective experience or psychological functioning from certain general norms for that individual during alert, waking consciousness' (1969: 9–10).

The One Who Suffers is Expanding God's Kingdom on Earth

Ogamisama, the prophet from Tabuse, had inverted the world-order. Members of the Dancing Religion came to understand that illness was not that bad, after all. They were not polluted and dangerous, but useful and important. Suffering was interpreted as a preparatory step towards fulfilment. A disease was nothing but a necessary preparation for salvation, a useful means for world peace. The best kind of *gyō*, or *shūgyō*, was illness. To purify the *hara*, a health problem was a must. The conception of illness as instrumental 'to eradicating pollution' was explicit. We can see in the movement's teaching a functional relevance of suffering (Lebra 1970: 46). In Kona, among Tensho-Kotai-Jingu-Kyo members, bad health was a means to expand God's kingdom on earth, to create more *tenshi* ('angels') than evil *senzo-no-rei* in the spiritual world. And it is worth recalling here that in Tensho-Kotai-Jingu-Kyo ancestor spirits means possession-afflictions.

The fancies associated with spirit possession are in a psychoanalytic sense a matter of defence mechanisms. With illness there was confinement, to be cured the sufferer had to be taken out of his or her daily routine, and the trip away from pain was in this case the prayer and *muga-no-mai* (the egoless dance). To escape the ego in the spirit world, where the face of Ogamisama hopefully would be seen and evil spirits chased away, made my informants forget about themselves, and their problems. A ritualized altered state of consciousness became a necessity and a temporary cure. The difference was a sense of healing, another 'whole-me'.

The members of Tensho-Kotai-Jingu-Kyo in Kona had visions and often auditory sensations, they knew how to put themselves in a hypnagogic state of mind and to them hypnagogia was well-being. The dancing-ritual was a formalized expression of inner salvation, it was attainable independently of the physical condition (cf. Lebra 1970: 49). And in fact, thanks to the physical condition, being ill and possessed.

The state of consciousness between wakefulness and sleep, called hypnagogia is on an equality with salvation. According to the converts: 'When we attain the state of ecstasy, God will come upon us and endow on us God's power, open Heavenly eyes and spiritual eyes, and acquaint us with the spiritual world, thereby making us perceive everything in the universe without study' (Tensho-Kotai-Jingu-Kyo 1950: 29–30). No matter who they are, human beings or evil spirits, there is body-wise and 'bodyless-entity-wise' no spatio-temporal difference between the other world and this world, it is only a matter of state of consciousness. The spiritual world is in the mind of the convert and so is psychosomatic illness. *Muga-no-mai* is a path into the spiritual world, a mind-transforming exercise. Ogamisama say's: 'You should understand that in a cross section of your real world is found an interrelation between the phenomenal and the spiritual world'

(Tensho-kotai-jingu-kyo 1986: 56). With a move from any kind of social-psychological ideas to physiology, salvation as liberation from pain is *muga-no-mai* and hypnagogia.

After the second world war the Japan-won-the-war group known as Hisshôkai in Kona, whose members refused to admit that Japan was defeated in 1945, found a new leader in Sayo Kitamura. With Amaterasu (who according to the teaching became one with the Shinto *kami* Kotai-jin) in possession of her *hara,* she would conquer the world while expanding the Kingdom of God. A new kind of imperialism in disguise of a religious movement with a strongly millenarian character was being advanced in a context wherein old nationalism, while still very much alive, could not be publicly expressed in a political, secular form. Explicit values and underlying feelings can create ambivalence, and the Hisshôkai members marginalized themselves even more after the convertion to the Dancing Religion. The solution to frustration was self-assertiveness by means of self-transcendence. *Muga-no-mai* was a happy-mood elevator.

The self-serving biases in social perception was inside this group a question of form. Among hard-working farmers a healthy body and good luck were often all you needed, and salvation was a 'body-thing', it was a matter of physique.

The very notion of self-assertion (or self-preservation) implies the assumption that there is some form of instinctual self-awareness. Fear and anger may have arisen out of this need for self-preservation and through the need to preserve itself as a more or less self-contained unit, an organism asserts itself on its environment: but without some form of awareness of itself as a separate unit, self-assertation would be meaningless, emotions like fear and anger would be meaningless and useless if they did not stem from some form of self-awareness.

The relevance of this to the nature and function of hypnagogia lies in the idea that the latter is a state characterized by integrative features and self-transcending tendencies, loosening of ego boundaries, pain-abandonment, the implicit assumption that the environment is not inimical, the tendency to incorporate (internalize) and merge with the environment, in this case with the big posters of Ogamisama and her voice from the tape-recorder, and the willingness to relinquish self-awareness, and therefore, absence of self-assertiveness. Now we have to correlate psychological aspects of hypnagogia with activities around the thalamus, since consciousness during hypnagogia is mainly concentrated in this area. Hypnagogia is characterized by relaxation and reduced respiration (and therefore, by increase in carbon dioxide in the blood), by inwardly turned, diffuse-absorbed attention, and by dreamlike mentation which is linked to a diminution in cortical and to an increase in mesencephalic activity. The feeling of loss of identity might be of the latter nature in that if no information from the senses is conveyed through the thalamus to the cortex the person is deprived of his 'reality anchorage' and the preservation of his 'ego schema' which normally enables him to relate himself to his mental and physical environment (Mavromatis 1991: 256–259). In *muga-no-mai* the convert meets Ogamisama in the spiritual world, evil spirits are leaving the body, pain is not present – and that is salvation because the convert is now a *tenshi*, a very important tool in God's hands. When self-transcending or integrative tendencies correlate with self-assertative tendencies, the induced state of hypnagogia brings self-confidence. In this case, salvation includes bad health and salvation *is* the happy moment when you do not feel the pain, being a dancing angel, and the realized eschatology leads us to the fen-like field of physiology, where the salvation dance is nothing but a pain-killer.

Conclusion

Björkqvist states that: 'Whatever the physiological basis of the experi-ence... we must not neglect the cognitive side. An experience is something that happens in our consciousness. We interpret in a certain way, depending on how we have been 'programmed' by our social background and past experiences' (1981: 84–85). When a person is using an ecstacy technique, he usually does so within a tradition. When he reaches an experience, a traditional interpretation of it already exists. During *reidō* (when evil spirits leave the body through the finger-tips) the member of Tensho-Kotai-Jingu-Kyo abandon pain, at least for awhile. The main thing is that the ancestors are capable of some immediate intervention in the realm of a mind that is in an altered state, in other words, the consciousness is the realm of personal relationships between living and dead. But the ritual is necessary to establish the right mood. This was something very important to the immigrant, who entertained feelings of guilt of having left the ancestors behind. The procedure for those fortunate enough to be chosen was: convert, be ill and meet your ancestors, and illness will be good to you. Health is a peaceful relationship with your ancestors. Health is *wa* (peace/harmony).

That suffering is a necessary preparation for salvation is supported by the idea of purification. It is good to be ill, according to my informants, because not until all filthy things are eliminated from the system can one live in God's Kingdom. The conception of illness as instrumental to eradicating pollution was something they learned from Sayo Kitamura. A convert must have his/her body, especially the *hara*, ready for the *kami* to enter. This means that salvation can be anticipated only after the body has been emptied and cleansed. Skin disease and other externally visible disorders shall be gratefully accepted since they signal internal purification having been completed.

The dance danced by a Tensho-Kotai-Jingu-Kyo member may serve as an activating agent for giving her-/himself temporarily to a supernatural being, i.e. embodying the supernatural in inner transformation, in other words, personal possession. Or it can be a way of merging with the supernatural toward enlightenment or self-detachment. The first case was exemplified by Sayo Kitamura. It was a matter of inviting spirit mediumship possession dances. In the case of my informants it was more a question of merging with the woman they have apotheosized. They strive to detach themselves from the world and divest themselves of ties to self in order to unite with a personified God.

According to the informants, Sayo Kitamura was a living goddess and at the same time an anthropomorphous shrine/tempel with a supernatural entity in her stomach, who could influence it to act on her behalf. The dance always indicates the deity's presence, both in the case of personal possesion and self-detachment through fusion.

Tensho-Kotai-Jingu-Kyo in Hawai'i is a manifestation of a transforma-tion. A pro-Japanese political group turns into a religion, and when it comes to the dance, the institutionalized dance is relaxed, here called a 'hypo-dance'. It is a transformed version of the wild, ecstatic dance that Sayo Kitamura performed when she, in the opinion of a number of anthropologists, acted like a shaman. The original dance in Tensho-Kotai-Jingu-Kyo was a 'hyper-dance'. But God's Kingdom on earth is the same, I was told by my informants. They see what the foundress saw. They all agree on that, since we are talking about the Absolute Real World. Besides, they are the chosen ones.

Here, dance is a vehicle that incorporates inchoate ideas in visible human form and modifies inner experience as well as social action. It can be both a metaphor, a dance in place of a mantra or a magic device, another expression that it resembles, and a metonym, the dance is connected with a larger whole. Where metonymi implies contiguity, metaphor depends upon asserted similarity. 'Gods Kingdom on earth' is all around the dancer and the larger whole is inside her. Besides contiguity, the anticipation of meaning in which the whole is envisaged becomes actual understanding when the parts that are determined by the whole themselves also determine this whole. The dancer who mentally steps in and out of herself, aware–unaware, aware–unaware, on her way to enlightenment in a 'non-ego state', has a parallel: the movement of understanding is constantly from the whole to the part and back to the whole. It is a circular relationship in both cases.

A monistic idealism is a necessesity in the case of the Dancing Religion. God's Kingdom has an absolute form of totality. It is an all-form. A dancer is someone who moves and does not move, in the dance all unity of consciousness transcends change and must be clearly unchanging; and change comes to arise from this. All things are unified by/in the 'true self', which is not something apart from this unification, but which is nothing more than this unification.

According to an abundance of research done on mysticism, during the mystical experience of oneness, there is no multiplicity, no distinctions, no concepts, and no words. There is only silence. It is afterwards we can contrast the two kinds of consciousness. I have been told that a paradox hides a mystical experience from the scrutiny required to help us understand what characterizes mystical experience. There is no way to get behind the full expression of the feelings, to compare, or even to understand. To sense the happiness behind the story about a pain that is now gone, thanks to Ogamisama, brings forth a feeling beyond understanding, and that will do.

Notes

1 The Polynesian word 'huna' means 'that which is hidden'. A *kahuna* conducted the ceremonies of the *heiau* (shrine), consulted the auspices for favorable omens, gave advice, healed, etc. and was the one who knew the hidden secrets about life and death.

2 Before 1964 Tensho-Kotai-Jingu-Kyo used the same *kanji* as the Nichiren sect to indicate *namu-myōhō-renge-kyō*, but ceased doing so as a consequence of a lawsuit initiated by the Nichiren Shoshu. Inside the Dancing Religion the formula has been interpreted as 'A woman with a little name has contacted the law of Heaven binding it into a teaching'. Nowadays the members are instructed that the words are untranslatable, reflecting in their sounds a transforming influence of evil or negative unredeemed spirits (Kerner 1979: 317).

3 The *katta-gumi* (Japan-won-the-war-groups) began to circulate their own beliefs concerning the war results. 'These Issei had relied on the mainland Japanese vernaculars for war news, which they got from Japanese sources and which was intended to keep morale high in Japan. When the mainland papers also reported the defeat of Japan, these Issei readers stopped reading all newspapers' (Kimura 1992: 244).

4 'The movement based on *Nōhonshugi* (doctrine making agriculture the source of well-being) came to emphasize the value to the State of the villages as viable economic units and helped to make them foundations of a fascistic state in the mid-30s. The instrumentality whereby communal spirit served state purposes rather than the needs of agricultural communities was embodied in Hokoku-kai and other patriotic organizations which submerged rural needs in supra-mural campaigns and movements' (Burton 1990: 161).

5 Because Sayo Kitamura's husband was a contract worker on Hawai'i for ten years, before their marriage, Hawai'i was very special to the foundress. Here Ogamisama would bridge over difficulties and, as previously mentioned, The Almighty God had decided that Hawai'i would be the bridge to the world, the point of departure for her missionary work.

References

Adams, E. (1992) Personal interview with prof. of Religion and Philosophy, University of Hawaii in Hilo. 1992.06.09.

Björkqvist, K. (1982) Ecstasy from a Physiological Point of View. In: *Religious ecstasy*, ed. Nils G. Holm; pp. 74–86. Stockholm: Almqvist & Wiksell International. (Scripta Instituti Donneriani Aboensis, 11).

Blaxter, M. (1995) What is health. In: *Health and Disease.*, eds. Basiro Davey, Alastair Gray and Clive Seale; pp. 26–32. Buckingham: Open University Press.

Fischer, R. (1971) A cartography of the ecstatic and meditative states, *Science*, Vol. 174, no 4012, 897.

—— (1972a) On the arousal state- dependent recall of 'subconscious' experience: State boundness. *British Journal of Psychiatry*, 120: 159–172.

—— (1972b) On separateness and oneness, An I-self dialogue. *Confinia psychiatry* 15: 165–194.

—— (1975) Cartheography of Inner Space. In: *Hallucinations: behaviour, experiences and theory*, eds. R. K. Siegel and L. J. West. New York: Wiley.

Jabbour, Millad E. (1958) *The Sect of Tensho-kotai-jingu-kyo: The Emergence and Career of a Religious Movement*. Honolulu. [Unpublished M. A. Thesis, University of Hawaii]

Kerner, K. (1979) *Building God's Kingdom: Society and Order in a Japanese Utopian Community*. New York. [Ph. D., Columbia university]

Kona Coffee (1993) *Kona Coffee. Cultural Festival* 23: 6. Hilo: Hawaii Dept. of Agriculture, Dept. of Business, Economic Development & Tourism, County of Hawaii, Hawaii Visitors Bureau.

Lebra, T.S. (1967) *An Interpretation of Religious Conversion: A Millennial Movement among Japanese-Americans in Hawaii*. [Unpublished Ph. D. Thesis, University of Pittsburg]

—— (1970) Logic of Salvation: The Case of a Japanese Sect in Hawaii. *The International Journal of Social Psychiatry* 16/1: 45–53.

Lindholm, C. (1993) *Charisma*. Oxford UK & Cambridge USA: Blackwell. [1990]

Ludwig, A.M. (1969) Altered States of Consciousness. In: *Altered States of Consciousness. A Book of Readings*, ed. Charles T. Tart. New York: Wiley, pp. 9–22.

Mavromatis, A. (1991) *Hypnagogia: The Unique State of Consciousness between Wakefulness and Sleep*. London: Routledge [1987].

Nakano, J. (1990) *Kono Echo. A Biography of Dr. Harvey Saburo Hayashi*. Kona: Kona Historical Society.

Nishiyama, Shigeru, & Fujii Takashi (1991) The Propagation and Spread of Tensho-kotai-jingu-kyo within Japanese American Society on Hawaii Island. In: *New Religions. Contemporary Papers in Japanese Religions*, red. Nobutaka Inoue. Tokyo: Kokugakuin University, pp. 125–161.

Noboru, M. (1988) Types of Maitreya Belief in Japan. In: Maitreya, the Future Buddha, eds. Alan Sponberg and Helen Hardacre. Cambridge: Cambridge University Press, pp. 175–190.

Obayashi, T. (1991) The Conceptions of the Soul among the Ancient Japanese and the Modern Ainu. Tokyo. [ms., Tokyo Woman's Christian University]

Odo, Franklin, & Kazuko Sinoto (1985) *A Pictorial History of The Japanese in Hawaii 1885–1924*. Honolulu: Departement of Anthropology. Bishop Museum.

Ogamisama's Sermon (1965) Ogamisama's Sermon. *Voice from Heaven* 67–68: 14.

Smith, R. (1985) *Ancester Worship in Contemporary Japan*. Stanford: Stanford University Press.

Tart, C.T. (1969) Introduction. In: *Altered States of Consciousness. A Book of Readings*, red. Charles T. Tart. New York: Wiley, pp. 1–8.

Tensho-Kotai-Jingu-Kyo

—— (1950) *Mioshie. The Divine Teaching*. Tabuse: Tensho-kotai-jingu-kyo.

—— (1954) *The Prophet of Tabuse*. Tabuse: Tensho-kotai-jingu-kyo.

—— (1960) *Key to Heaven. A Concise Explanation of God's Teaching*. Tabuse: Tensho-kotai-jingu-kyo.

—— (1986) *Ogamisama says ... Religious and Philosophical Teachings of the Prophet of Tabuse*. Tabuse: Tensho-kotai-jingu-kyo.

Yoshida, Teigo (1984) Spirit Possession and Village Conflict. In: *Conflict in Japan*, (eds.), Ellis S. Krauss, Thomas P. Rohlen och Patricia G. Steinhoff. Hono-lulu: University of Hawaii Press, pp. 85–104.

CHAPTER NINE

Shin Buddhism in the West

An Overview

Alfred Bloom

In recent years the western world has experienced a virtual inundation of new religions, mainly from Asia, offering new forms of spirituality and promising a variety of benefits. They have appealed to the individualism of the West, raising consternation among the more traditional individual and community oriented Christian traditions and denominations. Many of these newer movements are really representative of older traditions in Asia, but largely unknown in the West. Among these Asian religious movements is the Shin Buddhist sect. While it has been in the West perhaps longer than any other Buddhist community and constitutes the faith of the largest segment of Japanese immigrants and their descendants, it is among the least known of the religions generally accounted as new religions. This essay is an attempt to make clear the reasons for this anomaly and to assess the importance of the teaching.

Setting the Foundation

Shin Buddhism originated in thirteenth century Japan with the teaching of Shinran (1173–1263). It is noted for its emphasis on salvation by faith alone which is often compared with the Protestant Christian teaching of Martin Luther (1483–1546). Francis Xavier, the famous Catholic missionary to Japan, is said to have exclaimed on hearing of this teaching that 'the accursed Lutheran heresy had reached Japan.'

While Shin Buddhism remained an obscure sect of Japanese Buddhism for several centuries after its inception, the movement gained prominence through the efforts of Rennyo (1415–1499), the 8th Abbot. From that time forward Shin Buddhism (short for *Jodo Shinshu* or True Teaching of the Pure Land[1]) became the largest and most powerful Buddhist sect in Japan and has remained a major expression of Buddhism in Japan and in the West. It spread to the West in the latter part of the 19th Century with the migration of Japanese laborers to Hawaii and the North American mainland, as well as to South America, particularly Brazil.

The teaching is based on early Mahāyāna Buddhist Sutras which recount the myth of the Vows of Bodhisattva *Dharmākara* who aspired to save all beings by bringing them to the Pure Land, Nirvana or Buddhist Enlightenment through the merit of his sincere and pure discipline over many aeons of time. This story is related in the *Larger Pure Land Sutra*. (Inagaki 1994.) A popular movement developed in China from the 5th century through the work of the monk T'an-luan (476–542). The complex and arduous monastic practices of meditation in Buddhism were replaced by the recitation of the name of Amida Buddha (*nembutsu*). This practice was regarded as the chief means for rebirth into the Pure Land at death for ordinary lay people who could not leave society. The practice was based on the interpretation of Amida Buddha's 18th Vow.

The teaching arrived in Japan in the 6th century but flowered in a time of the upheaval and turmoil of the Kamakura Period (1185–1332), particularly during the 12th and 13th centuries, inspired by the work of Hōnen (1133–1212). Shinran was a disciple of Hōnen. In polemical dispute with other interpreters of Pure Land teaching, Shinran claimed that he only followed the teaching of his master Hōnen (1143–1212). While not regarding himself as the founder of a new movement, Shinran laid the doctrinal foundations of the teaching of Shin Buddhism, drawing on earlier Chinese and Japanese Pure Land sources, which he adroitly reinterpreted in conformity with his own religious experience.

Shinran formulated the theory of faith that became the hallmark of the Shin tradition. (Bloom, 1965) In comparison to the earlier teaching of recitation of the name for merit and purification, he taught that the *nembutsu* resulted from the Amida's gift of faith and expressed gratitude for the salvation which was assured. As a consequence, no special practices or meritorious good deeds are required for birth into the Pure Land. After trust in Amida's Primal Vow has arisen, all religious activities are viewed as expressions of gratitude and self-righteousness is negated. Further, awareness of the obligation one owes to the compassion of the Buddha is the foundation of ethic and morality. Confidence in Amida's universal compassion, liberated the faithful from all forms of all spiritual fear and magic.

Through the efforts of the 8th Abbot Rennyo (1415–1499) Shin Buddhism became the largest and most powerful Buddhist sect in Japan, a position it has held to the present time. (Rogers, 1991 and Dobbins, 1989) With deep roots in peasant society, as a result of Rennyo's efforts, Shin was particularly suited to the needs of a rural community in that it offered ordinary lay people a simple way to spiritual deliverance and affirmed ordinary, worldly life.

When the leaders of Hawaiian government in the 19th century sought for workers on the sugar plantations, they were impressed by the industriousness of Japanese labourers who were facing economic crisis. As a result of negotiations between the respective governments in 1885, contract laborers were recruited, primarily from the western regions of Japan where the Shin Buddhist denomination was very strong. Consequently, Shin Buddhism spearheaded the development of Buddhism in Hawaii and on the U.S. mainland, providing the strongest social base for Buddhism as it moved eastward over the Pacific ocean.

Japanese workers migrated to Hawaii and North America, bringing with them their Buddhist traditions, while other forms of Buddhism were beginning to permeate the more cultured classes in the West during the 19th century in a fragmentary and uninstitutionalized way.[2] Although various Buddhist sects later took root in Hawaii, the United States and Canada, by far the largest and best organized were the Honganji branches of Shin Buddhism.

However, because of the social situation of the Japanese immigrants as a segregated minority on the plantations, it was necessary for the immigrants to hold on to the customs, faith, and loyalties which they brought with them. Buddhist temples became social centers and the teaching a source of consolation for those experiencing the rigors of life on the plantations, on farms or in cities. In the face of the dominant Christian society, Buddhist temples in Hawaii and elsewhere developed educational and cultural programs. They also attempted to adapt their services to meet the needs of the new environment, manifesting the flexibility that had characterized the spread of Buddhism through Asia. However, with the annexation of Hawaii as a territory of the United States, Buddhists were often considered un-American for their efforts to maintain their revered traditions and language. The Japanese had to preserve an awareness of, and respect for, their ancestral cultures, since they were not permitted to become American citizens. However, they encouraged their children born in the United States to be good citizens.[3]

In the 1920s and 1930s, activities designed to meet the needs of the English speaking *Nisei* (second generation) members of the temples were initiated and expanded such as Sunday schools and Young Men's Buddhist Associations. These activities encouraged inter-community networking by the young people of the respective Japanese communities. Also in this period there was increasing awareness of the need for English speaking ministers.

The educational and social activities that might have led to broader integration into American society were obstructed by the onset of World War II. During this time all persons of Japanese ancestry (including United States citizens) and their ministers living on the West Coast were removed from their homes by the U.S. Government and interned in camps called 'relocation centers.' The community in Hawaii, though regarded with suspicion, was not generally uprooted, though temples were closed and clergy removed. Because of social isolation and developing ethnocentrism arising from these conditions, Shin Buddhism, as well as the other Japanese Buddhist traditions, has remained virtually unknown to the public at large, even to the present time. Nevertheless, the foundation for future development had been laid.

In recent decades, Zen, Tibetan or Theravadin traditions have been most popular and prominent in the West among youth through the efforts of individual teachers. They catch the attention of people seeking peace of mind in a turbulent world or a new approach to their fragmented lives through the practice of meditation. People of Japanese background would probably know the name *Shinshū* or Shin Buddhism, if not the teachings, because it has been so conspicuous in Japan and in the western Japanese community. However, it may appear to other western peoples to be one of the new religions that have appeared in recent decades as an alternative to traditional western religion.

In 1989 the Hawaii branch of Shin Buddhism celebrated its centennial, and the Buddhist Churches of America, the mainland U.S.A. branch of the Honganji in Japan, will mark its centennial in 1999. Despite its long, organized existence in the West, Shin Buddhism has been encountering problems of decreasing memberships, shrinking ministry, ambivalence to opening the faith to the wider community, and in interpreting the teaching in a way that is meaningful to modern, well-educated temple members, as well as inquirers from outside. Many problems arise from its history and the intertwining of Buddhism and Japanese culture. It may be said that Shin Buddhism is a victim of its own history and for the success of the ways it adapted to western society.

Particularity and Universality

A major factor in maintaining the social coherence and integrity of the immigrant community as been the cultivation of basic Japanese values in response to the new environment, contributing to the ethnocentrism which became characteristic of the Japanese Buddhist temples. In the immigrant situation, the family system and its coordinate respect for authority supported the cohesiveness of the family and the ethnic community as a whole, stressing social responsibility and obedience to the law. During World War II Ruth Benedict wrote her study, *Chrysanthemum and the Sword* based largely on studies of Japanese-Americans. (Benedict 1967) She investigated the basic ethical orientation of the first generation (*Issei*) immigrants who had come to America out of the background of the Tokugawa (1600–1868) and Meiji (1868–1911) periods. The concepts of *on* or *gir i* – obligation or duty – which had been central to Japanese society operated among the Japanese-Americans as the ethical foundation for human relations. The *on-giri* relationship is essentially conservative and can be stultifying for the individual, especially in the context of a status society and within a close family situation. The psycho-social functioning of these principles is that individuals tends to be more conscious of their external relations than their own inner promptings. There is, consequently, a disposition to be conformist, unquestioning, and prudent. The good is always determined by others to whom one has obligation. This tendency has given rise to the terms 'quiet Americans' or 'model minority' which, though seemingly positive, have negative implications and undermine Japanese-American critique of American society.

In addition to ethical values, there are other cultural attitudes which have been transferred from Japan. These are *shikata-ga-nai* which means to accept things over which you have no control; *mottainai* which generally suggests modesty, conveying a sense of unworthiness; *gaman* which means to endure and persevere in the face of difficulty; *enryō* which is a non-assertive restraint or reserve; and finally *okage-sama-de* or *arigatai* which express gratitude and appreciation to all those unseen factors supporting our lives. These cultural attitudes have contributed to the seemingly closed character of the Japanese-American Buddhist community. They have also conduced to more introspective and less aggressive personality formation, but also a flexibility in adapting to the changing conditions of society, while lessening tension with traditional values.

In the midst of its many vicissitudes experienced in the process of transplanting its spiritual and cultural heritage to the new American environment, Shin Buddhism has struggled seriously to discover its role in changing, modern society. When the immigrant Japanese were excluded from, and demeaned by the dominant society, its ethnic character and the values and attitudes transmitted from Japan were very important and effective in providing a rallying point for a community under siege.

The Japanese community, like most ethnic groups, attained a measure of solidarity through ethnocentrism, highlighting their own cultural attitudes and mores. Consequently, the transmission of such attitudes particularly through family relationships thwarts the universalism of Buddhism. Despite the popularity and seeming interest in, and attraction to, Buddhism by non-Japanese, Buddhist temples established by the immigrants have few members of other races. In such circumstances racial homogeneity, reinforced by language and culture, has made it difficult for outsiders to enter the heart of the Buddhist tradition. This situation persists because many Buddhist ministers are recruited from Japan or are second or third generation Japanese Americans who have spent many years of training in Japan and are deeply imbued with Japanese cultural attitudes. A fair number have problems speaking English and are often ill at ease outside the Japanese community.

The problem of outreach is further complicated by the personality characteristics of its ministers and leadership. A study of the psychological types among temple ministers reveals that Buddhists tend to be introverted and more introspective, while Protestant and Catholic ministers are generally more extroverted. (Imamura 1986, pp. 77–79, 102–103) Shin Buddhism and Japanese culture stress the values of harmony, interrelatedness, quiet reflection, patience, appreciation and humility. Differences in personality formation among leaders influence the stance of the group vis a vis the dominant society and any effort to reach out.

As all the branches of Shin Buddhism in the West approach their respective centennial celebrations, they face the enormous challenge of transcending its ethnic character to become more universal as a Buddhist tradition and thereby fulfill the meaning and potentiality of Shinran's teaching in the context of a highly competitive and aggressive religious environment.

There have been efforts, particularly among younger members, to distinguish the specifically Buddhist element in Shin teaching and temple life and what is a carry over from Japanese culture. As illustration, we may note that Buddhism is egalitarian, while Japanese culture is hierarchical. Hierarchy is not essential to Buddhism. A problem remains that while the teaching is universal, the organizations function to a significant degree according to Japanese cultural assumptions. In view of contemporary discussion about the differences between white Buddhists and ethnic, Asian Buddhists, it should be noted that, at least in the case of Shin Buddhists, the members have been Americans for several generations and educated totally in the American system. For all intents and purposes they are westerners who happen to be Japanese. Many seek the same goals as their white counterparts. There needs to be change within the temples to meet the spiritual and intellectual needs of these individuals, whether or not it seeks to reach out beyond the ethnic community.

Shin, like other ethnic religions in our diverse and pluralistic society, has to look beyond limited ethnic boundaries for adherents. The appeal to be Shin Buddhist simply because one is Japanese or out of some family loyalty has proven inadequate to stem the loss of adherents or to maintain the vitality of the community.

Shin Buddhism, as a facet of Mahāyāna Buddhism, has a clear mandate in the ideal of the Bodhisattva and in Shinran's teaching to reach out to all people. The translation of Shin texts and the increase in resources for study in recent years has reinforced this obligation, because Shinran clearly expressed a universal ideal.

Even though western society is multi-ethnic with various cultural heritages which should be respected and preserved, religious faith is not merely a cultural artifact. It goes beyond specificities of culture to deal with universal human issues. It is generally recognized that spiritual or religious truth must embrace all people. It cannot be limited simply to one ethnic group, if there is to be a robust and relevant spiritual community.

Consequently, in contemporary America, Shin Buddhism must develop its own well-defined form as a part of western culture, as Buddhism began to develop its own distinct character in Japan in the sixth century. Though twentieth century Shin Buddhism in America is indebted to Japanese sources and inspiration, it should not be entirely controlled from that source. Rather, the inspiration from the past must become the wellspring of change and renewal.

Moreover, younger Shin members, who have higher education and greater mobility in the society compared to earlier years, desire to participate in working toward the solutions to contemporary problems through their faith. Shin Buddhists are constantly asked the Shin view about women, race, ecological issues or political questions, etc. As the teachings have become more easily accessible to all people, more questions are being raised concerning the deeper meaning of Shin in society. The response requires thinking on a more universal plane.

Crisis in the Community

As we have earlier pointed out, the background of discrimination, war, incarceration and cultural transition have given rise to numerous problems and tensions within the Shin Buddhist community. However, in the absence of solutions, there continues to be an attrition of members and ministers which is reaching crisis proportion. We will review various issues that are significant for the future development of the movement in the west. We should note, however, that many aspects of the current crisis are influenced by problems and conditions affecting other religions in western societies. The relative small size of the Shin Buddhist organizations, perhaps, intensifies the significance of the crisis in comparison with the larger and more traditional Christian bodies which are also in a decline.

The figures we cite here indicate the depth of the current crisis in the Shin community particularly on the U.S. mainland.[4] It is evident in the obvious decline in general memberships and number of ministers. According to one study, the Buddhist Churches of America reached its peak in 1930 with 123 ministers. By 1981 there were 71. In 1977 the general membership stood at 21,600 families (approximately 65,000 persons). However, as of 1996, memberships have dropped officially to 16,902 (about 50,706 persons). (Buddhist Churches of America Annual Report 1996, pp. 27–29) Despite the vagaries of statistics, clearly gradual attrition has been going on for many years. It is also well known that in recent years 'outmarriage' (i.e. marriages with other ethnic individuals) of Japanese-American youth is more than 50 per cent. Yet, few of the children of mixed marriages or their parents are active in the temples.

Dharma schools are usually viewed as the seed-bed for the future development of the temples. Hence, temples educational programs focus on the children with little attention paid to adult education. The peak of Dharma school enrollment in 1940 for which there are records was 7,500 students. In 1972, the number had declined to 6,209. (Kashima 1977. p. 157) However, by 1983–1984 the total was approximately 2,550 students. Since that time the number has risen to 3,045 in 1992–1993. Though the numbers have risen and fallen over the years, from 1990 there has been significant increase which may be due to better organization and efforts of Dharma school parents and the encouragement of the ministers. With the improvement of teaching materials, methods and personnel, the downward trend may be reversed, and the Dharma schools can once again assure the future of the temples.

In addition to the attrition of members, there is also decrease in the number of ministers. The number of replacements has not kept pace with the number who have retired or left the ministry. It should be noted that in the early years of Shin presence in America the ministers were enlisted in Japan. Because of the large numbers of first generation Japanese in the community, this arrangement was optimal. However, Japanese priests who make the trip now have great difficulty culturally and linguistically in relating to the younger generations. In addition to problems of adapting to another culture, life for the priest is better in Japan than it is in the U.S. Priests in Japan are more or less in control of their temples, whereas in America priests are considered as employees of the congregation and they may receive lower wages and benefits than their Japanese counterparts.

Another aspect of the crisis is the difficulty in recruiting ministers among Japanese-American youth. It is evident that Japanese-American youth, observing the emphasis on death in the tradition, are not greatly challenged to become ministers, when there are many other options in society to fulfill themselves. In line with the general character of Buddhism in Japan a major function of Shin temples is holding funerals and memorializing the dead. Shin, with its belief in rebirth in the Pure Land after death, is generally regarded as an otherworldly religion and, like other Buddhist sects, dubbed as 'Funeral Buddhism'. This has not changed greatly in its transfer to the West and in a measure has contributed to the lack of appeal for youth.

Youth are also aware of the difficult working conditions and low remuneration of the ministers. Many temple members do not want their children to become ministers, preferring that they enter more lucrative professions.

There are non-Japanese individuals, however, who have entered the ministry at various times through its history. They have generally encountered Buddhism in its various forms through exposure to Asian spiritual and religious traditions in their own quest for meaning. They may have studied Buddhism in its more ideal forms or may have practiced other forms of discipline. They may even have participated in martial arts training. For deeply personal reasons, they turn to Shin Buddhism as the way to cultivate Buddhist experience and values. Shin welcomes those who make such a commitment and are willing to undergo the requisite training.

While progress has been made in the area of ministerial education, the life of the temples remains generally what it has been for decades. It is apparent that the focus of the temple is the traditional nuclear family, providing few specialized programs or activities for new styles of family life such as single-parent families, blended families, divorcees, singles or gender orientation.

Further, although a school, the Institute of Buddhist Studies, has been created to train English speaking ministers, trainees still go to Japan for a number of years to imbibe the traditional teaching and learn Japanese. Since the teaching given in Japan is shaped by issues of Japanese history and culture, the ministers who return may have difficulty translating the teaching culturally to interested inquirers. There is little discussion of Buddhism in relation to contemporary issues in sermons. Where doctrinal themes may be addressed, it is seldom that the further philosophical implications and meanings are explored. Lay members generally desire rather simple presentations. It should also be noted that there is a great emphasis on ceremony and ritual which results from Japanese cultural heritage. Much of the ritual is performed in Sino-Japanese language and understood by few members. Hence the ideals embodied in the text are not communicated. The future development of Shin Buddhism will require a more balanced approach, highlighting education and understanding of the teaching.

While external, historical circumstances are partially responsible for the attrition in Shin, it is also due to a lack of dynamic leadership within the tradition. An important element contributing to this problem is the high degree of professionalism of Japanese-Americans which encourages young people to become doctors, lawyers, dentists, scientists, engineers and business people. It has been pointed out that only 6 per cent of Japanese-American students in PhD graduate study take up the humanities which involve traditional academic disciplines that might lead to consideration of ministry.[5] The increased social and economic mobility of Japanese-Americans in the post-war period is also a factor in this trend.

As a consequence, Shin lacks a vibrant, intellectual core of members, despite the high degree of professionalization of its members. Few members have training and background in religious and philosophical studies to explore these issues critically and move the community in a more positive direction.

The broader dispersion of Japanese-Americans through American society after the war, higher education and greater professional mobility have supported the acculturation of the younger generations and loss of contact with the temples. However, at the same time, there has been a growing interest in Japanese heritage among many youth which is encouraged by emphasis on diversity and pluralism in the larger society, as well as by the persistence of racism in America. Nevertheless, these factors have not been sufficient to alter the trend of attrition within the temples.

Within the temples, some younger Japanese-American ministers also have become aware of the richness of their ethnic and religious heritage, as a result of study in Japan. In addition, through their educational experience they have become very articulate in dealing with issues facing the community. As a consequence of their religious and educational experience of the traditional religion, they sometimes appear to reinforce the conservative tendencies of the community which wishes to return to former times when temple life seemed more vital and cohesive. Hence, there is ambivalence toward developing practical programs for outreach.

There is a tension within the group between the efforts to appeal to all people and the responsibility not to abandon the cultural heritage of their parents, particularly the first generation immigrants who sacrificed so much to establish the teaching in America. The problem of seeking non-Japanese members lies in the latent anxiety of losing control over the institutions developed by the Issei forbears. Despite much discussion concerning outreach, there is no national policy, personnel or financial provision to carry out a continuous organized program of outreach.

Another major area of concern is the problem of religious education. There have been several attempts to upgrade and improve the educational resources in the temple over the years. However, Dharma school teachers are usually all volunteers, and there are few programs which offer systematic training for teachers. They tend to rely on the knowledge they received when they attended Dharma school. They are, however, to be commended for the efforts they make.

The young student is introduced to basic Buddhist teaching such as the four noble truths, the eightfold path and many stories about Sakyamuni and models of Buddhist piety, as well as ritual. The appeal is more to the affective aspect that conveys the feeling of being Buddhist. However, youth frequently leave the temple at adolescence or when they go to college. Their exposure to the basic principles of Shin Buddhism is very limited, leaving them with many questions. They may not return to the temple until middle age when they have their own families, if they return at all. When they return in later life, there are very few classes designed for adults which take up contemporary problems of religion and modern life. Sermons and occasional lecture programs are the main source for information.

The availability of literature on Shin Buddhism in English has increased greatly, but members are not noted for reading such materials. Consequently, the lay people, who should be taking the lead in sharing the teaching with others, have themselves only a hazy understanding of the relation of early Buddhism to Shin Buddhism or its content itself.

When we look at the problem of education, we can also observe that Shin Buddhism has an element of anti-intellectualism which derives in some degree from Japanese religious tradition generally, and because the founder and the successors emphasized that one should not try to rationalize the mystery of faith or exhibit the faith openly to flaunt one's spiritual superiority. Related to this issue is the stress laid on models of Shin piety called *myōkōnin*, wondrously good people, who are constantly held up for admiration in sermons and lectures. (Suzuki 1957) The stories about them reinforce the affective appeal of Shin Buddhism and tend to devalue intellectual issues.

These factors feed into an important theory which distinguishes philosophically between absolute and conventional truth which generally designates the two spheres of Buddha Dharma (Buddhist truth) and the Royal or Imperial Dharma, or the religious realm and the secular. The religious realm stresses the way to be born into the Pure Land through faith in one's mind or heart, while the secular realm requires the person, as a member of society, to obey superiors and maintain order. This perspective has unconsciously shaped the basic social understanding of the teaching among the members. An implication of the theory has been to disconnect spiritual concerns from the social arena, making it difficult for the temples and the leadership to take up social issues as a matter of religious concern and commitment. With decline in lively belief in the afterlife, the relevance of the religion is at stake.

Because of the many varied conditions, Shin Buddhism remains relatively isolated in American society where even after 100 years it appears to be a foreign religion. Recently, Mrs. Kimi Yonemura Hisatsune, a leading lay woman and writer, has written: 'Yet, our temples operate as if Jodo Shinshu is basically a Japanese religion, and some followers of Shinran Shonin even believe that it is vitally important or necessary to maintain or transmit the Japanese character of the Shin tradition.' (Hisatsune. 1993, 20/2 p. 4)

Charles Prebish in his volume American Buddhism notes this ambivalence of members in opening up to the wider community, commenting: 'As the issei (first generation) members of the congregation die, Buddhist Churches of America cannot seem to decide whether to follow the general wishes of the nisei members (second generation) and Americanize more fully, or honor the wishes of the clergy (and many young members) and reassert their Japanese heritage.' (Prebish 1979, p. 67) He also asserts: 'Consequently, the national organization finds itself in the curious predicament of having been present on American soil longer than any other Buddhist group and having acculturated the least.' (Prebish 1979, p. 68) He might also have noted that it not only has the longest history in America, but is the best organized, and endowed with human and financial resources. Yet it has not been able easily to make the transition.

The issue is not one merely of statistics and sociology or history. We have recounted the problems within the community that limit the impact of the teaching. However, the appeal of Shin Buddhism has been limited also by the perceptions of outside observers. Some scholars have questioned its authenticity as Buddhism. The eminent writer, the late Christmas

Humphreys was highly critical when he declared that Shin Buddhism 'is a form of Buddhism which on the face of it discards three-quarters of Buddhism. Compared with the Teaching of the Pali Canon it is but Buddhism and water...' (Humphreys, 1962, p. 164; also p. 165).

Paul Williams in his analysis of Shin teaching acknowledges the features of Mahāyāna Buddhism that shape Shin Buddhist teaching and its effectiveness and influence in the lives of followers. However, he describes it as *de facto* Buddhism, though it is rooted in the history and development of Mahāyāna tradition. The tenor of his detailed discussion leaves the subtle impression that its status remains unclear. The ambiguity of its status as Buddhism would naturally reduce interest in it by seekers. (William 1989, p. 275)[6]

It is true that Shin Buddhism rejects the disciplines such as meditation and precepts which had been, and still are for many, the core of traditional Buddhist practice as the way to enlightenment. It views those practices as compassionate means given by the Buddha to lead them to deeper insight into the depth of ego-centrism and its attachments. Humphreys overlooks the understanding of human nature underlying Shin and simply focusses on the issue of difficult and easy which has been used in the tradition to distinguish Pure Land teaching from other schools. Shinran went further than this distinction in probing human experience, as a result of his own religious experience in the monastery on Mount Hiei for twenty years. While the view may not be without its problems, it is an outgrowth of the logic of Mahāyāna Buddhist historical development and is, therefore, a serious interpretation of Mahāyāna Buddhism.

Further, the stress on the evil, defiled character of human life appears throughout Shinran's writings and in his confessions. This feature of Shin appears negative and would hardly appeal to westerners who have already given up beliefs in original sin, a term Humphreys uses to describe the basis of Shin teaching. However, what seems negative at first glance, may be a more realistic recognition of the passion-ridden character of human existence. This understanding led Shinran to a positive insight that if salvation were possible, it must derive from the side of the Buddha, not from his own finite, unstable mind and actions. Shinran gained insight into the complexity of motivation and sincerity, as well as the impossibility of building a bridge to infinity through finite acts, no matter how demanding in difficulty or quantity. According to Shinran, absolute Other-Power is the essence of life as it is rooted in the process of interdependence and symbolized in the structure of the Primal Vows of Amida Buddha. In any case, he may begin with a negative insight, but it opens the way to a positive approach to life and hope.

Another feature that distracts seekers is the apparent otherworldly character of Shin Buddhism. Occasionally Shinran employed the symbolism of the Pure Land to console grieving disciples with the hope of reunion in the Pure Land. Such statements imply a more concrete, literal or personal understanding of the Pure Land.

However, in his major scholarly text *Kyōgyōshinshō* Shinran describes birth into the Pure Land as the birth of non-birth or nirvana and beyond conceivability. He also connects it to the ideal of the Bodhisattva who returns to this world to save all beings, as well as immediate attainment of Buddhahood which has the same fundamental intention. We should note that there is no necessary contradiction between the literal, personalistic expressions and the more abstract, philosophical concepts. It is a question of the contexts in which the idea is being asserted. It is common that religious expressions are adjusted to the need of the listener. However, the strong otherworldly cast of traditional Shin Buddhism is the result of the popularization of the teaching and its institutionalization within feudalistic society. Similar developments may be seen in other traditions.

Finally, the apparent similarity of Shin Buddhism to Christianity also deflects interest for those who want something clearly different from what they had in western religion. However, the similarities between religions indicates their universality in dealing with common human problems and aspirations. Similarities are not to be completely discounted, even though differences among faiths are more decisive in evaluating their meaning.

Conclusion

In this presentation we have tried to offer a perspective on why Shin Buddhism, despite its prominence in Japan and its history in America, remains a relatively unknown and misunderstood Buddhist teaching. Part of the reason is due to historical conditions which Shin Buddhists have encountered; part is due to the reluctance of Shin Buddhists themselves to address the larger society; another part is the result of somewhat biased presentations in popular texts on Buddhism.

A ray of hope for better understanding is emerging from recent studies of Shin Buddhism. On the one had there is Galen Amstutz' detailed analysis of why Shin Buddhism has been underestimated in the studies by Japanese and western scholars in his recent work: *Interpreting Amida*. (Amstutz 1997) His study will provide a good corrective to future simplistic presentations of Shin Buddhism. Further, the study of Shinran's teaching by the Korean Christian theologian, Hee-sung Keel, *Understanding Shinran: A Dialogical Approach*, will encourage participnts in Buddhist-Christian dialogue studies to grapple more seriously with the dharmalogical principles and issues presented by Shinran. (Keel. 1997) Despite his criticisms of Shinran's teaching, he reveals implicitly the intellectual and spiritual viability of his teaching. Further, comparative studies are helping to clarify similarities and differences between Christianity and Shin Buddhism. As this process continues, it will eventually challenge and stimulate Shin teachers to interact more seriously with western culture and through this effort to discover the meaning and mission of Shin Buddhism within modern society.

The future of Shin ethnic organizations do not appear bright. Nevertheless, as Shin thought and insight engages the world of religious scholarship and discussion, its contribution to human spirituality will become clearer and may provide a new stimulus for the revitalization of Shin institutions.

Notes

1 The Jodo Shinshu sect is structurally divided into ten branches-the *Hompa* (Main branch) *Honganji, Otani-ha Honganji, Takada-ha, Kibe-ha, Bukkōji-ha Kōshō-ha* and the four branches in Echizen (*Sammonto-ha, Yamamoto-ha, Jōshōji-ha,* and *Izumoji-ha.*) The Mother Temples (*Honzan*) of the *Honganji* Branches are located adjacent to each other in Kyoto, Japan and are commonly called *Nishi* (West) *Honganji* (with respect to the Hompa Honganji) and *Higashi* (East) *Honganji* (with respect to the Otani Hinganji).

2 Buddhism initially became known to the intellectual and literary world in the United States through the writings of Ralph Waldo Emerson, Henry David Thoreau and Walt Whitman during the nineteenth century. The Theosophical Society founded by Madame H. P. Blavatsky and her associate Colonel Henry Steel Olcott further introduced Buddhism to Americans. In 1879 the first major treatment of Gautama's Buddha's life appeared in the very popular book The Light of Asia by Edwin Arnold. In 1893 as result of the World Parliament of Religions held in Chicago, Paul Carus, publisher of the journal Open Court, became deeply interested in Buddhism as a basis for resolving the conflict between science and religion. In editing the journal, Carus enlisted the aid of the youthful D.T. Suzuki who later became the foremost propagator of Zen Buddhism in the West.

3 Buddhism was often confused with Shinto, the Japanese native religion, by outsiders, and it incurred the resentment of Christians who found Buddhists resistant to conversion. Because of the confusion with Shinto, which was employed by the Japanese government as a cult of patriotism, there were suspicions as to the loyalty of Buddhists. Both traditions were viewed as foreign religions in America. This feeling escalated as World War II began, and temples were shut down and ministers arrested. Christian evangelists frequently stressed that Buddhism and Americanism were contradictory.

4 Membership statistics are very difficult to ascertain and interpret. The numbers given in the annual report indicate decline. However, there are a variety of reasons that the numbers have been pared down, such as removing the elderly from the count because they may not be able to pay the dues; or removing non-participants, and only retaining those who contribute. Since the assessment to the denomination is based on the number of members, such pruning of the rolls reduces the amount the temple owes.

Nevertheless, the decline in the number of ministers certainly reflects a real decrease in the number of members whom they would serve.

5 From a 1986 lecture by Prof. Yuji Ichioka. UCLA

6 It is to be noted that he does not address the question: 'But is it Buddhism' to such teachers as Nichiren who expressed very distinctive views concerning Buddhism and his position in it. It raises the question in the mind of the reader why is this question directed specifically to Shin Buddhism?

References

Amstutz, G. (1997) *Interpreting Amida: History and Orientalism in the Study of Pure Land Buddhism.*, Albany: State University of New York Press.

Benedict, R. (1967) *Chrysanthemum and the Sword,* Cleveland: Meridian Books

Bloom, A. (1965) *Shinran's Gospel of Pure Grace,* Tucson: University of Arizona Press.

Buddhist Churches of America *Buddhist Churches of America: 75 Year History 1899 to 1974. Vol 2.*

Buddhist Churches of America 1996 *Annual Report.*

Daniels, R. (1988), *Asian America: Chinese and Japanese in the United States Since 1950,* Seattle: University of Washington Press

Dobbins, J.C. (1989) *Jodo Shinshu: Shin Buddhism in Medieval Japan,* Bloomington: Indian University Press

Doi, J. Keynote speech reprinted in Institute of Buddhist Studies Newsletter, #49, April–June 1993.

Hisatsune, K. (1993) in *Wheel of Dharma,* February 1993, 20/2 p. 4.

Honda, Patti, ed., (1993), Higashi Honganji: 90th Year Anniversary booklet,

Humphreys, C. (1962) *Buddhism.* London: Penguin Books.

Hunter, L. (1971) *Buddhism in Hawaii: Its Impact on a Yankee Community.*, Honolulu: Hawaii University Press.

Imamura, Ryo Michael, (1986), *A Comparative Study of Temple and Non-temple Buddhist Ministers of the Jodo Shin Sect Using Jungian Psychological Types.* Ph.D. Dissertation, University of San Francisco.

Inagaki, H. (1994), *The Three Pure Land Sutras.* Kyoto: Nagata Bunshodo.

Kashima, T. (1977) *Buddhism in America: the Social Organization of an Ethnic Religious Institution.* Westport, Conn.: Greenwood Press.

Keel, Hee Sung. (1997) *Understanding Shinran: A Dialogical Approach.*, Fremont Ca.: Asian Humanities Press.

Prebish, C. (1979), *American Buddhism,* North Scituate, Massachussetts: Duxbury Press.

Rogers, Minor Lee and Ann T. (1991), *Rennyo: The Second Founder of Shin Buddhism.* Berkeley: Asian Humanities Press, pp. 434

Suzuki, D.T. (1957) *Mysticism: Christian and Buddhist.*, New York: Harper and Bros., pp. 214.

Tabrah, R. (1989), *A Grateful Past, A Promising Future,* Honolulu: Honpa Honganji Mission of Hawaii.

Tuck, D. (1987) *Buddhist Churches of America: Jodo Shinshu.*, Lewiston, N.Y., Queenston, Ontario, Canada: The Edwin Mellen Press.

Williams, P. (1989) *Mahāyāna Buddhism: The Doctrinal Foundations.*, London, New York: Routledge, 1989.

Wilson, R.A. and Bill Hosokawa. (1980) *East to America.*, New York: William Morrow.

CHAPTER TEN

'Success' and 'Failure': Japanese New Religions Abroad

Peter B. Clarke

The progress of Japanese new religions abroad has varied greatly from religion to religion and for the same religion in different contexts. Their presence abroad was due initially in most cases to immigration, and I will briefly describe that process before addressing the question of their actual development outside Japan before attempting to offer reasons for their successful expansion overseas on the one hand and their failure to take off on the other. In the conclusion I will comment on Stark's general theory of the success and failure of religions in the light of my own findings which cover research on the growth of Japanese new religions in the United States, Europe, Brazil and Japan, and on other religions elsewhere.

Immigration and the Early Expansion of Japanese New Religions Overseas

Japanese new religions are present today in over 80 countries in the world, and are most numerous in: North America, particularly the United States, where they are to be found mostly on the West Coast and Hawaii; Brazil, where over thirty have settled, mostly in the south of the country; Korea and Taiwan; Thailand; and western Europe.

In modern times large scale Japanese immigration began with the Meiji Restoration in 1868. No more than a trickle until 1885, it gathered momentum from then onwards and by 1963 a total of around one million Japanese had immigrated (Suzuki, 1969, Vol. 2: 14). The largest number of immigrants were eventually to settle in Manchuria, followed by Brazil, Hawaii, the United States mainland, southeast Asia, Australasia, Canada, Peru, Mexico and Columbia. The search for a livelihood was the principal motivation for immigration to the Americas, but not the only one in other instances such as Manchuria where demographic, political and strategic factors became important.

Initially, and until 1924, the year in which the Oriental Exclusion Act was passed by the United States Congress, a majority of immigrants went to Hawaii. The peak years of this first stage were between 1899–1910, and, overall, an estimated 231, 000 had entered Hawaii by 1924. 107,000 Japanese immigrants had also settled on the United States mainland by the same year, some of them from Hawaii, and 3,000 had arrived in Canada (Suzuki, 1969: 14). Peru, which had been host to over 30,000 by 1924 also closed the door on further immigration from Japan in that year. From 1908 Brazil, whose coffee industry as it expanded and contracted, would spasmodically require large amounts of labour between 1904–1931, began to attract increasing numbers of immigrants from Japan.

The flow of immigrants to Brazil reached its highest levels between 1924–34 when the total number of arrivals from Japan alone was over 135,000, compared with 35,000 between 1908–1923. This outward immigration to Brazil from Japan continued until the early years of World War II. By 1941 an estimated 234,000 Japanese immigrants were resident in Brazil (Suzuki, 1969: 14). Today there are approximately one million three hundred thousand citizens of Japanese origin and/or descent in Brazil, the majority of whom are settled in Sao Paulo, and elsewhere in the South of Brazil including Rio de Janeiro and Parana, with only a few isolated communities in the North of the country such as Tome D'Acu in the state of Para and Sao Joao de Mata in the state of Bahia.

Japanese immigration turned to Manchuria in 1920s and 1930s, and particularly after 1932 when the region came under Japanese control, reaching a peak of 51,000 in 1940 (Suzuki, 1969: 16). As is well known, Japanese also settled in Korea and Taiwan, as did several new religions including Tenrikyo and Omotokyo. The former is at present the largest Japanese new religion in South Korea with 78 churches and 69 mission stations. However, it appears to be growing faster in Taiwan where 1,385 took the Besseki pledge[1] in 1996 than in South Korea where the number was 871.[2]

Eventually both old and new Japanese religions were to follow these immigrants everywhere they settled to provide for their spiritual and moral well-being, although they were not always greatly sought after. If the concerns, preoccupations and lifestyles of the immigrants as described by the historians of Japanese immigration to Brazil, including Saito (1961), Handa (1980) and Yoshioka (1995), all immigrants themselves, can be used as a rough guide to the norm, then the Japanese in Brazil expressed little interest in religious matters, leaving these in the hands of the family back home. Almost all were committed to returning home and believed that if they were unlucky enough to die abroad before this could be arranged then their soul would find its own way back to Japan (Maeyama, 1983). Pre-World War II Japanese immigrants in Brazil spoke of death there as 'death in a foreign land (morte aldeia)' or as the 'death of a visitor, or 'morte do visitante' (Maeyama 1983). The fact that the departing soul was leaving kin behind in Brazil did not pose a problem for it was believed to be simply going on ahead to the common ancestral homeland.

Furthermore, there was no religious education as such, the emphasis being placed by the Japanese school on the Imperial Rescript on Education proclaimed in 1890, and on filial piety to the Emperor which it was designed to cultivate. A picture of the Emperor occupied the centre wall of the school entrance and all communal meeting places, and the school assemblies focused attention on him and on the imperial ancestors. As to religious ceremonies and rituals little was known. It was difficult to find anyone knowledgeable enough in the sutras to recite those appropriate to burial ceremonies. Those who were authorised to perform this rite were know as 'bonzos feitos na hora' (monks made on the spot, or substitute monks). Moreover, the ancestral tablets were rarely if ever cared for and were usually stacked up in the corner of the bedroom of the head of the household where they simply gathered dust.

Ethnic Religions

Old and new Japanese religions abroad were, until the 1960s, essentially ethnic religions. In the case of Brazil, the Japanese experienced little contact with the rest of society except by means of the Catholic church which made baptism a condition of entering its much sought after schools. Some of the Japanese who 'converted' were later to go half way to re-conversion by joining a Japanese new religion.

One informant, a second generation immigrant, from that still very Japanese town of Suzano east of the city of Sao Paulo told this writer that he always felt himself to be a Buddhist and knew he would remain a Buddhist despite the pressure from Catholicism at school.[3] Such people have found in the Japanese new religions present in Brazil a way of returning to Buddhism in a modern, practical and relevant form, in contrast to the Buddhism of their parents, the older Buddhist traditions, in which the focus is on death and funeral rites. New Religions, like the Sathya Sai Baba movement, appeal for similar reasons to second and later generations of Indian origin in Europe, the Caribbean, Australia the United States, South Africa and elswhere, who, while wanting to retain links with the culture of their parents and grandparents, also seek to express this desire in what they believe to be a more rounded, inclusive and contemporary style.

Even where the will and the desire to do so exist, the difficulties – historical, psychological, political, cultural and theological – encountered in seeking to become a more inclusive religion should not be understimated. Where, for example, the Japanese immigrants of the Jodu Shinshu or Pure Land tradition of Buddhism did interact and compete in the wider world of agriculture and commerce, as in California, the opposition could be extremely hostile strengthening an already existing tendency among the immigrants to remain together.

Moreover, though success stories in the business and commerical fields, and the professions, were later the norm, life could be extremely difficult for those Japanese immigrants, in particular the first generation, in Brazil, Peru, North America and elsewhere who encouraged their children to integrate and benefit from educational and other opportunities which were either not available or could not be taken up by themselves as the first generation. Emotional and material insecurity were reasons here. The fear of loneliness and the lack of anyone to care for them in later life was but one intractable problem.

A major shift in outlook among the Japanese immigrants in Brazil was already evident by the end of World War II; they had begun to look to Brazil as their home, and by the late 1950s, the idea of returning home had lost much of its force. It was greatly weakened by the numbers of Japanese who had returned to Japan either immediately before or immediately after that War, only to find that life there was too rigid and restrictive compared with their Brazilian experience, and so many of them retraced their steps. This, and their children's poor knowledge of Japanese, and the inevitable educational problems that this would bring with it, greatly influenced the older generation of immigrants' decision to accept Brazil as their permanent home, the place where they would die, and become, in their turn, *senzo* or ancestors.

It was this decision and the kinds of domestic and life-style changes that accompanied it that gave religion greater importance and significance in the life of the Japanese immigrant in Brazil, and similar developments occurred in the Japanese overseas communities elsewhere. This in turn impacted on the understanding and interpretation of belief and practice, widening their application and scope. For example, *ujigami* or protector deities of the land and the people, once confined in terms of their influence and power to the Japanese immigrant community, became the deities, not just of the Japanese in Brazil, but of all the inhabitants. The most typical of Shinto Shrines in Brazil today, The Great Shinto Shrine of Brazil, the *Kaminoya Yaoyorozu Kyo* (the Dwelling of the Myriad Deities) established in 1968 by the now nonagenarian Suzuko Morishita, daughter of a Shinto ascetic (*gyōja*), stresses the universal character of the Japanese Sun Goddess, Amaterasu.

The 1960s and the Appeal of Zen and Macrobiotics in the United States

By the 1960s a number of Japanese religions abroad sensed for the first time that they were on the verge of a breakthrough. In the United States Zen, Macrobiotics and Soka Gakkai, all began to attract large numbers of

275

adepts. The Japanese Zen practices that mostly appealed were those of the Soto and Rinzai traditions. The former was introduced to Japan from China by the Japanese priest Dogen (1200–1253) and sought adherents among the middle ranking Samurai and the commoners. Rinzai Zen was also brought to Japan by the Japanese priest Eisai (1141–1215) who built the Rinzai Zen temples of Kofukuji in Kamakura and Kenninji in Kyoto. In contrast with Soto Zen, Rinzai sought adherents primarily among the high ranking Samurai who held the reigns of power. The principal difference between the two traditions is that Soto Zen, following Dogen's counsel that his disciples should entertain no vagrant thoughts, but just sit in earnest contemplation, concentrates exclusively on meditation practiced while sitting erect in a cross-legged position, *zazen*. Rinzai, by contrast, makes use of the *kōan* or problem presented by the Zen master or Roshi to the student in the form of a cryptic utterance. The student must then give a satisfactory response to the problem.

Zen was introduced to the United States by Soen Shaku (1859–1919) the abbot of Enkakuji Temple in Kamakura who visited America in the late ninteenth century. It was initially intended that it should serve the Japanese-American community and only later were efforts made to reach out to the wider community culminating in the foundation in 1930 by Sokei-an Roshi of the First Zen Institute of America. Until the 1960s most practitioners of Zen in the United States belonged to the Rinzai tradition. But from that point in time Soto Zen became widely known in intellectual circles in particular, mainly through the writings of D.T. Suzuki (1870–1966). Jones and Melton (1994: 38) suggest that one of the main reasons for Zen's widespread appeal among intellectuals in the United States was '... because it is less embedded in cultural forms than other Japanese religions'. During the 1960s several new Soto Zen lineages were introduced to the United States from Japan, most of them by Japanese teachers. One exception was the Order of Buddhist Contemplatives started in San Francisco in 1969 by the British born Jiyu-Kennet Roshi. She was later to open centres in Canada and Britain.

Macrobiotics, was brought to the United States in 1929 by George Oshawa (1893–1966), and was the first Japanese religion to gain anything approaching mass appeal there, or, put differently 'the single most successful movement to permeate American Culture' (Jones and Melton, 1994: 41). Best known for its teachings on diet – and hence not a religion for many who either ignore or are unaware that the underlying Taoist principles are as important as the dietary prescriptions – Macrobiotics was developed as a synthesis of Chinese wisdom teachings in a Japanese Zen Buddhist context and western ideas by Ishizuka Sagen (1893–1910). Sagen passed on his synthesis to Nishihata Manubu who, in turn, interested Sakurazawa Yukikazu (alias George Oshawa). In the 1950s the movement began to experience success in the United States, beginning in New York, as the Oshawa Foundation, initially under the leadership of Kushio Michi, his wife Aveline, and Herman and Cornelia Aihara. It spread from New York to Boston as the East-West Foundation, and across America to California where it kept the name Oshawa Foundation.

Soka Gakkai's Rapid Take-Off in the United States

While never matching the strength of the appeal of Zen among American intellectuals or the mass appeal of Macrobiotics, Soka Gakkai in the United States experienced in the 1960s and 1970s one of the fastest take offs in modern times anywhere of any new religion. For more spectacular beginnings we have to look to movements such as the Harris Church which attracted more than a million converts in across the southern sectors of the Ghana and the Ivory Coast in less than two years between 1913–15. Soka Gakkai's recruits were in the main young Americans from middle and lower class backgrounds.

This lay movement of Nichiren Buddhism moved like a whirlwind through the streets of California in the 1960s. While at the beginning of that decade most members were of Japanese origin or descent, by the end of the 1960s, after a period of intense *shakubuku* activity – aggressive street evangelism directed at non Japanese-Americans – the membership stood at 200,000, according to official statistics produced by the Santa Monica headquarters (Inoue, 1983: 109). 41 per cent of members were Caucasian-American, 30 per cent Asian, 13 per cent Latin American and 12 per cent African-American (Yanagawa, 1983: 14). In terms of age, at the end of the 1960s, 17 per cent of members were under 20 and 71 per cent under thirty. From the perspective of the Santa Monica Headquarters, the rapid growth was a consequence of the involvement of the hippies 'because we preached at their communes and they joined collectively' (Yanagawa, 1983: 14). The Buddhist seminars held by the movement were also an important source of recruitment.

The situation in Hawaii was different due to the large population of Japanese on the islands, a substantial minority of whom were Catholics. There, the percentage of Japanese members equalled that of all other ethnic groups combined, with Caucasian members accounting for only 10 per cent of the total (Inoue, 1983: 109).

The second half of the 1970s were years of slower growth. The official estimates and some studies showed the movement had a membership size of 230,000 at the beginning of the 1980s (Inoue, 1981: 100–101). The character and strategy of recruitment had changed from that of hyperactive, militant evangelism to a more reflective philosophical and spiritual approach that included an emphasis on 'alternative' causes, including ecology and the environment. The balance of age in the movement had also changed. Compared with the high percentage of those under thirty years of

277

age at the end of the 1960s, by the end of the 1970s there was an even spread of Japanese-American male members in their twenties, thirties, forties and fifties, while the highest percentage of non-Japanese male members was in the 30–40 age category. The majority of American-Japanese female members was also in this category. Most of the non Japanese-female members were in the 30–35 age group, with a substantially minority in the 25–30 category (Inoue, 1983: 126). As to the composition of the movement based on gender, female members were now only marginally more numerous than male.

The leadership in California in November 1997 believed that, since both the figure of 200,000 for the beginning of the 1970s and that of 230,000 for the end of the decade, did not reflect the actual membership at those times the extent of the decline that has taken place since the mid-1980s has been exaggerated. Decline there has been but no massive haemorrhaging of members. The debate over the size of the membership, notwithstanding, Soka Gakkai's ability to attract non Japanese-Americans was unprecedented and surprised everyone concerned with the study of these religions outside Japan. As Inoue (1983: 101) observed with regard to the situation in the United States:

> The success of NSA (Soka Gakkai) in obtaining non-Japanese members is remarkable compared to other new religions of Japan

Important in a general sense to Soka Gakkai's early success was the new immigration law of 1965 which placed Asians on a par with Europeans in terms of immigration quotas. But this alone cannot explain its progress for it was legislation that Tenrikyo and other Japanese new religions benefitted from without attracting large numbers of followers. In the early stages, in particular, the Japanese wives of American soldiers who had formerly served in the Far East did much to build up the movement by bringing in their husbands and their husbands' families and friends. Leadeship was also crucial to the early success of Soka Gakkai. While leadership is rarely, if ever, entirely responsible on its own for the success of a new religion, in the case of Soka Gakkai in the United States the commitment, energy, and dynamism of Masayasu Sadanaga, alias George Williams, was crucial to its take-off among non Japanese-Americans. Sadanaga's contribution to Soka Gakkai's early expansion lay chiefly in familiarizing young Americans with the movement's teachings and practices. He organized *zadankai* or discussion meetings, lectured on university and college campuses across America, and in these ways laid the foundations for the take-off of the movement in 1960 which followed on the visit of its international President Daisaku Ikeda. Sadanaga's activities, supported by *shakubuku*, accounted for, in Inoue's words (1983: 110) 'a large number of new members from the late sixties to the mid-1970s'. The annual conventions held by Soka Gakkai also greatly helped recruitment bringing thousands of people together. In

Ellwoood's words they were 'splendid occasions full of fun and festivity. . . (and) Far removed from the usual staid church council, or the ordinary secular convention, they are at once innocent, sacred and human. . . countless pageants put across Nichiren Shoshu teachings through Japanese, African or outer space themes' (1974: 76–77).

The fall-off in recruits in recent times notwithstanding, Soka Gakkai continues to have high hopes of attracting a big following in the United States. The largest membership is still in California and is estimated at between 60,000 and 70,000, with 12,000 of these residing in Northern California and the remainder in the South. In addition, in the rest of the United States there are an estimated 50,000 members, making for a total of between 110,000 and 120,000.[4] As to the ethnic composition of the movement 75 per cent of the membership is Caucasian- and African-American, and less than 15 per cent is Japanese-American. The main means of recruitment since the ending of *shakubuku* or 'street shaku', as it was called, is through personal contact. According to one of the Californian leaders of the movement 'attracting one's friends who in turn attract their friends is considered to be the only sure and stable way to communicate our ideals, instead of chasing numbers. If numbers only increase there will be another collapse.'[5]

Back to the grass roots is the main theme of Soka Gakkai strategists at present and was one that was emphasised in my discussions with the leadership in Hawaii[6] where it is also the largest of the Japanese new religions. Between 10,000 and 12,000 have received the Gohonzon and five thousand members are active in Honolulu.[7] The growth of the movement in Hawaii, though on a smaller scale than the mainland, has also been impressive, increasing from 16 in 1960 to the above mentioned total of between 10,000–12,000 by 1997.[8] Soka Gakkai, however, has not had the same success in appealing to non-Japanese in Hawaii, or to the younger members of society, or to men, as has the movement on the mainland.

The proportion of Japanese-Americans – 80 per cent – in the movement in Hawaii remains high, but this notwithstanding it is the most multi-ethnic of the Japanese religions on the islands. The high percentage of Japanese-American members can be partly explained by the large Japanese-American population on the islands, which stands at just over 22 per cent of the total population, but is as high as 60 per cent on Oahu island. The average age of the membership is also unusually high with between 60 and 70 per cent over 45 years of age, as is the number of women members, estimated at 70 per cent.[9] The leadership in Hawaii is aware of these imbalances and, in particular, of the ethnic character of the movement, and for this reason is at present focusing its attention on culture and theatre 'to provide other ethnic groups with the opportunity to identify with some aspect of Soka Gakkai so that it becomes more international'.[10] This is all done within the context of a campaign to attract more recruits 'by returning to the grass roots'.[11]

Much has been said in relation to Soka Gakkai's rise and decline in the United States about the motives and ambitions of recruits and here I would like to discuss these briefly showing that they were more complex and more altruistic than is sometimes suggested by the local leadership, and by researchers who describe Soka Gakkai as a this-worldy religion (Wallis, 1984) with essentially hedonistic ambitions (Wilson and Dobbelaere, 1994).

The Appeal of Soka Gakkai

My data suggests that a substantial number of recruits to Soka Gakkai were attracted by its philosophy which endorses values essential to the well-being of the planet. I begin with testimony of a Californian member who joined Soka Gakkai in the 1960s and who recalled in an interview the philosophical and ideological reasons why he was first attracted to the movement:

> What we were objecting to in the 1960s was the insanity in which we found ourselves with governments supporting policies that were not good for life – and they still are to some degree. I personally was trying to find a philosophy that made sense – how to solve the world's problems, the misery of the people. The philosophy of Soka Gakkai basically answered the question – it made sense to me that individuals need to change the way they think and believe. That's why its concept of human revolution essential to the teaching made sense: people need individually to change the way they perceive things. And they do this through their daily ritual and chanting'.[12]

While Soka Gakkai endorses and pursues this-worldly values following its founders, Tsunesaburo Makiguchi (1871–1944) and Josei Toda (1900–1958), this should not necessarily be taken to imply that it affirms and upholds the values of contemporary society in their present form. Rather, its aim is to change in a radical sense the way we live now and turn the present value system upside down. It seeks a new basis to ethics (Holly, 1998) which it terms a virtue-based as opposed to a rule based ethics, a new foundation for global citizenship (Hudson, 1998), and a new interpretation and understanding of the self. Further, it seeks to provide an alternative interpretation of the meaning and purpose of life, derived largely from the teachings of the monk Nichiren Daishonin (1222–1282), founder of the Nichiren Buddhist tradition to which the movement belongs. Its list of the great enemies of the modern world that need to be slain before paradise can be established on earth include the widespread preoccupation with the self, or individualism and egoism, which it sees as rampant, and which mainstream culture is accused of encouraging and promoting at every opportunity. This interpretation of its orientation makes the designation of

Soka Gakkai as a world-affirming movement in the sense of a movement that endorses the ethos and life-style of contemporary society, highly problematic.

Soka Gakkai's cosmology is multi-layered and implies the mutual interdependence of the spiritual and material. The central practice of chanting is primarily a means of tapping into the latent power of a universal spiritual law that is believed to effect natural phenomena and events. An Augustinian would understand. Soka Gakkai appears this-worldy not only in it insistence that chanting works but also that paradise is to be found on earth. Paradise on earth, however, can only be realized on an earth that has been completely transformed by its practices. This is in keeping with Nichiren Daishonin's teachings in which he vehemently opposed Pure Land and other Japanese Buddhist traditions that spoke of an other-worldy paradise, chiefly because he contended that they undermined individual responsibility for turning Japan into the model human society by making it the land where true Buddhism prevailed. As Anesaki (1930: 202) comments: 'Japan, for Nichiren was the country where the Universal Buddhist Church was to have its seat; but Japan in an ideal sense meant the whole world – transformed in the light of the Scripture'. Inoue's study of the movement in California (1983) reinforces the point made above regarding the variety of reasons for conversion to Soka Gakkai. He states, for example, that the non-Japanese recruits 'all preferred the Buddhist way of thinking' to the Christian way on issues relating to destiny (Inoue, 1983: 123). Moreover, another cognitive aspect of motivation was expressed in comments on the compatibility between Buddhist teaching and scientific thought whereas Christian thinking was more deductive (Inoue, 1983: 123–124).

Those who joined the movement in the 1960s and 1970s may not have stayed for long but the movement's this-worldly philosophy, the opportunity it offered lay people to fully participate in saving the world by greening religion and through it politics, and in establishing lasting peace, were important elements of their motivation. Its alternative vision not withstanding, Soka Gakkai, like many sects in the past that opposed the mainstream, became a vehicle for the resocializing of its countercultural members into mainstream American values by inculcating in them a positive attitude toward work and by its stress on the necessity for individual responsibility as a precondition of enlightenment. Moreover, though a very Japanese form of Buddhism, it appears capable of universal application: no one is obliged to abandon their native culture or nationality in order to fully participate in the spiritual and cultural life of the movement.

While generally it can be said that a degree of failure is part of success, following on from it almost as certainly as night follows day, Soka Gakkai's decline in the United States had as much to do with centre-periphery

(Japan-United States) relationships, the movement's internal arrangements in America – it was certainly fast becoming an over-administered, bureaucratic organization – problematic interpersonal relationships, and the form and content of its local socialization programme. Over dependency on the *shakubuku* technique was also part of the problem in that its remarkable effectiveness may have made for a lob-sided recruitment strategy, obscuring the importance of friends and family members in attracting new recruits and in their continued involvement in the movement.

As Geertz (1968: 14) so eloquently and persuasively describes it the process of religious adaptation though indispensible to success is fraught with difficulties:

> Religious faith, even when it is fed from a common source, is as much a particularising force as a generalizing one, and indeed whatever universality a religious faith manages to attain arises from its ability to engage a widening set of individual, even ideosyncratic, conceptions of life and yet somehow sustain and elaborate them all. When it succeeds in this, the result may indeed as often be the distortion of these personal visions as their enrichment, but in any case, whether deforming private faiths or protecting them, the tradition usually prospers. When it fails, however, to come genuinely to grips with them at all, it either hardens into scholasticism, evaporates into idealism, or fades into eclecticism; that is to say, it ceases, except as a fossil, a shadow or a shell, really to exist. The central paradox of religious development is that, because of the progressively wider range of spiritual experience with which it is forced to deal, the further it proceeds, the more precarious it gets. *Its successes generate its frustrations* (my italics).

Adaptation: Enthusiasts and 'Discontents'

Religious movements are often more conscious of what they see as the perils of adaptation than of the necessity to adapt, as the following account of the debate on this subject within Soka Gakkai and Tenrikyo, principally, but also in the cases of Perfect Liberty Kyodan, Messianity, Seicho no Ie and Mahikari, will illustrate. Opinions in a movement on the degree of adaptation and the strategy to be employed vary greatly depending on the angle from which the process is being examined and experienced and how its ideological, psychological and social effects are perceived. As will be seen below, from one perspective adaptation has direct consequences for doctrine, ritual, identity and community participation. For some, it adversely affects the structure, character, operation and efficacy of their belief system which has come to serve for them as a social psychology providing explanations of the meaning and purpose of life, and especially of interpersonal and social relationships. For others, adaptation is a dynamic process that enables the spiritual content of their religion to emerge bereft of its cultural trappings and allows it to exert greater influence on individuals and society. Adaptation also has a bearing on authority, power, and control of capital, in its many forms, in a religious movement.

These broader issues raised by adaptation are often hidden beneath the debate that rages over apparently insignificant matters relating to rituals, as attempts to Americanize Soka Gakkai in the United States show. Apparently insignificant matters may well constitute an important element of the infrastructure on which the more formal doctrinal system rests. The traditional form and style of ritual, moreover, is often understood to be inextricably linked to its efficacy.

Most of the resistance to the process of domestication of Soka Gakkai in the United States came from the pioneers who had clear proof of the effectiveness of the traditional ways during the successful years of the 1960s and 1970s. Most opposition came from the Japanese-American women members. This was serious opposition as the Soka Gakkai leadership was quick to realise. All Japanese new religions whether in Japan or abroad would also have understood the seriousness of such protest for all are heavily dependent on their women members at the local and national levels, for their contribution to virtually all aspects of their activities. Women occupy all the important offices, and in several, including Shinnyo'en, are the spiritual leaders.

Among those seemingly trivial issues which caused disagreement and tension in the debate on the Americanization of Soka Gakkai was the introduction of chairs for chanting where the practice had been for members to simply enter a centre, kneel on the ground and chant. For many of the Japanese and Japanese-Americans it was inconceivable that there should be chanting sitting on a chair and not on the ground, for using a chair not only went against tradition but was not considered to be 'sincere enough'.[13] The idea that for a spiritual practice to be genuine it must involve discomfort or pain is of course widespread not only in Japanese culture but in many others. Moreover, by changing the form of chanting in this way the question arose as to whether the content and efficacy of the ritual would not also be affected at the same time, and members of many Japanese new religions, particularly those from a Shingon background such as Shinnyo'en, like the Japanese-American female members of Soka Gakkai, would have answered in the affirmative.

The attempt to translate the basic concepts of the teachings into English rather than using Japanese to relate the central ideas of Soka Gakkai also met with strong resistance. Those who opposed translation, again the majority were Japanese-Americans, maintained that a particular word, pronounced in a particular way, was the only effective means of ensuring the transmission of supernatural power or energy, and was, therefore, unchangeable. Moreover, the words of the ritual, it was pointed out, had an author whose message and will it carried and expressed; it was the personification of the one who gave it its original meaning and for this reason also could not be changed. In Shingon Buddhism there is also the belief that certain words clearly pronounced embody spiritual power, and in Shinto ritual prayers or *norito* this extends to the avoidance of certain terms which are believed to exercise a bad influence over people. A number of leaders of Japanese new religions, including Onisaburo Deguchi of Omotokyo (Young, 1988) became preoccupied with the esoteric dimension to words, or the practice of *kotodama*, as it is known, according to which a word has a spirit, or, certain kami or spirits reside in certain words.

The Japanese words and the ritual forms which they imbue with spiritual power were means of emotional and psychological contact for Japanese members with the world of Japan, of which Soka Gakkai was a model or miniature reflection. Clearly, this was not how those whe were pressing for change reflected upon these matters; they saw the arguments against change as empty formalism based on an attachment to a set of concepts and ways of doing things simply out of preference for the Japanese way which, with sufficient good will, could easily be changed with great benefit to the majority.

The defenders of change saw themselves separating out what they perceived to be the essentials of the religion from the cultural forms in which it was embedded. As one of those in favour of Americanization explained, the process would help everyone to go straight to the heart of the faith: 'A lot of it is just reading Nichiren Daishonin's writings and looking at what President Ikeda focuses on. The rest is simply what the original pioneers in America perceived faith to be'.[14]

Any resolution of the problems generated by Americanization was made more difficult by the split that occurred between Soka Gakkai and the Nichiren priesthood beginning in the late 1970s and ending in a schism in 1990–1991. In many ways it was inevitable for these two organizations were very different in style and purpose: the Nichiren priesthood's purpose was to provide Soka Gakkai, its lay arm, with authentic copies of the *Gohonzon* or sacred scroll inscribed by Nichiren and the object of worship, and perform funeral, memorial and posthumous naming ceremonies in return for financial support, while Soka Gakkai was determined to press ahead in a systematic way with *kōsen rufu* or the universal proclamation of Buddhism. It was a case of tradition being locked in conflict with instrumental rational action. Almost any move made by Soka Gakkai to introduce a more universal form of Buddhism was opposed by the Nichiren priesthood who saw no need for change in the form of ritual even outside Japan.

There is nothing more paralysing for a movement than uncertainty and inconsistency, and the greatest difficulty posed by this dispute – resolved by the early 1990s by the defection of a number of Nichiren priests to the side of Soka Gakkai – both for the Americanization and expansion of the movement, came from the hesitancy and wavering that prevailed as compromises were made by both sides and agreements reached, only to be later undone, and this over a long period. In these circumstances it was impossible to develop a clear set of policies on adaptation, recruitment and the above mentioned goal of *kōsen rufu*. The refusal by the Nichiren priesthood to grant copies of the *Gohonzon* to new Soka Gakkai members was a severe setback for it was through this object of worship, received by members in the *Gojukai* or faith affirmation ceremony, that believers were able to glimpse the Buddha nature within themselves, the very purpose of the movement. Its unavailability to new recruits led to an emphasis on internal dispositions and faith as opposed to ritual activity and symbolic forms which are crucial to its persistence and expansion.

With the resolution of the dispute the debate on Americanization changed in scope and depth; it was no longer simply about discerning whether the form and language used in a ritual was a matter of Japanese custom, but also about whether it was a 'matter for the priests only', and, therefore, not binding on the lay members of Soka Gakkai.[15] The discussion over the number of times it was necessary to recite extracts of the Lotus Sutra was carried on in the United States with this in mind. President Ikeda is said to have expressed the opinion that recitation several times in the morning and in the evening is a 'priestly practice'. Though Soka Gakkai International issued no official statement to this effect some concluded that numerous morning and evening recitations were not binding on them as lay members.[16] Nichiren's writings were also used to support this opinion for apparently nowhere did he say how many times the Lotus Sutra should be recited.

By the mid-1990s, despite the obstacles, many non-Japanese members in the United States had come to perceive Soka Gakkai as an 'American form of Buddhism'.[17] As one Caucasian-American member commented, 'I certainly think of it as an American organization, and I want to make it even more of an American organization by defining and refining exactly those practices and philosophies that are central and eliminate those that are formalities from the priesthood or simply brought over from Japan'.[18] Many in Brazil and Europe would echo this same sentiment for those regions also. Through a process of elective affinity not only have ritual forms and language undergone indigenization but so also has belief. When emphasising the 'positive and attractive' aspects of Soka Gakkai's teachings American informants could be reciting a list of those things they value highly as American citizens, including the absence of moralizing, the stress on individual choice and the need to take responsibility for one's own actions.[19]

The Development and Appeal of Soka Gakkai in Europe and Brazil

Looking further afield than the United States to Soka Gakkai in Europe, and in particular Britain, the single most important attraction for new recruits was the quality of the people they met in the movement – their vibrancy, liveliness, energy, enthusiasm and sense of purpose – and indirectly the teachings. Indirect, in that after observing the quality of the members they wanted to learn about the teachings which made it possible (Wilson and Dobbelaere, 1994: 53). Moreover, almost 50 per cent of recruits encountered spirituality and religion in Soka Gakkai for the first time (Wilson and Dobbelaere, 1994: 88). Also attractive to many was the idea of an ethic founded not on guilt but on the positive values to be enjoyed from behaviour that was in keeping with their own and others' fundamental interests and happiness (Wilson and Dobbelaere, 1994: pp57ff). My own research on Soka Gakkai in the Oxford City area points to its enabling powers, to the building up of self confidence largely through chanting and discussion groups.[20]

In Brazil, where it began to proselytise in 1960, Soka Gakkai has, according to official sources, a membership of around 150,000.[21] This has been accomplished without that most potent weapon of expansion in this part of the world, a healing ritual. With the exception of Soka Gakkai, Japanese new religions have used healing to launch themselves in Brazil, realizing later that, despite its initial appeal, this method was not adequate on its own to sustain commitment and ensure continuous growth (see chapter 5 pp. 129–81).

While it has made considerable progress in adapting to the local religious and cultural contexts Soka Gakkai has encountered several serious difficulties centring on matters of faith in Brazil, the problem of belief in God constituting a major obstacle for many to convertion to a Buddhist movement. To overcome this Soka Gakkai has spoken of the Buddhist form of God,[22] and with some considerable success. By the late 1980s some 60 per cent of members were Brazilians of other than Japanese origin and the majority of these are women (Clarke, 1995: 123).

The fact that Soka Gakkai is clearly a Buddhist movement also has its advantages in Brazil, as elsewhere. The focus on the individual and the stress on the idea that everyone can become a Buddha suggests to seekers that it has the capacity to be universal in outlook and spirit, in the sense of being capable of dealing with a wide range of spiritual experiences, and not only with those of its time and place of origin. As we saw, Soka Gakkai in the United States came to be perceived as being open and responsive to Americanization, and as having the capacity, even in its post-domesticated form, of integrating non Japanese-Americans into an authentic and dynamic form of Buddhism.

286

While Soka Gakkai has been relatively successful wherever it has established itself outside Japan, the fortunes of most other Japanese new religions abroad have been mixed. Several have so far enjoyed little success in the United States, Europe and Brazil, while others, though they have failed to take off in the United States and Europe, have achieved considerable success in Brazil.

Slow Growth in the United States and Europe and Rapid Success in Brazil

Among the Japanese new religions that so far have experienced great difficulty in becoming multi-ethnic religions with large memberships in United States and Europe are: Tenrikyo, Konkokyo, Omotokyo, Perfect Liberty Kyodan, Mahikari, Rissho Kosei-kai, Seicho no Ie and Messianity. While proclaiming a universal mission, these religions are identified as carriers of a specific identity which their cosmology, rituals, symbolism, mores, and organization are seen to protect. As a consequence, they are perceived as limited in terms of the range and scope of their concerns and ill equipped to address the wide range of experiences that new circumstances and situations inevitably force them to deal with in a multi-ethnic and pluralistic world. While I will attempt to illustrate this by reference to Tenrikyo in particular, limited coverage will be given to the other Japanese religions mentioned above that have, as yet, attracted only very few non-Japanese members in the United States and Europe.

Tenrikyo,[23] whose activities in the United States have been researched by Ellwood (1982), among others, was founded in Tenri city in 1838 by the charismatic peasant woman Miki Nakayama (1798–1887). It began proselytizing in the United States, in California, in 1896, and twelve years later it opened a church in Hawaii. Today Tenrikyo is active in thirty four countries including the Democratic Republic of the Congo, Kenya and Nepal.

Like all the earlier pre-World War II Japanese religions in the United States, Brazil, Peru, North America and other foreign countries Tenrikyo's mission was clear: to minister to the Japanese community. This missionary outlook persisted for a long time and continues on today among some in Tenrikyo's headquarters and this together with the highly specialized character of its ritual, the seemingly ethnocentric implications of its teachings, particularly those concerning the origins of human kind, the failure to indigenise its leadership abroad or to introduce the vernacular as the language of the services, has been the main reason for the movement's failure to attract non-Japanese abroad. Korea is an exception due largely to the domestication of the movement by the local membership.

Members on the spot are becoming increasingly aware of this. There are sixty Tenrikyo churches on the USA mainland and forty in Hawaii. Its oldest church in San Francisco, the Tenrikyo America West Church situated near Golden Gate Park – regarded locally as a dangerous area that limits the amount of proselytising that can be undertaken – is attended on average by forty members each month. The best frequented Tenrikyo church in the United States is its church in Fresno where three hundred attend monthly, a majority of whom are Japanese-Americans, the rest being made up of Chinese and Caucacian-Americans.[24] The pastor of the America West Church who insists that Tenrikyo is for all races, when asked to give his views on the main obstacles in the way of attracting other Americans to Tenrikyo commented: 'The main problem is that Tenrikyo was born in Japan and this gives us problems of style; when we try to get people to understand Tenrikyo some people say it is too Japanese. This is not Japan it is the United States'.[25]

In Hawaii, where it has been present since 1899, Tenrikyo is numerically stronger than on the mainland with around 3,000 members. Of these 85 per cent are Japanese-Americans, 8 per cent Chinese-Americans, 5 per cent Caucasian-Americans and under 2 per cent Hawaiian.[26] While there are no attendance records available informants speak of 'a lot of members only attending once a year'.[27] The most common reason given for this is that in many families both parents are working and have no time to go to Church.[28] The most active members are in the 40–60 age group, and a majority of these are Japanese-American women. The principal method of recruitment is the spreading of fragrance (nioigate) by members who go from house to house to offer assistance and discuss the movement's teachings. The most frequent response is one of no interest, 'particularly from among those who are healthy'.[29]

In Brazil, where it arrived in 1929, members with long experience of trying to atttract a wider public to Tenrikyo and change its image from an ethnic to a multi-racial church offer what is essentially the same explanation for its lack of success there also. Throughout its history in the United States and Brazil those who have encountered Tenrikyo have identified its primary goal as the conservation of Japanese customs and culture. The church's rituals, musical instruments, liturgical costumes, its symbolic interpretation of the relationship between the sexes through the different kinds of musical instruments men and women are allowed to play, and the parts they are assigned in the liturgical dramas acted out during ceremonies, and almost everything about Tenrikyo, reinforces the image people have of this movement as a model of traditional Japanese life. Ellwood (1982: 105) also stresses the negative effect on recruitment of the poor quality of the translations, where they exist, of Tenrikyo's teachings, and more seriously, the extent to which it privileges the *Jiba* in the origins and salvation of the human race.

The *Jiba* is to Tenrikyo what the Kaba is to Islam; it refers to the sacred centre of Tenrikyo located in the Oyasato or Village of the Parent, the common name for the Tenrikyo headquarters in Tenri city. It is believed to mark the site of *Kanrondai*, the pillar in the main sanctuary (*Shinden*) of the Oyasato, which in turn marks the site of the creation of humankind. Similar observations, particularly the centripetal forces which make all converge at the centre, are relevant to the slow development of several other Japanese new religions in the United States and elsewhere outside Japan. Assessing the problems the notion of the *Jiba* poses for Tenrikyo mission activity overseas Ellwood (1982: 105) comments:

> Not only do non-Japanese tend to find the *Jiba* harder to accept theoretically than do Japanese, but greater practical problems are obviously raised for overseas churches when such key rites of passage and opportunities for spiritual growth as *Shuyoka* (three months intensive training), the *Beseki* lectures (the nine lectures that must be attended in order to be initiated into Tenrikyo), the grant of *Osazuke* (a healing rite and the power granted by the Shinbashira to administer that rite), and the safe-childbirth grant – not to mention the privilege of worshipping before the *Kanrodai* during the service are available only in Japan (my italics).

Despite, or, paradoxicallly, on account of it its all pervasive Japanese character, Tenrikyo does have a limited appeal to the non-Japanese in the United States, Europe and elsewhere. In Europe, France has the largest membership. There are three hindred members in Paris, 60 per cent of whom are of European origin.[30] There is also a church in Bordeaux with a French born minister. The London church, opened in November 1998, is as yet numerically very small, though multi-ethnic, with members of Indian origin who first encountered the movement in Delhi, and Irish, Eastern European, and several British born members. In Europe and increasingly in the United States there is talk of following the Korean model. Not only by introducing the vernacular but also by allowing local instruments including the guitar.[31] Korea as we have seen, has the largest Tenrikyo membership outside Japan with over 100,000 followers and most opinion attributes this to the use of the vernacular in the services at the insistence of the Korean members and the establishment of a Korean leadership.

According to its Japanese minister at its Paris Church, the largest Tenrikyo church in the West, the difficulties in spreading Tenrikyo in France have less to do with the teachings which, he suggests, 'are easy to accept', and mainly to do with Japanese practices which create the impression that the Churh is an exclusive club established for Japanese only. When it does appeal, it tends to appeal to other minorities and the impression persists that it has nothing to offer the majority. This undermines its universal, salvific goal of transforming the whole world into a 'world of joy', a goal that constitutes the essence of the message of its main service, the *Kagura*

Service, which is performed as 'taught by *Oyagami* (God the Parent) out of God's parental love to save all mankind' (Sato, 1986: 157).

The Tenrikyo Paris minister singled out for special mention the following obstacles to growth in France: the Japanese musical instruments used at ceremonies, which are not only intended to provide music, but also an anatomical account of the bodily organs and their functions, the taking off of shoes on entering the shrine, the wearing of the black, Japanese blazer with the inscription, Tenri, in white Chinese characters, on the back, the practice of sitting on tatami mats, the use of Japanese as the language of prayer, and the accompanying hand gestures.[32] Regarding the language used in the services, it is worth pointing out that we are really speaking here of a sacred language or of a language that has acquired over time a sacred character, like Latin once had in the Roman Catholic church, for the Japanese used is not contemporary, widely spoken Japanese, but the dialect of the foundress, Miki Nakayama. Moreover, though it is not completely intelligible to all Japanese, the resistance to introducing modern Japanese in Japan is almost as strong as that mounted against the use of the vernacular outside Japan.

Tenrikyo, consequently, is able to offer little by way of a spiritual and social community to the average French citizen and this, as studies on the factors that make for long term membership of new religions show, suggests that it will become even less attractive with time to the non-Japanese in the country. If it remains unable to adapt its rituals, Tenrikyo will possibly exercise greater appeal as 'theatre' in the West than as religion by appealing to people interested in the Japanese style of music and dance which it performs. This, paradoxically, could have the effect of strengthening the position of those who are opposed, on theological grounds, to liturgical changes. But in the absence of a process of adaptation and domestication it will continue to be difficult for a non-Japanese person, other than one who is seeking a radical change of identity, to go beyond the intellectual and aesthetic stages of appreciation and admiration to commitment by entering fully into the spiritual life of this movement.

Considering their phenomenal success in Brazil (Clarke, 1995: 123) among the more surprising failures in the North American and European contexts are Seicho no Ie and Messianity. The former was founded in Kobe in 1932 by Masaharu Taniguchi (1893–1985) and was among the first Japanese new religions to evangelise in the United States. Previously a member of Omotokyo (Religion of Great Origin) Taniguchi claimed to have been the recipient of a revelation in 1929 which informed him that he was a child of the divine, and starting from this premise he constructed a theory in which he developed an understanding of the nature and relationship between devine and human reality (*Jissō*). Human beings are fashioned in their nature for a filial relationship with the divine and sin and illness are essentially symptoms of the breakdown of this relationship.

Healing comes by returning to the life of reality, by living as a child of the divine, of which the physical world is but a reflection. This core, Platonic, idea is supported by Shinto, Buddhist, Christian and New Thought sources.

Seicho no Ie prefers to define itself as a philosophy of life rather than a religion, and like a number of other Japanese new religions, including Kofuku no Kagaku (Institute for Research in Human Happiness), promulgates its message largely through its literature. Taniguchi's principal work, The Truth of Life, is the movement's 'sacred text' and consists of 40 volumes. Sales of this work total over 16 million copies. Its principal ritual is a form of meditation known as *shinsōkan*.

Seicho no Ie began proselytizing in Hawaii in the 1930s and occupied a privileged position there from 1943 until the end of World War 11. When all other Japanese new religions were obliged to discontinue their activities Seicho no Ie was granted permission through the good offices of a certain Dr Pemberton to continue to hold meetings and gained many converts from among the families of the members of the Japanese-American battalion who looked to it to provide memorial services and prayers for their relatives killed in battle.[33] In November 1943 an estimated 1,500 members attended the birthday celebrations of the movement's founder, Masaharu Taniguchi, in Honolulu.

After World War II recruitment slowed down and though Seicho no Ie had four centres in Hawaii by the end of the 1980s few young people were joining. Moreover, 95 per cent of the membership was Japanese-American, and 60 per cent of these were women in late middle age. The church had come to be identified by the young as an 'old person's church'.[34] After over 50 years of missionary effort in Hawaii, its present membership is estimated at around 2,500, 60 per cent of whom are women and the majority of whom are between the ages of 30 and 50. The disadvantage of being identified as Japanese was emphasised by leaders in Honolulu who recalled that 'only recently six non Japanese-Americans came to a service in Hawaii and received culture shock'. He added: 'But the older members are resistant to change and it is their church'.[35]

On the other hand, there is optimism about the future in certain quarters in San Francisco, and among activists in New York and the Mid-West. Ministers in New York are encouraged by the increasing numbers of African-Americans and Brazilians who are showing interest in the movement and point to the numerous adaptations that have been made in recent times to attract non Japanese-Americans generally.[36] These include services in English and Portuguese, the discontinuation of certain types of caligraphy such as the 'snake-like form which mid-Eastern Americans in particular object to' and 'the abandoning of the practice of bowing in church in Japanese style'.[37] These same ministers also support the recent emphasis by their leader on ecological and environmental issues.

What the younger ministers of the Seicho no Ie are now proposing with a view to the effective adaptation of belief and ritual to the United States is the abandonment of a uniform approach for the whole country and the introduction of a threefold strategy which takes into consideration the different conditions and needs on the East Coast, the West Coast and on Hawaii. Recent interviews with Tenrikyo ministers both in the movements headquarters at Tenri and in Europe indicate that they are also showing a cautious interest in this strategy.[38] In the case of Seicho no Ie, it is believed that more use can be made of Japanese in the form and content of the services on Hawaii, where the Japanese numbered 247,486 or 22 per cent of the total population (in 1996), than on the East Coast where it is much smaller and where, one minister believes, a 'more Christian-centred approach is needed; one with more comment on Jesus', and also, he added, as something of an afterthought, 'on Muhammad'.[39]

While seeing religious development in terms of personalities is dangerous I will, nevertheless, confine the discussion about the grounds for Seicho no Ie optimism in California to a brief account of the opinions and activities of its most energetic member, the lay preacher Mrs Uemoto, aged 85.[40] As in a number of other cases already cited above, Mrs Uemoto's record of her conversion to Seicho no Ie throws light on the outcome of the interaction between the global and the local, and on how they reshape each other until an acceptable version of both has been created. That is a version that will facilitate the juxtapositoning of two kinds of cultural and religious experience, one legitimising the religious narratives of primorial socialization and the other the wider experiences that come with birth, education and general upbringing in another culture than that of one's parents.

Mrs Uemoto, a nisei or second generation Japanese-American, was born in California of parents who had emigrated there from Hiroshima in the early 1900s. Her father worked as a labourer and her mother ran a small tofu business. Mrs Uemoto attended a Japanese school before World War II and speaks Japanese, 'but not fluently', and English.

She admits that the situation in California in general and in the town of San José where she lives and where the main Seicho no Ie church in the San Francisco region is situated, looks depressing from the outside. Even among the small membership there is little sign of the harmony and spirit of community which seekers find attractive. The Seicho no Ie movement in San José is composed of two groups that rarely interact, an English speaking, largely Japanese-American group which frequents the church, and a Japanese group that as yet has no church of its own. Mrs Uemoto, herself formerly a member of Jodo Shinshu or True Pure Land Buddhism, is the co-ordinator of the English speaking group. She found Seicho no Ie to be 'more open and inclusive' than Jodo Shinshu, and 'more in keeping with her determination to live as a Japanese-American, and not as Japanese in America'.

The 'open' and 'inclusive' character of Seicho no Ie is most evident, Mrs Uemoto believes, in its teachings about Christianity which are respectful and positive. The Japanese character of the movement is most obvious in its emphasis on harmony and gratitude and, ritually, in the service for the ancestors which takes place on the second Saturday of each month. This service, in particular, 'which expresses the belief that life is eternal and connects one to one's forebears', underpins, Mrs Uemoto explains, the Japanese dimension of her identity, while the teaching about Christ gives shape to her identity and self-understanding as an American. For Mrs Uemoto and her fellow members Seicho no Ie, like so many of the more ecumenical, eclectic new religions enables those of the second or later generations of immigrant families who feel a strong sense of belonging to two cultures, to integrate and harmonise these emotionally and intellectually.

Mrs Uemoto's optimism about Seicho no Ie stems from her contacts with the younger generation of Japanese-Americans, and particularly with those within her 'extended' family. While her own children and their spouses pursue their careers and 'employ' her as a carer Mrs Uemoto makes it a condition of her caring that she be allowed to introduce her grandchildren to the teachings and practices of Seicho no Ie. By this means seven of her grandchildren have become members, compared with two out of four of her own children, and she has recently begun 'working on' her great grandchildren, who, at nine, seven and five, are 'too young to join but already know how to pray'. Mrs Uemoto is persuaded that increasingly the responsibility for the socializing of the young will be taken over by grandparents and that this will lead to growth.

Seicho no Ie does not have any such back-up in Europe where its development has been even less impressive than in the United States. In Europe it has never enjoyed the benefits of having in its early years a strong immigrant base as a launching pad. Most of its tiny European membership is either Japanese or Brazilian. In Paris membership is less than 20 and there are no translations of Taniguchi's writings into French. Translation of these writings into Portuguese has not had much of an impact for in Lisbon there are only a dozen members who meet monthly in the home of a Portuguese devotee who worked for many years in Sao Paulo. In London the majority of the fifty or so members are Brazilian students or Japanese employees of Japanese companies some of whom due to the recession in Japan have had to return home. Recession has also affected other movements that rely on Japanese company employees as missionaries. In Germany the membership is estimated to be around 120, a substantial minority of whom are Brazilian. All of this must seem very puzzling to the movement's officials who count the membership in Brazil at over two million (Clarke, 1995). From the perspective of its success in Brazil and Thailand (Clarke pp. 129–81) Messianity's development in the

United States and Europe must also be extremely perplexing to its leadership.

Founded by Mokichi Okada (1882–1955) in Tokyo in the early 1930s, Messianity arrived in Hawaii in 1953 and in Los Angeles in 1954. The movement's teachings are based on three main principles; nature farming, faith healing through *johrei*, or purification of souls, in which the divine light (*ohikari*) is transmitted through the palm of the hand of the one administering the ritual to the sick person, and the cultivation of the artististic talents of the individual. Teaching the appreciation of the beauty of flowers is a salvific act, as is the administration of *johrei*. Members do both in the form of *gohōshi* or service. A member is one who has been converted through *johrei* and wears a pendant known as *ohikari*, believed to contain the Divine Light and to be a source of healing power. Other important sources of healing power are the *Miroku o okami* (the True God of Great Light) known as the *goshintai* (the Great Divine Body), and the ancestral altar, the *mitamaya* or Sacred Spirit House which contains the memorial tablet of the ancestors.

Messianity in Los Angeles began to attract non-Japanese members from the outset and by 1958 had introduced services in English and had also started a nature farm at Valley Center, followed later by the opening of a *Sangetsu* or Flower Arranging Academy. By the mid 1960s there were four non Japanese-American assistant ministers and a translation department was functioning to produce the writings of the founder in English. To adapt the movement to the expectations of the non-Japanese members rituals involving Shinto prayers were shortened and rubrics such as bowing and hand clapping were dropped, as were a number of traditional prayers, leaving only two Shinto prayers, the *Amatsunorito* and *Zengensanji*, and the Our Father.

These attempts at acculturation created tension, and at times the headquarters in Japan felt they could lead to a loss of central control over the periphery, a fear present in many other religions that pursue a global strategy of conversion. The fact that acculturation did not appear to be working did not help the cause of those who promoted it. By the late 1970s an estimated 85 per cent of the membership in Los Angeles was of Japanese ancestry – 60 per cent of whom were born in the United States and 40 per cent in Japan – while most of the remainder was composed of followers of Korean, Mexican and Thai origin (Yamada, 1983: 204). There were scarcely any Caucasian-American members, and those who had joined were on the whole middle-aged, middle class females preoccuppied with alternative spiritualities. There is no one perception of Messianity in the United States, but broadly it is seen either as an 'esoteric' movement attractive to those interested in mysticism, astrology and faith healing or as an 'ethnic' church, largely for Asian immigrants in California and for Brazilians in New York and on the West Coast.

There are those in the movement's headquarters who, with some justification, would dispute this negative interpretation of its history in the United States claiming that Messianity has exercised wide influence through its campaign to promote nature farming and spiritual healing or *johrei*. They tend to determine its success not only, or even principally, on the basis of the numbers of recruits gained, but according to the extent to which they feel they have been able to make others aware of their beliefs and practices through literature and conferences. Variations of this criterion of success are used by Seicho no Ie and Kofuku no Kagaku. Messianity, for its part, believes that by administering *johrei* and distributing flowers to millions who never became formal members, by encouraging *sangetsu* and natural farming in the United States and elsewhere for the past 50 years, it has made a major contribution to saving the world from disaster.

These activities are seen as crucial in the battle against crime, poverty and disease in Brazil and the developing world and against the destruction of the environment which is happening largeley in the developed world or, through the agency of the developed world, everywhere (see Clarke, 000). Thus, for Messianity a successful conference on nature farming that influences the thinking of those responsible for large scale agricultural projects, that introduces them to the benefits of what it terms Effective Microrganisms (EM) technology, to ways of protecting the soil and the forests and to beautifying their surroundings through the cultivation of flowers and shrubs is as successful a measure in 'saving' individual souls and the world as is a mass revivalist rally which leads to large numbers of actual conversions.

This notwithstanding, Messianity's numerical growth in the United States has been disappointing so far and does not look set to improve. On the West Coast where it has been present for almost 50 years its membership is less than 2,000 and its failure to display a more broadly based religious and cultural identity is the most common explanation offered by the movement itself for this.[41] Where it has attracted other ethnic groups than the Japanese these have tended to take over and, thus, in Los Angeles, for example, the Church has come to be identified as a Korean church. In New York, as was pointed out above, the membership is predominantly Brazilian, and the language of the ceremonies Portuguese. In one Messianity Church in New Jersey 201 out of the 206 'core members' are Brazilian. Organizational and leadership styles are also believed to be part of the problem of developing a wider appeal, particularly the casual style adopted that downplays the need for hierarchy and status.

Messianity's largest membership in Europe is in Portugal where there are about 1200 practioners, followed by Germany with 550, while in both France and Italy there an estimated 100 followers. In Britain most of the fifty or so members are Brazilian students. Of course, in Brazil itself, as has already been mentioned, Messianity's developement has been impressive, and the main reasons for this will be outlined later.

Rissho kosei-kai, Agonshu, Gedatsu-kai and Konkokyo have also made little headway in the United States. The last mentioned, Konkokyo, has remained one of the most Japanese of all the Japanese new religions outside Japan, though it has sought to attract non-Japanese members. In 1981, after 50 years activity in San Francisco all the church's officers, from head minister to ministers to assistant ministers, were of Japanese origin, as were the members of the board of directors, the presidents of the various organizations, including the youth organization, and the church representatives. Out of a total of 67 officials 100 per cent were Japanese or Japanese-American.[42] Its montly newsletter with the title 'The Japanese Spirit' reinforces the perception of the movement as an ethnic Japanese movement.

Even the latest forms of Japanese new religion which have never been identified with, dependent upon, or historically part of the Japanese immigrant community, have found it difficult to make a break through in the United States, and Europe. For example, Kofuku no Kagaku, the Institute for Research in Human Happiness, founded in 1986, began its activities in the United States in the early 1990s and by 1997 had attracted 200 members in San Francisco and 500 in Los Angeles, most of whom were of Japanese origin or married to a Japanese partner.[43] Searching through his experiences for an explanation for its slow progess a Kofuku no Kagaku minister believed that it had much to do with the fact that 'most members were women whose husbands did not understand, and so few whole families have joined'.[44]

Shinnyo'en, a Shingon derived movement, has fared somewhat better, though it has been present in the United States since 1982. Founded by Shinjo Ito and his wife Tomoji in 1935 the movement, composed in the main of lay followers, believes that the essence of the teachings of Buddhism are to be found in the *Mahaparinirvana* sutra, the 'last teachings' of the Buddha, while, by way of contrast, Agonshu claims to have discovered the earliest teachings in the form of the Agama sutra. It is claimed that the *Mahaparinirvana* was uncovered by Shinjo for the first time and breaking with Shingon tradition he taught that it could be made known to all. Shingon by contrast restricts its teachings to the initiated. Following Shingon tradition in other ways Shinnyo'en teaches that everyone and everything is an expression of Dainichi, the Great Sun Buddha, or Buddha-essence of the Universe, or of being itself as perceived by the enlightened mind. Its three main practices are: joyous offerings (kangi) which purify the mind, service (gohoshi) which purifies the body, and sharing the teachings with others (otasuke) which purifies speech. Through the perfect performance of these three practices one can identify with the essence of the universe and allow it to shine forth in one's person and so become a Buddha in this body and in this lifetime. By early 1997

Shinnyo'en had over 1,000 members in the United States, and, like Soka Gakkai, sees America as 'a universal training ground where all mankind can be saved, that is a place where harmony can be created and people saved from suffering'.[45]

Rissho Kosei-kai (Society of the Community of Believers in Accordance with Buddhist Principles), a Nichiren derived movement, like Soka Gakkai, was founded in 1938 by Nikkyo Niwano (1906-) and Myoko Nagawuma (1889-1957), both of whom were formerly members of Reiyukai (Association of Friends of the Spirit), which stresses in its teachings the virtue of the Lotus Sutra and the importance of ancestor worship, the neglect of whom is the cause of all misfortune. Also based on the Lotus Sutra and following the counsels of the founder of Nichiren Buddhism, Nichiren Daishonin (1222–82), Rissho Kosei Kai is primarily concerned with the revival of true Buddhism as the means to bring full enlightenment to every individual and make perfect Japanese society and the world at large. Since its establishment in 1938 it has divided history into three periods: 1938–1957 as the Age of Tactful Teaching; 1958–77 marked the Age of Manifestation of Truth, and 1978 ushered in the present dispensation called the Age of Unlimited Mainfestation of Compassion.

Active in the United States since the 1970s Rissho Kosei-kai's membership is around 1,000 members, the majority of whom are in Los Angeles, and Pacifica in the San Francisco area. The membership is mostly Japanese-American. As in Japan, this movement has great difficulty in retaining the active allegiance of its second generation members. A major obstacle to the recruitment of non-Japanese members, particularly Cauasian-Americans, it is believed, is their different attitude to the *hōza* system, Rissho Kosei-kai's distinctive form of discussion group. Traditionally, members sit (za) in a circle and attempt to find solutions to problems in the light of Buddhist principles (*hō*). According to Japanese-American informants 'while for the Japanese member it is a question of learning through listening the Caucasian places the emphasis on questions about self-understanding and is more concerned with 'self-revelation' than with hearing the voice of the other'.[46] There is also a language problem, and this became evident when one assistant in the church in Pacifica, on being asked to explain the purpose of the cult of the ancestors, replied that she could only speak about this in Japanese. Though progress has been slow there is no sense of failure, one of the leaders insisting 'we are very new, just babies'.[47]

Though its performance has been generally unimpressive so far in the United States compared with Brazil (Clarke, 1995: 123) this kind of confidence is also found in the Perfect Liberty Kyodan Church in Oakland, California, which is administered by the charismatic nonagenarian, the Reverend Sayama. This Church had its beginnings in Japan in 1912 as Shinto-Tokumitsu-kyo, the Divine Way as taught by Tokumitsu. Its founder Tokumitsu Kanada (1863–1924) was joined in 1912 by the former Zen priest, Miki Tokuharu (1871–1938) and his son, Tokuchika (1900–83). Together Kanada and Miki created a religion out of their experiences of Shingon and Zen Buddhism, Shinto, and Japan's ancient mountain faith. Kanada, in particular, was interested in a version of this last mentioned faith known as Mitake-kyo, and was himself a mountain ascetic or *yamabushi*.

Kanada had provided the movement with 18 principles for living and at his death predicted that a future leader would add three further principles to these. This was Tokuharu Miki who also planted at the request of Kanada a *himorogi*, a sacred Shinto tree, and meditated daily before it. He later formed the *Jindo Tokumitsu-kyo* (The Human Way as Taught by Tokumitsu), as a branch of the Shinto mountain sect *Fuso-kyo*, and laid more emphasis on corect family and social relationships than on the esoteric and ascetic aspects of the treaching. By 1931 there was another change of name to *Hito no Michi Tokumitsukyo*, the Tokumitsu Way of Man, and by this time the movement had an estimated one million members in Japan. However, like many another new religion, it was persecuted as it grew large and popular and was banned in 1937 for allegedly violating the Peace Presevation Law, teaching the heresy that Amaterasu was the Sun and not the Sun Goddess, and for lesè-majesté, or failing to respect and support the imperial system.

Miki died in prison and his son Tokuchika, on his release in 1946, established a temple in Kyushu and renamed the movement Perfect Liberty Kyodan, making use of English to emphasise the religion's universal mission. It formally began mission activity in the United States in 1960. In Europe it is present in France, in Paris, and in Portugal where it has recently (1996) opened a centre in Lisbon.

Perfect Liberty is led by the Oshieoya, or teaching-parent, commonly referred to as the Patriarch, who, following Kanada's example, and in a way similar to that in which Christ on the Cross took on the sins of the world. He takes on the illnesses of his followers in a healing ritual, performed monthly, known as *ofurigae*, a term which literally means transaction and is used commonly for a business arrangement. Although the present Oshieoya, Miki Tahahito (1957–), can be self-deprecating speaking belittlingly of his own capacities – for example in an address in 1996 which I attended he humorously commented on the great difficulties he experienced in coming to grips with basic computer technology – he is believed by followers to possess divine power and to be able to offer *mioshie,* or divine instuction, to those who request it. Wherever a service is held across the world the Patriarch is thanked for the blessings and benefits that he has brought mankind.

Members' understanding of the Patriarch's status differs widely. While, as will be seen in the discussion below on the Perfect Liberty Church in Oakland, California, he is believed to be a living god or *ikigami*, and the modern Jesus, the saviour for the present age, others equally devout and loyal to the Chruch, agreed with one well respected minister who explained:

> Our Patriarch is not a god. God is not a person. Everything is divine work. He directs us and takes our problems to God. He is not an *ikigami* either; he does not like this term. He is a man but with great intuition and perspicacity. He is very open, receptive and very spiritual.[48]

The Patriarch resides at the movement's headquarters at Tondabayashi, situated about forty five minutes drive to the southwest of Osaka, which houses a peace tower, a hospital that focuses on experimental research in psychosomatic medicine, a school that has become well known throughout Japan for its success in various sports including baseball, and three golf courses. The principal teachings of the movement are encapsulated in the first of its 21 principles: 'Life is Art', a Shingon idea which emphasises the role of art in spiritual development, an emphasis found in other new Japanese religions including Omotokyo (Great Origin) and Messianity (Clarke pp. 129–81). For the co-founder of Omotokyo, Onisaburo Deguchi, 'Life as Art' meant that human beings by following the divine model of creativity express their personality through their artistic endeavours. While in Perfect Liberty this understanding of 'Life is Art' is retained, the principle is also interpreted to mean the developed understanding of the total structure of life – birth, marriage, profession, leisure pursuits, and so on – as a single unit, as a composition similar to an artist's composition of a picture or painting.

Present in the United States since 1960, Perfect Liberty's progress at the beginning was impressive attracting as it did some 5,000 members within a decade (Ellwood, 1974: 184). The movement began evangelising on Hawaii islands in 1968 and by Janauary 1997 there were 300 registered members, 200 of whom were residents of Oahu island.[49] Almost 100 per cent of these converts were Japanese-Americans, and seventy per cent of them women. The average age of the present membership is between 50–60, although that is believed to be coming down.[50] At present the services are mostly in English but attendance is irregular, and increasingly limited to marriages and other rites of passage. The Church has no school, no leisure centre, no community centre. The recruitment strategy is based on personal contact, and, more recently, use has been made of the internet, but so far to little effect.[51]

While the Reverend Yano, the pastor in charge of the Perfect Liberty Church in Honolulu, believes the reasons why Perfect Liberty has not been successful so far are complex, he is of the opinion that one of the main obstacles to growth is the Christian character of the United States.[52] He gives the Japanese identity of Perfect Liberty as another important reason, while adding that 'these do not provide a complete explanation'.[53] Moreover, Perfect Liberty is not alone in failing to grow for, as Reverend Yano points out, the Japanese new religions, the Buddhist churches, of which there are over one hundred on Hawaii, and the Christian churches are all getting older, have few young people who wish to serve as pastors, and are failing to make progress.[54]

Nevertheless, some Perfect Liberty parishes in the United States are flourishing, and one of these is the Oakland Perfect Liberty parish administered by the nonagenarian, the Reverend Sayama, who is assisted by the former Catholic nun, the Reverend Margaret. Both Reverend Sayama's and Reverend Margaret's conversion to Perfect Liberty are worth describing briefly for they reveal how the intellectual and emotional difficulties which many seekers encounter in leaving one religion for another are resolved not by mentally and emotionally abandoning the old for the new, but by using the new to deepen their appreciation and understanding of the old.

Brought up a Christian in Japan where she graduated from an American Christian College in Tokyo Reverend Sayama was on the point of death from tubercolosis when she was 'miraculously' saved by the prayers of a Perfect Liberty pastor. Worried about abandoning Christianity for Perfect Liberty, the previously mentioned Tokuharu Michi, the Patriarch at the time, advised her that if she truly understood the movement's teachings she would then be a true Christian. This eventually helped her overcome her 'very funny feeling' as she came to believe firmly that:

> The God of the Christian is the same as that of other religions, for we all live in the same universe of which God is the cause and the one who gives us many kinds of saviour, Buddha, Jesus and many others, including Oshieoya, who is the saviour for the present age.[55]

Very many new movements stress the idea of a saviour for each age pointing out that the needs of each period in history requires this. That Oshieoya is right for the present age, the Reverend Sayama explains, is clear from the fact that he is 'the living Jesus, a modern, very scientific saviour, who can provide modern explanations of God's truth'. Having the saviour of the modern age means having the religion for the modern age, the religion which, Reverend Sayama emphasises, 'teaches those who practice it exactly how to live in their present situation'.[56]

In the Perfect Liberty Church in Oakland, California, many different ethnic groups have discovered a milieu in which they can participate in the ideal American community. Some have described it as a 'model American Church', that is a church of many races and classes.[57] When, in the 1960s, members of Perfect Liberty were reluctant to share their churches with African-Americans the Reverend Sayama sought and obtained the moral authority and financial aid of the Patriarch to set up the then Perfect Liberty church in Oakland with the help of the African-American, Papa Hughes, who was responsible for a large number of the conversions.

During the past 20 years Reverend Sayama's principal assistant has been the previously mentioned former Catholic nun, Reverend Margaret, who is also convinced that Perfect Liberty teaches the same fundamental truths as Christianity. She finds that her work in Oakland today bears a very close resemblance to the situation in which Jesus ministered. It is not about making people members of a Church, about enrolling them in Perfect Liberty – this is an 'old idea, an old way of thinking' – but about 'going from place to place to meet people, to talk to people, to save people'.[58] Perfect Liberty 'is today's religion' Reverend Margaret, who studied Theology in George Washington and Louvain universities, explains, 'for it offers not only that pure faith that I used to have in Jesus, in the sacraments and in the resurrection, but also the best combination of psychology and spirituality that I have ever known'. She continued: 'There is a reason for everything and you can find it out in Perfect Liberty.[59] Perfect Liberty rituals do not constitute a problem for Reverend Margaret being quite similar to Catholic ritual. The main difficulty encountered by her, and in her opinion by others, was cultural 'especially the language'.

Reverend Margaret claimed to speak from personal experience about the effects of Perfect Liberty. The divine instruction, *mioshie*, that she was given by the Patriarch, and the forgiveness of her sins which he provided, cured what she had begun to believe was her incurable back problem. The Patriarch diagnosed that this ailment was caused by her stubborness and her tendency to try to exert herself beyond her natural powers.[60]

In Europe Perfect Liberty has 100 adherents in France and about forty in Portugal where, as we have seen, it opened a Church in 1996 which consists of a three bedroom apartment in a private condominium of flats close to the centre of Lisbon. The minister is a woman, Senhora Elsa, who lived for many years in Brazil. Her husband and three children are also members. Senhora Elsa and others have made observations similar to those made in the United States concerning the difficulties in attracting recruits. One member, a 27 year old student of architecture, spoke of the problem of the younger generation who are less believing and less interested in organized religion, of the more closed (compared with Brazil) character of Portuguese society, and of the rituals which he described as 'a bit off-putting and scary at first'.[61]

Mahikari, discussed elsewhere in this volume (Bouma and Smith, pp. 74–112; Matsunaga, pp. 198–239) has found greater appeal in Europe than most Japanese new religions, although both there and in the United States it has been slow to take off. Like several of the other movements discussed it has enjoyed most success in Brazil (Clarke, 1995: 124), here discussion will be limited to the progress to date of its Dojo in San Francisco which was established in the early 1970s. By late 1996 when the research on which the following observations are based was undertaken there were between 200 and 300 active members in San Francisco.[62]

The 1990s have been the most successful years and have seen the membership change from a majority Japanese-American to an ethnically mixed membership of which the largest single group is Caucasian-American. At the beginning, an informant who has been a member for over 20 years explained:

'the drop out rate was high because it was too hard, too foreign, too Japanese. It was too big a step. The last thing I wanted to do when I came here to the Dojo was to get down on my knees and clap my hands and bow my head, the most obvious foreign features'.[63]

During the past five years a process of filtering out, as in Soka Gakkai in California, what is Japanese custom from what is essential to Mahikari faith and practice is in prgress and entails, 'throwing out the former and keeping the latter, for even in a liberal city like San Francisco it is thought foolish, especially by men, to join a movement like Mahikari with all its Japanese cultural baggage'.[64]

There is no overwhelming desire, however, to abandon everything Japanese. For example, not all Caucasian-American members want to make English instead of Japanese the language of the prayers recited during *okiyome*, the healing ritual. Those who are opposed to this change make the point that Japanese not only sounds better but has a 'mantric value'.[65] It is not the language, they argue, that has prevented Mahikari from growing but its Japanese character as a whole and its failure to attract the mainstream, 'the jacket and tie brigade who make things stick, who make a contribution and in turn get something out of it'.[66]

It is not easy to assess the impact of relativism on a Japanese new religion's progress in the United States. Soka Gakkai's success would seem to suggest that the stricter doctrinally a movement is the more successful. However, as we have seen, on the ethical and moral fronts Soka Gakkai does not impose detailed rules and regulations but emphasises individual responsibility (Wilson and Dobbelaere, 1994). Members involved in mission activity in situations where there is little obvious signs of progress, let alone of converting the entire world, interpret their teachings and activities in an inclusive rather than an exclusive sense. This relativism was expressed by a 22 year old female member of Mahikari who continues to identify herself as a Catholic. A former college graduate this member believed that the purpose of Mahikari 'was to make a contribution and not provide the total solution'.[67] Mahikari, she explained, was concerned with trying to purify the world and create a Garden of Eden by getting everyone to respect everyone else 'and to respect the environment and nature by not raping the land'.[68] Science can help in this and so can other religions for as my informant pointed out 'it is not necessary for everyone to practice this art (Mahikari); everyone has their own way of attaining their fullest potential'.[69]

Thus, seen from the perspective of the members themselves Japanese new religions should not continuously engage in competing with each other or with other religions for territory and members. Mission, Mahikari stresses, should be understood in a spiritual rather than in a purely numerical or geographical sense. While new members are eagerly sought what is almost as important is sympathy and moral support from the public at large, and where there are few visible signs of progress on either front there is the belief that their practices will influence the world in imperceptible but extremely vital and effective ways, thus reducing the meaning and content of success and failure to spiritual realities.

Conclusion

Stark's theory (1996), mentioned in the introduction as the lodestar of this presentation, has much to commend it and I have often encountered evidence in my research to support, at least in part, one or other of its ten propositions, though I was not able to operationalise all of these propositions during my research on Japanese new religions abroad for several reasons. Further, I would be inclined to add an eleventh proposition based on the notion of cultural interdependence. No cultural or social system is totally self-sufficient and all are in need of new theories and skills from 'outside'. Roughly formulated the eleventh proposition would read as follows: a religion to succeed must provide what are, or are perceived to be, essential or necessary benefits of a material and spiritual kind, and skills that are or are deemed to be inaccessible or unavailable.

Over and beyond the difficulties with the propositions themselves there is a degree of imprecision with the definition of success and failure. Stark surmises that of the hundreds of new religions that would come into existence 'this year' (1996, the year the article was published) 'probably no more than one religious movement out of 1,000 will attract more than 100,000 followers and last for as long as a century' (1996: 133). Does this mean 100,000 followers in total or 100,000 followers wherever the movement establishes itself?

If these criteria were to be applied to the Japanese new religions discussed above and were related to their development not only abroad but also in Japan, then many of them could be counted as outstanding successes. If the discussion were to be confined to Japanese new religions abroad during the past 50 years then, once again, several have to be counted as successful in that they have gained more than 100,000 followers at least in one country overseas and among these are: Tenrikyo in Korea, Seicho no Ie and Perfect Liberty in Brazil, Messianity in Brazil and Thailand, and Soka Gakkai in the United States and Brazil. The interesting question is why they have failed to take off in some countries while in others they have spread widely and rapidly. Soka Gakkai, as we have seen, is the only exception to date to this rule, enjoying relative success almost everywhere it has established itself, Germany being an exception. After 25 years its membership there stands at around 700 only. (Ionescu, 1998).

Turning to the propostions themselves the main reason why some of these could not be operationalised in this research on Japanese new religions abroad was chronological, and this applies to propositions 6 and 10 which refer to the maintenance of sufficient levels of fertility to offset member mortality, and the socializing of the young to ensure sufficient tension with the surrounding society respectively. In many cases movements are too new to be tested in this way. There are conceptual difficulties with propositions 3 and 9, and especially with the terms 'medium tension, 'strict, but not too strict' and 'sufficiently strict', and if these cannot be resolved satisfactorily it is difficult to see how these statements can be subjected to proof or disproof. Moreover, tension and strictness are extremely difficult to measure cross-culturally. These comments are not meant to suggest that propositions 3 and 9 are without any value; if treated as broadly sketched observations they can bring much constructive insight to bear on the analysis of the success and failure of religions.

My own research suggests a number of further comments on Proposition 10 which emphasises the importance of providing for the adequate socialization of the young, a process that must ensure that there is no diminution of strictness, that defections are kept to a minimum and involve only those who exercise a negative influence on the movement through their lack of commitment (Stark, 1996: 144). As previously noted, this can only be applied in the case of a minority of Japanese new religions abroad due to their relative short history outside Japan. But more importantly, even where there has been a relatively long history – several generations – in a cultural environment other than a religion's own the process of effective socialization is particularly complicated, as can be seen in the case of a Japanese new religion, and other religions, where the basic structure is the household or *ie*.

Traditionally, in Japan, it has been the head of the family who gains the necessary spiritual and ritual knowledge through a process of informal education to perform the ceremonies on behalf of the rest of the *ie* or household. Thus, once the head of a family decides to erect an altarpiece or symbol of a religious tradition in the home then all the immediate members of the family are counted as belonging to that faith, whatever their personal preference. Little of the doctrine or the purpose of the rituals is ever taught to children. Orthopraxy counts for far more than orthodoxy. Many of the Japanese new religions abroad continue to think traditionally along these lines – Tenrikyo still maintains the spiritual lineage system whereby a convert becomes a member of the church of the one who converts him or her though this may be geographically inconvenient – though the growth of the nuclear family and greater individual choice make it essential that they develop ways of socializing the young as believers in their own right with the knowledge and desire to pass on their faith to their children.

It has to be said, however, that where new approaches have been attempted, as in Hawaii, by the long established Japanese religious traditions such as Jodo Shu and Jodo Shinshu or Pure Land and True Pure Land Buddhism respectively, and by some of the older of the new religions, such as Tenrikyo which has been present there for over 100 years, effective socialization of the young continues to remain a serious problem. Opinion differs greatly as to why. Mrs Tokugawa Uemoto who, at 87, remains an active minister of the Jodo Shinshu main Temple in Honolulu and for whom religion is a psychology or in her own words 'a way to get to know oneself better', believes that greater choice of leisure activities is a major obstacle to the socialization of the young. Distracted by too many other interests students in the Temple school, she points out, lose interest in Temple services and activities by the age of twelve.[70] By this age they are no longer attending Sunday School regularly either. There is, however, a ray of hope, she believes, in the increasing numbers attending the service in English at 10 a.m. on Sundays.

Several other Japanese-American observers in Hawaii with long experience of the slow progress and in some cases stagnation of the Japanese religions there contend that at present Japanese old and new religions are failing to adapt adequately and point out that the older generation are by no means entirely responsible for this failure. Equally accountable are the later generations of Japanese-Americans in search of their roots. One observer, himself a third generation Japanese-American, believes that this search, which involves insisting that the Temples retain their Japanese character, is 'killing them of'.[71] The paradox, this researcher points out, is that a process of even limited Americanization by a previous generation has led to a demand for re-Japanization, thus preventing non-Japanese-American involvement. In Japan itself the situation is different and is, it would appear, more directly related to the question of the socialization of the second and latter generations, as interviews with Rissho Kosei-kai, Sekai Kyuesei Kyo and Seicho no Ie, confirm.[72]

To return to Stark's general theory and to proposition 1 in particular. which states that success neccessitates that new religions retain cultural continuity with the conventional faiths of the societies within which they seek converts (1996: 144). Deducted from the rational choice theory of religion (Stark and Bainbridge, 1987) this proposition contends that an individual prefers religions which demand little expenditure by way of cultural capital. This would appear to be the case in the United States where the degree of 'fidelity' of believers to the faith of their childhood in the Protestant, Jewish and Catholic traditions, and possibly also in others, is striking. As Greeley (1999) points out the vast majority of the members of these traditions remain with the denomination of their birth. According to Stark's theory such long term allegiance is not a matter of apathy or indifference but a calculated decision on the part of individuals for whom the advantages, psychological, social, emotional and spiritual for remaining in a faith, are seen to outweight the disadvantages that changing one's religious adherence could bring. For Greeley (1999), if I have understood him correctly, primary or primordial socialization is crucial to the maintenance of long term allegiance.

It would appear that the explanatory value of this first proposition is limited to certain kinds of cultural and historical contexts only. For example, so called modernizing religions operating in completely different cultural contexts from their own, and guiding the people among whom they were proselytizing away from their own religious culture, have had wide appeal. Examples are plentiful of successful 'new' religions of this kind including Christianity in sub-Saharan Africa and Soka Gakkai in the United States both of which have demanded from recruits considerable expenditure of cultural capital.

This same proposition also raises a problem regarding the internal consistency of the general theory as a whole. In stressing that a new religion's success necessarily depends on its retaining cultural continuity with the conventional faiths of the societies in which it seeks converts this proposition conflicts with several other propositions and, in particular, with propositions 3, 5, 9, and 10 that stress the importance of maintaining sufficient levels of tension with the surrounding society, and of the motivation to spread the message with commitment, enthusiasm and dedication. The principal reason for speaking of inconsistency here is that most conventional faiths, at least those that are church-like in character, tend to compromise with the world and maintain free-riders. Therefore, to make cultural continuity a prime factor in decision-making about one's religious allegiance, as Stark does, would involve similar compromises on the part of the new religion which to succeed would have to generate tension with the surrounding society, filter out the inactive and uncommitted, and inspire members to become world-savers. How would the highly successful sectarian, world-rejecting movements ever attract anyone?

There is also much evidence derived from the history of successful new religions which shows that a great variety of relationships have existed between these religions and 'the conventional faiths of the societies within which they seek converts'. Among the successful new religious movements that dismissed some of the fundamental values strongly upheld by the mainstream religions, is the Rajneesh Foundation whose views on the nuclear family ran completely counter to those of the Christian Church (Puttick, 1997). The very novelty and difference of this new movement, and the completely different life style that it offered potential recruits, was its greatest attraction. More generally, the idea of making all things new is central to the appeal of thriving millenarian movements. As we have seen, Soka Gakkai, during its most successful phase in the United States was perceived by new members as 'entirely strange' (Inoue 1983: 118).

Proposition 1 also overlooks the important role of religion in enabling communities to move out of a tradition or way of life which they feel confines and restricts them, or is incompatible with their new circumstances and way of life. Moving away from or out of tradition into a new culture is evident in the conversion process to Christianity in parts of sub-Saharan Africa and more precisely in places such as Eastern Nigeria, among the Igbo, in the early years of the twentieth century, and in South Korea, particularly since the rise of Communism in the North. In Japan many of the Japanese new religions as lay movements have rejected priestly and temple controlled Buddhism and State supported Shinto. They resemble the churches of the Protestant Reformation in Europe as they offer the possibility of full spiritual development to any individual, regardless of their previous and present relationships, without the mediation of a cleric.

Proposition 1 thus underestimates the dynamic and experimental character of religious belief. In no other area of cultural life has there been more innovation and fragmentation. Risk taking is common, people venture into new territory, and circumstances can be such as to demand a completely new start as the links between the rise of new religions and the counterculture of the 1960s illustrate. In Latin America, as Martin (1990) has shown, new, thriving evangelical Protestantism, the polar opposite of traditional, folk Catholicism, appeals essentially by offering the possibility of 'walking out' of Catholic culture. Staying in Latin America one of my most vivid and revealing experiences of the countercultural impact of 'new' religion in many contexts in Brazil was the sight of a young woman, aged about 22 and a convert to Evangelical Protestantism, sitting on a deck chair on a beech crowded with quasi-naked bathers on a Sunday afternoon. This young woman was wearing an arms and knee length black dress and drinking Coca Cola. In an interview this convert defined herself by contrasting her way of life with that of Catholics describing a Catholic as one who drinks, smokes, dances, wears revealing clothes, and does not regularly read the Bible or attend church.[73] Ritually, Evangelical Protestants also do, I was told, what Catholics do not do, and that is cast out devils and practice faith healing.

Of course, certain elemental beliefs and attitudes must be retained if a new movement is to enjoy success. In the Brazilian and Muslim contexts there must be respect for Jesus and Mary, his mother. But even in these cases there is a complication with the idea of cultural continuity if it implies adherence to the traditional theological and moral orthodoxies. For, as the Brazilian context makes evident, while a new religion, if it is to take off and become successful, must include Jesus in its theological, symbolic and ritual agenda, can without cost, offer an interpretation of Jesus' nature and salvific mission that is both original and even in conflict with the prevailing Catholic orthodoxy.

Stark's theory of the success and failure of religion is the best there is. However, the difficulties involved in developing a theory that can make sense of success and failure from a cross-cultural perspective are probably insurmountable. The evidence suggests that what makes for progress in one cultural and historical context does not necessarily do so in another. The one rule that seems to apply in most situations is that for a religion to succeed it must adapt in key areas such as language and ritual. Adaptation is undoubtedly extremely important although the amount or degree, the strategy employed, and the timing of it are crucial and, if ignored, can turn it into the enemy of success. And even when success comes as a result of getting all of this right, as Geertz's perceptive comments quoted above (1968) remind us, this in itself gives rise to another set of frustrations and obstacles. Religions unless they can continue to imbue life with meaning and explanation, after they have supplied the motivation to followers to rise above their anxieties, doubts, fears and material wants, have little possibility of maintaining their influence.

Notes

1 The Besseki lectures are a series of nine special lectures that complete the process of initiation into Tenrikyo, and are followed by the reception of the *Sazuke* or Divine Grant, the principal means a member has of helping to save mankind. Through it God works within members to save others from their physical torments.
2 Tenrikyo Magazine, 1997, January 26: 4.
3 Interview with a member of Kofuku no Kagaku, August 28th 1994.
4 Interview with Soka Gakkai administrator, alias Mr Y, San Francisco. November 18th, 1996.
5 Ibid.
6 Ibid.
7 Interview with Soka Gakkai members, Honolulu, January 7th 1997.
8 Ibid.
9 Ibid.
10 Ibid.
11 Ibid.
12 Interview with Soka Gakkai administrator, alias Mr X, San Francisco, November 18th, 1996.
13 Ibid.
14 Ibid.
15 Ibid.
16 Ibid.
17 Ibid.
18 Ibid.

19 Ibid.
20 Author's interviews with members of Soka Gakkai, Oxford, 1986.
21 Interviews with members of Soka Gakkai at the movement's Brazilian Headquarters, Sao Paulo, August 28th, 1994.
22 Interview with Soka Gakkai members at the movement's Brazilian Headquarters in Sao Paulo, September 4th, 1997.
23 A brief treatment of beliefs and practices are given here in the case of a movement that is not discussed in detail elsewhere in this volume.
24 Interview with Tenrikyo minister, San Francisco, November 21st 1996.
25 Ibid.
26 Interview with Tenrikyo members in Honolulu, January 4th, 1997.
27 Ibid.
28 Ibid.
29 Ibid.
30 Interview with Tenrikyo officials in Paris, February 25th 1997.
31 Interview with Tenrikyo members, London, November 14th 1998.
32 Interview with Tenrikyo members in Paris, February 25th 1997.
33 Interview with Seicho no Ie members, Honolulu, January 7th, 1997.
34 Ibid.
35 Ibid.
36 Ibid.
37 Ibid.
38 Interview with Tenrikyo members, London, November 14th, 1998.
39 Interview with Seicho no Ie members, Honolulu, Janauary 7th 1997.
40 Interview with Mrs Uemoto of Seicho no Ie, San Francisco, November 18th 1996.
41 Interview with senior members of Sekai Kyusei Kyo, August 1997.
42 This information is from the in house publication 1981 Fiftieth Anniversary of the Konko Church of San Francisco, 1981, p. 62.
43 Interview with Kofuku no Kagaku members, San Francisco, November 23rd, 1996.
44 Ibid.
45 Interview with Shinnyo'en ministers in Burlingame, California, November 19th 1996.
46 Interview with members of Rissho Kosei-kai, Pacifica, California, November 20th, 1996.
47 Ibid.
48 Interview with Perfect Liberty minister, Yumi Fujikura, Sao Paulo, September 17th 1996.
49 Interview with Perfect Liberty minister, Honolulu, January 3rd, 1997.
50 Ibid.
51 Ibid.
52 Ibid.
53 Ibid.
54 Ibid.
55 Interview with Reverend Sayama and Reverend Margaret, Perfect Liberty Church, Oakland, California, November 21st, 1996.
56 Ibid.
57 Ibid.
58 Ibid.
59 Ibid.
60 Ibid.

61 Interview with Perfect Liberty Church officials, Lisbon, March 1st, 1997.
62 Interviews with Mahikari members, Mr T and Ms Y San Francisco, November 16th 1996.
63 Mr. T, Ibid.
64 Ibid.
65 Ibid.
66 Ibid.
67 Ms. Y, Ibid.
68 Ibid.
69 Ibid.
70 Interview with Mrs Tokugawa Uemoto of Jodo Shinshu main temple in Honolulu, January 10th 1997.
71 Interview with Professor G. Tanabe, University of Hawaii, Janauary 10th 1997.
72 Ibid.
73 Interview with Ms W of the Igreja Evangelica, Salvador, Bahia, 18th August, 1991.

References

Anesaki, M. (1930), History of Japanese Religion, London: Kegan Paul, Trench, Trubner and Co.

Clarke, P.B. (1995), 'The Cultural Impact of New Religions in Latin and Central America and the Caribbean with Special Reference to Japanese New Religions', in Journal of Latin American Cultural Studies, Vol. 4, No. 1, pp. 117–126.

Ellwood Jnr, R.S. (1974), The Eagle and the Rising Sun. Americans and the New Religions of Japan, Philadelphia: The Westminster Press.

Ellwood, Jnr, R.S. (1982), Tenrikyo. A Pilgrimage of Faith, Tenri, Tenri University, Oyasato Research Insitute.

Geertz, C. (1968), Islam Observed, Chicago: Chicago University Press.

Greeley, A. (1999), 'The Tilted Playing Field: Accounting for Religious Tastes. A More General Model for the Sociology of Religion' in Journal of Contemporary Religion, Vol. 14, No. 2 May, pp. 189–203.

Handa, T. (1980), Memorias De Um Immigrante Japones no Brasil, Sao Paulo: Centro De Estudos Nipo-Brasileiros, T.A. Queiroz, Editor.

Holly, B. (1998), 'The Boddhisatva Virtues and the Global Ethic' in SGI Quarterly No.11 (Jan), pp. 2–8.

Hudson,W. (1998), 'Education for Global Citizenship', in SGI Quarterly, 14, (Oct), pp. 8–10.

Inoue, N. (1983) 'NSA and Non-Japanese Members in California' in Japanese Religions in California (ed) K. Yanagawa, Tokyo: University of Tokyo (Dept. of Religious Studies), pp. 99–161.

Ionescu, S. (1998), Women in Japanese New Religions in Germany: The Understanding and Construction of Self. Unpublished PhD Dissertation, Dept of Theology and Religious Studies, King's College, University of London.

Maeyama, T. (1983), 'Japanese Religions in Southern Brazil: Change and Syncretism' in Latin American Studies, 6, 1983 pp. 181–238.

Melton, J. Gordon and Jones, C.A. (1994), 'New Japanese Religions in the United States', in Japanese New Religions in the West, (eds) Peter B. Clarke and Jeffrey Somers, Eastbourne, Kent: Japan Library/Curzon Press, pp. 33–53.

Puttick, E. (1997), Women in New Religions. In Search of Community, Spirituality and Spiritual Power, Basingstoke and London: MacMillan.

Saito, H. (1961), O Japones no Brasil, Sao Paulo: Editora Sociologia e Politica.

Sato, K. (1986), 'Salvation Through Tenrikyo's Service (Tsutome)' in The Theological Perspectives of Tenrikyo, (ed) Oyasato Research Institute, Tenri: Tenri University, pp. 156–170.

Stark, R. and Bainbridge, W. S. (1987) A Theory of Religion, New York: Lange.

Stark, .R (1996), 'Why Religious Movements Succeed or Fail: A Revised General Model' in Journal of Contemporary Religion, Vol. 11 No. 2, pp. 133–146.

Suzuki, T. (1969), The Japanese Immigrants in Brazil (Vol. 2), Tokyo: Tokyo University Press.

Wallis, R. (1984), Elementary Forms of the New Religious Life, London: Routledge and Kegan Paul.

Wilson, B.R. and Dobbelaere, K. (1994), A Time to Chant. The Soka Gakkai Buddhists in Britain, Oxford: Oxford University Press.

Yamada, Y. (1983) 'Healing, Conversion and Ancestral Spirits: Religious Experiences among the Japanese-American Members of the Church of the Church of World Messianity in California' in Japanese Religions in California (ed) K. Yanagawa, Tokyo: University of Tokyo (Dept. of Religious Studies), pp. 197–239.

Yoshioka, R. (1995), Por Que Migramos Do E Para O Japao, Sao Paulo: Masao Ohno, Editor.

Young, R. Fox (1988), 'From Gokyo- to Bankyo-dokon: A Study in the Self-Universalization of Omoto' in Japanese Journal of Religious Studies, 15/4, pp. 263–286.

SELECT BIBLIOGRAPHY

Amstutz, G. (1997) *Interpreting Amida: History and Orientalism in the Study of Pure Land Buddhism.*, Albany: State University of New York Press.

Anderson, R. (1988) *Taiken: Personal Narrative and Japanese New Religions*, Ph.D. dissertation, Bloomington, In: University of Indiana.

Berthon, J-P. 1985, Esperance millenariste d'une nouvelle religion Japonaise, Paris: Cahiers d'etudes et de documents sur les religions du Japon, No. 6, Atelier Alpha Bleu.

Blacker, C. (1971) 'Millenarian Aspects of the New Religions in Japan', pp. 563–600 in D.H. Shively, (ed.), Tradition and Modernization in Japanese Culture, Princeton: Princeton University Press.

—— (1976), The Catalpa Bow, London: George Allen and Unwin Ltd, pp. 563–600.

Clarke, P.B. (1987), Black Paradise. The Rastafarian Movement, Wellingborough, Northants: Aquarian Press.

—— (1993), 'Why Women are priests and teachers in Bahian Candomble' in Puttick, E. and Clarke, P.B. (eds), Women as Teachers and Disciples in Traditional and New Religions, Lewiston, N.Y, Queenston, Ontario, Lampeter, Dyfed: Edwin Mellen Press.

—— (1994) 'Japanese "Old", "New" and "New, New" Religious Movements in Brazil' in: P.B. Clarke and J. Somers (eds): *Japanese New Religions in the West,* Kent, Japan Library: pp. 150–161.

—— (1995) 'The Cultural Impact of New Religions in Latin and Central America and the Caribbean with Special Reference to Japanese New Religions' in: *Journal of Latin American Cultural Studies.* Vol. 4, No. 1: pp. 117–126.

—— (1995a), Mahdism in West Africa. The Ijebu Mahdiyyat Movement, London: Luzac Oriental.

—— (1998), New Trends and Developments in the World of Islam, London: Luzac Oriental.

Clastres, H. (1995), The Land-Without-Evil, (translated from the French by Jaqueline Grenez Brovender), Urbana and Chicago: University of Illinois Press.

Cohn, N. (1970), The Pursuit of the Millennium, London: Paladin.

—— (1993), Cosmos, Chaos and the World to Come. The Ancient Roots of Apocalyptic Faith, New Haven and London: Yale University Press.

Cornille, C. (1991) 'The Phoenix Flies West: The Dynamics of the Inculturaltion of Mahikari in Western Europe', *Japanese Journal of Religious Studies*, 18(2–3): pp. 265–286.

—— (1994) 'Jesus in Japan: Christian Syncretism in Mahikari', in P.B. Clarke and J. Somers (eds), Japanese New Religions in the West, Kent: Japan Library/Curzon Press.

Davis, W. (1980) *Dojo, Magic and Exorcism in Modern Japan*. Stanford: Stanford University Press.

Ellwood, R. (1982) *Tenrikyo: A Pilgrimage Faith*, Tenri: Yenri University Press.

Flores, M. (1977) 'Japoneses no Rio Grande do Sul' in: *Veritas*, Porto Alegre, PUCRS: pp. 65–98.

Goszos Ooms, E. (1993), Women and Millenarian Protest in Meiji Japan. Nao Deguchi and Omotokyo, Ithaca, New York: Cornell University East Asia Program.

Handa, T. (1980), Memorias De Um Immigrante Japones No Brazil' Sao Paulo: T.A. Queiroz, Editora, Centro De Estudos Nipo-Brasileiros.

Hardacre, H. (1979) 'Sex-Role Norms and Values in Reiyukai', *Japanese Journal of Religious Studies*, 6(3): pp. 445–459.

—— (1984) *Lay Buddhism in Contemporary Japan: Reiyukai Kyodan*, Princeton: Princeton University Press.

—— (1988) *Kurozumikyo and the New Religions in Japan*, Princeton: Princeton University Press.

—— (1990), 'Gender and the Millennium in Omotokyo, A Japanese New Religion', in (eds) Umesao, T. et al., Japanese Civilisation in the Modern World VI, Osaka: National Museum of Ethnology

Hunter, L. (1971) *Buddhism in Hawaii: Its Impact on a Yankee Community*, Honolulu: Hawaii University Press.

Hurbon, L. (1986) 'New Religious Movements in the Caribbean', pp. 146–176 in J.A. Beckford (ed), New Religious Movements and Rapid Social Change, London: Sage.

—— (1991) 'Mahikari in the Caribbean', *Japanese Journal of Religious Studies* 18(2–3): pp. 243–264.

Inoue N. (1985) *Umi o Wattata Nihon Shukyo* (Japanese Religions that have crossed the seas), Tokyo: Kobundo.

—— (ed) (1991) *New Religions*, Tokyo: Kokugakuin University.

Inoue Nobutaka, Komoto Mitsugi, Tsushima Michihito, Nakamaki Hirochita, and Nishiyama Shigeru (1991) *Shinshukyo jiten* [Encyclopedia of the New Religions] Tokyo: Kobundo.

Inoue Nobutaka, Komoto Mitsugi, Tsushima Michihito, Nakamaki Hirochita, and Nishiyama Shigeru (1996) *Shinshukyo: Kyodan-Jinbutsu Jiten* (Dictionary of the New Religions–Groups and Personalities), Tokyo: Kobundo.

Jabbour, Millad E. (1958) *The Sect of Tensho-kotai-jingu-kyo: The Emergence and Career of a Religious Movement.* Honolulu. [Unpublished M. A. Thesis, University of Hawaii]

Kerner, K. (1979) *Building God's Kingdom: Society and Order in a Japanese Utopian Community.* New York. [Ph.D., Columbia University]

Kisala, R. (1994) 'Contemporary Karma–Interpretations of Karma in Tenrikyo and Rissho Koseikai', *Japanese Journal of Religious Studies* 21(1): pp. 73–92.

—— (1998), '1999 and Beyond: The Use of Nostradamus' Prophecies by Japanese New Religions', in Japanese Religions Vol. 23 Nos 1&2.

Kitagawa, J.M. (1987) *On Understanding Japanese Religion*, Princeton: Princeton University Press.

Knecht, P. (1995) 'The Crux of the Cross: Mahikari's Core Symbol', *Japanese Journal of Religious Studies*, 22(3–4): pp. 321–342.

Kobayashi S. (1960) 'Omoto, a Religion of Salvation', *Japanese Religions*, 2: pp. 38–50.

Koepping, K-P. (1967) 'Sekai Mahikari Bunmei Kyodan, A Preliminary discussion on a recent religious movement in Japan', *Contemporary Religions in Japan*, 8: pp. 101–134.

—— (1977) 'Ideologies and New Religious Movements: The Case of Shinrikyo and its doctrines in comparative perspective', *Japanese Journal of Religious Studies*, 4(2–3): pp. 103–149.

Lebra, T.S. (1967) *An Interpretation of Religious Conversion: A Millennial Movement among Japanese-Americans in Hawaii.* [Unpublished Ph.D. Thesis, University of Pittsburg]

—— (1970) Logic of Salvation: The Case of a Japanese Sect in Hawaii. *The International Journal of Social Psychiatry* 16/1: pp. 45–53.

—— (1986) 'Self-Reconstruction in Japanese Religious Psychotherapy', in T.S. Lebra W.P. Lebra (eds), *Japanese Culture and Behaviour*, Honolulu: University of Hawaii Press.

McFarland, H. (1967) *The Rush Hour of the Gods*, New York: Macmillan.

McVeigh, B. (1991a) *Gratitude, Obedience and Humility of Heart: the Cultural Construction of Belief in a Japanese New Religion*, Ph.D. dissertation, Princeton University.

—— (1991b) 'Gratitude, Obedience and Humility of Heart: the Morality of Dependence in a New Religion', *Journal of Social Science* (International Christian University, Tokyo), 30(2): pp. 107–125.

—— (1992a) 'The Vitalistic Conception of Salvation as Expressed in Sukyo Mahikari', *Japanese Journal of Religious Studies* 19(1): pp. 41–68.

—— (1992b) 'The Master Metaphor of Purity: The Symbolism of Authority and Power in Sykyo Mahikari', *Japanese Religions* 17(2): pp. 98–125.

—— (1992c) 'The Authorization of Ritual and the Ritualization of Authority: the Practice of Values in a Japanese New Religion', *Journal of Ritual Studies* 6(2): pp. 39–58.

—— (1993) 'Building Belief through the Body: The Physical Embodiment of Morality and Doctrine in Sukyo Mahikari', *Japanese Religions* 18(2): pp. 140–161.

—— (1995) 'Learning Morality Through Sentiment and the Senses: The Role of Emotional Experience in Sukyo Mahikari', *Japanese Religions*, 20(1): pp. 56–76.

Maeyama, T. (1983) 'Japanese Religions in Southern Brazil: Change and Syncretism', *Latin American Studies*, 6: pp. 181–238.

Marra, M. (1988 a), 'The Development of Mappo Thought in Japan (I)' in Japanese Journal of Religious Studies, 15/1, pp. 25–54.

Marra, M. (1988 b), 'The Development of Mappo Thought in Japan (II)' in Japanese Journal of Religious Studies, 15/4, pp. 287–305.

Martin, D. (1990), Tongues of Fire. The Explosion of Pentecostalism in Latin America, Oxford: Basil Blackwell.

Melton, G. and C. Jones (1994) 'Japanese New Religions in the United States', in Clarke, Peter and Jeffrey Somers (eds), *Japanese New Religions in the West*, Kent: Japan Library/Curzon Press.

Métraux, D. (1994) *The Soka Gakkai Revolution*, New York: University Press of America, 1994.

Miller, A.S. (1995) 'A Rational Choice Model of Religious Behaviour in Japan, *Journal for the Scientific Study of Religion*, 34(2): 234–244.

Miyata, N. (1988), 'Types of Maitreya Beliefs in Japan' in (eds) A. Sponberg and H. Hardacre, Maitreya, The Future Buddha, Cambridge: Cambridge University Press. pp. 175–190.

Nakamaki H. (1984) 'The Structure and Transformation of Religion in Modern Japan: In Search of a Civilisation Studies Perspective' *Senri Ethnological Studies*, 16: pp. 87–97.

—— (1991) 'The Indigenization and Multinationalization of Japanese Religion– Perfect Liberty Kyodan in Brazil', *Japanese Journal of Religious Studies*, 18(2–3): pp. 213–242.

Nattier, J. (1988), 'The Meaning of the Maitreya Myth: A Typological Analysis', in A. Sponberg and H.Hardacre (eds) Maitreya, The Future Buddha, Cambridge: Cambridge University Press pp. 23–47.

Nishiyama, Shigeru, & Fujii Takashi (1991) The Propagation and Spread of Tenshô-kôtai-jingû-kyô within Japanese American Society on Hawaii Island. In: *New Religions. Contemporary Papers in JJapanese Religions*, red. Nobutaka Inoue. Tokyo: Kokugakuin University, pp. 125–161.

Nehring, A. (1992) *Rissho Kosei-kai. Eine neubuddhistische Religion in Japan*, Erlangen: Verlag der Ev.-Luth Mission.

Ohnuki-Tierney, E. (1984) *Illness and culture in contemporary Japan–An anthropological view*, Cambridge: Cambridge University Press. Educational.

—— (1991), The Emperor of Japan as Deity (Kami): An Anthropology of the Imperial System in Historical Perspective, in Ethnology, 30 (3) pp. 199–215.

Peel, S. (1985) *The Pure Land. Journal of Pure Land Buddhism.*

Prebish, C. (1979), *American Buddhism,* North Scituate, Massachussetts: Duxbury Press.

Puttick, E. (1997) *Women in New Religions: In Search of Community, Sexuality and Spiritual Power,* London: Macmillan.

Pye, M. (1973) Zen and Modern Japanese Religion, London : Ward Lock Educational.

Reader, I. (1991) *Religion in Contemporary Japan*, Honolulu: University of Hawaii Press.

—— (1993a) 'The Rise of a Japanese "New New Religion" – Themes in the Development of Agonshu', *Japanese Journal of Religious Studies* 15(4): pp. 235–262.

—— (1993b) 'Recent Japanese Publications on the New Religions in the Work of Shimazono Susumu', *Japanese Journal of Religious Studies* 20(2–3): pp. 229–248.

Reader, Ian, Esben Andreasen and Finn Stefansson (eds) (1993c) *Japanese Religions Past and Present*, Honolulu: University of Hawaii Press.

Reid, D. (1996) 'Internationalization in Japanese Religion' in Noriyoshi, T. and Reid, D., eds, *Religion in Japanese Culture*, Tokyo: Kodansha International, pp. 184–198.

Shimazono, S. (1979) 'The Living Kami Idea in the New Religions of Japan,*Journal of Japanese Studies*, 6(3): pp. 389–412.

—— (1982) 'Charisma and the Evolution of Religious Consciousness: the Rise of the Early New Religions of Japan', *Annual Review of the Social Sciences of Religion*, 6: pp. 153–176

—— (1986a) 'Conversion Stories and their Popularization in Japan's New Religions', *Japanese Journal of Religious Studies*, 13(2–3): pp. 157–175.

—— (1986b) 'The development of millennialistic thought in Japan's New Religions: from Tenrikyo to Honmichi, pp. 146–176 in J.A. Beckford (ed), *New Religious Movements and Rapid Social Change*, London: Sage.

315

—— (1992) *Gendai Kyusai Shukyoron* [The Study of contemporary Salvationist Religions], Tokyo: Seikyusha.

—— (1993) 'The Expansion of Japan's New Religions into Foreign Cultures', pp. 273–300 in Mark Mullins, Shimazono Susumu and Paul Swanson (eds), *Religion and Society in Modern Japan*, Berkeley, Asian Humanities Press.

—— (1995) 'New New Religons and This World: Religious Movements in Japan after the 1970s and their Beliefs about Salvation' in: *Social Compass*, V. 42(2): 1913–205.

—— (1995) 'In the Wake of Aum: the Formation and Transformation of a Universe of Belief', *Japanese Journal of Religious Studies*, 22(3–4): 381–415.

Shupe, A. (1991) 'Globalization versus religious nativism: Japan's Soka Gakkai in the world arena', pp. 183–199 in R. Robertson and W. Garrett (eds), *Religion and the Global Order*, New York: Paragon House.

Smith, R.J. (1974) *Ancestor Worship in Contemporary Japan*, Stanford: Stanford University Press.

Smith, R. (1979), 'The Ethnic Japanese in Brazil' in The Journal of Japanese Studies, Vol. 5 No. 1 pp. 53–70.

Snow, D. (1987) 'Organization, Ideology, and Mobilization. The Case of Nichiren Shoshu of America' in D. Bromley and P. Hammond, *The Future of New Religious Movements*. Macon: Mercer University Press, pp. 153–174.

Spickard, J. V. (1995) 'Body, Nature and Culture in Spiritual Healing', in H. Johannessen, S. Olesen, J. Andersen (eds) *Studiesin Alternative Therapy 2: Body and Nature*, Gylling, Denmark: INRAT and Odense University Press: pp. 65–81.

Sponberg, A. and Hardacre, H. (eds) (1988), Maitreya, the Future Buddha, Cambridge: Cambridge University Press.

Stark, R. and Bainbridge, W. S. (1985) *The Future of Religion: Secularization, Revival and Cult Formation*, Berkeley: University of California Press.

Sutherland, S, and Clarke, P. B. (eds) (1991) *The Study of Religion, Traditional and New*, London: Routledge.

Swyngedouw, Jan (1978) 'Japanese Religiosity in an age of internationalization', *Japanese Journal of Religious Studies*, 5(2–3): pp. 87–106.

Tadao U., Hardacre, H., Hirochika N., eds (1990) *Japanese Civilization in the Modern World*, Osaka: Senri Ethnological Studies.

Tabrah, R. (1989), *A Grateful Past, A Promising Future*, Honolulu: Honpa Honganji Mission of Hawaii.

Tebecis, A.K. (1982) *Mahikari. Thank God for the Answers at Last*,Tokyo: Yoko Shuppan.

The Prophet of Tabuse (1954), Tabuse, Yamaguchi Prefecture: Tensho Kotai Jingu Kyo Publications.

Thomsen, H. (1963) *The New Religions of Japan*, Rutland, Vt.: Charles E. Tuttle.

Tsushima Michihito, Nishigama Shigeru, Shimazono Susumu and Shiramizu Hiroko (1979) 'The Vitalistic Conception of Salvation in Japanese New Religions: An Aspect of Modern Religious Consciousness', *Japanese Journal of Religious Studies*, 6(1–2): pp. 139–161.

Tuck, D. (1987) *Buddhist Churches of America: Jôdo Shinshû.*, Lewiston, N.Y., Queenston, Ontario, Canada: The Edwin Mellen Press.

Vasquez, M. (1998), The Brazilian Popular Church and the Crisis of Modernity, Cambridge: Cambridge University Press.

Waswo, A. (1996) Modern Japanese Society, 1888–1964, Oxford: Oxford University Press.

316

Select Bibliography

Ward, R. and Robert Humphreys (1995) *Religious Bodies in Australia: A Comprehensive Guide, third edition*, Melbourne: New Melbourne Press.

Wilson, B.R. (1970), Religious Sects, London: Weidenfeld and Nicolson.

—— (1979) 'The New Religions: Some Preliminary Considerations', *Japanese Journal of Religious Studies*, 6(1–2): pp. 193–216.

—— (1990) *The Social Dimensions of Sectarianism: Sects and New Religious Movements in Contemporary Society*, Oxford: Clarendon Press.

Wilson, B. & Dobbelaere, K. (1994) *A Time to Chant: The Soka Gakkai Buddhists in Britain*, Oxford: Clarendon Press.

Yamada Y. (1985) *Religious Experiences of Members of the Church of World Messianity in California*, Melbourne: Japanese Studies Centre, Working Papers No. 6.

Yamashita, A. (1998), 'The "Eschatology" of Japanese New and New New Religions: From Tenri-kyo to Kofuku no Kagaku' in Japanese Religions Vol. 23 Nos. 1&2, pp. 125–142.

Yasumaru, Y. (1977), Deguchi Nao, Tokyo: Asahi Shimbunsha

Young, R. (1988) 'From Gokyo-Dogen to Banko-Dokon. A Study of the Self-Universalization of Omoto' in *Japanese Journal of Religious Studies* Vol. 15 No. 4, pp. 263–286.

—— (1990) 'Magic and Morality in Modern Japanese Exorcistic Technologies: a study of Mahikari' in *Japanese Journal of Religious Studies* p. 17.

INDEX

Abbot Rennyo 257–258
acculturation 294,
altruism 82–3
ancestors and ancestral spirits 38,
    88–90, 163, 171, 226–230,
    244–248, 274–275, 293, 297,

Bodhisattva (in Mahayana someone
    who has achieved enlightenment)
    258, 269
Buddhism
    Funeral 264
    Nichiren 21–25, 188–190
    Pure Land 274, 292 *see also Shin
        Buddhism*
    Shin *see Shin Buddhism*
    Theravada 92, 97
    Zen *see* Zen Buddhism
business and religion Chapter 2 *see also
    Matsushita Electric, Yaohan*
butsudan (Buddhist household altar) 88,
    182

Candomblé 144, 151, 166, 170
Catholicism 117–118, 274, 307–308
centre
    Japan as the centre of the world
        18–24
    Jiba as the centre of the world 14–16
Church of World Messianity
    appeal of 118–120
    characteristics of 122–124
    in Brazil 113–128, 295–296
    in Europe 295–296

in Hawaii and North America
    294–295
in Japan 150–152
social representation of Japan in
    121–122
see also Sekai Kyusei Kyo
conversion 93–96, 249
cultural attitudes 260–263

daimoku (the invoaction of *Namu-
    myōhō-renge-kyō*) 21, 23, 191,
    247
Dancing Religion *see Tensho Kotai
    Jingu Kyo*
dōjō (training centre) 18, 79, 86–91

ecstasy dance 247–250
    *see also hypanogogia and spirit
        posession*
enlightenment 92, 98, 101
Espiritismo 17, 124
ethnocentrism 29, 260
evil spirits *see ancestral spirits*

founder *see role of founder and
    leadership*
Francis, Xavier 257

gender 191–192, 141–142
globalisation
    dimensions of 1–9
    'reverse' 1–9
    of conscience 183–186
    of religion 137–145

318

millenarianism
  in the Japanese context 133–137,
    145–150, 245, 251
  of Japanese New Religions 17–18
    and Chapter 5
miracles 82–83, 249
M.O.A (Mokichi Okada Association) 18

nationalism
  of Japanese 12
  of Mahikari 18–21
  of Tenrikyo 14
Nao Deguchi (spiritual foundress of
    Omotokyo) 138–142, 145–150,
    176
New Age City in Brazil – Solo Sagrado
    159–168
Nichiren Buddhism *see Buddhism*
Nichiren religions 21–25
Nichiren Shoshu 23, 25
Nihonzan Myohoji 21, 23
nisei (second generation Japanese)
  in Brazil 114–115, 125, 259, 267

Odori Shukyo 242
Ogamisama (Title of Sayo Kitamura,
    foundress of Tensho-Kotai-Jingu-
    Kyo) 240–248
ohikari (Medal of the Holy Light in
    Sekai Kyusei Kyo) 117, 124
Okada Mokichi (Okada Mokiti)
    (founder of Sekai Kyusei Kyo) 16,
    17, 150–152
  as a Prophet of the New Age
    154–159
Okada Yoshikazu (founder of Mahikari)
    19, 20
Okawa Ryuho (founder of Kofuku-no-
    Kakagu) 25–28
okiyome ('giving and receiving "light"'
    in Mahikari) 17, 81, 86, 89–90,
    170, 302
  meanings of 218–220
Omotokyo
  as a millenarian movement 132–145
  universalistic teachings of 16–21
  westernization 137–145
on-giri (obligation) relationship
    260–261
Onisaburo Deguchi (doctrinal founder
    of Omotokyo) 16, 19, 142–150,
    176

organisation
  of companies contrasted with NRMs
    36–43
  of Mahikari *see Mahikari*
paradise
  on earth 17, 20–21, 132, 162–168
  foundations of 150–152
  Okada's vision of 152–154
  *see also New Age City – Solo Sagrado
    and millenarianism*
peace
  Japan as the model for 24–25
  world 21–24
Perfect Liberty *see PL Kyodan*
PL Kyodan
  in United States 297–301
  in Europe 301
purification rituals
  in Mahikari 16–18, 87–88
  see okiyome
  in Tensho-Kotai-Jingu-Kyo
  see ecstasy dance and hypnagogia
  in Seicho-no-Ie
  see shinsōkan
  in Sekai Kyusei Kyo
  see johrei

Reiha no Hikari 40–41
reincarnation 118, 122, 124
Reiyukai 21–22
Rissho Kosei Kai 21–24, 297
role
  of founder/foundress in New
    Religious Movements 40–43 *see
    also under named individual
    founders*
  of founder in companies 40–43

salvation
  healing as 248–250
  Japan as the cradle of 18–21
  johrei as 120
  of the world 250–252
  through illness 252–254
Sayo Kitamura 240–248, 145–150,
    176
  see also Ogamisama
Seicho no Ie
  links with business Chapter 2
  in Brazil 290–294
  in Europe 293